Naturalizing Intention in Action

Naturalizing Intention in Action

edited by Franck Grammont, Dorothée Legrand, and Pierre Livet

A Bradford Book
The MIT Press
Cambridge, Massachusetts
London, England

© 2010 Massachusetts Institute of Technology

All rights reserved. No part of this book may be reproduced in any form by any electronic or mechanical means (including photocopying, recording, or information storage and retrieval) without permission in writing from the publisher.

MIT Press books may be purchased at special quantity discounts for business or sales promotional use. For information, please email special_sales@mitpress.mit.edu or write to Special Sales Department, The MIT Press, 55 Hayward Street, Cambridge, MA 02142.

This book was set in Stone serif by SNP Best-set Typesetter Ltd., Hong Kong.
Printed and bound in the United States of America.

Library of Congress Cataloging-in-Publication Data

Naturalizing intention in action / edited by Franck Grammont, Dorothée Legrand, and Pierre Livet.
    p. cm.
"A Bradford book."
Includes bibliographical references and index.
ISBN 978-0-262-01367-3 (hardcover : alk. paper) 1. Cognition. 2. Intention. I. Grammont, Franck, 1973– II. Legrand, Dorothée, 1975– III. Livet, Pierre.
BF311.N36 2010
153.4–dc22

2009020371

To Jacques Paillard, who died in 2006.

Our friend and a pioneer in "integrative cognitive neurosciences," who supported us at the beginning of our venture.

Contents

Acknowledgments   ix

Part I Introduction   1

1 Naturalizing Intention in Action: An Integrative View   3
Franck Grammont

Part II Philosophical and Scientific Overviews   19

2 Problems of the Contemporary "Theory of Action"   21
Pierre Livet and Jean-Luc Petit

3 Neural, Functional, and Phenomenological Signatures of Intentional Actions   39
Manos Tsakiris and Patrick Haggard

Part III Developmental and Comparative Perspectives   65

4 The Link between Action Production and Action Processing in Infancy   67
Jessica A. Sommerville and Amanda L. Woodward

5 Mirror, Mirror in the Brain, What's the Monkey Stand to Gain?   91
Colin Allen

Part IV Agent and Observer Perspectives   115

6 Can I Really Intend More than What I Am Able to Do?   117
Franck Grammont

7 Intention and Consciousness in Sensorimotor Automatisms   141
Jean Pailhous, Jozina B. De Graaf, and Mireille Bonnard

8 Bodily Intention and the Unreasonable Intentional Agent 161
Dorothée Legrand

9 Recursivity, Control, and Revisions in Intention in Action 181
Pierre Livet

Part V Interactionist and Social Perspectives 199

10 Of Goals and Intentions: A Neuroscientific Account of Basic Aspects of Intersubjectivity 201
Vittorio Gallese

11 Intersubjective Intentional Actions 227
Dorothée Legrand and Marco Iacoboni

12 Intention-in-Interaction 247
Albert Ogien

Part VI Intention and Intentionality: Neuroscientific and Philosophical Perspectives 267

13 Intention in Phenomenology and Neuroscience: Intentionalizing Kinesthesia as an Operator of Constitution 269
Jean-Luc Petit

14 Cognitive Neuroscience of Action and the Pragmatist Conception of Intentionalism 293
Jean-Michel Roy

Part VII Synthesis 321

15 Externalist Naturalization of Intention in Action 323
Dorothée Legrand

Contributors 337
Index 339

Acknowledgments

We wish to thank the "Cognitique" program from the French government for the financing of this international interdisciplinary project. It made possible our meetings and the writing of this book. We are particularly grateful to all the contributors to this book for their open-mindedness and their perseverance for having completed this project successfully. F.G. also wants to thank the Fyssen Foundation for its contribution to the financing of this project.

Part I Introduction

1 Naturalizing Intention in Action: An Integrative View

Franck Grammont

Note: In the following, the reader will find a schema presenting the main notions tackled in the chapters and short preambles on each of these notions. At the end of the book, an integrated reinterpretation of the main concepts is proposed (Legrand, chapter 15, this volume).

Naturalizing Intention in Action . . .

This book is the result of a series of meetings and collaborations between researchers interested in the topic of intention and belonging to various disciplines: cognitive neuroscience, psychology, philosophy, and sociology. The work presented here is thus a broad interdisciplinary integration of what we currently know and hypothesize about intentional processes naturalized through action. It aims at constituting a general model of intentional processes in their various dimensions.

Intention concerns nearly each moment of our everyday life, with executed or observed actions. We execute actions that we think we control (Tsakiris and Haggard, this volume). We can usually justify our motivations to act the way we did, even though our intentions may remain unformulated or unconscious (Pailhous et al.; Legrand, chapter 8, this volume). We are able to recognize the specific intentions of the people we are interacting with (Allen; Sommerville and Woodward; Grammont; Livet; this volume), and we build relationships with these people on the basis of our respective intentions. Both our basic motor behaviors and more social interactions are intimately linked to others' intentions (Legrand and Iacoboni; Gallese; Ogien; this volume).

Initially, intention was considered a philosophical concept at the epistemic level (Livet and Petit; Petit; Roy; this volume). Then, it was widely debated through psychological and social perspectives. It is only recently that cognitive neuroscience came on the scene with the purpose of tackling intention empirically at the level of its underlying mechanisms. This enterprise does not proceed unproblematically, though, since intention is typically considered a mental state, thereby raising the question of its naturalization.

What is it to naturalize (Roy, Legrand, chapter 15; this volume)? Literally, naturalizing an epistemic object is to make it "natural" in the sense of making it concrete and graspable by empirical sciences. This approach, though, does not aim at changing the nature of a mental state per se. Rather, it intends to indirectly assess the mental states we experience on the basis of their underlying mechanisms and behavioral expressions such as neuronal activities and actions—hence the title of this book!

The naturalization of a process requires genuinely interdisciplinary work, convening both theoretical and empirical approaches. This is what this book proposes by integrating research from various disciplines. However, this work would remain incomplete if it were to only merely juxtapose several independent disciplinary approaches tackling the notion of intention. On the contrary, both within the chapters and throughout the book, each expert of a domain takes into account and integrates into his or her reasoning the theoretical and empirical results obtained in other relevant disciplines. This approach allows for the development of genuine interdisciplinary accounts.

Like others, this book is not exhaustive and should rather be considered as a complement of other different perspectives (Malle et al. 2001; Johnson-Frey 2003). First of all, the notion of intention itself has frequently been used in different manners, potentially incompatible with each other, and not always distinct from other close concepts like will, desire, or intentionality. This has often been a source of confusion, and this book represents an attempt to clarify these concepts in order to make them helpful for concrete applications (Livet and Petit; Tsakiris and Haggard; Grammont; Petit; Roy; Legrand, chapter 15; this volume).

We consider that a complex process such as intention has to be studied at different and complementary levels in order to be better understood. In the present work, we start with a developmental approach, both ontogenetic (Sommerville and Woodward, this volume) and comparative (Allen, this volume). We then consider intention from two perspectives: the perspective of the agent of the intentional action and the perspective of the observer (Grammont; Pailhous et al.; Legrand, chapter 8; Livet; this volume). From there, we consider the relations between these two partners of intentional interactions (Gallese; Legrand and Iacoboni; Ogien; this volume).

Finally, beyond these different perspectives, approaches, and disciplines, the purpose of this book is to provide the reader with new theoretical and empirical elements on the different levels of intentional processes in order to go past the hazy and conflicting accounts of this notion. We aim at making intention a complex but integrated and useful concept in the various disciplines concerned (see below). To facilitate such integration, a reinterpretation of these concepts is proposed to the reader at the end of the book (Legrand, chapter 15, this volume).

An Integrative View . . .

Interdisciplinarity is not just a word. What does it mean? Usually, phenomena are only comprehended through disciplinary approaches, through restrictive methods or tools and within specific contexts. Although such approaches are rigorous and powerful, the results obtained are by definition patchy and relative. One of the consequences is that different disciplines often contradict each other on the same questions that they study at different levels and in different contexts. This is especially the case for the neurocognitive processes in which we are interested.

We cannot continue to propose a scientific description of phenomena in only reductionist and restrictive terms. It is now necessary to reassemble the pieces, and this is one of the aims of this book. We are far from being able to provide all the answers with respect to this concern, of course. However, most chapters integrate and combine at their level different perspectives and methods. The book as a whole thereby constitutes a genuinely interdisciplinary attempt at a general model of intentional processes and their links to action (see the schema shown in figure 1.1).

In the following, I present and define summarily the main notions tackled in this book with two key ideas in mind. First, I want to show that these notions cover most dimensions of intentional processes, for example, from sociological concepts to the activation of some specific classes of neurons. I intend to give evidence that the reunification of these dimensions constitutes an adequate basis for a general model of intentional processes and their links to action. The relevance of such an approach holds in the fact that the first step of the constitution of a model is to identify the variables constituting the studied system and their relationships. Second, and more pragmatically, the schema and the short definitions below should help readers to better find their way through the book according to their background and interests.

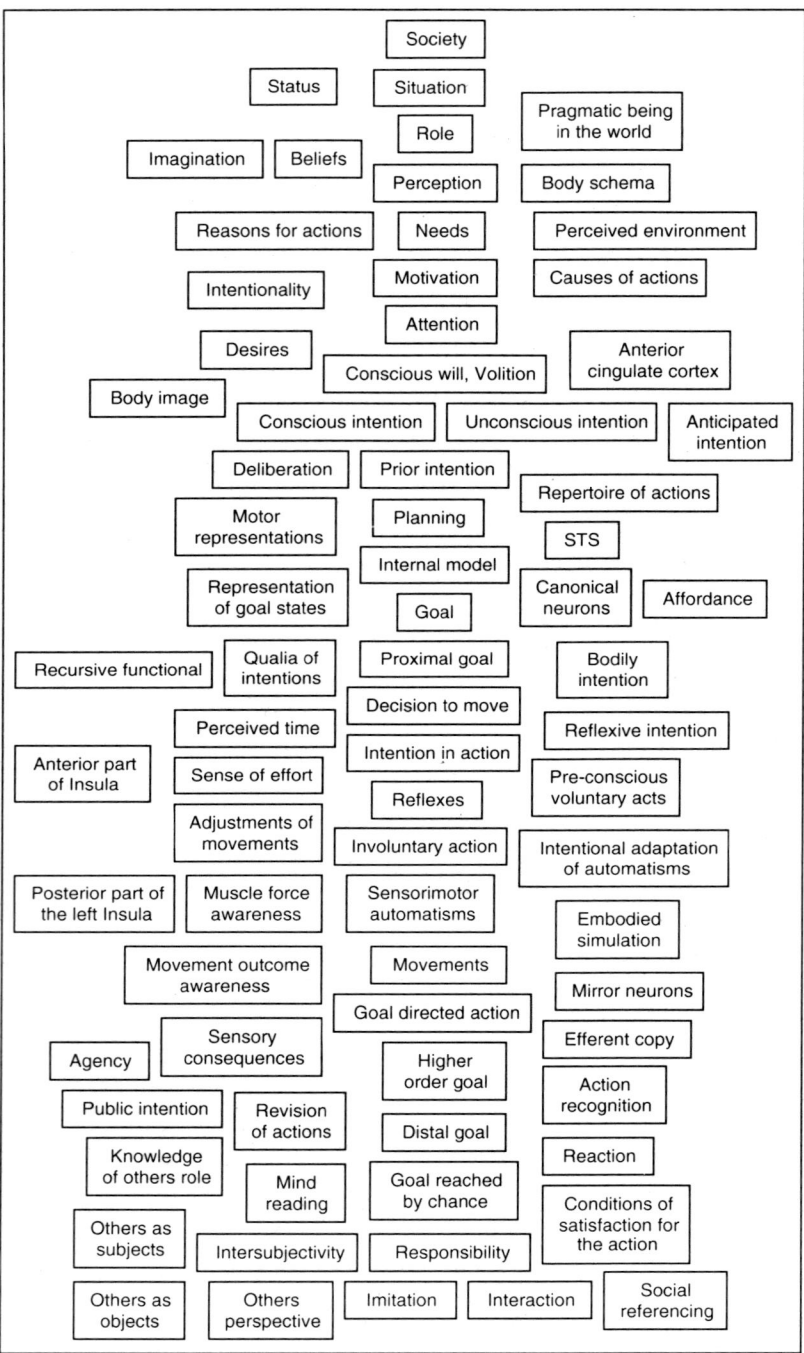

Figure 1.1
General model of intentional processes and their links to action. Boxes are located according to their degree of relation with their neighborhood, even if most of them also entertain more distant interactions. STS, superior temporal sulcus.

Each box in the schema shown in figure 1.1 refers to a short definition in the list that appears below; these short definitions, in turn, specify the authors treating the notion in this book. Obviously, such a presentation is by definition schematic, which means that some items may be reified and the relations between them reductive. Moreover, the short definitions proposed are not self-sufficient. They are, above all, an invitation to read the chapters to which they refer.

The fact that intention and its implementation in action constitute a multidimensional process means that very different types of notions appear in this schema, from philosophical concepts to cerebral structures. For that reason there is not a unique sense of order even if the principal one is from top to bottom, following the course of action in time, even if action is an ongoing process.

There are no connections between boxes, as it would have been more impressive than readable. Nevertheless, boxes are located according to their degree of relation with their neighborhood, even if most of them also entertain more distant interactions.

Authors are not equally represented in the schema. In the short definitions given, all content cannot necessarily be easily reduced into one term and a short definition. That is why there is obviously much more to read in the chapters, even if some are less mentioned here than others.

A few cerebral structures can be seen in the schema, but most neurobiological information will be found in the definitions below and in the chapters. The same goes for data from developmental psychology.

There is a notion which is not explicitly expressed in the schema and even in the definitions. It concerns the fact that certain processes, at different levels, may be contradictory and interfere with each other during the course of an intentional action (Livet and Petit, this volume). Indeed, one can easily imagine a situation in which a given desire would interfere with a more elementary need, with both of them being contradictory to some social expectations. The same is true for the underlying neuronal processes. This also has to be taken into account while reading this attempt to integrate intentional processes at different levels.

The main notions tackled in the chapters (see the schema in figure 1.1) are as follows:

action recognition   When an action is executed by others and recognized because it belongs to the agent's repertoire of actions (Sommerville and Woodward; Grammont). See also *Repertoire of actions*.

action understanding   When an action is executed by others and the observer understands what the higher order or distal goal is (Allen;

Sommerville and Woodward; Grammont; Gallese). See also *Higher order goal; Distal goal*.

adjustments of movements Movements have to be adjusted according to the goal of the action. Thereby, they indicate the presence of a goal-directed action (Livet). See also *Goal-directed action; Movements; Revision of actions*.

affordance The fact that we perceive objects according to the action we can perform on them (Gallese). See also *Canonical neurons*.

agency Refers to the feeling to be the one who does/did the action (Tsakiris and Haggard; Pailhous et al.; Legrand).

anterior cingulate cortex Its activation may reflect the degree of intentional effort, motivation, or volition that is needed to carry out a task (Pailhous et al.). It would constitute a relay between motivation and intention, between the limbic system and the cortex, notably the supplementary motor area (SMA; Tsakiris and Haggard). See also *Intention in action; Motivation; Prior intention; Supplementary motor area; Volition*.

anterior part of insula Is involved in the process of integrating one's sense of effort (Paihlous et al.). See also *Sense of effort*.

anticipated intention The intention one might entertain in a given situation has to be adequate to the kind of activity in which one is engrossed in a given situation (Ogien). See also *Situation*.

attention Focus of the perception and consciousness on a given static or dynamic object.

beliefs Our knowledge about things (Livet and Petit).

bodily intention It has notably two inseparable characteristics: (1) at the level of action, the body relates to the world in a meaningful, motor and nonintellectual way; (2) at the level of perception, the body as it is a power to act attributes a meaning to the perceived objects, in terms of action goal, and structures perceptual processes (Legrand). See also *Body schema*.

body image Conscious representation of the body (Legrand). See also *Body schema*.

body schema Unconscious representation of the body and sets of sensorimotor laws used by the system to execute actions (Legrand). See also *Body image*.

canonical neurons Neurons in the premotor cortex activated both during the execution of action on an object and the passive observation of the same object alone (Gallese). See also *Affordance*.

causes of actions Elements, external to the agent or not, provoking or influencing positively or negatively the action (Livet and Petit; Legrand). See also *Reasons for action*.

conditions of satisfaction for the action A goal-directed action must fulfill a certain number of criteria to achieve its goal (Livet; Gallese). See also *Goal-directed action*.

conscious intention The intention we are aware of in an explicit manner (Livet and Petit). See also *Intention in action; Unconscious intention*.

conscious will Concerns a feasible specific thing one wants to consciously do or obtain at a given moment (Tsakiris and Haggard). See also *Volition; Desire*.

decision to move Moment at which one decides to act. It is most probably the lateralized readiness potential (LRP), which is a specific signal of the chosen motor preparation, and not the readiness potential (RP) onset, that causes our awareness of the intention to move. The time difference between the conscious experience of intending an action and the conscious experience of execution of an action is restricted to a compressed time window of 120 ms. Given that the corresponding neural activity, from RP onset to muscle activity, extends over a much longer period (~700 ms), the subjective experience of intentional action is, in fact, temporally compressed relative to the underlying neural events. Therefore, our action awareness seems to be based on predicted rather than actual sensations, and it is dependent on the temporal interval between the intention to act and the initiation of that action. Thus, awareness of actions and effects showed an attraction in time toward each other, termed "intentional binding." The results showed that intentional binding occurred only when the movement was the *direct* consequence of a prior intention (Tsakiris and Haggard).

deliberation Choice between the different possibilities of action. Relations between the reasons previously evoked by the agent, the chosen goal, and the chosen means (theory of deliberation and choice; Livet and Petit). See also *Reasons for actions*.

desires Concerns the various things one would like to have or to do even if it is impossible (Grammont; Livet and Petit). See also *Imagination; Conscious will*.

distal goal   Refers to the long-term consequences of reaching a concrete and identifiable goal (Livet and Petit). See also *Goal; Proximal goal; Goal-directed action; Motivation*.

efferent copy   When a command to execute an action is sent, an efferent copy would also be sent in order to compare this copy with the reafferences and decide to correct the movement in course or not (Legrand and Iacoboni).

embodied simulation   Activation of the representation of an action with its goal, notably when an agent observes another one executing the given action (Allen; Grammont; Gallese; Legrand and Iacoboni). See also *Mirror neurons; Shared manifold space*.

goal   A concretely identifiable target of an action (Tsakiris and Haggard and most chapters). See also *Proximal goal; Distal goal*.

goal-directed action   More or less complex sequence of movements directed toward a concretely identifiable goal (Grammont; Livet; Gallese). Twelve-month-old infants interpret attentional behaviors (such as goal-directed points and eye gaze) in terms of the objects that they are directed toward (Sommerville and Woodward). See also *Goal; Proximal goal; Distal goal*.

goal reached by chance   When an agent reaches the goal of his or her action without having planned the action correctly (Livet and Petit; Livet). See also *Responsibility*.

higher-order goal   Refers to the final goal reached after a sequence of movements rather than to the intermediary steps. Twelve-month-old infants construe simple action sequences with respect to higher order goals (Sommerville and Woodward). See also *Distal goal; Proximal goal; Goal-directed action*.

imagination   Capacity of representation allowing the formulation of desires (Grammont). See also *Desires*.

imitation   Observation of other's action and reproduction of it. The superior temporal cortex would provide a visual description of the observed action to be imitated to posterior parietal neurons matching observation and execution of action (mirror neurons). The posterior parietal mirror neurons would provide additional somatosensory information regarding the action to be imitated, and this information would be sent to inferior frontal mirror neurons. Inferior frontal mirror neurons would code the goal of the action to be imitated. Efferent copies of motor commands providing the predicted sensory consequences of the planned imitative actions would be sent back to the superior temporal sulcus (STS). In STS a matching process would occur between the visual description of the action and the predicted sensory consequences of the planned imitative actions; if there is a good match, the imitative action is initiated; if there is a large error signal, the imitative motor plan is corrected until convergence is reached between the superior temporal description of the action and the description of the sensory consequences of the planned action (Legrand and Iacoboni). By 12 months of age, infants selectively imitate the goal of a sequence but often exclude the means of the sequence when it is not necessary for goal attainment. It has been shown that 18-month-old infants can imitate a human actor attempting to produce a target action even if he or she fails, suggesting that they readily construed the actor's actions with respect to an overarching goal (Sommerville and Woodward). See also *Mirror neurons; Superior temporal sulcus*.

intention in action Concerns the monitoring of the action according to the parameters originally determined at the level of the prior intention. This intention would be conscious (Livet and Petit; Tsakiris and Haggard). See also *Prior intention*.

intention understanding Other's intention can be understood through knowledge of other's beliefs and desires, according to traditional philosophical analysis (Livet and Petit; Allen), or through direct matching (Allen, Grammont) or simulation (Gallese). See also *Beliefs; Desires; Embodied simulation*.

intentional adaptation of automatisms Implies an articulation between a high-level controlled processing and a low-level automatic processing without a necessity for consciousness (Pailhous et al.). See also *Unconscious intention*.

intentionality In its philosophical sense, concerns the aboutness of consciousness (Livet and Petit; Roy).

interaction When two agents are involved in a common action (Gallese). Simply facing others in ecological situations may already involve an interaction. This is supported by data recorded during an experiment where the subject just had to look at movies showing people interacting. Interestingly, brain regions that are typically activated in nonecological laboratory situations are not activated by the presentation of the naturalistic social stimuli used in this experiment. The dorsolateral prefrontal cortex, often associated with reasoning, monitoring, and control; the anterior cingulate cortex, also associated with monitoring and control; and the lateral aspect of the posterior parietal cortex, often engaged in attentional tasks are not activated by the observation of the movie clips (Legrand and Iacoboni). Can also be referred to as joint action (Ogien). See also *Intersubjectivity*.

internal model Hypothesis stating that some neural mechanisms can model the input–output characteristics of the motor system. An inverse model retrieves the motor plan necessary to reach a desired sensory state. The input of the inverse model is the desired sensory state, and the output of the inverse model is the motor plan necessary to reach that desired sensory state. In the case of imitation, an efferent copy of the motor command (from frontoparietal mirror areas) is fed into STS to create a forward model that allows predicting the sensory consequences of the planned imitative action. A forward model is a model of the motor system, and if the prediction is confirmed by reafferent feedback, then the forward–inverse model pair is reinforced by a "responsibility signal" that assigns high responsibility for imitating that given action to that specific forward–inverse model pair (Legrand and Iacoboni). See also *Imitation, Superior temporal sulcus*.

intersubjectivity Refers to the shared meanings and here the shared motor representations between two agents engaged in an interaction (Gallese; Legrand and Iacoboni). See also *Interaction*.

involuntary action Can be produced experimentally thanks to transcranial magnetic stimulation. It refers also to reflex movements (Tsakiris and Haggard). See also *Reflex*.

knowledge of other's role Knowledge of the behavior others are supposed to express in a given situation (Ogien). See also *Role; Situation*.

mind reading Attribution of intentions or mental states to others when the agent builds a theory of the other's mind ("theory of mind") or direct understanding of them ("simulation theory"; Livet and Petit; Allen; Grammont; Gallese). In this context, mirror neurons can be conceived as "mental states detectors" (Allen). See also *Mirror neurons*.

mirror neurons Neurons in F5, in the premotor cortex, are activated both during the execution of action and the observation of the same action executed by other (Allen; Grammont; Gallese). See also *Repertoire of actions; Embodied simulation*.

motivation General or specific drive to do something, but also motive for doing something. (See also *Reasons for actions*.) A proximate motivation (i.e., for doing a given action) can be distinguished from a distal one (referring to the longer term consequences; Livet and Petit; Livet). See also *Goal*.

motor representation Representations of the different kinds of actions one is able to perform (Grammont; Gallese). See also *Repertoire of actions*.

movement outcome awareness The end state of the executed movement, which is a function not only of active forces but also of passive ones. The awareness of the action can occur because of a discrepancy between kinetic and kinematic feedback (Pailhous et al.). Ten- and 11-month-old infants showed a novelty preference for disrupting sequences, indicating sensitivity to the intentional structure of the ongoing stream of behavior (Sommerville and Woodward). It seems that parietal cortex plays a pivotal role in detecting mismatches between the intended and the actual movement, especially in cases where there is ambiguous visual feedback (Tsakiris and Haggard). See also *Muscle force awareness; Posterior part of the left insula*.

movements Elementary components constituting actions (Grammont; Legrand; Livet; Gallese). By 6 months of age, infants develop the ability to reach proficiently under a variety of conditions. They can adjust their grasp to the size of an object (Sommerville and Woodward). See also *Goal-directed action*.

muscle force awareness The force one is aware to use to reach a certain movement outcome. The awareness of the action can occur because of a discrepancy between kinetic and kinematic feedback (Pailhous et al.). See also *Movement outcome awareness; Posterior part of the left insula*.

needs Elementary physiological or psychological lack which has to be compensated.

observer perspective How an observer recognizes a goal-directed action by detecting that movements are (1) oriented toward a target, an aspect of which is motivating for the agent, (2) adjusted as soon as necessary when the relations between the environment and the agent change (the relations relevant for the motivational aspect), and (3) controlled in such a way that the deviations are corrected and the obstacles either removed or bypassed. These characteristics of intention can be used as criteria for the intentionality of a movement (Livet).

others as objects When others are considered from an external, observational point of view (Legrand and Iacoboni). See also *Others as subject*.

others as subjects When others are considered in an interactional manner as agents "like me" (Legrand and Iacoboni; Gallese). See also *Others as object*.

perceived environment Subjective representation of the world depending on our capacities of perception, attention, intention, action, conceptualization, and so forth: *Umwelt* (Grammont; Petit).

perceived time The perceived, or psychological, time between one's action and the consequences of one's action may appear different as a function of different experimental conditions (Tsakiris and Hagard). Ongoing research suggests that 4-year-olds' ability to recall the agent of a given action within a sequence is importantly influenced by the temporal proximity of the action to the goal of the sequence: agent recall decreases linearly with each step away from the goal (Sommerville and Woodward).

planning The commands of actions are prepared before action execution, even if actions are finally not executed (Grammont). Frontoparietal neural loops are necessary for the generation, execution, and perception of intentional actions (Tsakiris and Haggard).

posterior part of the left insula The most significant difference in brain activity between Muscle force awareness and Movement outcome awareness was found for the posterior part of the left insula (Pailhous et al.). See also *Movement outcome awareness; Muscle force awareness*.

pragmatic being in the world Our way of being in the world can be conceived as primarily pragmatic (based on actions and interactions according to environmental and contextual factors), rather than mentalistic or conceptual (based on prediction and attribution, mediated by mental contents; Legrand; Legrand and Iacoboni).

preconscious voluntary act Nonconscious voluntary acts which are predisposed to appear in the field of consciousness (Pailhous et al.).

prior intention Intention leading to the execution of an action at a given moment. Intention as a cause of the action (Livet and Petit; Tsakiris and Haggard).

proximal goal Refers, for example, to the fact of concretely reaching a given and identifiable goal (Livet and Petit). See also *Goal; Distal goal; Action; Motivation*.

public intention What one is able to intend in a given circumstance is an element of commonsense knowledge and is therefore probably shared by all the partners in interaction (Ogien). See also *Role; Status*.

qualia of intentions Refers to the subjective experience (the "what it is like") of entertaining an intention (Tsakiris and Haggard).

reaction A reaction can be considered as an action which answers to another action, often in a rather automatic way, which gives to it a less intentional character (Legrand and Iacoboni).

reasons for actions Elements that the agent uses to justify his choices of goals. Allows also answering the "why" question: "Why did you do what you just did?" (Livet and Petit; Legrand; Grammont). See also *Causes of actions; Prior intention*.

recursive functional This philosophical concept that gives an idea of the formalization of the action gives also the relation between reason and control: reason is given by the motivational parts of the functional, and control is given by the effect of these motivational functions on the movement, and, reciprocally, by the specifications that the real movements impose recursively on their own determination by the motivation (Livet). See also *Motivation; Movements*.

reflexes By definition, reflexes are automatic movements produced by the medulla, but the notion can also refer to other kinds of automatic movements (Paihlous et al.). See also *Involuntary action*.

reflexive intention The goal one initially aims at can be radically modified in the course of an interaction to match unexpected events and new orientations. It follows the evolution of one's role according to the evolution of the situation (Ogien). See also *Role; Situation*.

repertoire of actions Stock of representations of the different kinds of actions one is able to perform (grasping, pulling, etc.) (Sommerville and Woodward; Grammont; Gallese). See also *Mirror neurons*.

representation of goal states Representation of the final state reached after a sequence of movements (goal) but without the representation of these movements (Tsakiris and Haggard; Livet; Gallese). See also *Goal; Goal-directed action; Reward system*.

responsibility Refers to the question of being the aware cause for one's own actions (Livet and Petit; Grammont). See also *Goal reached by chance*.

revision of actions Corrections needed when the anticipated action encounters obstacles and incompatibilities and need to be reorganized. Revisions indicate thus the presence of a goal-directed action (Livet). See also *Adjustments; Goal-directed actions*.

reward system Reinforces the behaviors allowing the agent to reach certain goal states satisfying physiological or psychological needs (Gallese). See also *Representation of goal states*.

role Refers to the type of behavior that should be adopted by the agent who puts his or her rights and duties in application (Ogien). See also *Status*.

sense of effort Refers to what we feel while executing a movement, according to the force involved and the complexity of the task. The awareness of the produced force would be essentially based on the activation of primary and associative somatosensory structures (Pailhous et al.). See also *Anterior part of insula*.

sensorimotor automatism Sequence of movements controlled by the medulla with or without involvement of the brain, such as the sequence performed for locomotion (Pailhous et al.).

sensory consequences The execution of an action produces sensory consequences (reafferences) which can be anticipated and used as a criterion to determine whether the action was correctly performed (Pailhous et al.). See also *Efferent copy*.

shared manifold space Refers to our capacity to conceive of the acting bodies inhabiting our social world as *goal-oriented persons* like us, which would depend on the constitution of a "we-centric" shared meaningful interpersonal space (Gallese). See also *Embodied simulation*.

situation The notion of situation qualifies, for Goffman, a typical and relatively stable frame which organizes beforehand the kind of behavior that must, at a certain time, occur in it. These frames preexist to the engagement of individuals in an interaction and survive to its termination. However the situation is also variable among time (Ogien). See also *Role*.

society System of norms and values of the society (or social group) an individual belongs to (Ogien).

social referencing It has been shown that around 6 months of age infants visually "check back" to the mother's emotional reaction in order to disambiguate ambiguous or uncertain events (Gallese).

status Qualify the sum of rights and duties structurally attached to an institutionalized position in a social system (Ogien). See also *Society, Role*.

superior temporal sulcus In the case of imitation, the imitator wants to imitate the action of the actor, and an inverse model is created by STS inputting the visual description of the observed action into frontoparietal mirror areas that produce the output of the inverse model, the motor command necessary to imitate the actor (Legrand and Iacoboni). See also *Imitation; Internal model; Mirror neurons*.

supplementary motor area It is activated during preparation for action and 1.2 seconds before the primary motor cortex (M1) for self-generated movements. When subjects perform a complex automated sequence of finger movements, activation in rostral SMA occur 0.7 seconds earlier than in M1. When subjects perform the same sequence of movements at a time of their own free choice, activity in rostral SMA is observed 2 seconds earlier than in M1. Rostral SMA and M1 are both activated during the execution of movements. SMA is a necessary area for the sensory suppression to occur, and it is probably the brain area from which the efference copy originates (Tsakiris and Haggard).

unconscious intention The intention we are not aware of (Paihlous et al.). See also *Intentional adaptation of automatisms; Conscious intention*.

volition Concerns a feasible specific thing one wants to consciously do at a given moment (Livet and Petit). See also *Conscious will*.

References

Johnson-Frey, S. H. (Ed.). (2003). *Taking action: Cognitive neuroscience perspective on intentional acts*. Cambridge: MIT Press.

Malle, B. F., Moses, L. J., and Baldwin, D. A. (Eds.). (2001). *Intentions and intentionality*. Cambridge: MIT Press.

Part II Philosophical and Scientific Overviews

2 Problems of the Contemporary "Theory of Action"

Pierre Livet and Jean-Luc Petit

Movement and Intention

Most of the issues of the contemporary theory of action[1] have been raised by Wittgenstein's question, "When I raise my arm, what is left over if I subtract the fact that my arm goes up from the fact that I raise my arm?" (*Philosophical Investigations*, §621; see Wittgenstein 2001 and also Legrand, this volume). This question has been interpreted as emphasizing the distinction between an action and a movement without an intention (for a neuroscientific consideration of this distinction, see Tsakiris and Haggard, this volume). The answer seems obvious: if I subtract my movement from my action, what is left is my intention. However, a number of problems then arise. How can we distinguish an intentional movement from a nonintentional one? The criterion cannot be that the agent can tell us that he or she had an intention when doing the intentional movement: it would not be a criterion, because it would be circular. If I have the intention first, before the action, I am not sure that the action will happen. And if I can separate the intention from the action, then we are left with two intentions, the intention before the action and the intention in the action, so that the first intention is not the intention to do this very action, contrary to the definition of this intention, because the intention to do this action is the second intention. If we accept making a distinction between two kinds of intention, the prior intention and the intention in action, as Searle (1983) has done in *Intentionality*, the problem is then the relation between the two intentions. Is it a third intention (the intention of transmuting the prior intention into an intention in action)? However, an infinite regress is lurking there. Is it volition? But volition raises the same problems as intention, because volition cannot be the conative impulsion leading to pass from prior intention to execution of action and, at the same time, the active control of the action during its execution. Perhaps we think that it is possible to identify the real intention with the prior intention which is the cause of the movement? However, the cause of the physical event that is the movement cannot be but another physical event—for instance, the activation of the motor preparation area. And is this activation an intention? When asked what my intention is, I do not answer, "The activation of my motor preparation area." I answer by giving the reason why I am doing that action. Now reasons seem very different from causes. Even if some reasons could be causes, we have no means of identifying which reasons are causes and which are not.

In what follows, we will first come back to the Aristotelian approach. Anscombe (1959), as well as Davidson (1982), has taken it as a source of reflection for the contemporary theory of action. Action was problematic for modern philosophers like Spinoza, because they want to avoid finalism. But a teleological aspect is intrinsic to action. We first focus on diverse versions of this teleological aspect, the ones of Aristotle (1998), Anscombe (1959), Von Wright (1971), and Larry Wright (1976). Then, we will show that inasmuch as the possible cases in which action fails to reach its goal imply the interference of diverse causes, the normal stream of action can be thought of as a cause that also can be taken as a reason. This perspective may throw a different light on the causes–reasons debate. Finally, we will show that our usual notion and representation of action are focused on a summary of the real action, a summary that is mainly concerned with the satisfaction of the teleological aspect (reaching our goal). However, the real action is much richer and is mainly dealing with adjusting movements to particular situations and unexpected obstacles, with revising too simplified expectations of the execution of action and even schematic representations of the conditions of success of action. Such a difference between represented and real action is implicit in the contemporary debates on the intentionality of lucky actions, on the difference between prior intentions and intention in action, on volition as being prior to action or being a part of action by itself, or on the difference between proximate and distal motivation of action.

Aristotelian and Teleological Approach to Action

The difference that could explain why questions about causes and reasons were not raised in the ancient theory of action is that this theory was a teleological one, not oriented toward the relation between intention and movement but toward the relation between action and its goal or whatever the action was aiming at. The theory of action consisted mainly of two parts: an examination of what are the relations between the reasons previously evoked by the agent, the chosen goal, and the chosen means—this part was a theory of deliberation and choice; and an examination of what is the suitable way of assigning the responsibility of a previously done action and how the agent could give acceptable justifications for his action—or have acceptable excuses. The distinction between movement and action was mainly raised in this context: if my movement has been caused by someone who has pushed me, I am not responsible for the causes of that movement. However, if I have a trembling hand and do not take care of my erratic movements, I am responsible for their effects, even if in a weak way (this distinction was supposed to deal with marginal cases and was not useful for the central ones).

This quest for ends and responsibility was not considered as incompatible with a naturalist analysis of action as a movement. For Aristotle, *praxis* is made up of movements even though it might not be the equivalent of their total sum (a convincing demonstration of this view is made by Carlo Natali 2004, who rejects the interpretations of Aristotle of Wittgensteinians like Anscombe, who puts the emphasis on the end as answering "why" questions). However teleological might be his concept of *physis*, Aristotle is no less a materialist and causalist when he claims that desire for vengeance, manifest in an influx of blood and heat in the heart (*De Anima* 403b), is *the efficient cause* of the movements one makes to be avenged. Pressing these analogies still further, in a compatibilist trend of interpretation, David Charles (1984) has given us reasons for criticizing a *homogeneous* causal theory of action–event (Davidson's model takes reasons as causes and can be supposed homogeneous) and suggesting a *heterogeneous* model of equivalence classes of events, whether physiological or psychological, a model he derives from a close reading of Aristotle (Charles 1984, p. 223).

Aristotle has considered causes and reasons as entangled together. This could explain why he assumes that for most actions, we can reconstruct what he calls a "practical syllogism." It is a strange syllogism (Aristotle tells us that is it a syllogism only by analogy) because while the premises are logical, the conclusion is an action. For example, I take cherries for desirable fruits, I believe that these red fruits in front of me are cherries, and I eat these cherries. The first premise is a general desire, justified by the belief that cherries are good to eat, the second one is a particular premise (the belief that in this particular situation, I am seeing cherries), and the conclusion is an action. Aristotle examines several failures to achieve this logicopractical sequence. First, I may not realize that the universal premise is relevant in my case. Second, I may not realize that these red fruits are cherries. Third, I may not be able to make a practical use of my knowledge. Fourth, some obstacle may inhibit the normal development of the sequence. However, in this case, the question is the following: are agents still responsible when inhibited? Aristotle claims that agents are still responsible if they act for a reason, but with a desire that blocks their best reason. This desire does not prevent them from entertaining the general desire that is related to their best reason. It prevents them from articulating this general desire and their particular action in this situation. An agent knows that it is better not to drink because he or she has to drive, but his or her desire when seeing this glass of fresh beer relates another general desire (drinking a fresh beer when it is warm) with the particular situation, and this desire blocks the efficiency of the agent's best reason. Aristotle was quite conscious of the complex articulation of desires and beliefs, of final causes (desired ends), formal and logical causes (reasons), and efficient causes (practical articulation between desires and movements), as his analysis of the possible failure of the practical reasoning shows us. In our opinion, the practical syllogism was mainly a way to analyze these possible failures, in order to define different degrees of responsibility, and in no way the naive idea that reasons are by themselves causes in action or that weakness of the will is only a matter of ignorance (Socrates's thesis that Aristotle precisely criticizes).

Anscombe (*Intention*) has suggested that one might extract from the scholastic doctrine of the "practical syllogism" a formal framework for any practical reasoning drawn from an intention to do to the action itself. This framework, applied in the reverse order, would apply equally to any attempt to justify retrospectively an already completed action. Action is then linked with intention, and intention is linked with the answer to a "why" question. Insight into this intelligible structure underlying the language of action was accredited to Wittgenstein.

So far, so good. However, when modern philosophers are not satisfied with staying in the domain of language, of questions and answers, and try to expand their analysis to the domain of causes, they no longer have at their disposal the articulated network of causes (and reasons) that Aristotle has woven. In their intellectual framework, final causes have been excluded, making it difficult to think through the articulation between causes and reasons. Since Galileo and Descartes, founders of an exact natural science which radically revises the traditional view of the world, *final causes* are once and for all banished, and only *efficient causes* are left. From this time on, in fact, movement and action have been dramatically separated with the result that the explanation of effects on the basis of their physical causes no longer has anything to do with the projection of action on the basis of a goal. Likewise, the retroactive judgment of an expert who establishes the objective causes of an event no longer has anything to do with the practical reasoning of the agent who is preoccupied with his or her subjective reasons for doing something. At least, all this remains relatively clear as long as one sticks to bodies falling through space or trajectories of canon balls. But a machine–man is not an agent who can be held responsible for intentional actions.

Do we need to come back to Aristotle to understand action? Could we on the one hand make room in our explanations for a teleological schema alongside the standard causal schema and, on the other hand, find in Aristotle a remote precursor for our causal conception of movement? By bringing into the debate the examples of action mentioned by Aristotle (the man who goes somewhere not of his own free will but because he is carried there by the wind *Eth. Nic.* 1110a), one can, in fact, find in his thinking the equivalent of "nonintentional movement," in which causes are distinct from action. Indeed, an influential line of interpretation has grown according to which Wittgenstein's distinction of reasons and causes could be traced back to Aristotle. However, this distinction is in our times rooted in a fundamental epistemological dualism concerning the explanatory systems operative in physics and in the human sciences. Some philosophers have tried to define the distinction in a way independent of this dualism—and, by the way, better suited for thinking about action. Von Wright sought to clarify it in *Explanation and Understanding* and other essays by proposing a quasi-formal schema for the practical syllogism covering the interpretation of the teleological reasoning (or rather quasi-teleological as well as quasi-causal) employed by historians and sociologists. Von Wright used the idea of an "anankastic" constraint. "Unless I use this mean, this goal cannot be obtained; I desire to obtain this goal, so I use this mean." The anankastic constraint relates the mean as a cause and the goal as an effect, but it is used by the agent in a counterfactual and modal reasoning that exceeds the pure domain of efficient causality. In a different perspective, Larry Wright has given new credit to the notion of a teleological function. He wanted to present a general analysis of the notion of function, applicable also to artifacts, but his notion has been developed mainly in the biological domain: "in an organism O, X has F as a function if X causes F and the fact that X causes F gives the organism O a selective advantage in the evolution." Here, counterfactual reasoning is replaced by evolution, which selects among all the possible paths of evolution some path of reproduction and competition with another species. But this teleological analysis cannot be applied to only one occurrence of an action. It requires repetitions of actions of the same kind.

Causes and Reasons

Our conscious experience of action is a teleological one: our intention is to reach our goal by our action. Now, when we have to explain after the action how it has been possible and has been realized, we have to reconstruct this teleological experience by using only causal relations. In order to do that, the sequence of action has to be reconstructed in a linear way, following the arrow of time, starting from the cause and not from the effect. The obvious way to do that seems to assume that there is, in our brain, a first event that is supposed to be the physical basis of a representation of the goal, linked with another neuronal activation that is supposed to be the basis of a desire for this goal. These activations also are representations, some of which anticipate the end of the action. If there are several desires and possible goals, deliberation takes first place, then choice, then volition and execution of action. As this reconstructed sequence follows the order proposed by the first part of the classical theory of action (the part about deliberation and choice), things seem to be in order. However, the intention conceived as such (the combination of the representation of the goal and the desire to reach this goal) is separated from the movement, because the anticipating activations are representations whose content can be defined apart from the actual motor activation of the body. Dualism is lurking here, because we are tempted to put movement and physical causes on one side (following the time order) and intention and representational content of the goal on the other (reversing the time order). Problems arise from the conjunction of the antifinalism of the causalist and naturalist perspective, of the representational status of the triggering mental event, and of the dependence of the control of the movement upon the intentionality.

Note that Wittgenstein, when asking his famous question, had no dualistic perspective in mind. His point was to focus attention on the fact that examination of movement is not by itself our way of access to action. For example, we are not able to repeat a movement only by imagining the kinaesthetic sensations proper to this movement. It is better to visually imagine the target and trajectory of the movement (*Remarks on the Philosophy of Psychology*, §389; Wittgenstein et al. 1980). The executed movement is not the primary access to the intentional movement. This is a profound observation, but it has not been correctly interpreted.

The duality between the examination of the sequence leading to action, which can be supposed to follow the arrow of time as the causal relations do (most of the time), and the examination of retrospective processes assigning responsibility and giving justification to the action is summarized in the opposition between causes and reasons. Anscombe (*Intention*) is reminiscent of the second perspective when she says that the content of an intention as such is the answer to a "why" question. However, can intention be at the same time the justification, the reason of the action, *and* its cause? Melden (1961) argued in *Free Action* that the relation between reasons is a logical relation, while the causality relation requires logical independence.

In a sense, Davidson has used the very difficulty of the possible separation between intention and executed action as a way to defeat this argument. From my "wanting to turn on the light," it does not logically follow that "I turn on the light." And my wanting is not directed to a precise movement executed in such and such manner (Davidson 1982, p. 6). Another argument is that in order to identify a movement as an intentional action, we have to redescribe the movement as linked with an intention. This seems to be a redescription in terms of reasons. Davidson objects that we can redescribe an event in terms of its cause (e.g., when "this man is hurt" is redescribed by "this man is burned"). And the very perspective of justification and assignment of responsibility requires that the reason we ascribe to the action is its cause. If we argue that a causality relation implies a causal law, and that we are unable to exhibit here such a law, Davidson answers that we can make the plain assumption that there exists *some* law under some redescription.

These are smart answers, but Davidson's theory raises other problems. First, in this theory the cause of action is not the agent but one of his or her mental states (or events). This can be endorsed by the naturalist position, but then the notion of agent has to be reconstructed. Second, if the reason for the action is also its cause, then the better the reason, the stronger has to be the cause. However, cases of weakness of the will are counterexamples. Third, the reason can be activated, it can be the cause of the movement, and nevertheless the chain of causality can be a wayward one (such as when one is climbing and loses hold of the rope not directly because of one's reason and intention to get rid of the weight and the danger of one's partner hanging on the rope and possibly falling, but because this thought unnerves the climber). Fourth, a perfectly well-formed intention is not automatically followed by action. Davidson has not given solutions for these problems, but rather he has drawn their consequences: our mind can function in a divided way; weakness of the will does not imply that the action is irrational; wayward causations are not eliminable; perfectly well-formed pure intentions may not be followed by actions.

We suggest that admitting these difficulties might be taken as the main contribution made by Davidson to the theory of action. Pure pratical reason is related to a representation of action that forgets the peculiarities of its real performance. Causes are focused on mainly when in real action we consider interferences with the satisfaction of the represented condition of the success of the action. It is only by extension and for the sake of completion that "normal" and successful action is also considered as the effect of a cause, which has, in order not to interfere, to be consubstantial with its reason.

If we interpret the duality between causes and reasons as a duality between possible interferences and the normal stream of action, the difficulties admitted by Davidson turn out to be essential properties of action. Normally, there is no discrepancy between the agent and his or her presently activated mental state, but sometimes, it could be the case (when I find myself acting in a strange way). Normally my better reason is controlling my action, but sometimes, a worse reason prevails. Normally, there is no part of my action that is in conflict with its monitoring by my intention, but sometimes, some trouble occurs. Normally, as soon as my intention is well formed and activated, nothing prevents it from being executed, but sometimes, other causes interfere. Reasons are causes but only by default: they are supposed to be causes only when no appreciable discrepancy between the teleological representation of action and the real action is noted and has to be referred back to its cause.

Other Problems of the Contemporary Theory of Action

Intention is supposed to include the reason for the action. However, intention has two faces: first, the reason as the cause by default that is assumed when the action is normally performed and reaches its goal and, second, the intention that monitors the execution of the action and has to revise this execution when some unexpected obstacle or difficulty occurs. The two characterizations—"by default" and "revisable"—are two faces of the same coin. If we assume something only by default, we have to be ready to deal with situations in which the default option is not satisfied, and we need revision policies in order to have a chance to reach our goal even in these troublesome situations. In the same way, intention has two faces: one is the reason (cause by default), and the other is the revising activity that controls and resolves the possible discrepancies between the conditions of success of the action and the evolution of the situation during the execution of the action.

If the two faces of intention are normally not separated, problems arise when we interpret Wittgenstein's question as a separation between intention and movement. If the intention is separated from the execution of the action, we need other kinds of intention in order to fill the gap between the pure intention and the executed action. If prior intention is different from intention in action, we need, then, another intention or representation—Bach (1978) and Pacherie (Pacherie 2000; Jeannerod and Pacherie 2004) call it "executive representation"—in order for the prior intention to be effective. However, how can a nonexecutive intention be transformed into an executive representation?

Wittgenstein's question ("What is left if I subtract my movement from my action?") didn't have the aim of separating movement and intention. The answers to this question seem absurd, and this shows that intention as a function is not separable from movement. From the first-person perspective, the distinction between an intentional movement and a nonintentional one is obvious. A nonintentional movement has no personal motivation; it is difficult to see what would be called a discrepancy with its realization. It exhibits no monitoring and, above all, no corrective control. From the third-person perspective, this distinction can be made only if observers are able to evoke by themselves a reason by default for the behavior and have at least some of the monitoring abilities related to the intentional movement. This is another proof, if necessary, of the dual character of intention.

Pacherie, following a similar but slightly different line of reasoning, proposes to distinguish three types of intention: a prior intention, a future-directed one; intention in action, a present-directed one; and motor intention. The third and the second ones differ because the second is perceptual and the third has a motor format and because the control and monitoring of the second is conscious, whereas for the third it is mainly unconscious and not subjected to rationality constraints as are the first and second ones. Our dual schema can admit this threefold structure: the two faces have to be made coherent. Most of the time, in normal conditions, the motor schema is sufficient for the action to satisfy the success conditions. However, when obstacles and troubles occur, we have to shift to different motor schemas, and the relevance of the chosen shift has to be checked against the success conditions. The two faces of the intention have to be matched against one another. Then, the "present-directed intention," the intention in action, becomes conscious. Most of the time, as the congruence between the represented success of the action and the motor schema goes without any problem, we become conscious of a quasi-automatic action after its completion and success. We perceive the goal (e.g., our cup of tea) and then find ourselves grasping our cup. In her threefold distinction, Pacherie merges two types of distinction: the difference between the representational aspect and the implementational one and the difference between the future-directed intention and the present-directed intention. In our perspective, the present intention has two faces, and most of the time the distinction between the two is not explicitly conscious. When difficulties occur, the relation between the two has to be restored, and this relation may appear as a third type of experience.

However, if the problem of the relation between intention and execution is solved by the two-faces conception of the intention, then we have another and dual problem to solve, a problem related to the first type of distinction used by Pacherie between the future-directed and the present-directed intention: how can there be a prior intention, an intention before the action, a future-directed one? If this intention also has two faces, how can we evoke this future-directed intention without executing a movement? Is not intention automatically bringing forth movement? Inhibition is one part of the answer. In fact, we have to inhibit our action schema even when we see another person making a specific movement (e.g., kicking a ball). As the motor implementation part is inhibited, we are left with the representational part (the goal and the success condition) and with the stored marks of the past adjustments, corrections, and revisions. In the prior intention these marks of our past actional experience play the role of the implementation face of intention.

We can evoke the intention of a future action in different ways. First, do not forget that we can activate the motor schema inside our mind—as Jeannerod (1994) has shown, this activates a specific motor mental imagery. Motor imagery may replace here motor activity. However, it can be objected that we can have a future intention without activating motor imagery. Then, second, we can evoke only the goal of the action and the success of the action, not at all in a detailed way, but only as the event of reaching the goal, without another specification. In the same way, when the action is a rather complicated one, and has to be planned, we can evoke the subgoals of the plan (e.g., taking a tool). Such an evocation is the representational face of the intention. But in order to have a real prior intention, its dual implementation face has to be present, at least in an inchoative manner. If mental imagery is not activated, we need to have at our disposal the past traces of the congruence between motor activity and representational conditions. We need to keep as a disposition the learned experience of adjusting this kind of action to particular situations. If we are not able to begin the execution of the action, and if we are not able to have the disposition to correct some of our mistakes and to learn to improve our imperfect execution, we have no real actional intention—we have a desire to reach some goal, but this is not sufficient for having an intention of action. Moreover, prior intentions are not complete intentions of action. They are always incomplete, but this is only a matter of degree: the implementation part cannot be absent; it is always present, even if faint and unconscious. When the implementation part is very sketchy, the representational part is also incomplete to a high degree. On the contrary, the implementation part can be very rich, and the representational part not very detailed, precisely because we are confident in our practical ability.

It is important to realize that neither the implementation part nor even the representational one are well fitted for descriptive and observational uses. We are most of the time only implicitly aware of the implementation part—we have access to parts of its content only when difficulties happen—but the representational part itself is most of the time reduced to a "by default" success condition—reaching our goal. Anscombe's famous remark that our knowledge that we are acting intentionally is knowledge without observation (*Intention*) is, of course, true for the implementation content, but it could be partly extended even to the representational aspect of intention. By observation, we get descriptive contents. By action, we get actional contents, and the histories of their acquisition are very different.

This dual status of intention could explain our reactions in front of actions in which chance takes a part. According to Mele (1997), the folk concept of intentional action implies that an action is less likely to be judged intentional if the agent has to be lucky in order to succeed. This could imply that in order to believe that I intentionally do A, I would have to lack the belief that I probably will not be able to carry out A and expect on the contrary to achieve A without the help of chance. But this is not the case. In addition, the folk concept of intentional action seems to have a lower threshold for the intentionality of "lucky" actions deemed morally wrong than for the intentionality of equally lucky actions deemed morally neutral (Malle, Moses, and Baldwin 2001, pp. 32, 34, 40).

If some luck is needed, this simply implies that the representational part of the intention can be activated while the implementation part is not sufficient for ensuring the normal success of the action. We can have the representation of the success (reaching the goal) while not being able to make all the adjustments, corrections, and revisions that are needed in the situation in order to reach it. If we are beginners in a sport, we do not have in our repertoire all the adjustments that would give us the best probability of reaching our goal. If we are champions, but try to beat our record, some adjustments are still missing. If we succeed, it can be said either that now we have put these adjustments in our repertoire or that our success was pure luck. We have to be able to repeat our performance in order to be sure that we have acquired a real skill. If we cannot, this will show that the implementation part of the intention was not rich enough to cope with the task. Our folk judgments about the intentionality of lucky actions are, in fact, judgments about the extent to which the dual content of some agent's intention is complex enough to cope with the task. The purely cognitive belief of the subject is not relevant here, in contrast with the dual content of intention as it is revealed not only by the present performance of the agent but by his or her past actions. This explains why the fact that the agent believes that he or she will not do A is not an obstacle to his or her acting intentionally if the agent has the required implementation abilities. The third effect (actions deemed morally wrong are judged more intentional than morally neutral actions) is only a consequence of the fact that we ask more easily the question of responsibility and that stronger justifications and excuses are needed when the action is wrong than when it is good.

Volition has been considered as a kind of moral force that makes us able to reach our goals even when we encounter obstacles or bad luck. However, the status of volition has itself been subject to debate. Volition, says Davidson, cannot be a third step between the formation of intention and the execution of intention if we want to avoid infinite regress, and he thinks we had better avoid using the concept of volition. On the contrary, Ginet (1990, *On Action*) thinks that volition is an action, as a part of the global action. Then, we have the difficult task of distinguishing in action a part that is volition and other parts that are not volition. O'Shaughnessy (2007, *The Will*) claims that will is striving. If I kick a ball, even unintentionally, there is a physical event—moving my feet—and a mixed event, both nonpsychological and psychological, which is striving to kick. There is always a psychological residue, which is striving or trying. This kind of will does not have to be conscious and is a conative phenomenon, not a cognitive one.

Apparently, the words volition or will point toward various phenomena. The first one might be the monitoring of the movement—which can be reduced to the unconscious matching between expected proprioceptive as well as perceptual reafferences of the movement and observed ones when the movement is quasi-automatic. Another one is the transition from prior intention to action. Normally, this is triggered by the evolution of the situation that becomes proper to the action. But sometimes we are still activating another kind of activity—even rest, maybe—and we have to find roundabout means to overcome this prevalent activity. Most of the time, what we call volition or will is the activity of adjusting, correcting, and revising our movements during the action in order to overcome obstacles and reach our goal in spite of them. This is nothing but to ensure practically and not only cognitively the convergence between the two faces of intention in action. If routines are sufficient for these tasks, volition is phenomenally silent.

When we are phenomenally conscious of volition, it corresponds to an activity of self-motivation and self-control. It may be the focalization on a specific motivational aspect, blocking access to other motivational aspects. It may be the act of inhibiting the triggering of a motor schema by its target, by our posture and our motivation (in this case, it could be called "nolition"). It can be the act of inhibiting a tendency to activate a motor schema when the environment has changed and is no longer suited to the situation. It can be the inhibition of an inhibition of an executive intention ("Jump, please jump!"). It can be the act of triggering a new motor schema if the first one has obviously failed to reach its target during the execution of an action. Or it can be the act of trying to find a new combination of motor schemata in an attempt to fulfill the conditions of satisfaction of a conceptual representation of intention. These are very different kinds of acts. Then, volition seems to be a name for a class of acts, not for a specific act. However, in any case, no "explicit" volition is needed when the goal, the motivation, and the motor ability are present and there is no inhibition.

If volition consists just in strengthening the process of adjusting the implementation of action in order to satisfy both the representational success conditions and the peculiarities of the actional situation, and if, for an activity to be an action, this reciprocal checking between the two faces of action is required, then we can understand the following intriguing fact, noticed but left unexplained by Anscombe. On the one hand, it is always possible to repeat the question "Why have you done A?" for each answer we obtain. "Why have you taken poison with you?" "Because I wanted to pour it in the reservoir." "Why have you poured it in the reservoir?" "Because I wanted to poison the population of the city." "Why did you want to poison the population of the city?" "Because I hate its inhabitants." And so on and so forth. On the other hand, the only "why questions" that can be called questions *about action* are the questions that precede the answer "Because I wanted to poison the population." The reason is that this answer is the last one for which we can evoke the two faces of action, and mainly possible implementations of the action, among which we find the means that have been really used. The answer "Because I hate its inhabitants" is an explanation of the proximate motivation of the action by a more distal motivation. Hating the inhabitants is a motivation that could be satisfied by very different actions, but poisoning them is a motivation that is directly satisfied by pouring the poison into the water tank (the proximate target is the reservoir). This implies that the intention of the action cannot be reducible to its "why," as Anscombe seems to suggest, because the intention of the action puts limits and constraints to the why contents, and not the other way round.

If we now come back to the difficulties that Davidson has brought to light, the dual conception of intention helps us to make them tractable. The question about "pure intention" is the following: Is pure intention, which is a prior intention, only representational, or is it already equipped with its implementational dispositions suitable to be triggered when the situation will make the action possible? If it is only representational, it can be an "all-out judgment" in a "conceptual representation" format. If it is equipped with implementational dispositions, it can be a "ready to action" intention. Obviously, only the latter can trigger the action, and "all-out judgment" is not a sufficient condition for action.

What about wayward causations (backward deviations), like the unnerved climber losing his hold on the rope, or forward deviations, like the nephew killing his uncle by accident, but in conditions that satisfy his plan (he plans to run over him with his car in a given street, thinks he is late, drives very fast in another street, and runs over a pedestrian who proves to be his uncle)?

Losing your grip because you are unnerved is being unable to make the right adjustments and corrections. It is losing one's control, and some steps of the intention in action are not satisfied. The other example of the uncle, who gets run over by his nephew driving his car, when the nephew, being late in his plan of murdering his uncle with his car, runs over this unnoticed pedestrian, is a combination of the absence of adjustments and control and of a "lucky" action.

The reinterpretation of the weakness of the will may be more interesting. Remember that Aristotle has given three causes for the weakness of the will. (1) The agent does not identify in the properties of the situation the aspect that would trigger his or her motivation for the better action. (2) The agent has no "knowledge in act" of the better action to be done. (3) The agent has another desire, causally stronger than his or her better one. The progression of Aristotle's analysis makes plausible that for him these three causes could be present conjunctively.

We could add a motor aspect to the problem. (1) The agent is not able to match the motivating aspect of the better action onto the relevant movement in his or her repertoire (but the agent does not have this problem for the worse action). (2) The agent does not have in his or her repertoire the adjustments, rearrangements, and corrections needed for the better action (but has the ones needed for the other action). (3) The motivation for the better action has been presented in the descriptive or evaluative aspect format ("this action is good") and not in the actional aspect format ("this action is good to do"); the motivation for the other action has been presented in the actional format. Each of these causes is sufficient for the action to present a case of weakness of the will. However, in order to justify the blame on the acrates (the people subject to the weakness of the will) step 1 is not sufficient. In order to be blamed, the second step has to be a consequence of bad practices, and only the third one corresponds to the blame that Aristotle finds justified.

Note that Aristotle insists on the fact that the belief concerning the particular situation is "the master of the action," as he says. The whole action can be reconstructed as follows. The conjunction of the desire and the universal maxim produces a motivation. The belief concerning the particular situation activates this motivation and gives rise to action. The desire provides the impulse and energy needed for the motion; the particular belief guides the movement. This is the forward role of the particular belief. It triggers and guides the action as "a master of the action." However, it is also possible that the belief concerning one attractive part of the situation—an affordance—results in backward activation of the universal maxim and the desire. For a plainly rational agent, this backward activation is consistent with the forward guidance and the chosen action. In the case of the acrates, the guidance of the action is not consistent with the better maxim. Normally, the particular belief would have activated the better universal maxim. But there were no desires related to this maxim, only a desire related to the other and worse one. Thus, the presence of a motivation activating the worse maxim and the absence of the conjunction of a desire with the better universal maxim prevented the particular belief to activate the better universal maxim. This activation could still have been possible if the agent would have taken time to consider the situation, looking for the better reasons: the agent would have sooner or later activated the relation between the particular belief and this better maxim, and as this maxim is better evaluated than the other, the agent would have followed it. The fault of the acrates is that its particular belief, the guide of the action, has been deviated from its backward path to the better maxim by the salience of the worse maxim, which is due to its conjunction with the present desire.

The reason and cause of the weakness of the will is that the belief that guides and controls the action fails to activate a coherent and rational loop between its forward guidance of action and its backward activation of the relevant motivations. The actional and motor aspect of "the master of the action" does not activate all the evaluative representations. It just activates the one that is linked with a desire. It is only when the actional and motor guidance is at work that the conflict and the moral weakness of the acrates is revealed by its disconnection with the hierarchy of reasons and by the impossibility of finding a stable and coherent loop that takes into account all the reasons.

This approach of intention as a relation between two faces, the representational and the motor and implementational one, gives us several ways to escape the problems that have been raised in the contemporary theory of action. These problems were caused in part by the emphasis on the difference between causes and reasons, between justification and causal explanation of action, and the separation of intention from action that has been one of its consequences. But our approach is not only a remedy to these difficulties. It can also provide a conceptual grid for investigating new and more subtle aspects of our phenomenological experience of action.

Note

1. Most of the philosophical literature that goes by the name of "theory of action" has been developed independent of any dialogue with physiology and mainly with a view to clarify "the logic of language" in a field freed up for conceptual analysis through a relaxation of the methodological constraints of logical positivism: ordinary language as it bears on human action. To be sure, Alvin Goldman (after having become the theoretician of action with his work of 1971) has done a great deal from the middle of the 1980s to reorient the "philosophy of mind" toward cognitive

science. What is meant by "theory of action" today has to be developed henceforward on the basis of this kind of discussion with neurophysiology. One could prefer to keep the word *theory* for what stays within the sphere of the formal or empirical sciences and so avoid using it for what is mainly a discussion of arguments. Analyses based only on conventional examples and linguistic analyses (which owe much to Wittgenstein's own "Viennese" literary style) have to be anchored in analyses based on a critical review of the experimental work of the physiologists and on reinterpretation of the conclusions that are the result of their work.

References

Anscombe, E. (1957). *Intention*. Oxford: Oxford University Press.

Aristotle. (1998). *Nicomachean ethics*. London: Oxford World's Classics.

Bach, K. (1978). A representational theory of action. *Philosophical Studies, 34*, 361–378.

Charles, D. (1984). *Aristotle's philosophy of action*. London: Duckworth.

Davidson, D. (1982). *Essays on action and events*. Oxford: Clarendon Press.

Ginet, C. (1990). *On action*. Cambridge: Cambridge University Press.

Goldman, A. (1971). The individuation of action. *Journal of Philosophy 68*, 761–774.

Jeannerod, M. (1994). The representing brain: Neural correlates of motor intention and imagery. *Brain and Behavioral Sciences, 17*, 187–245.

Jeannerod, M., and Pacherie, E. (2004). Agency, simulation and self-identification. *Mind and Language, 19*, 113–146.

Malle, B. F., Moses, J., and Baldwin, D. A. (Eds.). (2001). *Intentions and intentionality: Foundations of social cognition*. Cambridge: MIT Press.

Melden, A. I. (1961). *Free action*. London: Routledge & Paul.

Mele, A. (1997). "Introduction" and Mele and Moser, "Intentional Action." *The philosophy of action*. New York: Oxford University Press.

Natali, C. (2004). *L'Action efficace: Etudes sur la philosophie de l'action d'Aristote*. Dudley, MA: Peeters.

O'Shaughnessy, B. (2007). *The will: Dual aspect theory* (2nd ed.). Cambridge: Cambridge University Press.

Pacherie, E. (2000). The content of intentions. *Mind and Language, 15*, 400–432.

Searle, J. (1983). *Intentionality: An essay in the philosophy of mind*. Cambridge: Cambridge University Press.

Von Wright, G. (1971). *Explanation and understanding*. Ithaca, NY: Cornell University Press.

Wittgenstein, L. (2001). *Philosophical investigations*. Oxford: Blackwell.

Wittgenstein, L., Anscombe, G. E. M., and Wright, G. H. V. (1980). *Remarks on the philosophy of psychology*. Oxford: Blackwell.

Wright, L. (1976). *Teleological explanations: An etiological analysis of goals and functions*. Berkeley and London: University of California Press.

3 Neural, Functional, and Phenomenological Signatures of Intentional Actions

Manos Tsakiris and Patrick Haggard

> [...] my body is the only object of which I know not merely the one side, that of representation, but also the other, that is called *will*.
> —Arthur Schopenhauer (1969, p. 126, italics in original)

We normally experience our own actions as being caused by our intentions that are formed on the basis of our beliefs and desires. However, it is still debated whether intentions are indeed the true causes of our own actions. Libet (1985), who pioneered the experimental study of "free will," suggested that it is neural states preceding our conscious decision to act that cause the action, rather than our conscious intentions. Recently, Wegner (2002) suggested that free will is an illusory reconstructive perception of the relationship between unconscious brain processes and events that occur in the world around us at the right time and the right place. The main argument against the causal role of intentions derives from the commitment of cognitive neuroscience to a form of physicalism that excludes the very possibility of mind–brain causation. Having said that, (conscious) intentions seem to be an integral part of human experience and activity. In fact, it would be difficult to imagine how the human condition would be if intentions did not really exist. Consequently, even if we were to prove that intentions do not have causal power, we would still need to account for their very existence not only in phenomenological terms but also in functional and neural terms. To that extent, a naturalistic neuroscientific study of intentional states should account for both the underlying brain processes and for the phenomenology of what it is to have an intention and act accordingly.

Intentional behavior is characterized by the presence of a reason (i.e., motive, desire, belief) to act in a way that will bring about the intended effect. Two elements are constitutive of the phenomenology of intentional behavior: the source of the action (i.e., the intention to act) and the perception of the effects of the given act. The link between the two is made possible through embodiment. We communicate our intentions to the world through the efferent signals that are conveyed into voluntary bodily movements, and we understand the world through the interpretation of the reafferent and ex-afferent signals. The body is this "intentional arc" (Merleau-Ponty 1962) between the agent and the world, between intentions, actions, and effects, between the self and the other. To that extent, our sense of self is critically dependent on the processing of the sensorimotor signals that make possible this interaction. From a neuroscientific perspective, the emphasis on the role of motor and sensory signals may provide a viable framework for the naturalization of intention in action. In fact, any cognitive theory of "free will" and intentional states must start from a *motor* model of intention, because freedom begins from the ability to move at will our own body. We will therefore focus on the study of intentional actions rather than on intentions as mental states.

Intentional actions are characterized by a series of distinct neural, functional, and phenomenological properties that differentiate them from other types of movements (e.g., reflexes or involuntary movements). Their differentiation lies in their neural origins, their functional properties, and their phenomenological content. Implicit in this characterization of intentional actions is the definition of intentions as those conscious states that are generated during the translation of motives, desires, and goals into motor behavior that causes effects in the world (Haggard 2005). We review relevant empirical data that characterize the *neural, functional*, and *phenomenological* signatures of intentional voluntary actions.

The neural signature of intentional actions reflects the distinct neural networks underpinning the generation, selection, execution, monitoring, and perception of voluntary motor behaviors. A viable empirical approach is to compare the neural correlates of internally generated actions to those of externally defined actions (e.g., reactions to a "go" signal) and/or involuntary movements. For the purposes of the present review, emphasis will be given to two aspects of intentional actions that are also constitutive of the phenomenology of agency: the source of the actions (i.e., the intention) and the perception of its effects. Therefore, we first address the role of frontal areas and, in particular, the contribution of the supplementary motor area (SMA) in the early stages of action generation. Second, we focus on the role of parietal cortex in the formation of a neural work space that integrates efferent, reafferent, and ex-afferent signals.

The functional signature of intentional actions represents the distinctive way in which actions are structured and, at the same time, the way actions structure perception. A critical question for the cognitive neuroscience of action is the way in which intentional content modulates the awareness and perception of the sensorimotor signals that constitute every self-generated action. This question is intelligible only if we accept that action and perception do not stand apart at the two far ends of a serial cognitive processor that receives perceptual input to produce motor output. On the contrary, recent neuroscientific evidence suggests that sensorimotor coupling constitutes an organizational principle of brain function. Moreover, we become aware of such sensorimotor signals in various ways, all of which coconstitute our sense of agency, the feeling of being the owner of the action. Awareness of time is one critical dimension, not only because actions are temporally structured but also because intention is principally "a property of action, an action whose end is *anticipated*" (Pachoud 1999, p. 197, italics added). The very possibility of anticipating the end of an action introduces another time dimension in the serial temporal structure of action. We intend to show that this predictive informational power of intentional states can be used for modulating the time- and sensory-perception of the effects of our actions.

Finally, the investigation of the phenomenological signature of intentional action will attempt to bridge the neural and functional descriptions of the underpinning processes and their corresponding phenomenal states. A central theme is the way we experience agency. Almost always, we experience our actions as the realization of our own intentions, and usually there is no need to reassure or represent ourselves as the agents of our own actions. Our actions are experienced as self-owned and agentic by virtue of our conscious intentions. However, pathological conditions such as the "anarchic hand syndrome" and schizophrenia suggest that the phenomenology of being the owner of an intention is not self-evident. In neuroscientific terms, the problem of agency becomes a question of whether the sense of being the agent of an action is a correlate of pre- or postaction neural processing.

The Neural Signature of Intentional Actions

From Motives to Intentions

We usually act intentionally according to our motives, goals, desires, and beliefs. A first step toward the realization of the action is to translate these motivational states into an "intention in action" (Searle 1983). Anterior cingulate cortex (ACC), often considered as part of the limbic system that regulates emotion and motivation, has been implicated in the processes underlying the initiation of voluntary movements. The anatomical location of ACC, at the interface between limbic structures and frontal and motor cortices, suggests that the intact function of this area is integral to the early stages of the generation of endogenous behavior. The rostral parts of ACC are intimately connected with prefrontal, premotor, and orbitofrontal areas, and it has been suggested that their role is to modulate interactions between motivational processes and motor output (for a review, see Paus 2001). Interestingly, bilateral damage in the ACC results in a condition known as akinetic mutism. Such patients show a lack of initiating spontaneous movement and verbal communication and, usually, an inability to suppress externally triggered motor responses (Németh, Hegedüs, and Molnár 1988). Such observations provide further support for the crucial role of ACC in the very early stages of action motivation.

If ACC is the region that underpins the motivational states preceding intentional actions, the SMA is considered to be the brain structure responsible for translating these motivational states into intentional motor programs, a region that provides "the royal avenue, into the cerebral cortex, of the limbic input that pertains to willed movement" (Damasio 1985, p. 589). The following review of neuroscientific data aims at highlighting the engagement of SMA activity in processes that precede and/or alter the execution of self-generated movement.

The distinctive role of SMA in the generation of intentional motor behavior is supported by the studies of Deecke and colleagues on the characteristics of *Bereitschaftpotential* (i.e., readiness potentials; RPs). The RP is a prime example of a neural signature of intentional states preceding voluntary actions. RP is a negative shift in cerebral DC waves recorded over SMA, starting as early as 1 to 2 seconds prior to the onset of voluntary muscle activity (for a review, see Deecke 1996).

Libet, Wright, and Gleason (1983) recorded a vertex-centered RP while subjects were planning to move but did not subsequently commit an overt act. This suggests that SMA is critically involved in the planning of actions, independent of whether the intention will be translated into overt motor output. Deecke and colleagues (1997), in reviewing studies on movement-related potentials obtained with various techniques (DC-EEG, magnetoencephalography, and functional magnetic resonance imaging), conclude that the earliest recording of an RP in a voluntary movement occurs over the SMA and the cingulated motor area, and that only later can it be found over primary motor cortex (M1). Their hypothesis is that SMA is upstream "in the final motor cascade when it comes to channeling motivation, intention or the act of will into motor execution" (Deecke et al. 1997, p. 3).

These observations were replicated in recent neuroimaging studies. The anterior part of SMA and premotor areas were found to be active during motor preparation, whereas the posterior portion became active during motor execution along with M1 (Lee, Chang, and Roh 1999). Cunnington et al. (2002) found that activation latencies in SMA precede by 1.2 seconds those found in M1 during self-generated movements. Weilke and colleagues (2000) showed that when subjects performed a complex automated sequence of finger movements, activation in rostral SMA occurred 0.7 seconds earlier than it did in M1. When subjects performed the same sequence of movements at a time of their own free choice, activity in rostral SMA was observed 2 seconds earlier than in M1.

Equally interesting, though, is the correlation between activity in SMA and actual motor output. Single-cell recordings from the SMA in monkeys during a precision grip of the thumb and forefinger and consequent maintenance of constant force revealed that only 2 of 134 neurons recorded significantly increased firing frequency with increased finger force (Smith 1979). In a positron emission tomography study, Dettmers and colleagues (1995) investigated the relationship between regional cerebral blood flow (rCBF) in motor areas and exerted force during an index finger flexion. Primary somatosensory and motor cortices, SMA proper, and the dorsal cingulated motor area showed a high correlation between rCBF and the degree of force exerted. Interestingly, no evidence of a correlation was found in any of the subjects between rCBF in the pre-SMA and exerted force. The fact that the pre-SMA activity was force independent suggests that this area provides motor execution areas with the necessary raw efferent information to be specified before execution, while activity in the SMA relates to the more concrete description of the actual motor program. The nature of this *raw efference* might reflect the most abstract representation of intention-in-action.

The exact relationship between SMA and overt motor behavior becomes even more perplexed by the fact that transcranial magnetic stimulation (TMS) over SMA seems to affect the selection of motor response. Ammon and Gandevia (1990) instructed subjects to perform extensions of either the left or right index finger. Subjects were instructed to avoid repetitive responses and to act within 2–5 seconds after listening to the audible click produced by the stimulator. Ammon and Gandevia placed the TMS coil over the FCz point according to the international 10–20 system of electrode placement, which is assumed the appropriate location for stimulating the SMA. Interestingly, when the direction of the current inside the magnetic coil was anticlockwise, participants showed a 64% preference for extending the right index finger, whereas when its direction was clockwise, they showed a 57% preference for extending the left index finger. Moreover, the participants reported that they felt as if their decisions were made in an entirely natural way.

More direct evidence regarding the role of SMA in translating intentions into actions comes from Fried and colleagues (1991), who studied the functional organization of SMA in 13 patients with intractable epilepsy. Direct electrical stimulation, below the threshold of afterdischarges, elicited complex movements, vocalization and speech arrest, as well as various sensations. In six sites in three patients, stimulation elicited the subjective experience of movement in the absence of overt motor behavior. Even more interestingly, four patients reported a subjective "urge" to move or an anticipation that a movement was about to occur. At some of the sites where this "urge to move" was elicited, higher current stimulation produced overt motor behavior. This observation seems compatible with previous studies showing alteration in the ability to initiate or continue voluntary activity during stimulation of SMA (Penfield and Welch 1951).

To recap, SMA activity precedes M1 activation during the generation of voluntary movement, and it is present even when no actual movement occurs. Moreover, its activity seems to reflect a higher level representation of motor preparation and execution, since it is not correlated to the actual muscle activity. Finally, it has been documented that magnetic stimulation over SMA can alter the choice of the movement to be executed. Overall, these observations argue in favor of Goldberg's view that SMA "functions in a 'supramotor' (Orgogozo and Larsen 1979) fashion, participating earlier than M1 in the translation of motive to intention to action and exerting control over M1" (Goldberg 1985, p. 586).

Selecting an Action

Given that a certain goal can be achieved in various ways, the selection of the motor program that will be executed is a central problem in the generation of intentional actions. In fact, the early neuroimaging work on willed actions was based on the assumption that actions are willed only if we consciously pay attention to their selection (Frith et al. 1991). Frith and colleagues (1991) asked subjects to make routine acts as response to stimuli or to perform open-ended willed actions. The subject's responses were done in two different modalities, either by saying a word or by lifting a finger. Under both conditions, the results showed increased activation in the left dorsolateral prefrontal cortex (DLPFC) only for the internally generated responses (i.e., "willed" responses). According to Frith (2000), these results suggest that the role of DLPFC is that of "sculpting the response space" from which the subject can actively choose an action according to his or her own will.

However, a possible confounding factor in the interpretation of the DLPFC activation is the attentional load required for carrying out "willed" responses. An attempt to dissociate between attentional load and "willed" selection was reported by Lau, Rogers, Ramnani, and Passingham (2004), who designed a task where an internally determined response had the same attentional load as an externally determined response. The critical comparison between these two tasks showed significant activation in ACC, pre-SMA, right medial parietal cortex, and right intraparietal sulcus. Interestingly, no significant activation was observed in DLPFC, suggesting that "freedom of choice" is not crucial for its activation.

Planning and Perception of Self-Generated Actions

Parietal structures are also involved in the generation of intentions and the planning of the movement. Parietal cortex is a multimodal area, in which both efferent and multimodal afferent signals converge in order to represent accurately the current state of the organism in relation to its environment. Such representations seem indispensable for the generation of appropriate intentional behavior to the extent that they inform the organism about the current state of itself and the world, but also because they enable the online monitoring of the action and its effect. To interact successfully with the external world, we often need to transform spatial information of visual origin into appropriate motor plans. Previous studies have shown that parietal cortex, located between visual cortex and motor cortical areas, is an important integration site for multimodal information including visual and proprioceptive signals (for a review, see Graziano and Botvinick 2001).

In primates, posterior parietal cortex (PPC) provides the signals that predict impending motor activity. Andersen and Buneo (2002) argue for the presence of various "intentional maps" in PPC. In this context, intention corresponds to a goal for orienting action and is quite different from the sense of intention (i.e., free will) as studied in experiments on humans. These "intentional maps" are localized in different subregions within PPC and are dedicated to different types of movement (e.g., grasping, reaching, eye movements). For example, the lateral intraparietal area (LIP) is more specialized for saccade planning, whereas the medial intraparietal area (MIP) is more specialized for reaching. Moreover, single neurons are discharged in these areas, even if the intention does not become an actual movement. The common functional principle of the PPC is to transform multisensory signals into appropriate motor plans. This transformation is facilitated by the existence of a distributed spatial representation that enables transformations between different coordinate frames. However, in humans, PPC is thought to be involved in evaluating the motor significance of sensory stimuli, independent of any possible response, a process that Toni, Thoenissen, and Zilles (2001) named "motor intention."

Parietal cortex is also involved in the online monitoring of actions and their consequences. Fink and colleagues (1999) used the Luria bimanual coordination task to investigate neural responses during a conflict between the intention to move and the afferent feedback. Subjects moved both hands either in phase or out of phase, and the visual feedback of either the left or the right hand was manipulated so that in the critical condition subjects saw in-phase movements while they were performing out-of-phase movements. This mismatch between intention, proprioception, and visual feedback caused cognitive conflict. The main effect of out-of-phase movements was associated with increased activity in PPC and DLPFC bilaterally. Analysis of the critical interaction revealed that the mismatch between intention and sensory feedback led to a specific activation in the right DLPFC alone. Similarly, Leube and colleagues (2003) identified a right frontoparietal network activated when subjects observed a mismatch between the performed movement and the visual feedback. Farrer et al. (2003), following the paradigm first reported by Franck et al. (2001), introduced spatial distortions (i.e., angular deviations) in the visual feedback of the subject's voluntary movement. Activation in the right inferior parietal lobe was positively correlated with the degree of spatial distortion. It seems, therefore, that parietal cortex plays a pivotal role in detecting mismatches between the intended and the actual movement, especially in cases where there is ambiguous visual feedback (for a review, see Blakemore and Sirigu 2003).

Finally, activation in the parietal cortex has been linked to the sense of agency (Farrer and Frith 2002; Lau, Rogers, Haggard, and Passingham 2004). Lau and colleagues asked the subjects to press a button at a time of their own choice. In different conditions, they were asked to report either the time at which they felt their intention to move (will judgment), or the time at which they actually moved (movement judgment). Their hypothesis was that the task of attending to one's own intentions would engage brain areas relevant to the generation of intentions per se. The comparison between the will and the movement judgments showed increased activation in pre-SMA, right DLPFC, and left intraparietal sulcus.

To recap, parietal cortex functions as a neural work space that facilitates the integration of efferent, reafferent, and ex-afferent signals. As such, it is involved in both action generation and action monitoring.

Overall, it is suggested that the intact function of frontoparietal neural loops is necessary for the generation, execution, and perception of intentional actions. However, it is still unclear where exactly along this information chain the conscious experience of intention arises. From the empirical evidence reviewed, only the observation made by Fried and colleagues seems to directly answer this question by showing that direct stimulation of SMA generates the conscious feeling of an "urge" to act. It is possible, though, that a more concrete answer can be given by studies that investigated the functional correlates of intentional actions.

Functional Signatures of Intentional Actions

A critical question for the cognitive neuroscience of action is the way in which intentional content modulates the awareness and perception of the sensorimotor signals that constitute every self-generated action. We focus on three functional signatures of intentional actions: anticipatory awareness of action, intentional binding across time between the action and its effect, and sensory suppression of self-generated sensory effects. These functions can be used as implicit measures of agency (Haggard 2005), and as such they are particularly relevant to the quest for the functional correlates of intentional action.

Time Awareness of Intention and Anticipation

Libet's work on the time awareness of intentions and actions was the first neuroscientific study investigating the neural mechanisms underlying conscious intention and free will. In Libet's experiment (Libet, Gleason, Wright, and Pearl 1983) participants watched a clock hand on a monitor rotating with a period of 2,560 ms, and they were asked to make a simple manual movement at a time of their own choice. Their task was to report retrospectively the time at which they first "felt the urge" to make the movement (will judgment) or the time that they actually moved (movement judgment). Participants' will judgments preceded the onset of muscle activity by an average of 206 ms, while movement judgments preceded the onset of movement by an average of 86 ms. Surprisingly, the RP started at about 700 ms before the EMG onset. The fact that the RP was recorded almost 400 ms before the participants reported being aware of their urge to move led Libet to conclude that conscious intentions are caused by unconscious brain events, namely the RPs. Since the initiation of the movement (RP) started long before participants became aware of their own will (will judgment), the role of conscious will is not to initiate a specific voluntary act. Libet's interpretation of these data assigned a rather limited role to conscious will: "Conscious will can function in a permissive fashion either to permit or to prevent the motor implementation of the intention to act that arises unconsciously" (Libet, 1985, p. 529). In the light of Libet's suggestion, "free will" might be described as "free won't."

Both the methodology and the interpretation of Libet's experiments have been fiercely criticized on various neuroscientific and philosophical grounds (see Libet 1985, commentaries). Nevertheless, this study paved the way for a systematic investigation of awareness of action. Haggard and Eimer (1999), based on Libet's paradigm, showed that most probably it is the lateralized readiness potential (LRP), which is a specific signal of the chosen motor preparation, and not the RP onset, that causes our awareness of the intention to move. By instructing participants to choose between a left or a right key press, Haggard and Eimer showed that the will judgment covaried with the onset of the LRP, but not with the onset of RP. LRP onset occurred significantly earlier on trials with early awareness, whereas the opposite correlation was found for the RP. Therefore, the puzzling temporal discrepancy between RP and will judgments found in the original Libet experiment can be reduced to a much smaller discrepancy, namely the one between LRP and will judgment. Moreover, it seems that conscious intentions are related to specific rather than general preparation for action.

Two important conclusions, which have often been neglected, can be drawn from these studies. First, the time difference between the conscious experience of intending an action (will judgment) and the conscious experience of execution of an action (movement judgment) is restricted to a compressed time window of 120 ms. Given that the corresponding neural activity, from RP onset to muscle activity, extends over a much longer period (~700 ms), the subjective experience of intentional action is, in fact, temporally compressed relative to the underlying neural events (Frith 2002; Haggard 2005). Second, the movement judgments obtained in these studies suggest that the awareness of initiating the movement is much too early to be based on the sensory feedback associated with the movement, which under normal circumstances would occur about 100 ms after the movement of the limb. Therefore, our action awareness seems to be based on predicted rather than actual sensations, and it is dependent on the temporal interval between the intention to act and the initiation of that action. Both observations may reflect a common phenomenon: conscious awareness of intention and action represents a compressed time scale, which does not match the neural time scale of these events nor the actual time scale of the events as occurred. This compression of objective time in action makes an interesting contrast with perception, where the "specious present" (James 1840, 1981) can be interpreted as a temporal dilation of subjective experience.

Time Awareness of Action and Intentional Binding

As aforementioned, the intention to act and the perception of the effects of the action are the two fundamental elements of the phenomenology of intentional action. The experiments by Libet and colleagues and Haggard and Eimer suggested that a temporal compression occurs between the perceived time of the intention to act and the perceived time of the actual action. A similar mechanism might underlie the time awareness of the actions and its effects.

By using a modified version of the Libet method (Libet, Gleason, Wright, and Pearl 1983), Haggard and colleagues (2002) asked subjects to make time judgments for manual actions (such as a key press) or for sensory stimuli caused by the action after a short delay. Subjects judged the perceived time of voluntary actions and of involuntary movements induced by TMS over the motor cortex (single-event conditions), as well as the perceived times of these events (voluntary action or a TMS-induced movement) when they triggered an auditory stimulus (operant conditions). Judgment errors were defined as the difference between the actual time of occurrence of the judged event and the perceived time of its occurrence, and they were calculated for each trial and averaged. By subtracting the judgment error for an event in the single-event condition from the perceived time of the same event in a causal, operant context, Haggard and colleagues calculated the perceptual shifts for each context. These perceptual shifts represent the effect of operant context on the perceived time of each event.

The analysis of perceptual shifts showed that the perceived times of voluntary actions and their sensory consequences (auditory tones) were attracted toward each other. Participants perceived voluntary movements as occurring later and their sensory consequences as occurring earlier when these events occurred together compared to when they occurred in isolation. Approximately comparable involuntary movements caused by TMS over the motor cortex reversed this attraction effect between the movement and the auditory tones, producing a perceptual repulsion in the opposite direction. It seems that only operant intentional actions can elicit these perceptual attraction or binding effects between the action and its sensory auditory consequence.

Tsakiris and Haggard (2003) compared the perceived times of voluntary actions or involuntary movements and of a subsequent somatic effect. In one condition, subjects were asked to press a key with their left index finger at a time of their own free choice. The key was connected to a transcranial magnetic stimulator, and, therefore, 270 ms after the key press, subjects experienced a twitch of their right index finger. Here, TMS played the role of inducing afferent somatic sensations, as a consequence of voluntary action (Ellaway et al. 2004). In another condition, the key was pressed involuntarily by means of a motor that pressed the subject's left index finger on to the key. As before, the key press resulted in a twitch of the right index finger. Subjects had to judge each one of these events when they occurred in isolation (baseline conditions) and also when they occurred in an operant context. In this experiment, the aim was to manipulate the sense of agency by altering the voluntary nature of the key press. Participants perceived voluntary actions as occurring later and their bodily effects as occurring earlier in the agency context, compared to single-event baseline conditions. When the voluntary action was replaced by a passive, involuntary movement, this attraction effect reversed. Again, the results suggest that the time perception of somatic effects is modulated by the intentional context of a prior action.

Consistent results obtained from these studies suggest that the volitional character of the movement modulates not only the perception of the action, but also the perception of the sensory stimulus following that action. By manipulating both causality (Haggard et al. 2002) and agency (Tsakiris and Haggard 2003), it was shown that the perceived times of voluntary actions and their effects are bound together. Briefly, voluntary actions that produced an external or somatic effect were perceived to occur later than voluntary actions that produced no effect. Conversely, external events produced by one's own voluntary action were perceived to occur earlier than comparable events, which occurred without agency. Thus, awareness of actions and effects showed an attraction in time toward each other, termed "intentional binding" (Haggard et al. 2002; see figure 3.1).

Recently, the same methodology was used to assess whether conscious experience of agency derives from the intention to act or whether it is simply a reconstructive, perhaps illusory (Wegner 2002), process. According to the former view, the sense of agency seems to be largely dependent on the processing of signals that precede the actual action. The latter view suggests that conscious experience of action is, in fact, a perceptual recon-

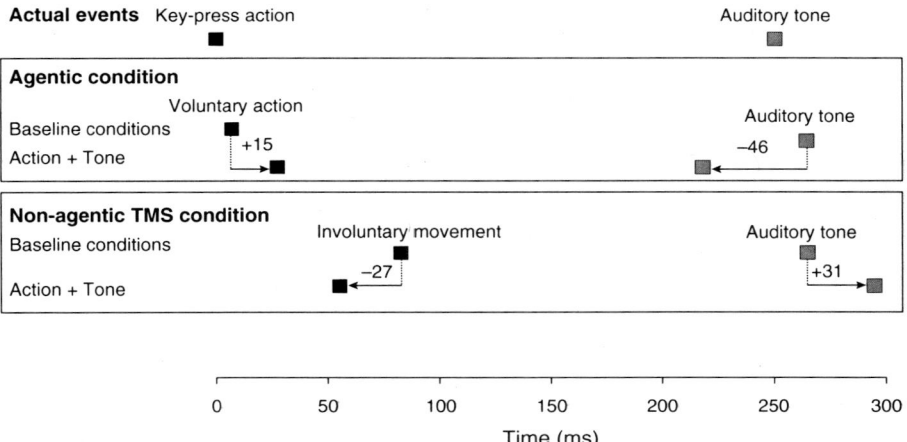

Figure 3.1
Changes in time perception when actions cause external events. A simple button press causes an auditory tone. In baseline conditions, participants note on a rotating clock the time at which they press the button in the absence of a tone or at which the tone occurs in the absence of a button press. In agency conditions, the time of action and tone are perceived as shifted from their baseline values toward each other. The magnitude of each shift is shown in milliseconds. In a nonagency control condition, the voluntary key press was replaced by an involuntary contraction of the same muscles used to press the key, caused by transcranial magnetic stimulation (TMS). This produces a perceptual repulsion, in contrast to the shifts found in the agency condition. Data are taken from Haggard, Clark, and Kalogeras (2002).

struction that is based on a retrospective inference of the origin of the action. Wegner and Weatley (1999) reported an experiment in which participants retrospectively attributed to themselves intentions in order to explain actions that were, in fact, performed by someone else. These two alternative hypotheses were tested within the experimental framework of intentional binding. If intentional binding would occur in cases where subjects had the intention to move, but the movement itself and the subsequent sensory stimulus were externally generated, then the reconstructive view of conscious intention would provide the best account for the conscious experience of agency.

Haggard and Clark (2003) asked participants to produce a voluntary movement, which was followed by an auditory tone. In some trials, the process of translating the intention into an actual voluntary movement was interrupted by applying TMS over the motor cortex. TMS was used to produce an involuntary movement similar to the voluntary movement.

Both kinds of movements were followed 250 ms later by an auditory tone. Participants were asked to judge the onset time of any of these events in an operant context (both movement and auditory tone occurred) or in baseline context (only one event occurred). The results showed that intentional binding occurred only when the movement was the *direct* consequence of a prior intention. The mere presence of preceding but incomplete intention and the consequent externally generated movement did not elicit intentional binding.

If the reconstructive account of action awareness was true, then one would expect some intentional binding to occur also when the intention was followed by an externally generated movement: a prior intention to produce a tone was present, and the tone was produced, albeit by an indirect way which involved TMS. The absence of such an effect suggests that intentional binding occurs only when effects are caused by actions that are produced by intentions in the predicted manner.

To conclude, the "intentional binding" effect suggests that "the conscious experience of our actions is an integrated and compressed version of the underlying neural events that cause our actions" (Haggard and Johnson 2003, p. 77). A series of experiments has consistently shown that this process is specific to actions, underlying therefore its intentional nature, and does not reflect general perceptual attraction. This "intentional binding" mechanism might underlie the way in which the mind constructs a strong association between intentions, actions, and consequences so as to generate the unique and private phenomenological experience of self-agency (Tsakiris and Haggard 2004). Moreover, intentional binding may structure our experience of our own bodies. Indeed, the sense of ownership of one's own body, which is seen as central to modern theories of embodied self-consciousness, could arise as a consequence of binding somatic effects to motor actions.

Sensory Suppression

Sensory suppression is a key phenomenon in sensorimotor neuroscience. Numerous studies have shown that the perceptual consequences of self-generated actions are attenuated compared to comparable sensory effects that are externally generated (for a review, see Blakemore, Wolpert, and Frith 2000). The reasons for sensory attenuation are probably twofold. First, in the case of self-generated movements, the internal models of the motor system are able to predict the sensory consequences by using efferent information. By perceptually attenuating the reafferent signals, the system avoids a computational overload of redundant self-related sensory information. Second, during action, what is crucial is to divert our attention to externally produced sensory stimulation—namely, ex-afference. Therefore, thanks to sensory suppression, we attenuate reafference, and accentuate ex-afference.

Two critical processes support the mechanism underlying sensory attenuation. First, whenever a motor command is issued, an efferent copy of this command is produced in parallel. Second, this efference copy is then used by internal models of the motor system to predict the sensory consequences of the movement. Thus, the efference copy and a motor predictor, which jointly constitute the forward model (Wolpert 1997), make possible the anticipation and at last the cancellation of self-produced sensory consequences. Given that only self-generated sensory stimulation is attenuated according to this view, sensory suppression can also serve as an *index of the origin* of the afferent signals. This process of separating and distinguishing self-generated from externally generated sensory events has been linked to the sense of selfhood and agency (Blakemore, Frith, and Wolpert 2002). Therefore, the conditions under which sensory suppression occurs may shed light on the functional properties of intentional voluntary movements.

Blakemore and colleagues (1998, 1999), following Claxton's (1975) idea, investigated the way somatosensory consequences of our own actions are perceived differently from identical somatosensory inputs that are externally generated. In one study by Blakemore and colleagues (1999), tactile stimulation was applied on the participant's right hand. The stimulation was either produced by a voluntary movement of the participant's left hand or it was externally generated. Crucially, for the self-generated condition, a robotic interface mediated between the movement of the left hand and the stimulated right hand, so that the experimenters could manipulate and parametrically vary (1) the delay between movement and stimulation and (2) the degrees of trajectory perturbations. Participants perceived the tactile stimulation as significantly less ticklish when it was self-generated, compared to the externally generated condition, suggesting that relevant perceptual attributes of stimulation were attenuated. When a time delay of 200 ms was artificially introduced between the self-generated movement of the left hand and the resulting sensation, the attenuation effect was absorbed. The sensory discrepancy, or the error between the predicted and the actual sensory feedback, can account for the absence of attenuation. Therefore, even in the case of self-generated stimulation, for the attenuation to take place, the tactile sensation and its causative movement should correspond in time and space.

A neuroimaging study on a similar paradigm showed decreased activation in the cerebellum and bilaterally in the parietal operculum, which is thought to be the secondary somatosensory cortex, during self-generated movements that led to sensory stimulation (Blakemore, Wolpert, and Frith 1998). According to the authors, the cerebellum is crucially involved in the comparison between predicted and actual sensory feedback (Blakemore, Frith, and Wolpert 2001), and it provides the signal used for sensory attenuation in the somatosensory cortex (Blakemore, Wolpert, and Frith 1998).

Where Does the Efferent Signal Used for the Sensory Suppression Come From? Recently, Haggard and Whitford (2004) reported a study in which the main focus was on the neural source of the efferent signal that is used in the attenuation of self-produced sensory consequences. The hypothesis tested was whether transient magnetic stimulation of SMA prior to the stimulus would disrupt the generation of the efferent signals.

Subjects were instructed to make or withhold a voluntary flexion of their right index finger in synchrony with an instructional stimulus. On each trial, TMS was delivered at the optimal location over left M1 for eliciting twitches of the right index finger. This produced a motor evoked potential (MEP) that was superimposed on any voluntary action the subjects made. On half of the trials, a conditioning TMS pulse was also delivered over SMA 10 ms before the TMS pulse over left M1. Then, the subjects were instructed to relax, and 3 seconds later a second pulse over left M1 at fixed intensity was delivered, producing a second MEP. The second twitch served as a reference against which the first twitch had to be compared. Subjects had to judge whether the first twitch was more intense compared to the second one. During the second TMS pulse, no voluntary movement was made by the subject. During the first TMS pulse, subjects made a voluntary movement on half of the trials.

The results showed that subjects perceived the first twitch to be less intense when they made a voluntary action than in trials where they did not move. This effect demonstrated that sensory attenuation for self-produced sensory effects did occur. However, for the trials where the SMA was stimulated prior to voluntary movement, the sensory attenuation effect was almost abolished. That is, subjects did not perceive the test MEPs to be less intense than the reference MEPs even when they had made a voluntary movement. This suggests that SMA is a necessary site for the sensory suppression to occur, and it is probably the brain area from which the efference copy originates. This result also contrasts with previous suggestions that sensory suppression arises in the motor cortex as part of the descending motor command itself.

Does Sensory Attenuation Occur Only for Predicted Afferent Events? The forward model hypothesis is strongly committed to the point that sensory attenuation occurs only when the afferent events can be predicted. The studies by Blakemore and colleagues showed that spatiotemporal congruency between the movement and the sensory consequence is necessary for sensory suppression to occur. However, it is still unclear whether similar attenuation would occur in situations where the agent performs a self-generated movement whose sensory consequence cannot be predicted across all dimensions (e.g., it may be temporally predictable, but its sensory intensity may not be).

This question was addressed in a recent experiment where the action of the left hand could not predict the sensory consequence on the right hand (Tsakiris and Haggard 2003). In this study, comparable somatic effects (i.e., TMS-induced twitches of the right index finger), whose intensity was unpredictable, were caused either by a voluntary or an involuntary key press made by the subject's left hand. The results showed that subjects judged the sensory effects to be less intense in the voluntary condition, compared to the involuntary one, even though the motor system could not use any motor information to predict the actual intensity of the stimulus, and despite the fact that across both conditions the intensity of the stimulus was similar and externally controlled (see figure 3.2). The fact that sensory suppression occurred even in the case where the efferent information did not carry enough information so as to accurately predict the sensory consequence suggests that intention and efference may act as a general context for perceptual awareness.

Similar contextual modulation of sensory perception was reported in a neuroimaging study of pain perception. Salomons and colleagues (2004) showed the neuronal activity in anterior cingulate, insular, and secondary somatosensory cortices, areas that are all linked to pain processing, is modulated by the cognitive context, such as the perceived controllability that the subjects erroneously thought to exert over painful stimuli.

To recap, the studies on sensory suppression of self-generated sensory consequences highlight two important elements of intentional actions. First, in the case of a self-generated action, the efferent copy, originating from SMA, is used by the forward model of the motor system to predict and therefore anticipate the sensory consequences. Second, recent evidence suggests that sensory suppression might also occur as a result of the

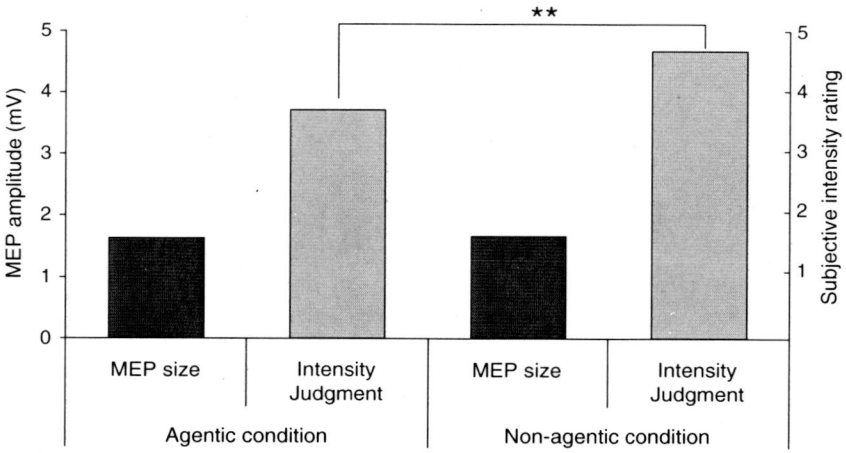

Figure 3.2
Sensory consequences of voluntary action are perceptually attenuated. In the agentic condition, subjects made a voluntary key press with the left hand. This caused an involuntary movement of their right hand shortly afterwards (a motor evoked potential [MEP] caused by transcranial magnetic stimulation). In a nonagentic control condition, the key press was applied by an external force to the participant's passive hand. Participants estimated the magnitude of the MEP. The physical size of the MEP did not differ across conditions (left-hand scale), but agency significantly reduced the perceived magnitude of MEPs (right-hand scale). Data are from Tsakiris and Haggard (2003).

intentional context within which the action takes place and in the absence of accurate predictions regarding the consequent sensory feedback. We have argued that this context effect could be applied in the form of a "sensory bias" that arises at an early stage in the initiation of action, before the precise details of the impending movement are determined (Tsakiris and Haggard 2004). Such a bias would also denote the forthcoming event as being "mine," before the motor system commences the prediction and monitoring of various sensorimotor parameters of the movement. The mere presence of raw efferent information could therefore constitute a possible correlate of the sense of agency.

The Phenomenological Signature of Intentional Action

The phenomenological signature of intentional action is the sense that one is the conscious agent of one's own action, an action whose source and ownership can be traced back to the acting subject. But what exactly is the nature and content of such phenomenology? Numerous studies have demonstrated that various motor aspects of our actions do not enter awareness. We are able to correct automatically our own movements, and if we are asked to comment on our performance, we are unaware of any corrections we made (Fourneret and Jeannerod 1998). It has also been argued that our phenomenology of agency is thin and elusive in the sense that our voluntary actions are not accompanied by an explicit representation of self-agency. For example, when I switch on the light, I do not explicitly represent myself as a conscious agent. This subtle, but not absent, phenomenology of agency might be accounted for by the fact that in the case of a self-generated action, intentions and efference copy should predict the consequent visual, auditory, and somatosensory signals produced by the movement. However, the exact neural and functional correlates of the sense of agency are still debated. In particular, a key empirical question is whether the sense of agency results from pre- or postaction processes. For example, it could be possible that all the processes preceding the action are agent neutral and, as such, they do not suffice for the experience of agency. Alternatively, it may be argued that preaction processes, such as the translation of an "intention in action" into an efference copy, are sufficient conditions for the experience of agency.

Reconstructing Agency

Jeannerod and colleagues (de Vignemont and Fourneret 2004; Georgieff and Jeannerod 1998) have argued for the necessity of a neural system that would function as a discriminator between the self and the other, namely, the "who system." The thrust of the argument is based on accumulating evidence suggesting that action representations are independent of the agent who is performing them. It has been shown that the representations of both self-generated and observed actions activate overlapping neural networks (for a review, see Grèzes and Decety 2001). Similarly, the discovery of mirror neurons (Rizzolatti and Craighero 2004) argues for the presence of "shared representations" during execution and observation of actions, and that these representations are agent neutral (Jeannerod 2003a, 2003b).

According to the "shared representations" model, the "who did it?" question can be answered in computational terms only by disentangling the nonoverlapping areas that are active during self- and other actions. Recently, Jeannerod and Pacherie (2004) suggested that the existence of shared representations for actions is evidence for the existence of "naked intentions." In an attempt to specify what they mean by naked intentions, they write, "It could be the case either that intentions—or rather the specific variety of intentions we are concerned with here—are impersonal representations or that, although their form is <agent, action, goal>, the agent parameter can be left unspecified" (p. 139). This line of argument can only imply that the sense of agency arises as a postaction reconstructive metarepresentation.

This model can be criticized on two grounds. First, whereas it is true that the mirror neuron system contains an action vocabulary that operates in an agent-neutral fashion, it is not the same to say that this vocabulary includes all the intentional descriptions that define a certain action. For example, the action representation of grasping will be similar, irrespectively of whether I want to grasp the object in order to hold it or throw it at someone else. This is obviously not true for the intentional representation of the given act of grasping in these two different situations.

Moreover, the "who system" seems to be strongly committed to a representational model of agency and self-consciousness, within which the problem is no more that of *being* the agent but is rather that of *knowing* who is the agent. In that sense, the model ignores all the processes that precede the execution of intentional actions and instead focuses on the perception of action as an objective manifestation of naked intentions. However, the acting body is perceived both from the inside, and it is therefore given in an epistemologically immediate fashion, and from the outside through the perception of objectively manifested events. For the "who system," the default mode of operation seems to be "no agent." In effect, the "shared representations" model and the conceptualization of mirror neurons raise an epistemological problem, because they leave no room for a self. If "shared representations" is the brain's basic model, then we need to either abandon the concept of an agentic self or postulate a "who system" to recreate it.

Constructing Agency

On the other hand, it has been argued that "efferent consciousness" might be a more parsimonious solution to the problem of agency (Tsakiris et al. 2005; Tsakiris and Haggard 2004). This alternative view of agency focuses exactly on the dynamic unfolding of intentional action, namely, from intention to action, to the resulting sensory feedback and the perception of its effects. Moreover, it may be argued that it is by virtue of the preaction processes (i.e., motivation, intention, motor command and efference, prediction) that our bodily movements acquire the right psychological qualities that enable their characterization as agentic.

The empirical evidence reviewed in the section entitled "The Neural Signature of Intentional Actions" highlighted the presence of certain functional signatures of intentional actions—for example, the intentional binding effect and the sensory suppression effect that are modulated by intentional self-generated actions. The presence and the processing of the efferent copy of the motor command were shown to play a critical role for eliciting these functions. Overall, the results suggest that the sense of agency is at least partly efferent driven.

From a conceptual point of view, the raw efferent copy can be thought of as the interface between the psychological and the physiological content of our actions. The psychological content is the intention-in-action, and the physiological content is given by the descending motor command and the sensory feedback. In addition, the mere presence of efference reflects the processing of a *self*-generated voluntary movement and predicts the impending arrival of *self*-related sensory feedback. Therefore, it seems unjustified to suggest that all these processes are agent neutral. In fact, for the constructive accounts of agency (Frith et al. 2000; Tsakiris and Haggard 2004), the default mode of operation seems to be bound to the acting self.

Moreover, the outcome of the comparison between the predicted and the actual sensory feedback will provide a pragmatic index of the efficiency of the self-generated action. Therefore, by virtue of the anticipatory function of our motor system, the automatic detection of congruence between intention and effect may not require the formation of an explicit representation of agency for our actions. Thus, this constructive account of agency may also account for the observation that the phenomenology of intentional actions is thin and elusive.

Quite often, philosophers remind neuroscientists that the concept of intention as used in many empirical studies may still betray some sort of commitment to dualistic traditions. One way of dealing with this paradox is to argue that intentions are ontologically bound to actual bodily movements. Schopenhauer (1969) denied the existence of volitions as mental willing by replacing them with "acts of will" that are physical actions of the body. The act of will and the action is one and the same event that is given to the agent in two distinct ways: epistemologically immediately as willing, and immediately through the perceptual systems (e.g., vision, proprioception) as movement. The advantage of this view is that one can identify the bodily movement of a certain act with the psychological event of trying or willing to do this act (O'Shaughnessy 2004).

In that sense, intention or will is to be understood as "the activation of the motor-system that is blessed with the right psychological ancestors" (O'Shaughnessy 2004, p. 208). Some of the neuroscientific data reviewed here suggested that the awareness of intentions, awareness of actions, and awareness of their effects are temporally bound to each other. This implies that the conscious experience of agency is an integrated and compressed version of the underlying neural events. This binding process may underpin this "blessing" of the activation of the motor system with the right psychological ancestors.

References

Ammon, K., and Gandevia, S. C. (1990). Transcranial magnetic stimulation can influence the selection of motor programmes. *Journal of Neurology, Neurosurgery and Psychiatry, 53*, 705–707.

Andersen, R. A., and Buneo, C. A. (2002). Intentional maps in posterior parietal cortex. *Annual Review of Neuroscience, 25*, 189–220.

Blakemore, S.-J., Frith, C. D., and Wolpert, D. (1999). Spatio-temporal prediction modulates the perception of self-produced stimuli. *Journal of Cognitive Neuroscience, 11*, 551–559.

Blakemore, S.-J., Frith, C. D., and Wolpert, D. (2001). The cerebellum is involved in predicting the sensory consequences of action. *Neuroreport, 12*, 1879–1884.

Blakemore, S.-J., Frith, C. D., and Wolpert, D. (2002). Abnormalities in the awareness of action. *Trends in Cognitive Sciences, 6*, 237–242.

Blakemore, S.-J., and Sirigu, A. (2003). Action prediction in the cerebellum and in the parietal lobe. *Experimental Brain Research, 153*, 239–245.

Blakemore, S.-J., Wolpert, D. M., and Frith, C. D. (1998). Central cancellation of self-produced tickle sensation. *Nature Neuroscience, 1*, 635–640.

Blakemore, S.-J., Wolpert, D. M., and Frith, C. D. (2000). Why can't you tickle yourself? *NeurReport, 11*, R11–R16.

Claxton, G. (1975). Why can't we tickle ourselves? *Perceptual and Motor Skills, 41*, 335–338.

Cunnington, R., Windischberger, C., Deecke, L., and Moser, E. (2002). The preparation and execution of self-initiated and externally triggered movement: A study of event-related fMRI. *NeuroImage, 15*, 373–385.

Damasio, A. (1985). Understanding the mind's will. *Behavioral and Brain Sciences, 8*, 589.

Deecke, L. (1996). Planning, preparation, execution, and imagery of volitional action. *Cognitive Brain Research, 3,* 59–64.

Deecke, L., Lang, W., Beisteiner, R., Lindinger, G., and Cui, R. Q. (1997). Movement-related potentials and magnetic fields: New evidence for SMA activation leading MI activation prior to voluntary movement. In *Proceedings of the 14th International Congress of EEG and Clinical Neurophysiology,* Florence, Italy, http://cogprints.ecs.soton.ac.uk/archive/00000010/00/FlorenzPap.html.

Dettmers, C., Fink, G. R., Lemon, R. N., Stephan, K. M., Passingham, R. E., Silbersweig, D., Holmes, A., Ridding, M. C., Brooks, D. J., and Frackowiak, R. S. J. (1995). Relation between cerebral activity and force in the motor areas of the human brain. *Journal of Neurophysiology, 74,* 802–815.

de Vignemont, F., and Fourneret, P. (2004). The sense of agency: A philosophical and empirical review of the "who" system. *Consciousness and Cognition, 13,* 1–19.

Ellaway, P. H., Prochazka, A., Chan, M., and Gauthier, M. J. (2004). The sense of movement elicited by transcranial magnetic stimulation in humans is due to sensory feedback. *Journal of Physiology, 556,* 651–660.

Farrer, C., Franck, N., Georgieff, N., Frith, C. D., Decety, J., and Jeannerod, M. (2003). Modulating the experience of agency: A positron emission tomography study. *NeuroImage, 18,* 4–33.

Farrer, C., and Frith, C. D. (2002). Experiencing oneself vs. another person as being the cause of an action: The neural correlates of the experience of agency. *NeuroImage, 15,* 596–603.

Fink, G. R., Marshall, J. C., Halligan, P. W., Frith, C. D., Driver, J., Frackowiak, R. S., and Dolan, R. J. (1999). The neural consequences of conflict between intention and the senses. *Brain, 122,* 497–512.

Fourneret, P., and Jeannerod, M. (1998). Limited conscious monitoring of motor performance in normal subjects. *Neuropsychologia, 36,* 1133–1140.

Franck, N., Farrer, C., Georgieff, N., Marie-Cardine, M., Daléry, J., d'Amato, T., and Jeannerod, M. (2001). Defective recognition of one's own actions in patients with schizophrenia. *American Journal of Psychiatry, 158,* 454–459.

Fried, I., Katz, A., McCarthy, G., Sass, K. J., Williamson, P., Spencer, S. S., and Spencer, D. D. (1991). Functional organization of human supplementary motor cortex studied by electrical stimulation. *Journal of Neuroscience, 11,* 3656–3666.

Frith, C. D. (2000). The role of dorsolateral prefrontal cortex in the selection of action, as revealed by functional imaging. In S. Monsell and J. Driver (Eds.), *Control of cognitive processes: Attention and performance XVIII* (pp. 547–565). Cambridge: MIT Press.

Frith, C. D. (2002). Attention to action and awareness of other minds. *Consciousness and Cognition*, *11*, 481–487.

Frith, C. D., Blakemore, S.-J., and Wolpert, D. M. (2000). Abnormalities in the awareness and control of action. *Philosophical Transactions of the Royal Society of London, Series B, Biological Sciences*, *355*, 1771–1788.

Frith, C. D., Friston, K., Liddle, P. F., and Frackowiak, R. S. (1991). Willed action and the prefrontal cortex in man: A study with PET. *Proceedings of the Royal Society London, Series B, Biological Sciences*, *244*, 241–246.

Georgieff, N., and Jeannerod, M. (1998). Beyond consciousness of external reality: A "who" system for consciousness of action and self-consciousness. *Consciousness and Cognition*, *7*, 465–477.

Goldberg, G. (1985). Supplementary motor area structure and function: Review and hypotheses. *Behavioral and Brain Sciences*, *8*, 567–616.

Graziano, M. S. A., and Botvinik, M. M. (2001). How the brain represents the body: Insights from neurophysiology and psychology. In W. Prinz and B. Hommel (Eds.) (2002), *Common mechanisms in perception and action: Attention and performance XIX* (pp. 136–158). New York: Oxford University Press.

Grèzes, J., and Decety, J. (2001). Functional anatomy of execution, mental simulation, observation, and verb generation of actions: A meta-analysis. *Human Brain Mapping*, *12*, 1–19.

Haggard, P. (2005). Conscious intention and the sense of agency. In W. Prinz and N. Sebanz (Eds.), *Disorders of volition* (pp. 69–86). Cambridge: MIT Press.

Haggard, P., and Clark, S. (2003). Intentional action: Conscious experience and neural prediction. *Consciousness and Cognition*, *12*, 695–707.

Haggard, P., Clark, S., and Kalogeras, J. (2002). Voluntary action and conscious awareness. *Nature Neuroscience*, *5*, 382–385.

Haggard, P., and Eimer, M. (1999). On the relation between brain potentials and the awareness of voluntary movements. *Experimental Brain Research*, *126*, 128–133.

Haggard, P., and Johnson, H. (2003). Experiences of voluntary action. *Journal of Consciousness Studies*, *10*(9–10), 72–85.

Haggard, P., and Whitford, B. (2004). Supplementary motor area provides an efferent signal for sensory suppression. *Brain Research: Cognitive Brain Research*, *19*, 52–58.

James, W. (1840/1981). *The principles of psychology*. Cambridge: Harvard University Press.

Jeannerod, M. (2003a). The mechanism of self-recognition in humans. *Behavioral Brain Research*, *142*, 1–15.

Jeannerod, M. (2003b). Consciousness of action and self-consciousness: A cognitive neuroscience approach. In J. Roessler and N. Eilan (Eds.), *Agency and self-awareness: Issues in philosophy and psychology* (pp 128–149). Oxford: Oxford University Press.

Jeannerod, M., and Pacherie, E. (2004). Agency, simulation and self-identification. *Mind and Language, 19,* 113–146.

Lau, H. C., Rogers, R. D., Haggard, P., and Passingham, R. E. (2004). Attention to intention. *Science, 303,* 1208–1210.

Lau, H. C., Rogers, R. D., Ramnani, N., and Passingham, R. E. (2004). Willed action and attention to the selection of action. *NeuroImage, 21,* 1407–1415.

Lee, K. M., Chang, K. H., and Roh, J. K. (1999). Subregions within the supplementary motor area activated at different stages of movement preparation and execution. *NeuroImage, 9,* 117–123.

Leube, D. T., Knoblich, G., Erb, M., and Kircher, T. T. (2003). Observing one's hand become anarchic: An fMRI study of action identification. *Consciousness and Cognition, 12,* 597–608.

Libet, B. (1985). Unconscious cerebral initiative and the role of conscious will in voluntary action. *Behavioral and Brain Sciences, 8,* 529–566.

Libet, B., Gleason, C. A., Wright, E. W., and Pearl, D. K. (1983). Time of conscious intention to act in relation to onset of cerebral activity (readiness-potential): The unconscious initiation of a freely voluntary act. *Brain, 106,* 623–642.

Libet, B., Wright, E. W., Jr., and Gleason, C. A. (1983). Preparation- or intention-to-act, in relation to pre-event potentials recorded at the vertex. *Electroencephalography and Clinical Neurophysiology, 56,* 367–372.

Merleau-Ponty, M. (1962). *The phenomenology of perception.* London: Routledge.

Németh, G., Hegedüs, K., and Molnár, L. (1988). Akinetic mutism associated with bicingular lesions: Clinicopathological and functional anatomical correlates. *European Archives of Psychiatry and Neurological Sciences, 237,* 218–222.

O'Shaughnessy, B. (2004). Theories of bodily self. In T. Pink and M. W. F. Stone (Eds.), *The will and human action: From antiquity to the present day* (pp. 197–211). London: Routledge.

Pachoud, B. (1999). The teleological dimension of perceptual and motor intentionality. In J. Petitot, F. J. Varela, B. Pachoud, and J.-M. Roy (Eds.), *Naturalizing phenomenology: Issues in contemporary phenomenology and cognitive science* (pp. 196–219). Stanford, CA: Stanford University Press.

Paus, T. (2001). Primate anterior cingulate cortex: Where motor control, drive and cognition interface. *Nature Reviews Neuroscience, 2,* 417–424.

Penfield, W., and Welch, K. (1951). The supplementary motor area of the cerebral cortex: A clinical and experimental study. *Archives of Neurology and Psychiatry, 66*, 289–317.

Rizzolatti, G., and Craighero, L. (2004). The mirror-neuron system. *Annual Review of Neuroscience, 27*, 169–192.

Salomons, T. V., Johnstone, T., Backonja, M.-M., and Davidson, R. J. (2004). Perceived controllability modulates the neural response to pain. *Journal of Neuroscience, 24*, 7199–7203.

Schopenhauer, A. (1969). *The world as will and representation* (Vol. 1, E. F. J. Payne, Trans.). New York: Dover.

Searle, J. (1983). *Intentionality: An essay in the philosophy of mind.* New York: Cambridge University Press.

Smith, A. M. (1979). The activity of supplementary motor area neurons during a maintained precision grip. *Brain Research, 172*, 315–327.

Toni, I., Thoenissen, D., and Zilles, K. (2001). Movement preparation and motor intention. *NeuroImage, 14*, S110–S117.

Tsakiris, M., and Haggard, P. (2003). Awareness of somatic events following a voluntary action. *Experimental Brain Research, 149*, 439–446.

Tsakiris, M., and Haggard, P. (2004). Experimenting with the acting self. *Cognitive Neuropsychology, 22*, 387–407.

Tsakiris, M., Haggard, P., Franck, N., Mainy, N., and Sirigu, A. (2005). A specific role for efferent information in a self-recognition task. *Cognition, 96*, 215–231.

Wegner, D. M. (2002). *The illusion of conscious will.* Cambridge: MIT Press.

Wegner, D. M., and Wheatley, T. (1999). Apparent mental causation: Sources of the experience of will. *American Psychologist, 54*, 480–492.

Weilke, F., Spiegel, S., Boecker, H., von Einsiedel, H. G., Conrad, B., Schwaiger, M., and Erhard, P. (2000). Time-resolved fMRI of activation patterns in M1 and SMA during complex voluntary movement. *Journal of Neurophysiology, 85*, 1858–1863.

Wolpert, D. M. (1997). Computational approaches to motor control. *Trends in Cognitive Sciences, 1*, 209–216.

Part III Developmental and Comparative Perspectives

4 The Link between Action Production and Action Processing in Infancy

Jessica A. Sommerville and Amanda L. Woodward

Central to our ability to process and interpret the actions of others is the tendency to view action as directed toward goals or end states. Presented with a stream of ongoing behavior, we construe single actions within the stream as directed toward objects, and interpret actions within a sequence as directed at higher-order goals or outcomes. Imagine an evening out at a local restaurant with a dinner companion. We readily perceive our social partner's reach toward and grasp of the fork as directed at attaining a utensil but also recognize this act as one step among many in enjoying a meal. The ability to construe action as directed toward proximate and ultimate goals is key not only to interpreting the actions of others but also for predicting future actions based on past actions, for learning from and describing novel actions to others, and for categorizing action sequences in terms of the event representations to which they belong.

Empirical work has focused on adults' ability to build goal-centered event representations (for a review, see Zacks and Tversky 2001). When asked to describe naturalistic behavior, adults rely on behavioral episodes (e.g., driving to work) that correspond to events consisting of action parts (e.g., leaving the house, getting into the car, etc.; Barker and Wright 1954). In laboratory tasks, adults readily identify goal-relevant action units in commonplace behavior. These action units are consistent both within and across individuals (e.g., Newtson and Engquist 1976). Moreover, adults describe ongoing action to others with respect to its partonomic or hierarchical structure, parsing ongoing behavior both with respect to action-based goals (e.g., grasping a fork) and with respect to higher order goals (e.g., eating a meal; Zacks, Tversky, and Iver 2001). Goal-relevant actions are remembered more strongly than goal-irrelevant actions in the context of text processing (Black and Bower 1980), and prior segmentation of videotaped activity with respect to partonomic structure makes action content more memorable than unsegmented activity (Boltz 1992). These findings suggest that adults (1) create behavioral representations that parse activity at the level of action goals and (2) appreciate the organization of these action units and their relevance to the overarching or event goal.

Action Processing in Children

Recent work with children suggests that their ability to process human action shares many features with that of adults. Preschoolers spontaneously create hierarchically organized event schemas when asked about their everyday activities (e.g., Slackman, Hudson, and Fivush 1986). When asked to imitate the actions of another person, preschoolers selectively reproduce the highest order goal of the action (Bekkerring, Wohlschlager, and Gattis 2000). In addition, preschoolers' and toddlers' memories for action sequences often exclude actions that do not bear directly on the goal of the sequence (Travis 1997). Ongoing research suggests that 4-year-olds' ability to recall the agent of a given action within a sequence is heavily influenced by the temporal proximity of the action to the goal of the sequence: agent recall decreases linearly with each step away from the goal (Sommerville and Hammond, 2007). These findings suggest that children construct action representations that are, in many ways, similar to those of adults.

The State of Action Processing in Infancy

Findings on the relative sophistication of children's action processing and representation have sparked interest in the roots of this ability. In a landmark study, Meltzoff (1995) showed 18-month-old infants a human actor attempting to produce a target action but failing. For instance, one of the sequences that toddlers viewed involved the actor trying to pull apart the ends of a miniature barbell. However, the actor's hands repeatedly slipped off of the barbell before he could complete the target action. Other infants watched the actor successfully complete the target action. When given the opportunity to act on the barbell, both groups of infants successfully reproduced the target action, despite the fact that the former group had never viewed this action before. These findings suggest that 18-month-olds readily construed the actor's actions (grasping the barbell, pulling at the ends, etc.) with respect to an overarching goal.

Other studies have investigated younger infants' ability to segment everyday activities into action units that are commensurate with those of adults. Baldwin, Baird, Saylor, and Clark (2001) showed infants video clips of familiar action sequences, into which still frame pauses had been inserted. These pauses either preserved or disrupted the intentional structure of the activity. For instance, in some cases the pause occurred after the actor had picked up a towel (preserving sequences), and in other cases the pause occurred in the midst of the actor's reaching for the towel (disrupting sequences). Ten- and 11-month-old infants showed a novelty preference for disrupting sequences, indicating sensitivity to the intentional structure of the ongoing stream of behavior.

Recent research suggests that even young infants show goal-biased processing of simple, single actions. Five-month-old infants shown an event in which an actor reached for one of two toys showed selective attention to the relation between the actor and the object that she was grasping over other properties (such as spatial location and path of motion; Woodward 1998). Several months later (by 12 months of age) infants also interpret attentional behaviors (such as goal-directed points and eye gaze) in terms of the objects that they are directed toward (Woodward 2003; Woodward and Guarjardo 2002). These findings suggest that over the first year of life infants begin to create action representations that highlight goal-relevant information.

In this chapter we discuss research that further explores the development of infants' action processing in the first year of life (Sommerville and Woodward 2005; Sommerville, Woodward, and Needham 2005). In doing so, we focus on two different time points that mark developmental achievements in goal processing: the ability to construe a simple reach and grasp as goal directed and the ability to construe actions within a sequence as directed toward a higher-order goal. We discuss these achievements with respect to a key mechanism that we believe underlies infants' ability to view the actions of others with respect to an underlying goal structure. Although it is likely the case that many innate and developing capacities contribute to infants' ability to view action as goal directed, we consider the rich information that infants' own developing motor capabilities and action skills may play in their perception and interpretation of the actions of others.

Action Production and Perception: Birds of a Feather?

Recently evidence has been mounting to suggest that action production and perception are intimately related. Studies suggest that action observation, simulation, and execution may rely on a common computational and neural code both in human and nonhuman primates (see Decety and Sommerville 2007 for a review).

Behavioral research reveals that action production and observation share a common computational code (e.g., Hommel et al. 2001; Prinz 1997). When subjects are asked to identify arrow directions presented on a monitor using already prepared left- and right-key responses, their ability to perceive the direction of an arrow is reduced when the response required matches the arrow direction (Muessler and Hommel 1997). The findings from these spatial compatibility tasks suggest that interference occurs because action and perception try to simultaneously access the same representation. Interestingly, these spatial compatibility effects extend to situations in which the response is split across two participants (e.g., one participant responds to right-facing arrows and the other to left-facing arrows), suggesting that other's actions are represented in a fashion similar to one's own (Sebanz, Knoblich, and Prinz 2003).

Prior motor observation also facilitates action production, suggesting that the perception of action primes a representation, making it in turn more readily available to action. Viewing compatible motor responses prior to responding speeds action production, whereas viewing incompatible motor responses prior to responding slows action production (Brass, Bekkering, and Prinz 2001), and observing prehension primes subsequent execution (Castiello et al. 2002). Action production also affects action perception: perceptual judgments of arm movements affect subsequent motor learning (Hecht, Vogt, and Prinz 2001).

Further evidence suggests that individuals may use their own action plans when observing the actions of others. In one study, individuals asked to predict the next marking in a handwriting sequence of another person benefited from having performed those sequences earlier (Knoblich, Seigerschmidt, Flach, and Prinz 2002). Moreover, individuals watching the actions of others appear to produce eye movements similar to those produced when they are performing similar actions themselves (Flanagan and Johansson 2003).

Shared representation for action production and processing also exist at a neural level. In monkeys, the presence of "mirror neurons," which discharge during the performance and observation of a particular action, suggests a system that links observed events to internally generated actions (e.g., Rizzolatti and Arbib 1998; Rizzolatti and Fadiga 1998). Research with human subjects provides evidence for a similar action observation–execution matching system in humans. Functional magnetic resonance imaging studies indicate overlapping areas of activation during action observation, execution, and simulation (e.g., Grèzes and Decety 2001). Transcranial magnetic stimulation studies suggest a selective increase in motor-evoked potentials during action observation (specific to muscles used to perform those actions; Fadiga et al. 1995) that closely follows that of movement execution (Gangitano, Mottaghy, and Pascual-Leone 2001). Similar to behavioral findings, some investigators report that the neural processes involved in preparing one's own action are also involved in predicting the future actions of others (Ramnani and Miall 2004).

Taken together, the findings from behavioral and neural studies give teeth to the long-standing speculation that action production, simulation, and understanding may be closely intertwined (e.g., Baldwin, 1897; Cooley 1902; Goldman 1989; Gordon 1986; Harris 1989; Heal 1998; Mill 1867). Indeed, many have suggested that observation–execution matching system may underlie our ability to understand the actions of others (e.g., Blakemore and Decety 2001; Gallese and Goldman 1998; Keysers and Perrett 2004).

Action Production as an Engine in Development

Researchers have speculated that the relation between action production and action understanding serves as a powerful engine in development. For instance, some investigators have argued that infants' understanding of others as intentional agents depends in large part upon their own newly emerging forms of intentionality in sensorimotor actions (e.g., Frye 1991; Tomasello 1999) or that imitation of others' actions allows infants to determine their intentions (Meltzoff and Moore 1995). Indeed, even neonates spontaneously imitate the actions of others (Meltzoff and Moore 1977). These speculations and findings raise the possibility that action processing and production may be tightly interconnected from early in development. However, to date there are few studies that have directly investigated the relation between action production and processing in infancy.

Regardless of the exact role that action production may play in action perception, this perspective predicts that the interrelation between action perception and production should be apparent in at least two ways. First, natural variability in action production during periods of development should be related to variation in action perception. Second, providing infants with action experience should facilitate goal-directed action perception. To assess these claims, we have investigated the relation of infant action production and perception with two different age groups. We focused on the role of action experience in (1) infants' ability to construe simple actions (e.g., a reach and grasp) as goal directed in 3.5-month-old infants (Sommerville, Woodward, and Needham 2005) and (2) infants' ability to perceive action sequences as directed toward a higher order goal in 10-month-old infants (Sommerville and Woodward 2005). With respect to older infants, we present work that examined the relation between naturally occurring variability in infants' action production and perception. With respect to younger infants, we present work that has explored the impact that providing infants with action experience has on action perception. Our research suggests that action production and action processing truly are birds of a feather: action production and perception are interwoven starting early in development (cf. Meltzoff 2004).

The Relation between Natural Variability in Action Production and Action Perception

Previous work suggests that 9 to 12 months of age marks a transitional time in infants' ability to spontaneously generate goal-directed action sequences (e.g., Bates, Carlson-Luden, and Bretherton 1980; Piaget 1953). It is throughout this time that infants develop the ability to solve a variety of simple means–end tasks (tasks which require producing an initial action in order to obtain a goal object), such as pulling a cloth to obtain a toy, opening a box to obtain a toy, and pulling a string to get a toy. This ability has been considered a hallmark of intentional behavior, as it requires the ability to separate a goal state from the means to achieving it (Piaget 1953; Tomasello 1999).

Over this same time period, infants demonstrate the ability to construe the action sequences of others in terms of their goal structure. By 12 months of age, infants selectively imitate the goal of a sequence but often exclude the means of the sequence when is not necessary for goal attainment (Carpenter, Call, and Tomasello 2005). Studies implementing infants' visual assessment of events have yielded similar findings. To illustrate, after 12-month-old infants watched an actor perform a box-opening sequence in which she opened a translucent box to grasp a toy inside, infants represented the actor's subsequent touch to the box lid as directed toward the toy inside the box rather than as directed toward the box lid itself (Woodward and Sommerville 2000). Taken together with the action production findings, these results suggest that infants' abilities to produce and perceive goal-directed action sequences share a similar developmental trajectory.

In one series of studies, we investigated whether this shared developmental trajectory between action perception and production reflects a functional relation between the two abilities. Our goal was to develop action and perception measures involving the same sequence. We chose a cloth-pulling sequence (one in which a cloth that supports an out-of-reach toy can be pulled in order to obtain the toy) for three reasons. First, adults readily construe this action sequence as hierarchically organized: they view an individual's actions on the cloth as directed at the toy rather than at the cloth itself. Second, cloth-pulling sequences may be familiar to infants: they may have seen siblings pull a blanket in order to obtain a toy resting on top of it or seen their parents pull a newspaper to retrieve their keys. Third, decades of literature on infant problem solving suggests that infants are able to solve a variety of simple means–end sequences by 1 year of age (Diamond 1985; Piaget 1953; Willatts 1999). Our first goal was to test whether 12-month-old infants would respond to these observed sequences in the same way as in the box-opening study. This then enabled us to investigate younger infants, who were likely to be transitional with respect to their comprehension of these sequences and their ability to produce them.

Infants were tested using a visual habituation paradigm. During this paradigm, infants watched live events presented on a puppet stage, and an online observer who was unaware of the particular events that infants were viewing timed their looking to the outcome of these events (see figure 4.1). During the habituation phase of the task, infants saw an actor sitting between two different colored cloths, each of which supported a different toy. On each trial a screen was lowered and infants saw an actor pull a cloth that supported an out-of-reach toy, then grasp the toy once it came into reach. This action was performed once per trial, and infants were shown this event on multiple trials until their looking to the event declined to half its initial level. As such, infants saw a minimum of 6 and a maximum of 14 identical habituation trials. At this point, all infants proceeded to the test phase of the study.

Prior to the test phase, we switched the locations of the toys (so that each toy now sat on a different cloth than it initially had). This enabled us to show infants two new types of test events. In the *new toy* test events, the screen was lowered and infants saw the actor grasp the same cloth that she had on habituation trials that now supported a new toy. This event featured a disruption in the relation between the actor and her ultimate goal. In the *new cloth* test events, the screen was lowered and infants saw the actor grasp a new cloth (e.g., the cloth that supported the same toy

Habituation Events

New toy event New cloth event

Figure 4.1
The cloth-pulling habituation paradigm.

that she had acted on during habituation trials). This event featured a disruption in the relation between the actor and the intermediary that she acted on. Infants saw these test events in alternation, three times each (for a total of six test trials). The prediction here was that if infants construed the actor's actions on the cloth as directed toward the toy (after having seen the completed cloth-pulling sequence), they should show a novelty preference for the new toy events. In contrast, if they misconstrued the actor's actions on the cloth as directed toward the cloth itself, they may prefer the new cloth events.

Our findings provided further evidence that 12-month-old infants construe simple action sequences with respect to higher order goals. Infants looked significantly longer to the new toy event, indicating that they represented the actor's actions on the cloth as directed toward the toy. Thus, taken together with evidence suggesting that it is also by this age that infants can solve a range of means–end sequences (e.g., Piaget 1953), these findings suggest that it is by 12 months of age that infants' view both their own and others' actions as directed toward a higher order goal.

These findings positioned us to investigate younger infants' representations of the cloth-pulling sequence both in their own actions and the actions of others. We next sought to assess 10-month-olds' interpretation of the cloth-pulling sequence. Based on previous work (Sommerville and Woodward, unpublished data), we suspected that 10-month-old infants would be transitional with respect to their ability to perceive the cloth-pulling sequence as directed toward the toy. Previous work suggested that infants' own means–end behavior is also transitional at this time (e.g., Piaget 1953). To assess 10-month-old infants' ability to construe another person's cloth-pulling actions as directed toward a higher order goal and their ability to solve a cloth-pulling sequence in their own actions in an apparently planful manner, we tested infants on an action production task (action task) and an action perception paradigm (habituation paradigm).

During the action task, infants were given multiple opportunities to pull a cloth in order to obtain an out-of-reach toy. Infants' ability to solve this task was gauged by coding their solutions to the task. Specifically, we were interested in trials on which infants solved the task in ways that appeared planful and clearly directed toward the ultimate goal of the sequence: obtaining the toy. Previous work suggests that cloth-pulling sequences can be solved by infants as young as 7 months, using strategies that can best be described as accidental (e.g., Willatts 1990, 1999). For instance, infants might play with the cloth and inadvertently bring the toy within reach. As such, we considered as planful strategies those trials on which the infant looked at the toy, maintained focus on the toy while pulling the cloth, and quickly and immediately grasped the toy once it came into reach.

Infants also took part in the cloth-pulling habituation paradigm (see figure 4.1). This paradigm was identical to that used with 12-month-old infants. These tasks were presented in a counterbalanced order such that half of the infants received the habituation paradigm first, whereas the other half of infants received the action task first.

We first assessed infants' group-level performance on the action task and the habituation paradigm. We found that infants' ability to (1) produce planful strategies to solve the action task and (2) perceive the actor's actions on the cloth as directed toward the toy in the habituation paradigm was variable. Specifically, on the action task infants produced planful strategies on just over half of all codable trials. In the habituation paradigm infants' looking to the two test events did not differ significantly: about half the infants looked longer on new goal trials, and the other half looked longer on new side trials. These findings suggest that, unlike 12-month-olds, 10-month-old infants (as a group) do not systematically use goal-directed strategies to solve the cloth-pulling task in their own actions, nor do they systematically perceive the actions of another as goal directed when that person performs a similar sequence. Thus, 10 to 12 months of age marks a transition in infants' ability to perceive the goal directedness of action sequences and to reliably produce goal-directed action sequences.

The variability that was naturally present in infants' action and habituation performance enabled us to investigate the relation between action and habituation performance at an individual level. We first looked at the correlation between the frequency of planful strategies that infants produced on the action task (a measure of how goal directed infants' own actions were) and the magnitude and consistency of their preference for the new toy test event (a measure of the extent to which infants were sensitive to the goal of another person's actions). This correlational analysis revealed that action task performance and habituation task performance were significantly related, even when controlling for age. Infants who showed a greater novelty reaction to test events that featured a disruption between the actor and the toy produced more planful strategies on the action task than infants who demonstrated a lesser preference (or the reverse preference).

In a second analysis, we explored habituation task performance for the top and bottom performers on the action task. We categorized infants who performed in the top 25% with respect to how frequently they produced planful strategies as "planful infants." We categorized infants who scored in the bottom 25% with respect to how frequently they produced planful strategies as "nonplanful infants." We then compared infants' looking time preference on the habituation task as a function of action task performance. We found that both groups of infants showed systematic and opposite patterns in their looking times. Planful infants showed a significant preference for the new toy test events, whereas nonplanful infants showed a significant preference for the new cloth test events. These findings suggest that planful infants understood that the actor's touch to the cloth was directed toward the ultimate goal of attaining the toy. In contrast, nonplanful infants may have been focusing on the relation between the actor and the intermediary that she acted on: they may have construed her actions as directed toward the cloth itself.

These findings suggest that there is an intimate relation between the ability to process and produce at least one simple action sequence in infancy: pulling a cloth to get a toy. As such, our results provide some of the first empirical evidence for a link between action production and processing in infancy and are consistent with the speculation that infants' own action production may provide a powerful source of information for their ability to understand the actions of others (Meltzoff 2004; Tomasello 1999; Woodward, Sommerville, and Guajardo 2001). Such a perspective also predicts that providing infants with action experience may facilitate their ability to detect goals in the actions of others. In another line of studies, we assessed the impact of an action experience intervention on young infants' action perception.

The Impact of Action Production on Action Perception

Our findings point to a tight link between action production and perception by the end of the first year of life. However, because our results are correlational, they raise questions regarding the generality, directionality, and nature of the relation between action processing and action production. With respect to generality, it is possible that a lurking third variable accounts for the observed relation between action production and processing (such as general intelligence or developmental level). Although our present results argue against this possibility (neither age nor habituation rate, a proxy for general intelligence, accounted for the relation between action processing and perception), it is difficult to rule this possibility out entirely. Furthermore, if the relation between action production and action processing reflects a causal one, the question arises as to whether developments in action processing lead to developments in action production, whether developments in action production lead to changes in action processing, or whether action processing and action production have a reciprocal influence on one another.

In a second line of studies, we sought to assess the effect of providing infants with action experience on action perception and vice versa. To do so, we tested younger infants using a habituation paradigm similar to that implemented by Woodward (1998). In this paradigm, during habituation trials, infants watch an actor reach for and grasp one of two toys sitting side by side on a stage. Once infants reach the habituation criteria, the position of the toys is reversed and infants see events in which the actor reaches for a new toy (new toy event) in alternation with events in which the actor reaches for the same toys she did initially now in a new location (new side event). Adults seeing a similar event would be predicted to focus selectively on the relation between the actor and her goal object over other superficial changes of the event. Thus, this paradigm assesses infants' ability to construe a simple, single action (a reach and grasp) as goal directed, by comparing looking times to the two test events.

Using this paradigm, Woodward (1998) demonstrated that it is by roughly 5 months of age that infants look significantly longer to the new toy event. In contrast, at 3 months of age infants attend equally to a change in the superficial perceptual properties of a reach and grasp (e.g., change in spatial location of reach) as to a change in the goal object of the reach (Sommerville, Woodward, and Needham 2005). Thus, this time period marks a transition in infants' ability to attend to the object directedness or goal directedness of another person's reach.

Research on infants' ability to produce goal-directed reaches in their own actions reveals similar developmental trends. Infants' interactions with objects change both qualitatively and quantitatively over the first 6 months of life. By 6 months of age, infants show changes in exploratory behavior in the presence of objects, such as an increase in the amount of object manipulation (Bakeman, Adamson, Konner, and Barr 1990; Rochat 1990). Over this same time frame infants develop the ability to reach proficiently under a variety of conditions. By 6 months, infants can adjust their grasp to the size of an object (Clifton, Rochat, Litovsky, and Perris 1991; von Hofsten and Ronnqvist 1988), reach under differing conditions of illumination (Clifton, Rochat, Robin, and Berthier 1994), adjust their body position when reaching for objects placed just beyond their grasp (Yonas and Hartman 1993), and anticipate an object's trajectory (Robin, Berthier, and Clifton 1996).

This similarity in developmental trajectory led us to investigate whether providing infants with a reaching intervention would impact action perception. We first sought an intervention that would enable prereaching infants to successfully apprehend and move objects. To do so, we utilized an action intervention task created by Needham, Barrett, and Peterman (2002). In this task, prereaching infants were given play sessions with "sticky mittens" (mittens with palms that stuck to the edges of toys and allowed the infants to pick up the toys) that increased infants' object engagement and exploration strategies. We (Sommerville, Woodward, and Needham 2005) investigated the impact of sticky mittens experience on infants' perception of the goal directedness of another person's reach and grasp.

To this end 3.5-month-old infants took part in an action intervention task (sticky mittens task) and a habituation paradigm (Sommerville et al. 2005). Half of the infants received the action intervention task prior to the habituation paradigm, and half of the infants received the tasks in the reverse order. Thus, we hoped to assess (1) the impact of action intervention on action perception and (2) the impact of action perception on action intervention.

During the action intervention task, infants sat on their parent's lap in front of a white, height-adjustable table that was set at approximately waist height. For approximately 2 minutes, infants were given the opportunity to look and interact with small toys barehanded. These toys (a ball and a teddy bear) were miniature versions of the toys that were implemented in the habituation paradigm. During this initial 2 minutes, infants typically looked at, and occasionally made contact with, the toys. The experimenter changed the position of the toys from time to time to ensure that infants were equally attentive to both toys.

After this initial period elapsed, the experimenter fitted a pair of small mittens on the infants. These mittens were made of a sheer fabric through which infants could see the back of their hands. The palm of the mittens was made of felt and covered with Velcro. Because the toys were also Velcro covered, the mittens would attach to the toys when infants made contact with a toy, allowing infants to apprehend the toys. Infants were given the action intervention task for approximately 3 minutes. During this time, the experimenter removed each toy from the mitten after it had been attached for several seconds, enabling the infant to have multiple opportunities to apprehend the toys. Again, the experimenter changed the position of the toys from time to time to ensure that infants were equally attentive to both toys.

Infants also took part in the habituation paradigm (see figure 4.2). This paradigm was identical to that of Woodward (1998), with the exception that the actor wore a white mitten identical to the one the infant wore during the action intervention task.

We first sought to establish whether we successfully intervened on infants' reaching experience. To do so, we calculated the amount of time that infants spent in contact with the toy while also looking at the toy for both the barehanded and mittens phase of the action intervention. Infants spent a significantly greater proportion of time in coordinated eye gaze and manual contact with the toys with the mittens on than when they were off. These findings suggest that our intervention was indeed successful: infants interacted with the objects in a more clearly goal-directed manner as a result of the sticky mittens experience. Further analyses revealed that infants' action production was unaffected by whether they received the action intervention task first or whether they received the habituation paradigm first.

Habituation event

New toy event

New side event

Figure 4.2
The mittens habituation paradigm.

We next assessed the impact of action intervention on action perception by investigating infants' looking times to the test events. We predicted that the action intervention should help infants focus on the goal of another person's reach. As such, we predicted that infants who received the action task prior to the habituation task would show a significant preference for new object test trials over new side test trials but that this effect would be absent for infants who received the tasks in the reverse order. Our findings bore out these predictions. Infants who received the action intervention prior to the habituation paradigm looked significantly longer at the new object events than at the new side events. In contrast, infants who received the tasks in the reverse order looked equally to both types of test events. Moreover, we conducted a series of correlational analyses examining the relation of infants' habituation response (their preference for the new object event) and various aspects of their mittened experience. These analyses revealed a selective relation between infants' overall amount of coordinated gaze and manual contact on objects while wearing the mittens and the extent of their preference for the new object events, indicating that the effects of action production on action perception were not reducible to perceptual highlighting of the toys or individual differences in motor development. Thus, action experience with the sticky mittens impacted infants' subsequent perception of the action of others.

Our findings suggest that experience producing goal-directed reaches facilitates infants' perception of the goal-directed reaches of others. In contrast, however, there was no evidence for an impact of action perception on action production. It is possible that action production and action perception exert a mutual influence on one another but that this bidirectionality is difficult to measure in young infants. It may also be the case that the perceptual information that infants received in the habituation paradigm was not rich enough to influence their action production. Nevertheless, these results provide further evidence for a tight link between action perception and production. In the following section we consider the different ways in which action production may contribute to action perception.

Information Gleaned from Action Production and the Role of Agency

There is no doubt that multiple factors contribute to infants' ability to detect the goal structure of ongoing behavior. Our findings suggest that chief among these factors is infants' own experience as goal-directed agents (Sommerville and Woodward 2005; Sommerville, Woodward, and Needham 2005; Woodward 2005). Infants' own action experience appears to exert a role in action perception from very early in life. Ongoing work is seeking to establish whether observational experience also plays a role in developing action perception, and whether that role is similar to or different from observational experience. Self experience may exert an influence on action perception at a variety of different levels. Below we consider three possibilities.

Action Experience Facilitates the Detection of the Behavioral Manifestation of Goals

Self experience may play a role in action perception by providing infants with exemplars of action from which cues to goal directedness can be detected. Baldwin and colleagues (Baird and Baldwin 2001; Baldwin et al. 2001) have argued that infants' ability to parse ongoing action into goal-relevant units may be based on their capacity to detect structural regularities in the stream of ongoing behavior that signal the completion of action goals or intentions. Indeed, bodily cues such as eye gaze, direction of motion, and contact with object and release may signal an actor's intent. Such cues are present in both infants' own actions and the actions of others. Thus, infants' developing ability to produce particular actions may provide them with an increased number of exemplars from which to detect these behavioral cues. According to this account, it is not critical that experience be self-produced: observing exemplars of another person acting may have a similar effect on action production. Although this possibility sounds like the simplest explanation of our data, it is worth pointing out that gleaning structural information from one's own actions is not trivial. It requires the ability to take an objectified, unembodied view of the self's actions and also entails a perspective switch when applying this knowledge to the actions of others.

Action Experience Restructures Representations of Other's Actions

Another possibility is that infants' developing ability to produce specific action sequences allows them to build action representations that relate particular actions to an end state. In the case of the cloth-pulling sequence, this would entail building a representation that related the action of cloth pulling to the goal of toy attainment. Some authors have proposed that motor representations may help an individual monitor prospective actions online and thus could function similarly in representations of others' actions (Rizzolatti et al. 2000). Indeed, Wilson and Knoblich (2005) have suggested that covert motor activation during action observation serves just this purpose: the internal simulation of perceived ongoing movements allows individuals to generate perceptual predictions.

Although representations of this nature could be similarly structured based on observational experience, self-produced experience could provide a privileged source of prospective organization. Infants' developing mastery of simple action sequences may necessitate attentional shifts to the goal of an action sequence. Consider acquiring a skill in adulthood, such as learning to serve a tennis ball. Initially a tennis novice may focus on each component of the serve at a time—bending his or her knees, throwing the ball up, and pulling the racket back—with little attention to the overarching goal of hitting a winning serve. Over time, as mastery is attained over each component, the player will allocate greater attention to hitting the ball and directing it to the correct place on the court. A similar account may be applied to infants: as they come to solve the cloth-pulling sequence, their attention may be increasingly focused toward the ultimate goal: attaining the toy. This reorganization of attention in infants' own action may then lead to a restructuring of action representations that are accessed when performing self actions and observing the actions of others.

Action Experience Yields Introspective Insight

A final possibility is that infants may glean important subjective information through their developing ability to produce a given action sequence. It is just this information that simulation theorists would argue forms the basis of our understanding of others' actions. For instance, the action of reaching for a highly desired object is accompanied by a particular intention: to obtain the toy. Under this view, infants are aware of this intention when they act on the cloth, attempting to get the toy, and then apply this awareness to the behavior of others when they see others perform similar actions. Although such an account may appear untenable at first glance, as it presumably requires that infants have awareness of their intention while acting and access to prior intentions, it is possible that such a simulation process may occur at an automatic and unconscious level rather than as a result of conscious cognitive effort (cf. Metzinger and Gallese 2003).

Conclusions

The ability to construe human action as directed at objects and outcomes in the world is integral to mature social reasoning. The findings presented in this chapter suggest that by the end of the first year of life, infants' processing of human action is in some ways commensurate with that of adults and older children. Specifically, over the first year of life, infants develop the ability to perceive the goal structure of simple actions and action sequences. These findings raise interesting and important questions regarding the nature of infants' action representations and subsequent developments in infants' goal understanding.

Adults not only recognize goals as the physical end states of action sequences but also can distinguish their own goals from those of others, understand goals as private attributes of individuals, and construe goals as mental representations of outcomes that guide and motivate human behavior. Ongoing work is aimed at investigating when and how subsequent developments in goal understanding are achieved and the functional relation of these more elaborate and sophisticated goal representations to early perceptual sensitivities to goals in the actions of others. One possibility is that a more abstract and mentalistic understanding of goals may emerge from these initial sensitivities. Infants' ability to structure action sequences with respect to a seen goal may provide the framework for redescriptions of human behavior with respect to unseen mental states.

Consistent with a burgeoning literature suggesting a common basis for both the production and perception of action, infants' own active experience contributes to their ability to view others as goal-directed agents. As such, these findings provide some of the first empirical evidence for a link between action production and action processing in infancy. Thus, our results not only have implications for the ontogeny of shared representations but impact theories of cognitive development more broadly. In demonstrating that infants *acquire* knowledge early in life based on their concrete experiences in the world, we push the field beyond accounts that focus singularly on rich innate knowledge versus those that suggest that infants possess no cognitive abilities whatsoever. In addition, our findings provide points of continuity with classic theories of cognitive development as well as points of expansion and departure. Consistent with Piaget's claim regarding the primacy of sensorimotor actions in forming the bedrock of cognitive capacities, our findings document that motor skill acquisition helps to structure cognition. More specifically, our results address the content of early action representations and the manner in which these action representations become structured at a microgenetic level.

Finally, our findings suggest continuity in action–perception mapping from infancy to adulthood. In doing so, they raise fundamental and profound questions surrounding core issues in cognition. From the vantage point of infants' action representations, we can begin to approach questions concerning the differences and similarities in procedural and declarative knowledge, the accessibility of representations to different systems, and the role of active experience in conceptual acquisition and change. Assessing infants' understanding of others' behavior provides not only a snapshot of the developing mind of the child but also a panorama of the very nature of cognition itself.

Acknowledgments

We are grateful to Elizabeth Perkowski, and all members of the Social Understanding Program at the Center for Infant Studies at the University of Chicago for their help with data collection and coding, as well as to the infants and parents who participated in our research. This work was supported by an NIH grant (HD35707) to the second author.

References

Baird, J. A., and Baldwin, D. A. (2001). Making sense of human behavior: Action parsing and intentional inference. In B. F. Malle, L. J. Moses, and D. A. Baldwin (Eds.), *Intentions and intentionality: Foundations of social cognition* (pp. 193–206). Cambridge: MIT Press.

Bakeman, R., Adamson, L. B., Konner, M., and Barr, R. G. (1990). Kung infancy: The social context of object exploration. *Child Development, 61*, 794–809.

Baldwin, D. A., Baird, J. A., Saylor, M. M., Clark, M. A. (2001). Infants parse dynamic action. *Child Development, 72*, 708–717.

Baldwin, J. M. (1897). *Social and ethical interpretations in mental development: A study in social psychology.* New York: Macmillan.

Barker, R. G., and Wright, H. F. (1954). *Midwest and its children: The psychological ecology of an American town.* Evanston, IL: Row, Peterson.

Bates, E., Carlson-Luden, V., and Bretherton, I. (1980). Perceptual aspects of tool using in infancy. *Infant Behavior and Development, 3*, 127–140.

Bekkerring, H., Wohlschlager, A., and Gattis, M. (2000). Imitation of gestures in children is goal-directed. *The Quarterly Journal of Experimental Psychology, 53*, 153–164.

Black, J. B., and Bower, G. H. (1980). Story understanding as problem solving. *Poetics, 9*, 223–250.

Blakemore, S. J., and Decety, J. (2001). From the perception of action to the understanding of intention. *Nature Reviews Neuroscience, 2*, 561–567.

Boltz, M. (1992). Temporal accent structure and the remembering of filmed narratives. *Perception and Psychophysics, 57*, 1080–1096.

Brass, M., Bekkering, H., and Prinz, W. (2001). Movement observation affects movement execution in a simple response task. *Acta Psychologica, 106*, 3–22.

Carpenter, M., Call, J., and Tomasello, M. (2005). Twelve- and 18-month-olds copy actions in terms of goals. *Developmental Science, 8*, F13–F20.

Castiello, U., Lusher, D., Mari, M., Edwards, M., and Humphreys, G. W. (2002). Observing a human or a robotic hand grasping an object: Differential priming effects. In W. Prinz and B. Hommel (Eds.), *Common mechanisms in perception and action: Attention and performance XIX* (pp. 315–333). Oxford: Oxford University Press.

Clifton, R. K., Rochat, P., Litovsky, R. Y., and Perris, E. E. (1991). Object representation guides infants' reaching in the dark. *Journal of Experimental Psychology: Human Perception and Performance, 17*, 323–329.

Clifton, R. K., Rochat, P., Robin, D. J., and Berthier, N. E. (1994). Multimodal perception in the control of infant reaching. *Journal of Experimental Psychology: Human Perception and Performance, 20*, 876–886.

Cooley, C. H. (1902). *Human nature and the social order*. New York: Scribner's.

Decety, J., and Sommerville, J. A. (2007). Motor cognition and mental simulation. In S. Kosslyn and E. Smith (Eds.), *Cognition: Mind and brain* (pp. 451–481). New York: Prentice Hall.

Diamond, A. (1985). Development of the ability to use recall to guide action, as indicated by infants' performance on AB. *Child Development, 55*, 868–883.

Flanagan, J. R., and Johansson, R. S. (2003). Action plans used in action observation. *Nature, 424*, 769–771.

Fadiga, L., Fogassi, L., Pavesi, G., and Rizzolatti, G. (1995). Motor facilitation during action observation: A magnetic stimulation study. *Journal of Neurophysiology, 73*, 2608–2611.

Frye, D. (1991). The origins of intention in infancy. In D. Frye and C. Moore (Eds.), *Children's theories of mind: Mental states and social understanding* (pp. 15–38). Hillsdale, NJ: Erlbaum.

Gallese, V., and Goldman, A. (1998). Mirror neurons and the simulation theory of mind reading. *Trends in Cognitive Science, 12*, 493–501.

Gangitano, M., Mottaghy, F. M., and Pascual-Leone, A. (2001). Phase-specific modulation of cortical motor output during movement observation. *Neuroreport, 12*, 1489–1492.

Goldman, A. (1989). Interpretation psychologized. *Mind and Language, 4*, 161–185.

Gordon, R. M. (1986). Folk psychology as simulation. *Mind and Language, 1*, 158–171.

Grèzes, J., and Decety, J. (2001). Function anatomy of execution, mental simulation, observation and verb generation of actions: A meta-analysis. *Human Brain Mapping, 12*, 1–19.

Harris, P. (1989). *Children and emotion*. Oxford: Blackwell.

Heal, J. (1998). Co-cognition and off-line simulation: Two ways of understanding the simulation approach. *Mind and Language, 13*, 477–498.

Hecht, H., Vogt, S., and Prinz, W. (2001). Motor learning enhances perceptual judgment: A case for action-perception transfer. *Psychological Research/Psychologische Forschung, 65*, 3–14.

Hommel, B., Muessler, J., Aschersleben, G., and Prinz, W. (2001). The theory of event coding (TEC): A framework for perception and action planning. *Behavioral and Brain Sciences, 24*, 849–937.

Keysers, C., and Perrett, D. I. (2004). Demystifying social cognition: A Hebbian perspective. *Trends in Cognitive Sciences, 8,* 501–507.

Knoblich, G., Seigerschmidt, E., Flach, R., and Prinz, W. (2002). Authorship effects in the prediction of handwriting strokes: Evidence for action stimulation during action perception. *Quarterly Journal of Experimental Psychology: Human Experimental Psychology, 55A,* 1027–1046.

Meltzoff, A. N. (1995). Understanding the intentions of others: Reenactments of intended acts by 18-month-old toddlers. *Developmental Psychology, 31,* 838–850.

Meltzoff, A. N. (2004). The case for developmental cognitive science: Theories of people and things. In G. Bremner and A. Slater (Eds.), *Theories of infant development* (pp. 145–173). Malden, MA: Blackwell.

Meltzoff, A. N., and Moore, M. K. (1977). Imitation of facial and manual gestures by human neonates. *Science, 198,* 75–78.

Meltzoff, A. N., and Moore, M. K. (1995). Infants' understanding of people and things: From body imitation to folk psychology. In J. Bermúdez and N. Eilan (Eds.), *The body and the self* (pp. 43–69). Cambridge: MIT Press.

Metzinger, T., and Gallese, V. (2003). The emergence of a shared action ontology: Building blocks for a theory. *Consciousness and Cognition: An International Journal, 12,* 549–571.

Mill, J. S. (1867). *Examination of Sir William Hamilton's philosophy.* London: Longmans.

Muessler, J., and Hommel, B. (1997). Blindness to response-compatible stimuli. *Journal of Experimental Psychology: Human Perception and Performance, 23,* 861–872.

Needham, A., Barrett, T., and Peterman, K. (2002). A pick-me up for infants' exploratory skills: Early simulated experiences reaching for objects using "sticky mittens" enhances young infants' exploration skills. *Infant Behavior and Development, 25,* 279–295.

Newtson, D., and Engquist, G. (1976). The perceptual organization of ongoing behavior. *Journal of Experimental Social Psychology, 28,* 28–38.

Piaget, J. (1953). *The origins of intelligence in the child.* London: Routledge and Kegan Paul.

Prinz, W. (1997). Perception and action planning. *European Journal of Cognitive Psychology, 9,* 129–154.

Ramnani, N., and Miall, C. (2004). A system in the human brain for predicting the actions of others. *Nature Neuroscience, 7,* 85–90.

Rizzolatti, G., and Arbib, M. A. (1998). Language within our grasp. *Trends in Neurosciences, 21*, 188–194.

Rizzolatti, G., and Fadiga, L. (1998). Grasping objects and grasping action meanings: The dual role of the monkey rostroventral premotor cortex (area F5). *Novartis Foundation Symposium, 218*, 81–95.

Rizzolatti, G., Fogassi, L., and Gallese, V. (2000). Cortical mechanisms subserving object grasping and action recognition: A new view on the cortical motor functions. In M. S. Gazzaniga (Ed.), *The new cognitive neurosciences* (2nd ed., pp. 539–552). Cambridge: MIT Press.

Robin, D. J., Berthier, N. E., and Clifton, R. K. (1996). Infant's predictive reaching for moving objects in the dark. *Developmental Psychology, 32*, 824–835.

Rochat, P. (1989). Object manipulation and exploration in 2- to 5-month olds. *Developmental Psychology, 25*, 871–884.

Sebanz, N., Knoblich, G., and Prinz, W. (2003). Representing others' actions: Just like one's own? *Cognition, 88*, B11–B21.

Slackman, E. A., Hudson, J. A., and Fivush, R. (1986). Actions, actors, link and goals: The structure of children's event representations. In K. Nelson (Ed.), *Event knowledge: Structure and function in development* (pp. 47–69). Hillsdale, NJ: Erlbaum.

Sommerville, J. A., and Hammond, A. J. (2007). Treating another's actions as one's own: Children's memory of and learning from joint activity. *Developmental Psychology, 43*, 1003–1018.

Sommerville, J. A., and Woodward, A. L. (unpublished data).

Sommerville, J. A., and Woodward, A. L. (2005). Pulling out the intentional structure of human action: The relation between action production and processing in infancy. *Cognition, 95*, 1–30.

Sommerville, J. A., Woodward, A. L., and Needham, A. (2005). Action experience alters 3-month-old infants' perception of others' actions. *Cognition, 96*, B1–B11.

Tomasello, M. (1999). Having intentions, understanding intentions and understanding communicative intentions. In P. D. Zelazo, J. W. Astington, and D. R. Olson. *Developing theories of intention: Social understanding and self-control* (pp. 63–75). Mahwah, NJ: Erlbaum.

Travis, L. L. (1997). Goal-based organization of event memory in toddlers. In P. W. van den Broek, P. J. Bauer, and T. Bovig (Eds.), *Developmental spans in event comprehension and representation: Bridging fictional and actual events* (pp. 111–138). Mahwah, NJ: Erlbaum.

von Hoftsten, C., and Ronnqvist, L. (1988). Preparation for grasping an object: A developmental study. *Journal of Experimental Psychology: Human Perception and Performance, 14*, 610–621.

Willatts, P. (1990). Development of problem-solving strategies in infancy. In D. F. Bjorklund (Ed.), *Children's strategies: Contemporary views of cognitive development* (pp. 23–66). Hillsdale, NJ: Erlbaum.

Willatts, P. (1999). Development of means-end behavior in young infants: Pulling a support to retrieve a distant object. *Developmental Psychology, 35*, 651–667.

Wilson, M., and Knoblich, G. (2005). The case for motor involvement in perceiving conspecifics. *Psychological Bulletin, 131*, 460–473.

Woodward, A. L. (1998). Infants selectively encode the goal object of an actor's reach. *Cognition, 69*, 1–34.

Woodward, A. L. (2003). Infants' developing understanding of the link between looker and object. *Developmental Science, 6*, 297–311.

Woodward, A. L. (2005). The infant origins of intentional understanding. In R. V. Kail (Ed.), *Advances in child development and behavior* (Vol. 33, pp. 229–262). Oxford: Elsevier.

Woodward, A. L., and Guarjardo, J. J. (2002). Infants' understanding of the point gesture as an object-directed action. *Cognitive Development, 17*, 1061–1084.

Woodward, A. L., and Sommerville, J. A. (2000). Twelve-month-old infants interpret action in context. *Psychological Science, 11*, 73–77.

Woodward, A. L., Sommerville, J. A., and Guajardo, J. J. (2001). How infants make sense of intentional action. In B. F. Malle, L. J. Moses, and D. A. Baldwin (Eds.), *Intentions and intentionality: Foundations of social cognition* (pp. 149–169). Cambridge: MIT Press.

Yonas, A., and Hartman, B. (1993). Perceiving the affordance of contact in four- and five-month-old infants. *Child Development, 64*, 298–308.

Zacks, J. M., and Tversky, B. (2001). Event structure in perception and conception. *Psychological Bulletin, 127*, 3–21.

Zacks, J. M., Tversky, B., and Iver, G. (2001). Perceiving, remembering, and communicating in events. *Journal of Experimental Psychology: General, 130*, 29–58.

5 Mirror, Mirror in the Brain, What's the Monkey Stand to Gain?

Colin Allen

Here are three mutually incompatible propositions:

1. To understand the intentional actions of others requires knowledge of the intentional states (i.e., beliefs and desires) that (rationally) motivated those actions.
2. Monkeys do not have knowledge of the intentional states (beliefs and desires) motivating the actions of others.
3. Monkeys understand the intentional actions of other monkeys.

Proposition 1 is based on the received Aristotelian analysis of intentional action and a commonsense view about understanding. Proposition 2 represents a consensus view among primatologists about the absence of higher order "theory of mind" capacities in monkeys. Proposition 3 reflects a common interpretation of the functions of so-called "mirror neurons" found in the ventral premotor (F5) cortex of macaque monkeys (e.g., Gallese and Goldman 1998; Rizzolatti and Craighero 2004; Fogassi et al. 2005).

Taken at face value, then, this inconsistent triad presents a paradox for understanding the contribution of F5 neurons in macaques to their cognitive capacities. This paradox does not arise for humans because the human analogue to proposition 2 is the obvious candidate for rejection. Nevertheless, the considerations relevant to resolving the paradox for monkeys are also important for a properly skeptical interpretation of the neurological evidence about the mirror neuron system in humans (see Debes, forthcoming).

In this chapter I discuss each of the possibilities for resolving the paradox by rejecting one of the three propositions. Although my philosophical sympathies presently lie with rejecting proposition 1, some of the arguments depend on empirical knowledge that is presently lacking. Nevertheless, I describe an approach to understanding the functions of F5 mirror neurons in macaques which entails a nontraditional understanding of the relationship between intentionality in its ordinary English sense of "purposefulness" and intentionality in the philosophers' technical sense of "aboutness" or representational content. Because my aim is to put the most pressure on the most philosophical leg of the inconsistent triad, this chapter discusses the propositions in reverse order, from 3 to 1.

Proposition 3: Monkeys Understand the Intentional Actions of Other Monkeys

A subpopulation of the neurons of the ventral premotor cortex (area F5) of rhesus macaques appears to play a dual role in action and perception of action by these monkeys (di Pellegrino et al. 1992; Gallese et al. 1996). These neurons are active during the premotor and motor phases of specific actions as well as during observation of similar actions performed by other individuals, earning them the moniker "mirror neurons." Prior to the discovery of these neurons in rhesus macaques in the 1990s, proposition 3 would have been the most likely candidate for rejection. Even given what is now known about these neurons, it may retain that status. Nevertheless, rejection comes at the cost of making the neural findings quite puzzling.

F5 mirror neurons in macaques are specialized by body part (e.g., hand vs. mouth), and they show a moderate to strong degree of specificity for particular actions (e.g., grasping vs. holding vs. tearing). This specificity is congruent between motor tasks and vision—that is, the same neurons are active when the monkey is grasping and when perceiving grasping, when holding and perceiving holding, and so forth. This congruence is "strict" in about one-third of the F5 mirror neurons and "broad" in the remainder, meaning that their activation during perception does not require exactly the same action as in their motoric role (Rizzolatti and Craighero 2004). It is also important to note that the level and pattern of activation of these neurons is generally not identical between the motoric and perceptual cases. Of particular interest to proposition 3 is that F5 mirror neurons appear to be sensitive to the goal directedness of action. For instance, neurons that are activated during perception of goal-directed grasping motions are not activated by similar grasping motions which do not result in an object being touched (Gallese et al. 1996). Remarkably, the completion of the goal does not have to be directly observed; the sequence of showing a monkey an object, obscuring it from view, and then initiating a reaching motion to grasp the object behind the obstruction is sufficient to activate F5 neurons in the observing monkey (Umiltà et al. 2001).

While single-cell recordings of F5 neurons have thus far been limited to monkeys, a variety of evidence derived from EEG and functional magnetic resonance imaging (fMRI) exists to support the claim of the homologous brain region in humans serving similar functions (Fadiga et al. 1995; Rizzolatti and Craighero 2004; Iacoboni et al. 2005). Indeed, the evidence for "mirroring" properties in other parts of the brain has led to the idea of a human mirror neuron system (Rizzolatti and Craighero 2004; Iacoboni et al. 2005). On the basis of their fMRI study, Iacoboni et al. claim that ascribing intentions by inferring the goals of actions is something that the human mirror system does automatically.

In light of these discoveries, philosophers and neuroscientists have found it tempting to speculate that F5 mirror neurons may support higher order intentionality in monkeys. Thus, for example, Gallese and Goldman write as follows: "One possible function is to enable an organism to detect certain mental states of observed conspecifics. This function might be part of, or a precursor to, a more general mind-reading ability" (1998, p. 493). Similarly, Rizzolatti and Craighero (2004) identify "action understanding" as the perceptual function of F5 mirror neurons in macaques. (See also Fogassi et al. 2005.)

The dual role of F5 mirror neurons in perception and action is reflected in their classification as "visuomotor" neurons. As such, they would seem to provide the perfect neural mechanism for the proverbial "Monkey see; monkey do." Aphorisms aside, however, most comparative psychologists think that "monkey see" is a poor predictor for "monkey do"—the general consensus is that monkeys are not good imitators, with the possible exception of neonates (Ferrari et al. 2006). Definitions of imitation are controversial (see Thorpe 1956; Whiten and Ham 1992; Heyes 1994; Tomasello and Call 1997; Miklosi 1999; Byrne 2004), but successful cognitive imitation of an action is often taken to require both a close match of the motor patterns between model and imitator and recognition of the purpose or intention underlying the action (Tomasello and Call 1997). What is not controversial is that, regardless of definition, the imitation skills of monkeys that have been tested are much poorer than those of humans and the great apes (Byrne 2004). In humans, fMRI imaging reveals that regions included in the mirror neuron system are significantly active during human imitation (Iacoboni et al. 1999). However, in light of the absence of strong evidence for imitation in monkeys, the reasoning of most neuroscientists is represented by Rizzolatti and Craighero (2004, p. 172), who write, "Therefore, the primary function of mirror neurons [in monkeys] cannot be action imitation." Byrne (2004) also remarks, "Monkeys are, pace conventional wisdom, not great imitators (Visalberghi and Fragaszy 1990); mirror neurons are unlikely to have evolved originally as part of an imitative learning system, but rather as part of social comprehension, allowing subtle dispositions and objectives of social companions to be discerned."

Action imitation nicely connects perception to action and exploits the congruence between visual and motor tasks to explain successful imitation as a result of perceptual priming of imitators' own actions. On abandoning imitation as the primary function of F5 mirror neurons in macaques, Rizzolatti and Craighero fall back on the more generic notion of "action understanding." However, this notion shares a common deficit with Gallese and Goldman's (admittedly tentative) suggestion that mirror neurons function to detect mental states. Neither of these functional descriptions yields specific predictions for monkey behavior. Without operationalizing these ideas about function beyond measurements of the neurons' responses to action-related stimuli, it would be circular to claim that the neural responses settle the question of whether F5 mirror neurons serve action understanding.

Neither Gallese and Goldman nor Rizzolatti and Craighero operationalize the notions of mental state detection or action understanding, but they do appeal to additional evidence to bolster their claims about function. Rizzolatti and Craighero refer to two studies to support their claim that mirror neurons in monkeys serve the function of understanding actions. They cite the study by Umiltà et al. (2001), mentioned above, to argue that because similar movements do not evoke the same response in F5 mirror neurons unless the goal is the same (i.e., picking up an object), it is the meaning of the action, not the visual features specifically, which is responsible for activating the neurons. To support this claim about meaning, Rizzoli and Craighero cite a study by Kohler et al. (2002) in which it was shown that an auditory cue (the sound of ripping) was sufficient to activate about 15% of the F5 mirror neurons normally activated by directly observing ripping. While these results are interesting, they would seem to be equally well predicted by a first-order association between auditory and visual stimuli (seeing ripping and hearing ripping). No understanding of the intentionality of the ripping agent seems to be required. Without identification of further behavioral consequences of "action understanding," the encoding of such events by macaque F5 neurons does not provide a strong basis for asserting that monkeys understand the intentional actions of others.

Gallese and Goldman cite a study of free-ranging rhesus macaques who were observed withholding food vocalizations when vocalizing would have required them to share the food with others but where there was also a reduced chance of getting caught by other group members (Hauser 1992; see also Hauser and Marler 1993a, 1993b). Hauser (1992) describes the withholding of food calls as deception, and Gallese and Goldman assert that deception "calls for the existence of second-order intentionality" (1998, p. 499), but they don't explain their reasoning. While it is true that some philosophical analyses of deception invoke second-order intentionality, biologists also recognize a category of functionally deceptive behavior that does not commit them to higher order states in deceivers (e.g., Munn 1986). Monkeys who fail to alert their troop mates to the presence of food may have succeeded in functionally deceiving them about the presence of food, but the withholding of food vocalizations might be explained, without invoking higher order intentionality, as the result of a first-order assessment of the likelihood of being caught with the food.

Nevertheless, there is some evidence from human fMRI studies that neurons related to the mirror system are activated during assessment of deceptive behavior (Grèzes et al. 2004). To connect F5 neurons to intentionally deceptive abilities in monkeys, there would need to be plausible grounds for thinking that the visuomotor congruence of these neurons facilitates deceptive behavior or the detection of such behavior in others. If the congruent properties of F5 neurons in monkeys do support deception, then we should predict that the ability of a monkey to engage in deception would be different for actions which involve neurons with congruent visuomotor properties than for actions for which there is reduced or no congruent visuomotor neural activity. For example, we would expect there to be a difference between a monkey's deceptive capacities with respect to its grasping intentions and its capacity to engage in deceptive actions for which there are no specific mirror neurons, or the activated F5 neurons are much less specific. A contrast between deceptive hand movements and deceptive vocal communication might be especially interesting in light of Rizzolatti and Craighero's (2004) discussion of mouth-related F5 neurons that respond when communicative mouth movements are observed but which are more strongly connected to ingestive functions than to vocalization on the motor side. If the "mirroring" function of F5 neurons is significant for deception, then the looser linkage for actions involving mouth movements should have functional consequences when compared to actions involving hand movements.

The important point here is that the evaluation of proposition 3 is a matter for further empirical investigation, requiring appropriately designed behavioral tasks. If monkeys engage in intentional deception, we should seek evidence that their deceptive abilities are somehow structured by the properties of F5 neurons along the lines suggested in the previous paragraph. If there is currently a lack of evidence for imitation by monkeys, perhaps scientists can design more specific experiments in light of predictions that would follow from our knowledge of F5 neurons. One might propose, for example, that monkeys would perform better on imitating actions for which there is a specific, measurable mirroring response during perception of the action to be imitated. A hint in this direction is provided by Kumashiro et al. (2003), who reared Japanese macaques in a home environment that provided intensive interactions with humans, including extensive use of pointing gestures and extensive work to establish shared attention between the human caregivers and the monkeys. They report that these monkeys are more capable of imitating human actions spontaneously than monkeys housed and raised in more typical laboratory conditions. Their experiment is fascinating, but given the apparent need for special rearing, it adds to the mystery about the role of F5 neurons for monkeys raised without the same kind of deliberate human enculturation. Laboratory experiments testing the linkage of F5 neurons to imitative abilities are yet to be developed. It is worth remarking, too, that we have no evidence about the extent to which the development of F5 neurons in laboratory animals is a good model for the neural development of free-ranging monkeys in the wild. Studying the latter would provide better information about F5 neuron function if the relatively impoverished social and ecological conditions of captive animals result in decreased functionality. However, free-ranging studies would require new technologies for collecting neural data in naturalistic conditions.

Because the attention to mirror neurons has been largely driven by excitement about their potential for grounding higher order intentionality—intentional states representing the mental states of others—there has been little philosophical discussion of their role for the ordinary purposefulness (what I'll call the "basic intentionality") of actions. F5 neurons are active just prior to and during grasping, holding, and so on, and the purposefulness of these actions is generally just assumed. Any claim that F5 neurons serve higher order intentional functions in observers during perception depends on these neurons' serving a basic intentional function in the observed individuals. If what's detected by F5 neurons during perception is not appropriately "mental," then the detection doesn't count as "mind reading." I do not wish to challenge the claim that the (pre)motor functions of F5 neurons are relevant to the basic intentionality of action, although a denial of this claim provides a route to denying proposition 3 (i.e., one could join the strict behaviorists in denying that monkeys are intentional agents; it is a corollary of proposition 3 that monkeys act intentionally). Nevertheless, one might suspect that any correlation between the activity of F5 neurons in an observer and the intentional properties of the observed individual is a happy coincidence that is only of indirect cognitive significance to the observer. Furthermore, given that monkeys typically can see their own hands when reaching for things, there is an associative explanation for the visuomotor congruence of F5 neurons (Keysers and Perrett 2004).

Compare what we might say about the neural responses of a predator to the high bounding (stotting) of an antelope that is running away. Antelopes stott when they have seen a predator, so the neurons in the predator that detect stotting are also correlated with the mental state of the prey having seen the predator. Does this mean that it is a function of these neurons to detect the prey-has-seen-predator mental states of prey? How one answers this question depends, in part, on some conceptual issues about what one means by "function" (Allen and Bekoff 1994), but (almost) whatever position one takes on those issues, it seems that focusing on the perceptual side alone provides an inadequate basis for an answer. We need to know whether there are any behavioral consequences of having a prey-seeing-predator detector that aren't predicted by having a stotting detector. All other things being equal, a predator that has learned to give up the chase when it detects stotting is as biologically fit as one that has learned to give up the chase when it is informed by the prey's stotting that it has been seen by the prey. A deflationary account of the neural responses to stotting, which does not invoke any understanding of intentionality, seems quite adequate. Similarly for F5 neurons, when the focus is on the perceptual side only, it is far from clear what consequences there are for monkeys' behavior if F5 neurons are mental state detectors.

Nevertheless, there are significant differences between the stotting example and the responsive range of F5 neurons. Stotting seems to be an evolved behavior that has characteristics which are specifically designed to be salient to predators, making it easy for operant conditioning in the predator to work to the advantage of prey and predator alike. Furthermore, there is no reason, neurological or behavioral, to think there would be a positive answer to the question of whether the lioness observing a stotting antelope has mapped the antelope's behavior onto her own behavioral repertoire. (This is, of course, an empirical question whose answer it would be preferable to know, instead of guessing, but I'm not holding my breath on this one.) Any attempt to take a similar deflationary approach to F5 neuron function in macaques would be forced to explain away the fact that the actual visuomotor congruence would play no direct functional role. Without a way of connecting the perceptual function of F5 neurons to their motor functions in macaques, we would have two domains of activity for F5 neurons in macaques—a perceptual domain and a motor domain—each of which would be functional, but whose functions would be perhaps no more related than the reproductive and eliminative functions of the male urethra. It just happens to be the case that the same channel gets used for two purposes, but any similarity between the two is due to the architectural constraints built into the channels.

On such a view, a possible evolutionary scenario is that the common ancestor of macaques and humans had independently functioning perceptual and motor systems using the same F5 machinery, but that somewhere along the way to the great apes and humans, the congruence between the visual and motor functions of F5 neurons was co-opted for imitation and other higher order capacities. In this case, there is a sense in which it would be accurate to say, with Gallese and Goldman, that the congruent F5 activity during action observation and action performance in monkeys is a precursor to "mind-reading" abilities. However, this tells us no more about the current cognitive abilities of monkeys than the fact that fins are evolutionary precursors to legs tells us anything about the walking abilities of fish. A more radical possibility that is also compatible with the co-option account is that the activity of F5 neurons during perception is strictly functionless in macaques—that is, it is epiphenomenal with respect to the macaques' cognitive capacities. While this single-function thesis has not been ruled out, I will assume that the specificity of F5 mirror neuron responses during perception makes it unlikely. Nevertheless, because the term "mirror neuron" appears to prejudge the issue of function, we should prefer to refer to these neurons by their location (F5) whenever there is a danger of overinterpretation.

In light of all this uncertainty, the rejection of proposition 3 may seem like a reasonable option. However, at least two considerations motivate considering the rejection of the other propositions. First, the empirical chips may yet fall in favor of the claim that monkeys have some kind of understanding of intentional agency, albeit more limited than that in humans. Indeed, Fogassi et al. (2005) presented evidence that F5 neuron activity in monkeys is sensitive to differences of intention in otherwise identical grasping actions (grasping to eat vs. grasping to place a food

Mirror, Mirror in the Brain

item). If the chips do fall this way, then something else will have to go, and it's worth considering the options now. Second, even if proposition 3 does seem like the most likely candidate for rejection, other options present a greater challenge to the status quo, making them philosophically more interesting. More specifically, the *simulationist* view of social cognition favored by Gallese and Goldman (1998; see also Gordon 2004) suggests that understanding of intentional actions need not be implemented as the kind of theoretical knowledge envisaged in the standard "theory theory" account of human folk-psychological competence. In other words, mental simulation may enable a kind of understanding of intentional action that does not depend on explicit knowledge of the beliefs and desires alleged to be motivating the actions of others.

Proposition 2: Monkeys Do Not Have Knowledge of the Intentional States (Beliefs and Desires) Motivating the Actions of Others

What do macaque monkeys understand about the intentionality of others? "Very little" would seem to be the consensus answer among primatologists, given the repeated failure of monkeys (many species) to perform well on various behavioral tests, such as "false belief" tasks (Wimmer and Perner 1983), laboratory tests of imitation, and other instruments of the "theory of mind" industry, such as mirror self-recognition (Gallup 1970; Gallup et al. 2002). Cognitive ethologists studying free-ranging populations were also skeptical that evidence in monkeys would be forthcoming. For instance, careful ethological observation of vervet monkeys communicating about predators led Cheney and Seyfarth (1990) to conclude that vervets do not distinguish whether conspecifics are knowledgeable or ignorant of a predator's presence. However, more recent work by Laurie Santos (Santos et al. 2006) with free-ranging rhesus macaques points in the opposite direction and will be described below.

The tasks that were originally used to test primates' understanding of the mental states of others come from a tradition within comparative psychology which seeks general methods that can be applied to a variety of species. A more ethologically oriented approach might be to devise experiments that challenge animals in ways that are more ecologically relevant given the evolutionary history of their species. This kind of approach has, in fact, been taken by Hare and colleagues (see Hare and Wrangham 2002 for an overview) in challenging the negative theory of mind results reported by Povinelli (2000). Hare's innovation was to investigate chimpanzees' knowledge of what others do and do not see under socially competitive conditions. Hare and Wrangham (2002) write that

> when two pieces of food were placed in view of both competitors, the dominant subject retrieved the majority of food. If one piece of food was hidden behind an occluder from the dominant while the subordinate could see both, as subordinates, subjects preferred to retrieve the hidden piece of food that the dominant could not see. In addition, if one piece was hidden behind an occluder from the subordinate but the dominant could see both, as dominants, subjects preferred to retrieve the visible piece of food first to assure they obtained both pieces. (p. 366)

They argue that Povinelli's negative results are due to the use of a "cooperative-communicative paradigm" that is less natural for chimpanzees—that is, Povinelli asks his chimps to engage in cooperative communication about food, whereas competition for food is the more normal problem that they face.

The point here is not to enter the debate about Povinelli's deflationary claims regarding chimpanzee theory of mind (for that, see Allen 2002). Rather, the point is that one might hold out similar hope that novel species-appropriate tests for macaques might provide evidence for knowledge that beliefs or desires motivate (at least some of) the actions of others and that macaques can use this knowledge to guide their own behavior. Such an approach is being pursued by Santos in her studies of free-ranging rhesus macaques on the island of Cayo Santiago in Puerto Rico (Santos et al. 2006). Like Hare, Santos places her subjects in a situation in which they are competing for food (in this case with humans) and finds that the monkeys appear to be sensitive to what the humans can or cannot see and hear. These innovative experiments go part way toward providing a case against proposition 2 and of resolving the paradox in this fashion (see also Lyons, Santos, and Keil 2006).

Nevertheless, there remains widespread skepticism about the claim that monkeys have knowledge of the beliefs and desires of others, and even if pursuing other ideas generated by the study of F5 neurons revealed that limited forms of imitation and deception are within the range of macaques, these results would not provide strong evidence for knowledge of beliefs and desires as this is traditionally understood (although such results might, as Kristin Andrews pointed out to me, provide further support for proposition 3). If macaques understand something about the intentional actions of other macaques, and it is not because they have knowledge of beliefs and desires of the other animal, what are we to make of the remaining proposition?

Proposition 1: To Understand the Intentional Actions of Others Requires Knowledge of the Intentional States (i.e., Beliefs and Desires) That (Rationally) Motivated Those Actions

Proposition 1 presupposes a traditional philosophical analysis of intentional action according to which intentional action is behavior that is appropriately (rationally) motivated by beliefs and desires. This traditional analysis links the two notions of intentionality that are in play throughout the discussion of F5 neuron functions. First, actions are said to be intentional in the ordinary English sense of "purposefulness." Second, beliefs and desires are said to be "intentional" in the philosophically technical sense of being states with representational content. On the traditional analysis, intentional (purposeful) action is motivated by intentional (contentful) states according to an ends–means reasoning process that has been represented by philosophers since Aristotle in the format of a "practical syllogism."

One may reject proposition 1 either by accepting the presupposed analysis of intentional actions, and offering a different condition for understanding them, or by rejecting the traditional analysis. The first approach yields an attenuated notion of understanding action. The second approach yields a novel understanding of intentional actions.

It might seem implausible to accept the traditional analysis while denying that knowledge of the underlying intentional states is required for understanding of intentional actions. If intentional action is appropriately motivated behavior, then how could one understand the action without having knowledge of the motivating states? The notion of understanding is, however, vague enough to allow this as a possibility. Water is a product of hydrogen and oxygen, and while one might deny that someone who knows nothing of hydrogen and oxygen can have a *full* understanding of water, nevertheless, one can understand quite a lot about water without knowing its chemical composition. Likewise, then, perhaps monkeys can partially understand each other's intentional actions without knowing anything about the intentional states assumed to produce them. I concede that the traditionalist might want to dig in his or her heels at this point and reject this notion of partial understanding. Such a traditionalist—a Davidsonian for instance—has probably already decided that to reject proposition 3 is the way out of the paradox. However, I am exploring the consequences of not making that move and so will proceed with the idea of partial understanding to see how it might be applied to monkeys.

(See also Hunt et al. 2006 for discussion of the importance of a concept of partial understanding for interpreting animal cognition.)

One way in which such understanding might be manifested is in predicting or anticipating the visible or tangible outcomes of actions rather than representing their mental causes (this suggestion is made by several of the participants commenting on Gallese 2004—see, e.g., the commentaries by Proust and Csibra [Forum 2004]). On such a view, the macaque uses its F5 neurons during perception to anticipate that (e.g.) an object will end up in the grasp of another, and it does this by using the same machinery that would initiate and sustain a movement that would cause the object to end up in its own grasp. Such anticipation can be generated without any knowledge of the reasons the other has for grasping the object. Indeed, the results of Schubotz and von Cramon (2004) implicate F5 neurons in anticipating the outcomes of abstract nonbiological movements.

So long as the ability to anticipate the outcome of other monkeys' actions counts as understanding their intentional actions, then this approach to rejecting proposition 1 is compatible with accepting proposition 3, although the significance of the latter is attenuated. Certainly, the functional description of F5 neurons in terms of "mind reading" would be misleading if this meant nothing more than the ability to anticipate the physical outcome of an organism's movements. Furthermore, deflating action understanding in this way makes it harder to see how this function of F5 neurons would constitute a precursor to the full-blown folk-psychological mind-reading capacities that simulation theory is supposed to explain.

In his response to this kind of deflationary proposal, Gallese (in Forum 2004) proposes that prediction of action outcomes—to avoid connoting a verbal performance, we should prefer "anticipation" to "prediction"—is an important component of identifying intentions; hence, showing that F5 neurons serve an anticipatory function is perfectly compatible with saying that they also function as intention detectors. I'm sympathetic to Gallese's position, but it is important to emphasize that without some way of behaviorally operationalizing the difference between anticipation of action outcomes and detection of intentions, it is unclear whether macaques are capable of the latter as well as the former.

Gallese (2004) also proposes that there is a phenomenological accompaniment to the latter, a feeling of familiarity that comes from what he calls "intentional attunement." Perhaps such a feeling would serve to maintain attention, enhancing learning by social facilitation. The spread of potato washing in Japanese macaques, described by Imanishi in 1952 (de Waal

2001) shows that monkeys acquire behaviors from those around them. (This is not generally considered direct imitation because it seems that there is a significant trial-and-error component involved in each individual's acquisition of the new behavior.) If Gallese is right that intentional attunement plays a role over and above anticipation of physical outcomes, social facilitation is one domain of monkey competence in which the difference might be operationalized.

The conservative approach to rejecting proposition 1 does not challenge the traditional analysis of intentional action in terms of intentional states (propositional attitudes such as belief and desire) interacting according to a rational calculus of abstract content. On the traditional analysis, to say that a monkey acts intentionally in, say, reaching for a food container, is to say that he believes there is a food container within reach and he desires to hold the container (perhaps because he desires to eat what he believes is in the container) and he believes that reaching for the container will enable him to satisfy his desire(s). The monkey is conceived as having all these beliefs and desires even if he does not realize that he has them (i.e., he has no second-order awareness of his own intentional states). In such a case, his understanding of his own intentional actions may be as partial as his understanding of the actions of others. Perhaps the monkey reaching for the container is cognitively capable of nothing more than anticipating that the container ends up in his grasp or that the food ends up in his mouth, even though (because it is intentional, according to the traditional analysis) his behavior is the outcome of an unconscious (or, at least, unself-conscious) reasoning process that computed over beliefs and desires with propositional content.

One might think this view unstable, teetering as it does between a deflationary understanding of the monkeys' cognitive capacities and an inflationary view of the basis for those capacities as implemented by something like the traditional propositional attitudes. Indeed, insofar as alternative approaches to modeling or explaining the behavior of animals and prelinguistic infants—for example, dynamical models (Thelen et al. 2001; Beer, in press) or Bayesian models (Luttbeg and Langen 2004; Valone 2006; Courville et al. 2006)—do not make use of folk-psychological notions, one might take the monkeys' inability to rationalize their own actions as a *reductio* of the view that one should appeal to rational relations among propositional attitudes in explaining those actions. Nevertheless, the elimination of the propositional attitudes may not be as direct a consequence as proponents of alternative (connectionist, dynamical, causal, or probabilistic) models have sometimes suggested. Eliminativist arguments based on such models typically depend on a general antirepresentationalist claim to the effect that representational notions play no explicit role in formulating the preferred models. However, Beer (in press, ms. p. 19) argues that while the "situated, embodied, dynamical" approach to cognitive modeling encourages "representational skepticism," it is an unsettled empirical question whether the internal states of dynamical systems are representational. Dynamical models are not, in his view, inherently antirepresentational. I concur with this, and I believe that a similar point could be made about the other types of nonclassical models. For reasons given below I am more inclined than Beer to think that some of the cognitive and behavioral sciences will continue to need and use representational ideas to explain (animal) behavior. But even if representational notions can be rehabilitated within nonclassical models of cognition, it does not follow that those models will preserve the aspect of folk psychology which holds that discrete beliefs and desires interact within the framework of the Aristotelian practical syllogism. The familiar folk-psychological notions might disappear even if intentionality survives as a useful concept.

There are reasons, therefore, to consider a more radical approach to proposition 1 that rejects the traditional analysis of intentional action (radical, that is, to many philosophers but increasingly less so to cognitive scientists). Of course, for a monkey successfully to reach out and grasp a food container, it must know something about the container's location and other properties. However, that knowledge may already be represented in the premotor cortex in such a way that it is intrinsically tied to action. For example, Murata et al. (1997) showed that some F5 neurons encode the shapes of three-dimensional objects even when the monkey is not immediately required to perform any action. Likewise, an abstract desire may not be what underlies the action. Instead, it may be possible to distinguish intentions from desires by the involvement of concrete motor plans in the former but not the latter (Franck Grammont, personal communication). Intentional action, on such an account, results from intentions and representations of external situations that are embodied concretely in motor patterns rather than from beliefs and desires whose propositional contents are abstract and impersonal. A full understanding of the intentional actions of another agent, rather than consisting in being able to reason via the practical syllogism using abstract characterizations of knowledge and goals that are decoupled from specific actions, would involve the activation within the observer of a concrete motor plan that is below the threshold for actual motor output but that responds to environmental cues and has temporal dynamics similar to the states of the agent. How best to model the dynamics of such a process—for example, whether to use statistical methods such as dynamic Bayesian networks (Ghahramani 1997) or the differential equations of dynamical systems theory (Beer, in press)—remains an open scientific question.

On this account, the observer macaque whose F5 neurons more or less mirror the F5 neurons of the observed actor knows more or less all there is to know about the intentions of the actor. That is, there are no further beliefs and desires to which the observer is not privy. Rather, by activating corresponding representations, grounded in motor schemas, the observer is in more or less the same intentional mental state as the actor. The repetitions of "more or less" here are deliberate, for there can be varying degrees of correspondence between the representations of action between observer and observed. By the same token, the congruence between visual and motor responses of F5 neurons can be more or less precise (recall the distinction between strict and broad congruence in the discussion of proposition 3). A whole host of social, motivational, genetic, and developmental factors are likely to contribute to the degree of matching that can be accomplished between any two individuals, and for functional reasons it may be that precise matching would be too inflexible to support social transmission of skills. It is unsurprising that experiments that look for a generalized capacity for imitation in monkeys without taking such factors into consideration have produced negative results. And from this perspective, the success of Kumashiro et al. (2003) in producing monkeys who are adept at imitation is what one would predict from an experiment that explicitly manipulated social and developmental factors. The recent evidence for neonatal imitation in rhesus macaques (Ferrari et al. 2006) might also provide a further avenue for developmental studies, but the claim that mirror neurons play a role in the neonatal behavior is highly speculative. Jones (2005), coming from her perspective as a developmental psychologist, has argued that the evidence that mirror neurons play a role in neonatal imitation is very weak, including for humans, and she goes on to point out that such a role would be especially puzzling with respect to nonhuman primates, for "if mirror neurons *are* the mechanism underlying newborn behavioral matching, then newborn behavioral matching goes nowhere developmentally and is consequently less interesting than we thought" (Jones 2005, p. 209; emphasis in original).

If we give up the traditional analysis of intentional action, what is left of the idea that behavior is to be explained by mental states that are intentional in the philosophers' technical sense? I believe that the philosophers' notion of intentionality continues to have a place in our current best explanations of monkey cognition. Cognitive ethologists, cognitive neuroscientists, and developmental psychologists all continue to describe cognitive–neurological states in terms of their representational content, and it is important that the activation of motor schemas in animals, even though they may facilitate action, doesn't automatically entail that the animal will act. Hence, there seems to be a need to attribute cognitive representations that are prior to action, even if the content of these states intricately involves the animals' own possibilities for action.

The new neuroscientific approaches to the premotor states of intentional agents are relevant to the philosophical debates insofar that they suggest alternative ways of describing the content and function of such states in terms of the organisms' own ways of interacting with the world. Part of our problem in describing the intentional states of nonhuman animals is that we lack easy conceptual access to their own ways of dealing with the world. Any propositional content described in a human language seems to import layers of meaning that are implausible when applied to other animals. By understanding the ways in which the motor system contributes to the brain's own ontology (Murata et al. 1997; Metzinger and Gallese 2003), the neurosciences hold out the prospect of purposive action as the result of states involving intentional content, without presupposing that such content is as abstract as our sentences and words suggest.

Conclusions

We have now considered each of the three mutually incompatible propositions with which I began this essay. Perhaps all three should be rejected, as suggested by the eliminative materialists, but I don't believe that such a radical step is required by the data at hand. However, those data are not adequate to make any of the three propositions the obvious target for elimination. More research is needed, and the importance of an integrated approach to behavioral and neuroscientific experimentation cannot be stressed too strongly. It is significant that Gallese and Goldman (1998) turn to cognitive ethology to support their claims about monkeys' capacities for understanding intentions. Even though I argued that their specific example was not conclusive, it is nevertheless the case that a proper understanding of neural–cognitive functions requires these functions to be investigated in the kinds of rich social and ecological contexts that ethologists use and that are only rarely found in the lives of captive laboratory animals (although there are exceptions).

There is also conceptual work to be done. Proposition 1 describes a conceptual framework within which the behavioral and neurological evidence for the other two propositions can be assessed, but this does not place it out of the reach of empirical evidence. For instance, a study by Sommerville and Woodward (2005) indicates that in human infants the capacity for intentional understanding may precede the attribution of mental states to others, suggesting that the conceptual connection between intentional actions on the one hand and beliefs–desires on the other might not be as tight as is suggested by the traditional philosophical account. These empirical results may push us away from the traditional and toward new conceptions of intentionality. Those new conceptions do not come ready made and will themselves be shaped by the empirical discoveries subjected to philosophically reflective analysis.

What about the question implied by my title: "Does the mirroring property of macaques' F5 neurons serve an important function for them?" I'm reasonably confident that the answer is "yes"—although this may not mean what we might have thought under the traditional account of intentional action. Most of the discussion of macaques' F5 mirror neurons has been focused on their implications for "mind reading" in humans. In this discussion, macaques are sometimes merely proxies for humans, enabling us to extrapolate findings from experiments that would not be approved for human subjects. When attention is turned toward the cognitive capacities of macaques themselves, the negative behavioral findings that support proposition 2 are usually taken at face value, and proposition 3 is called into question. The pressing questions become "What else do humans have that distinguishes them from macaques?" and "What are F5 mirror neurons for in macaques?" Taking a different tack and challenging proposition 1 has the potential to provide a more unified account of neuronal function between humans and macaques.

Finally, I want to emphasize the importance of continued dialogue between neuroscience, ethology, and philosophy. Ethology, with its historical concern for many nonprimate species of animal, can help to provide a broader perspective on intentionality than is usually provided by primatology, with its sometimes too-neat tripartite hierarchy of monkeys, great apes, and humans, all presumed to be sitting above the rest of the animal kingdom. Many nonprimates show social and cognitive skills that exceed primate abilities (see Emery and Clayton 2004 for a direct comparison of intelligence in corvids and apes, and Hare and Tomasello 2005 for a comparison of dogs and chimpanzees; see Bekoff et al. 2002 for discussions of cognition in a wide variety of species). Imitation does not seem all that difficult for many birds, at least for some common activities, and dolphins seem to be good general imitators, even across species boundaries (Herman 2002). Social play provides an especially rich area for studying intentional understanding in a wide variety of species because the social dynamics of play require constant signaling of intentions, monitoring of social rules and expectations, and turn taking and interactive matching of behaviors for a common purpose (Bekoff and Allen 1998; Flack et al. 2004; Bekoff 2004; Allen and Bekoff 2005). The study of nonprimate species would provide a much broader comparative perspective for evaluating claims about neural function. The discovery of mirror neurons shows how neuroscience can shake ethologists, comparative psychologists, and philosophers out of their dogmatic slumbers, suggesting new paths for behavioral investigation of old topics. In this vein, too, Gallese's (2004) bold suggestions about the phenomenology of intentional attunement should not be dismissed as automatically untestable or empirically vacuous but rather taken as a stimulant toward further cognitive ethological investigation of all aspects of mental continuity among the nonhuman and human animals. Finally, philosophy can act as both brake and accelerator by taking its traditional concerns as explananda as criteria for judging the success of scientific theories (Debes, forthcoming) and as a source of ideas for new approaches to old topics, such as how any organism can know the mind of another.

Acknowledgments

I thank Franck Grammont for the initial impetus to write this chapter and for his valuable suggestions, instruction, and encouragement. Kristin Andrews and Marc Bekoff also provided helpful suggestions (the latter on a lightning-quick turnaround). Members of the Biology Studies Reading Group in my own department also provided useful feedback, and I wish especially to thank Lisa Lloyd for her extensive written comments on the manuscript. I am also grateful to Remy Debes and an anonymous referee for suggestions incorporated into the final version of this chapter.

References

Allen, C. (2002). A skeptic's progress. *Biology and Philosophy, 17*, 695–702.

Allen, C., and Bekoff, M. (1994). Function, natural design, and animal behavior: philosophical and ethological considerations. In N. S. Thompson (Ed.), *Perspectives in ethology: Vol. 11. Behavioral design* (pp. 1–47). New York: Plenum Press.

Allen, C., and Bekoff, M. (2005). Animal play and the evolution of morality: An ethological approach. *Topoi, 24*, 125–135.

Beer, R. (in press). Dynamical systems and embedded cognition. In K. Frankish and W. Ramsey (Eds.), *The Cambridge handbook of artificial intelligence*. Cambridge: Cambridge University Press (preprint at http://mypage.iu.edu/~rdbeer/Papers/AIHandbookChapter.pdf)

Bekoff, M. (2004). Wild justice and fair play: Cooperation, forgiveness, and morality in animals. *Biology and Philosophy, 19*, 489–520.

Bekoff, M., and Allen, C. (1998). Intentional communication and social play: How and why animals negotiate and agree to play. In M. Bekoff and J. A. Byers (Eds.), *Animal play: Evolutionary, comparative, and ecological perspectives* (pp. 97–114). Cambridge: Cambridge University Press.

Bekoff, M., Allen, C., and Burghardt, G. M. (Eds.). (2002). *The cognitive animal: Empirical and theoretical perspectives on animal cognition*. Cambridge: MIT Press.

Byrne, R. W. (2004). Detecting, understanding, and explaining animal imitation. In S. Hurley and N. Chater (Eds.), *Perspectives on imitation: From mirror neurons to memes* (pp. 255–282). Cambridge: MIT Press.

Cheney, D. L., and Seyfarth, R. M. (1990). *How monkeys see the world: Inside the mind of another species*. Chicago: University of Chicago Press.

Courville, A. C., Daw, N. D., and Touretzky, D. S. (2006). Bayesian theories of conditioning in a changing world. *Trends in Cognitive Sciences, 10*, 294–300.

Debes, R. (forthcoming). Which empathy? Limitations in the "mirrored" understanding of emotion.

de Waal, F. B. M. (2001). *The ape and the sushi master: Cultural reflections of a primatologist*. New York: Basic Books.

di Pellegrino, G., Fogassi, L., Gallese, V., and Rizzolatti, G. (1992). Understanding motor events: A neurophysiological study. *Experimental Brain Research, 91*, 176–180.

Emery, N. J., and Clayton, N. S. (2004). The mentality of crows: convergent evolution of intelligence in corvids and apes. *Science, 306*, 1903–1907.

Fadiga, L., Fogassi, L., Pavesi, G., and Rizzolatti, G. (1995). Motor facilitation during action observation: A magnetic stimulation study. *Journal of Neurophysiology, 73*, 2608–2611.

Ferrari, P. F., Visalberghi, E., Paukner, A., Fogassi, L., Ruggiero, A., and Suomi, S. J. (2006). Neonatal imitation in rhesus macaques. *PLoS Biology, 4*, e302. DOI: 10.1371/journal.pbio.0040302.

Flack, J. C., Jeannotte, L. A., and de Waal, F. (2004). Play signaling and the perception of social rules by juvenile chimpanzees (*Pan troglodytes*). *Journal of Comparative Psychology*, *118*, 149–159.

Fogassi, L., Ferrari, P. F., Gesierich, B., Rozzi, S., Chersi, F., and Rizzolatti, G. (2005). Parietal lobe: From action organization to intention understanding. *Science*, *308*, 662–667.

Forum (2004). Discussion of Gallese (2004) at http://www.interdisciplines.org/mirror/papers/1/1/printable/discussions.

Gallese, V. (2004). Intentional attunement: The mirror neuron system and its role in interpersonal relations. Accessed at http://www.interdisciplines.org/mirror/papers/1/ on Jan 15, 2007.

Gallese, V., Fadiga, L., Fogassi, L., and Rizzolatti, G. (1996). Action recognition in the premotor cortex. *Brain*, *119*, 593–609.

Gallese, V., and Goldman, A. (1998). Mirror neurons and the simulation theory of mind-reading. *Trends in Cognitive Science*, *2*, 493–501.

Gallup, G. G., Jr. (1970). Chimpanzees: Self-recognition. *Science*, *167*, 86–87.

Gallup, G. G., Jr., Anderson, J. R., and Shillito, D. J. (2002). The Mirror Test. In M. Bekoff, C. Allen, and G. M. Burhgardt (Eds.), *The cognitive animal: Empirical and theoretical perspectives on animal cognition* (pp. 325–333). Cambridge: MIT Press.

Ghahramani, Z. (1997). Learning dynamic Bayesian networks. In C. L. Giles and M. Gori (Eds.), *Adaptive processing of temporal information: Lecture notes in artificial intelligence* (pp. 168–197). New York: Springer-Verlag.

Gordon, R. M. (2004). Folk psychology as mental simulation. In E. N. Zalta (Ed.), *The Stanford encyclopedia of philosophy* (Fall 2004 ed.), http://plato.stanford.edu/archives/fall2004/entries/folkpsych-simulation/.

Grèzes, J., Frith, C. D., and Passingham, R. E. (2004). Inferring false beliefs from the actions of oneself and others: An fMRI study. *NeuroImage*, *21*, 744–750.

Hare, B., and Tomasello, M. (2005). Human-like social skills in dogs? *Trends in Cognitive Sciences*, *9*, 439–444.

Hare, B., and Wrangham, R. (2002). Integrating two evolutionary models for the study of social cognition. In M. Bekoff, C. Allen, and G. M. Burghardt (Eds.), *The cognitive animal: Empirical and theoretical perspectives on animal cognition* (pp. 363–369). Cambridge: MIT Press.

Hauser, M. D. (1992). Costs of deception: Cheaters are punished in rhesus monkeys (*Mucaca mulatta*). *Proceedings of the National Academy of Sciences USA*, *89*, 12137–12139.

Hauser, M. D., and Marler, P. (1993a). Food associate calls in rhesus macaques (*Mucaca mulatta*): I. Sociological factors. *Behavioral Ecology, 4*, 194–205.

Hauser, M. D., and Marler, P. (1993b). Food associate calls in rhesus macaques (*Mucaca mulatta*): II. Costs and benefits of call production and suppression. *Behavioral Ecology, 4*, 206–212.

Herman, L. (2002). Exploring the cognitive world of the bottlenosed dolphin. In M. Bekoff, C. Allen, and G. M. Burhgardt (Eds.), *The cognitive animal: Empirical and theoretical perspectives on animal cognition* (pp. 275–283). Cambridge, MA: MIT Press.

Heyes, C. M. (1994). Social learning in animals: Categories and mechanisms. *Biological Review, 6*, 207–231.

Hunt, G. R., Rutledge, R. B., and Gray, R. D. (2006). The right tool for the job: What strategies do wild New Caledonian crows use? *Animal Cognition, 9*, 307–316.

Iacoboni, M., Molnar-Szakacs, I., Gallese, G., Buccino, G., Mazziotta, J. C., and Rizzolatti, G. (2005). Grasping the intentions of others with one's own mirror neuron system. *PLoS Biology, 3*, 529–535.

Iacoboni, M., Woods, R. P., Brass, M., Bekkering, H., Mazziotta, J. C., and Rizzolatti, G. (1999). Cortical mechanisms of human imitation. *Science, 286*, 2526–2528.

Jones, S. S. (2005). The role of mirror neurons in imitation. In S. Hurley and N. Chater (Eds.), *Perspectives on imitation: From neuroscience to social science: Vol. 1. Mechanisms of imitation and imitation in animals* (pp. 205–210). Cambridge: MIT Press.

Keysers, C., and Perrett, D. I. (2004). Demystifying social cognition: A Hebbian perspective. *Trends in Cognitive Science, 8*, 501–507.

Kohler, E., Keysers, C., Umiltà, M. A., Fogassi, L., Gallese, V., and Rizzolatti, G. (2002). Hearing sounds, understanding actions: Action representation in mirror neurons. *Science, 297*, 846–848.

Kumashiro, M., Ishibashi, H., Uchiyama, Y., Itakura, S., Murata, A., and Iriki, A. (2003). Natural imitation induced by joint attention in Japanese monkeys. *International Journal of Psychophysiology, 50*, 81–99.

Luttbeg, B., and Langen, T. A. (2004). Comparing alternative models to empirical data: Cognitive models of Western scrub-jay foraging behavior. *American Naturalist, 163*, 263–276.

Lyons, D. E., Santos, L. R., and Keil, F. C. (2006). Reflections of other minds: How primate social cognition can inform the function of mirror neurons. *Current Opinion in Neurobiology, 16*, 230–234.

Metzinger, T., and Gallese, V. (2003). The emergence of a shared action ontology: Building blocks for a theory. *Consciousness and Cognition, 12,* 549–571.

Miklosi, A. (1999). The ethological analysis of imitation. *Biological Review, 74,* 347–374.

Munn, C. A. (1986). The deceptive use of alarm calls by sentinel species in mixed-species flocks of neotropical birds. In R. W. Mitchell and N. S. Thompson (Eds.), *Deception: Perspectives on human and nonhuman deceit* (pp. 169–175). Albany: State University of New York Press.

Murata, A., Fadiga, L., Fogassi, L., Gallese, V., Raos, V., and Rizzolatti, G. (1997). Object representation in the ventral premotor cortex (Area F5) of the monkey. *Journal of Neurophysiology, 78,* 2226–2230.

Povinelli, D. J. (2000). *Folk physics for apes: The chimpanzee's theory of how the world works.* Oxford: Oxford University Press.

Rizzolatti, G., and Craighero, L. (2004). The mirror-neuron system. *Annual Review of Neuroscience, 27,* 169–192.

Santos, L. R., Nissen, A. G., and Ferrugia, J. (2006). Rhesus monkeys (*Macaca mulatta*) know what others can and cannot hear. *Animal Behaviour, 71,* 1175–1181.

Schubotz, R. I., and von Cramon, D. Y. (2004). Sequences of abstract nonbiological stimuli share ventral premotor cortex with action observation and imagery. *Journal of Neuroscience, 24,* 5467–5474.

Sommerville, J. A., and Woodward, A. L. (2005). Pulling out the intentional structure of action: The relation between action processing and action production in infancy. *Cognition, 95,* 1–30.

Thelen, E., Schöner, G., Scheier, C., and Smith, L. B. (2001). The dynamics of embodiment: A field theory of infant perseverative reaching. *Behavioral and Brain Sciences, 24,* 1–86.

Thorpe W. H. (1956). *Learning and instinct in animals.* London: Methuen.

Tomasello M., and Call, J. (1997). *Primate cognition.* Oxford: Oxford University Press.

Tomasello, M., Carpenter, M., Call, J., Behne, T., and Moll, H. (2005). Understanding and sharing intentions: The origins of cultural cognition. *Behavioral and Brain Sciences, 28,* 675–691.

Umiltà, M. A., Kohler, E., Gallese, V., Fogassi, L., Fadiga, L., Keyers, C., and Rizzolatti, G. (2001). I know what you are doing: A neurophysiological study. *Neuron, 31,* 155–65.

Valone, T. J. (2006). Are animals capable of Bayesian learning? An empirical review. *Oikos, 112,* 252–259.

Visalberghi, E., and Fragaszy, D. (1990). Do monkeys ape? In S. Parker and K. Gibson (Eds.), *Language and intelligence in monkeys and apes: Comparative developmental perspectives* (pp. 247–273). Cambridge: Cambridge University Press.

Whiten, A., and Ham, R. (1992). On the nature and evolution of imitation in the animal kingdom: Reappraisal of a century of research. In P. J. B. Slater, J. S. Rosenblatt, C. Beer, and M. Milinski (Eds.), *Advances in the study of behaviour* (pp. 239–283). New York: Academic Press.

Wimmer, H., and Perner, J. (1983). Beliefs about beliefs: Representation and constraining function of wrong beliefs in young children's understanding of deception. *Cognition, 13*, 103–128.

Part IV Agent and Observer Perspectives

6 Can I Really Intend More than What I Am Able to Do?

Franck Grammont

Following common sense, we are used to wondering, "Will I be able to do what I intend to do?" And yet, the true question to ask could rather be "Knowing what I am able to do, what can I intend to do?" This is the question I will try to justify and answer in this text at the theoretical and experimental level. Why would answering such a question allow us to participate in the approach of naturalizing intention? Because the answer to this question implies showing how intention is, constitutively, linked to action and how action is necessarily intentional. Now, by embodying intention in action, we objectify it, we make it natural and comprehensible by empirical sciences.

One of the ideas supported in this text is that our ability to represent the world and others' behavior depends on our ability to act. Indeed, logically, one cannot intend to do something for which one has no representation, something one cannot conceive and conceive how to do. In other words, we should not theoretically be able to intend more than what we are able to do at a given moment. And yet, we, humans, are able to *imagine* that we are able to do incredible things such as flying like Superman or using telepathic powers like Professor X! As a matter of fact, the circularity of this proposition (I act, thus I represent, thus I intend, thus I act) is only apparent and formal as within reality; these elements are generated in an interactive and progressive manner and not in a strictly sequential, potentially circular, way.

It seems thus necessary to clearly distinguish the concept of intention from what can rather refer to our abilities of imagining or desiring. As the popular wisdom says, "One shouldn't engage in wishful thinking"! We will thus have to redefine certain concepts linked to action and intention in order to more clearly express our working framework. Redefining basic concepts is necessary in an interdisciplinary context like that of the study of intention and action. Indeed, it is essential to avoid the risks of ambiguity with the specialists from other disciplines working on the same topic, precisely if we want these different disciplines to benefit from each other. In the following, I will thus detail the relationships that the components of the action-representation–intention–action system entertain, notably by founding my work on the research on mirror neurons and mirror systems.

From Movement to Action and Beyond . . .

First of all, what are we talking about when we refer to action? What characterizes action is its goal. An action is oriented toward a goal. It is a function of this goal. To take a glass of water is a typical example of action. The goal of this action is to drink the water inside the glass. It is the kind of simple action which is easy to adapt to experimental conditions. However, actions can be even simpler or more complex. An action can be made up of one unique element—an elementary movement (e.g., moving horizontally from left to right to reach a target)—or, on the contrary, can be made up of numerous movements (involving several limbs, sequences, etc.). Moreover, the same action can be achieved thanks to different movements, for what's important at the level of action is, first of all, the achievement of its goal and not so much how precisely this goal has been achieved at the more elementary levels. We can grasp a glass and drink it in different ways. We can grasp it more or less rapidly, following a more or less direct trajectory, eventually avoiding an obstacle placed on this trajectory, and so on.

Such a distinction between actions and movements is justified from the logical and behavioral point of view. But it is above all justified because there are specific neuronal correlates for each of these subdivisions. For example, we have known for a long time that avoiding obstacles can be accomplished thanks to different subcortical structures of the central nervous system. At the extreme, a cat with his medulla severed at the cervical level is still able to walk on a treadmill and to avoid obstacles placed on the trajectory of his limbs. Such avoidance reactions are made possible thanks to polysynaptic medullar reflexes. Of course, the more sophisticated the strategy of avoidance is, the more involved are the structures that evolve. Indeed, a monkey becomes unable to avoid a sheet of glass between him and the target of his action if the anterior part of his supplementary motor area has been injured.

Concerning elementary movements, we have known, for instance, since the beginning of the 1980s that the primary motor cortex is involved in the coding of the direction of ballistic movements (Georgopoulos et al. 1982). Neurons in the motor cortex can increase their firing rate in a specific direction of movement, their preferred direction. By calculating the vector sum of all these activities at the level of an entire population of neurons, it is possible to represent the exact direction in which the animal executes his movement. During the preparation of such movements, it is also possible to observe some particular moments of synchronization of neuronal activity which are notably correlated with the amount of information and the moment at which the animal has to prepare and execute his movement (Grammont and Riehle 1999, 2003; Riehle et al. 2006). Other types of neuronal activity linked to the elementary parameters of movements such as force or amplitude have also been discovered in the primary motor cortex (Riehle and Requin 1989, 1995).

The discovery of neuronal correlates involved in action per se is more recent. Here I refer to the discovery of the famous mirror neurons (di Pellegrino et al. 1992; Gallese et al. 1996) in F5 in the premotor cortex of the macaque monkey (Matelli et al. 1985). This discovery has been corroborated in humans on a more macroscopic scale (Fadiga et al. 1995; Rizzolatti et al. 1996; Buccino et al. 2001). These neurons increase their activity when the animal executes a given action and, surprisingly, when he observes a similar action being executed by someone else. However, in order for these neurons to be activated, the observed action has to actually be executed. Indeed, if one only mimics the given action in front of the subject, without the goal of the action's being actually performed, mirror neurons do not discharge (Gallese et al. 1996; Umiltà et al. 2001). This shows their involvement in topocinetic actions, that is, actions oriented toward a goal, rather than in elementary movements alone. The fact that action has necessarily to be oriented toward a goal, concretely identifiable, and has to reach this goal in order to activate these neurons shows how much action is necessarily intentional at this level. Moreover, the involvement of these neurons in the execution of different specific actions (grasping, pulling, displacing, tearing, etc.) allows one to consider that there exists in the premotor cortex a kind of motor repertoire in which we can choose the most suited actions depending on the circumstances (for a synthesis, see Rizzolatti et al. 2001; Rizzolatti and Craighero 2004; Fabbri-Destro and Rizzolatti 2008).

One could think that the neuronal correlates of goal-oriented actions necessarily correspond to those of goals and intentions themselves. However, intention cannot be necessarily reduced to the goal of the action, and the goal itself not necessarily to the action. Indeed, as different movements can allow performing the same action and reaching the same goal, an intention can also be achieved through different types of actions and movements. I can, for example, intend to displace an object and then use different types of actions. I can push it, pull it thanks to another object, and so forth. On the other hand, different intentions can be achieved through the same action, without these different intentions being necessarily directly readable and interpretable on the basis of the observation of the action and the fact that its concrete goal has been reached. In this case, it is actually the consequences of the action in the short or long term which will allow an observer to determine the true intention of the observed action. For example, I can press the enter key on my computer ten times in the same way (in motor terms), having, however, a different intention each time and producing different consequences on my screen. This relation, potentially ambiguous, between actions, goals, and intentions, constitutes also the basis of the judicial work when a court has to prove the intention behind the committed action.

From the Observation of Another's Action to the Attribution of Intentions

Remarkable works have recently explored the question of intention in macaque monkeys, on the one hand, and in humans, on the other hand. Fogassi and collaborators (Fogassi et al. 2005) have trained monkeys to grasp some food or an equivalent object in size and form in order to eat it or place it in a container close to the location of the grasping. The recordings of the neuronal activity of the inferior parietal lobe (where neurons have the same properties as mirror neurons in F5; Fogassi et al. 1998; Tanaka et al. 2004) showed that certain neurons discharged differently if the grasping (executed or observed by the monkey) led to the ingestion of the food or just the placement of the object in an adjacent container. The fact that these two kinds of activity are different according to the final outcome of the action (eating or placing) could correspond to the intention linked to the given action. However, as the authors themselves mention, the action of grasping itself was different according to the rest of the action, either a flexion of the arm in order for the hand to reach the mouth or no flexion if the hand had to place the object in the adjacent container. That is why a third experimental condition has been added in which the object had to be placed in a container on the left of the animal's mouth, above his shoulder. And in this condition also, the activity of a proportion of neurons remained different compared to the first condition

Can I Really Intend More than What I Am Able to Do?

in which the animal swallowed the grasped food. The authors interpreted this as meaning that because the action of the first condition (grasping of the food and ingestion) is almost identical to the last described (grasping of the object and placing it in the container above the shoulder), the only really different thing is the final goal of the action, which means here the intention of the action (in one case, eating, and in the other case, placing). In the end, the authors conclude that the difference of activity must necessarily correspond to the difference of intention. Thus, at least a part of the activity of mirror neurons (here in the inferior parietal lobe) would be linked to the intention of the subject.

However, a certain confusion is maintained in this study between a concept of intention which answers the question "Why are we doing this action, for what reason?" and another concept which answers the question, "What is the next action or movement?" (in this study, "What occurs after grasping, placing, or eating; what is the sequence, and how many actions are there to select in the motor repertoire?"). And this last question is not necessarily synonymous with intention, as has been seen before. Concretely, would it perhaps be possible to elaborate a protocol in which one could compare two actions that are "strictly identical" but have different consequences, as is the case when one presses the enter key of one's computer? One possibility is a protocol in which a monkey would have to press a button (red or green), allowing two different mechanisms to switch on depending on the given color, and producing, respectively, two clearly distinct consequences for the animal. Such a protocol in animals could perhaps enable researchers to evaluate more precisely and rigorously the respective part of action and intention in mirror-neuron activation (in inferior parietal lobe or F5).

A protocol inspired by these kinds of concerns, and considering intention primarily as the answer to the question "Why do we do this action," has been conducted in humans using functional magnetic resonance imagery (fMRI). In this protocol (Iacoboni et al. 2005), subjects had to observe three types of videos: either a static context, an action without context, or the same action with a context. In this last condition, subjects should theoretically be able to deduce from the context what the actor's intention was while doing an action: grasping a cup from a table ready for breakfast (understand: in order to drink) or grasping a cup from a table in disorder (understand: in order to clear it). The hypothesis formulated by the authors is that if the mirror systems from premotor and parietal cortex are only linked to the goal-directed action (grasping the cup) and do not take into account the global intention of the given action (drink or clear), then one should not be able to note any difference in activation in the last experimental conditions in which the same action is executed in two different contexts, implying two different intentions. And precisely, results have shown a different activation at the level of the premotor cortex between the condition in which the actor grasps the cup seemingly in order to drink and the condition in which he grasps it seemingly in order to clear the table (note that two different grips were used in the two conditions: precision and whole-hand grip). These data thus show once again that the mirror system in humans integrates the context of the action and not only the concrete action.

It remains difficult, however, to further interpret such a difference in cerebral activation. Indeed, why should taking a cup in a given context produce a more important activation than taking a cup in another context? Why should taking a cup in order to drink its contents be more costly than taking a cup in order to clear a table? Authors answer that there are more neurons activated in relation to actions involving food in monkeys (Fogassi et al. 1998). Another difference between the two experimental conditions lies in the fact that the expectable next actions to prepare in both conditions are different. Precise motor representations are more easily evocable in the "drinking context" than in the "clearing context." This would make the system activate more representations in the first condition. Theoretically, one should even expect qualitatively different patterns of activation at more microscopic levels (e.g., extracellular recordings), but not at the level of the entire structure (fMRI). To conclude, these results show that, in one way or another, the human mirror system seems to take into account, at a minimum, the context in which a goal-directed action is achieved and what kind of actions can follow and, at a maximum, the intention of the actor doing the action as it can be understood from the context.

In addition, it seems that humans cannot help attributing intentions to others, not to mention even to the things around them (for a synthesis, see Blakemore and Decety 2001). Two different theories tend to disagree concerning the attribution of intentions to others, the theory of the "theory of mind" and the theory of "simulation." The former defends the idea that we understand others' intentions by producing hypotheses, logical deductions, and inferences on the basis of what we know rationally about them and their behavior. The latter defends the idea that we simulate in ourselves the behavior we observe in others and are automatically able to understand the intentions we would have ourselves in the same situations. Actually, a simple consensus could be found between these two theories if one considers that they both have a place but at different levels. We would use a theory of others' minds principally at a conscious level, in rather complex situations, whereas we would use simulation in an automatic and nonconscious manner when we observe others' actions and, more generally, their behavior. Obviously, the discovery of mirror neurons brought forth arguments in favor of the simulation theory (Gallese and Goldman 1998), even if it remains a rather controversial issue (Csibra 2005; Gallagher 2007; Dinstein 2008; Dinstein et al. 2008). We can also refer to some other results. Indeed, our brain deals with biological movement in a specific way. A specific structure in the brain, the ventral part of the superior temporal sulcus (STS), is activated during the observation of actions and not during the observation of objects in movement (Grossman and Blake 2001). Such a distinction also works even if stimuli are only light points in movement (points placed at the level of the articulations of what would be a human model). The observation of light points simulating biological movements activates the posterior part of STS, whereas light points moved in a rigid and mechanical manner activate the occipitotemporal junction (Grèzes et al. 2001), showing that the brain is able to process biological movements in a specific manner.

To summarize all these experimental results in a few words, we could say that it seems that there are a certain number of automatic processes which allow us, when we observe another individual acting, to activate our own motor representations among others and to attribute, in one way or another, some intentions. However, are these processes as automatic and, above all, as systematic as it seems? And if not, how should we interpret this? This is what we are going to tackle now.

Does the Observation of Another's Action Always Activate Our Own Motor System in the Same Way?

Stevens and collaborators (Stevens et al. 2000) described with positron emission tomography a condition in which the activation of motor representations is not systematic when the subject observes another individual acting. In their protocol, they present different types of videos to their subjects. In the first condition, subjects can see an actor, foot on a chair, moving an arm from left to right and back going around the knee. In the second condition, thanks to a special effect, the arm seems to pass through the knee. In both conditions, visual areas like MT, for instance, are activated. However, premotor and parietal areas are activated only in the first condition, the condition which is concretely feasible. Indeed, in the second condition, although the movement of the arm is actually biomechanically possible, it remains obviously impossible to pass through one's knee. Thus, these data again show that the motor system is able to take into account the context in which an action is performed by others. However, here, the activation of the appropriate motor representations is made impossible because the action is not realistic enough. Yet, we are all able while observing the arm passing through the knee to represent, to visualize, to imagine that we can do the same thing even if we know that it is concretely not feasible. Moreover, movies nowadays, with all their special effects, show us situations that are completely unrealistic but still imaginable. That is why we must distinguish what we can represent visually and eventually desire to do from what we can represent in a more complete manner, that is, by integrating our capacity of motor representation (Jeannerod and Decety 1995). We are going to develop this question in the following.

Numerous works have shown up to now the rich capacities of representation of mirror neurons. As described above, mirror neurons are activated both when a subject executes an action and when he observes another subject doing the same action, insofar as the goal of the action is reached, achieved (Gallese et al. 1996). These neurons can also be activated by the sound usually produced by the execution of a given action alone, even if the animal does not see the action (Kohler et al. 2002). They are activated even if the final part of the observed action is hidden behind a panel, insofar as the animal has knowledge of what is behind the panel (Umiltà et al. 2001). Moreover, it has been shown that other brain areas could "work in mirror-like fashion." That is why the notion of mirror neurons has been generalized to that of "mirror system" (Gallese et al. 2004; Rizzolatti and Craighero 2004). It is, for example, in the case of the secondary somatosensory cortex. Indeed, this structure is activated both when subjects are touched somewhere on their body and when they observe someone else being touched at the same location (Keysers et al. 2004). The insula is also activated both when subjects are disgusted by a nauseating odor and when they observe the face of someone else being disgusted himself or herself (Wicker et al. 2003).

These different studies show that mirror neurons can be activated by the observation, in a broad sense, of actions executed in numerous and various conditions. Such a neuronal processing must participate in our rich and flexible representations of others' actions, goals, and intentions. Yet, there is an experimental condition in which mirror neurons are not activated when a monkey observes another individual executing an action. This case has been reported by Gallese et al. (1996). Indeed, when an experimenter

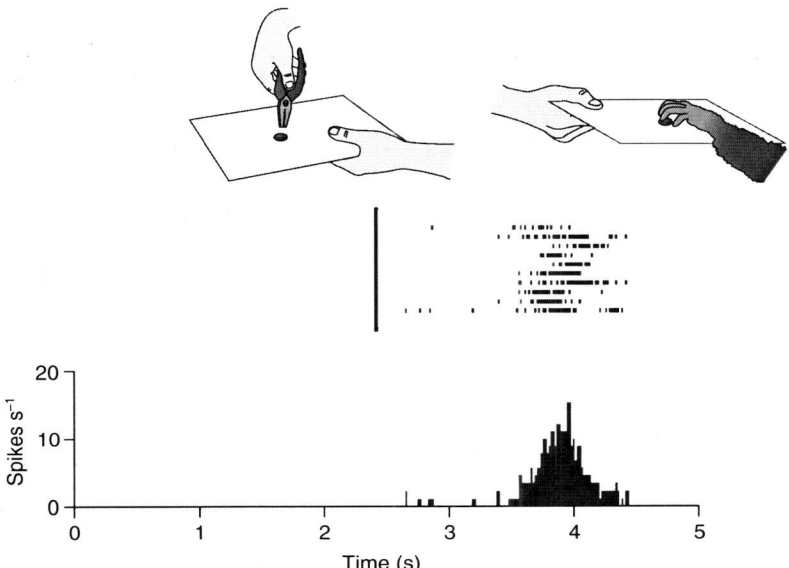

Figure 6.1
From top to bottom: raster (each point represents an action potential, each line a trial executed by the monkey); frequency histogram of the activity of the recorded neuron. A piece of food is placed on a tray. The experimenter grasps the food with some pliers and then presents the tray with some food to the monkey and lets him grasp. The neuronal response is absent when the monkey observes the grasping with the pliers. On the contrary, the neuronal discharge increases when the monkey grasps the food himself with his hand. The raster and the histogram show the neuronal activity before and after the moment when the experimenter touches the food (vertical line).
Figure adapted from Rizzolatti et al. (2001; itself adapted from Gallese et al. 1996).

grasps an object with pliers in front of the animal, the mirror neurons recorded in F5 do not increase their firing rate (see figure 6.1).

This case is particularly surprising given all the other conditions in which mirror neurons are activated. Indeed, the movement of grasping of the pliers closing on an object is visually very similar to the movement of a hand or to the one or two fingers closing on the object. So why in these conditions do mirror neurons not fire? Would the reason be limits to mirror neurons' capacity for representation? The hypothesis that was formulated in order to clarify this question is that it is not a question of visual representation but rather a question of "resonance" of the motor system. Indeed, if one considers that our perspective on the world is also a motor perspective, this means that our perspective on the world depends on the specificity of our own motor system. It means that it concretely depends on the presence or absence of certain populations of neurons usually involved in the execution of certain actions. In other words, the idea is that a monkey who is not able to grasp with the pliers is not supposed to possess a population of neurons involved in such an action. If there is no such population in F5, there is no possible resonance when the monkey observes this action executed by the experimenter, even if the monkey remains, of course, able to visually analyze the scene, this involving other structures like STS among others. Moreover, note that macaque monkeys are not supposed to be able to manipulate complex tools in their natural environment.

If this hypothesis is true, then the acquisition by the monkey of the ability to use pliers in order to grasp should be linked with the adaptation of a population of neurons in F5 involved in the execution of such an action. The presence in F5 of such a population for the execution of this new ability could then be the basis of the process of resonance that was lacking before the acquisition of the new ability by the monkey. In other words, in order to better perceive and represent others' actions, one should first begin with being able to act oneself!

What Makes It Possible for the Observation of an Unknown Action to Activate Our Own Motor System?

The fact that macaque monkeys do not express in nature behaviors involving the use of complex tools does not necessarily imply that it is impossible to teach them how to do so in an experimental context. Indeed, the opposition between the thumb and the rest of the fingers allows them to easily manipulate pliers, and their cognitive capacities are particularly developed. Yet, learning how to manipulate pliers required several months of training for each of the monkeys who participated in this protocol at the department of neuroscience of the University of Parma in Italy. This constitutes an important indication that such an action was particularly difficult for them to perform from a cognitive point of view, despite its simplicity in biomechanical terms (press–release the hand on the pliers in a coordinate manner in relation to the object to grasp). Two types of tools were used in order to distinguish that which is concerned with the level of movements and muscular contractions from that which is concerned with the level of action. The first tool is a pair of reverse pliers (see figure 6.2a). The contractions required in order to manipulate them and grasp an object are

Can I Really Intend More than What I Am Able to Do? 127

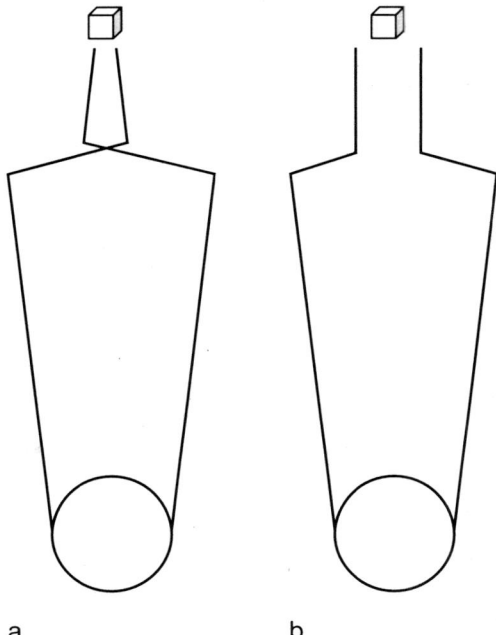

Figure 6.2
(a) Schema of the reverse pair of pliers. Pressure on the handles allows opening the pliers. Releasing this pressure allows the automatic closure of the pliers. (b) Schema of the normal pair of pliers. Pressure on the handles allows closing the pliers. Releasing the pressure allows the automatic opening of the pliers.

the inverse of those required to grasp an object with the hand itself. The pliers open when one presses the handles and close automatically when one releases the pressure on them. The second tool is a normal pair of pliers (see figure 6.2b). The pliers close when one closes the hand on the handles.

With these two types of tools, it was possible to make the monkey execute the same goal-directed action, grasping an object, using two different movements, in this case two sets of muscular contractions precisely inversed. Thanks to this experimental trick, we could evaluate for the first time with precision to what extent the activity of mirror neurons is linked to the movement and to its neuromuscular characteristics versus to what extent it is linked to a superior level of abstraction that is linked to the course of the action itself. Finally and above all, it was possible in this way to check the hypothesis according to which if a monkey learns how to use a given tool, his mirror neurons will be activated significantly when he observes afterwards another individual using the same tool.

The results obtained with these two types of tools demonstrated that the time course of mirror-neuron activity in F5, their dynamics during the execution of action, was independent from the succession of muscular contractions required for the tools (see Umiltà et al. 2008 for a demonstration on F5 motor neurons). As can be seen in figure 6.3, the firing rate of the recorded neuron increases significantly when the tool touches the food, regardless of the tool used (i.e., normal pliers or reverse pliers), that is, independently from the state of contraction or relaxation of the hand (see the mecanograms in figure 6.3). Indeed, this neuron is activated during the second part of the action, while the monkey at this moment is pressing the hand on the normal pliers or, on the contrary, releasing the pressure on the reverse pliers. Thus, the activity of this neuron is correlated with the performance of the end of the action, however it is executed.

Actually, movements and action were mostly superimposed in the previous experimental protocols studying mirror neurons so that it remained impossible to delimit with precision the involvement of these neurons at the neuromuscular level of the movement. With such results, it is possible to confirm today that it seems that there is no direct link between the activity of mirror neurons and the neuromuscular aspects of movement. Yet, the electrical stimulation of certain zones of the ventral premotor cortex triggers the execution of movements in monkeys (Hepp-Reymond et al. 1994). However, as was already hypothesized by the authors of this

Figure 6.3
From top to bottom: rasters (each point represents an action potential, each line a trial executed by the monkey); frequency histogram of the activity of a neuron recorded while the monkey grasps a piece of food with the normal pliers (a) and with the reverse pliers in (b). Below: mecanograms of the grasping actions with the two types of tools, respectively. (a) The neuron increases its firing rate when the normal pliers reach the piece of food (vertical line). From this moment, the monkey's hand increases its pressure on the handles and the pliers close on the food. The mecanogram indicates the space between the handles which diminishes at this moment. (b) The same neuron again increases its firing rate from the moment when the reverse pliers reach the piece of food; however, this time the hand of the monkey releases its pressure on the handles. The mecanogram shows that the space between the handles increases at this moment, which implies that the space between the two tips of the pliers diminishes and that the pliers close on the piece of food. At the very end of the action, the monkey slightly releases the pressure on the handles in order to grasp the piece of food with the mouth.

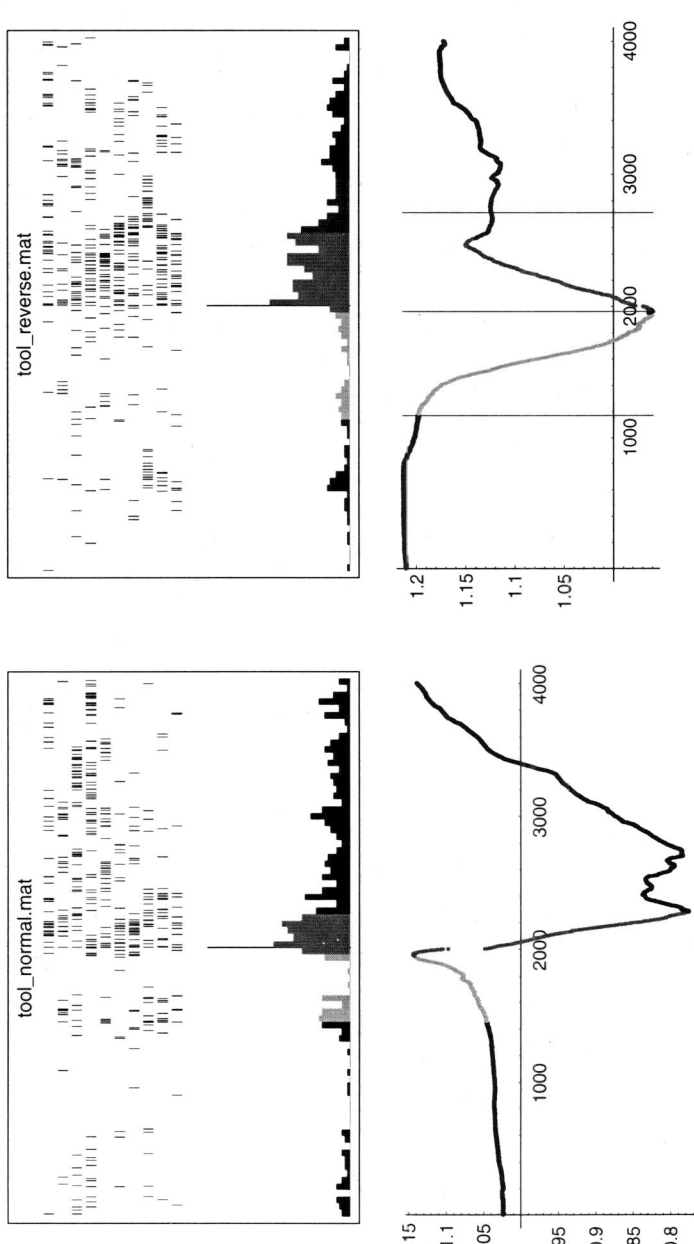

study, our results seem to confirm that F5 would be composed of several types of neurons with only certain of them having relatively direct contact with the medulla, as in the primary motor cortex with the Betz cells (representing only about 20% of all the cells of the primary motor cortex).

Moreover, and above all, we finally were able to observe that mirror neurons increase their firing rate when the monkey observes the experimenter grasping some food with a tool he has learned how to use. We thus confirm our starting hypothesis according to which if mirror neurons were not significantly activated by the observation of the use of a tool in the previous studies (Gallese et al. 1996), it was because the monkey was not able to execute such an action by himself, because he did not have the appropriate motor representations which thus could logically not be activated, could not resonate. An example is presented in figure 6.4. First, the neuron increases its firing rate when the monkey grasps an object with the hand (see figure 6.4a) and with a tool (see figure 6.4b), given that he knows now how to use it. It is interesting to note that the temporal dynamics of the neuronal activity adapts to the length of the executed action, the grasping with the pliers being much slower than the grasping with the hand. This constitutes a supplementary argument showing that mirror neurons are involved in the action and its dynamics rather than in the neuromuscular aspects of movements. One can observe in the same figure that the neuron increases its firing rate when the monkey observes the experimenter grasping a piece of food with his hand (see figure 6.4c), which is completely normal for mirror neurons, but also when he uses the tool in order to grasp (see figure 6.4d). The mirror neurons of this animal are finally activated by the observation of the use of a tool that he learned how to use himself. In the condition of observation also, the dynamics of the neuronal activity follows that of the observed action. The experimenter

---

Figure 6.4
From top to bottom for each part: raster (each point represents an action potential, each line a trial executed by the monkey); frequency histogram of the activity of the recorded neuron. (a) The neuron increases its firing rate when the monkey grasps a piece of food with the hand. (b) The neuron increases its firing rate when the monkey grasps a piece of food with the reverse pliers. (c) The neuron increases its firing rate when the monkey observes the experimenter grasping a piece of food with the hand. (d) The neuron increases its firing rate when the monkey observes the experimenter grasping a piece of food with the reverse pliers.

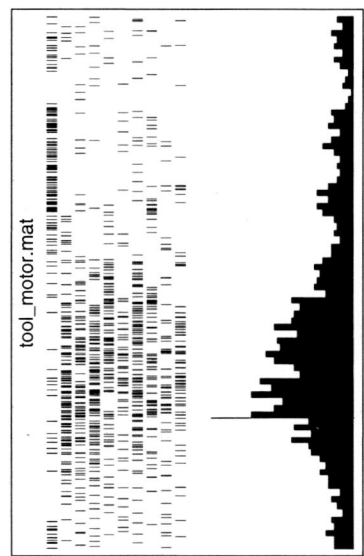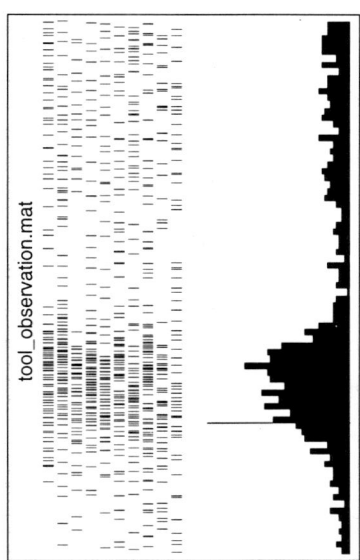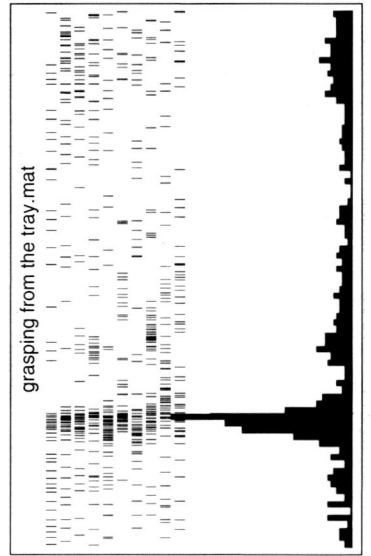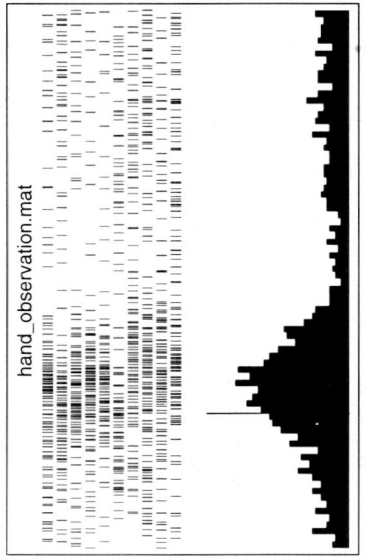

executes his action at a slower rhythm than the animal does but is equally slow with the hand and the tool.

In these data, we can note that the same neuron is activated for both the action–observation with the hand and with the pliers. In this study, no neurons were found to be activated only for the use of the pliers, without being activated for the action with the hand. This indicates that the neurons involved in the action of grasping with the hand have extended their repertoire up to grasping with the pliers. It shows that mirror neurons are capable of plasticity according to the practice of the subject.

Nevertheless, some results that may appear contradictory showed that mirror neurons can in some cases be activated when the monkey observes another individual using a tool, even if this monkey had not learned how to use the tool previously (Ferrari et al. 2005). However, we must highlight here that in this last study, several years of observation of tool manipulation by another individual were necessary in order to get such a result. Even more interesting in this study, the neurons activated by the observation of tool manipulation do not fire significantly for the observation of the same grasping action with the hand. This aspect of these results allows for an understanding of the relation between this study and our study. The protocol by Ferrari et al. involved only the observation by the monkey of the use of the tool, and thus the animal did not have the opportunity to extend the motor repertoire of his own hand. This is quite different from our study because our monkeys concretely learned how to use the pliers with their hand, and that is why the mirror neurons involved in this training fire subsequently, both when the monkey observes an action executed with a tool and when he observes one executed with the hand. To conclude, the results obtained by Ferrari and collaborators show that in some particular cases (observation of a complex action for years), it remains possible that mirror neurons acquire a representation of others' actions that the animal does not master himself. However, this kind of representation does not seem to be functional in motor terms. Indeed, the fact that in Ferrari et al. the neurons which fire for the observation of actions with a tool do not fire for the observation of actions with a hand may precisely be the explanation of the incapacity of the macaque monkeys to learn by imitation. The acquired representation by way of vision only is not able to link the hand to the tool.

It seems thus that the "normal" process of acquiring a representation of an action that we do not master requires at least a minimum of motor training at the beginning. This is what our study has shown, and this is consistent with most of the other studies in this domain.

The results we obtained are actually in line with Stevens and collaborators' works quoted above (Stevens et al. 2000). They showed that the motor system of human subjects was not activated when these subjects observed an action that was feasible at the biomechanical level but impossible because of the context. In our study, the context of the observed action was absolutely normal, but the action itself was not feasible by the observer because it was not part of his repertoire of actions. Thus, it seems that if an observed action is not feasible because of the context (Stevens et al. 2000) or because of the physical limits of the observer (our study), the mirror system of this subject will not be significantly activated during the observation of such an action. And given the necessary relation between action and intention (see also Fogassi et al. 2005; Iacoboni et al. 2005), everything leads us to believe that, in consequence, it would be difficult for such an observer to integrally understand the action observed and the intentions of the one executing the action. Moreover, what can be hypothesized here is that what is true for other's action and intention understanding should also be true for oneself, that is, one should logically not be able to intend to do something that one cannot represent, represent how to do, and finally cannot do at all, even if it should still be possible for the individual to desire or imagine it. This is something we can observe in everyday life during sports practice, for instance. If tennis players do not master the technique used by their adversaries, it will be very difficult for them to anticipate and read the trajectory of the balls. In the same way, they will not be able to intend to use their adversaries' techniques, as they will not, by definition, be able to activate motor representations they do not possess.

Other recent works which, once again, have yielded results in the same direction as our own have shown that subjects who possess a specific expertise in a given physical activity activate their motor system more than control subjects when they observe the physical activity in question. This is the case with professional dancers in classical ballet or capoeira (Calvo-Merino et al. 2005). When these subjects observe some movements from the dance in which they are expert, their motor system (premotor and parietal cortex) is more activated than when they observe a dance they have not mastered. This study in humans shows that the activation of our mirror system when it is confronted with actions we master more or less can be gradual. Similar results have also been obtained with professional pianists (Haslinger et al. 2005). A fronto–parieto–temporal circuit is more activated in pianists than in control subjects during the observation of hands playing on a piano. Finally, our data are fully compatible with the results obtained by Sommerville and Woodward (this volume). Indeed, they show that children who have previous experience with a given action are able to understand the goal directedness of that action when they observe it in others, contrary to other children who do not have such previous experience.

Conclusion

We have known since the 1990s, thanks to the discovery of mirror neurons among others, that our motor system is also involved in the perception and understanding of others' actions and behaviors. Our results, like those of other studies we have introduced here, allow us to more precisely understand how our mirror system and our capacity to perceive and understand others' behavior are constrained and limited by the diverse capacities of action that each of us has. In other words, if we are not able to perform a particular action, we should not be able to represent it integrally (see also Sommerville and Woodward, this volume) because our mirror system will not be activated during such an action. Moreover, it is not an all-or-nothing rule. Indeed, if we are more or less able to do a given action without being an expert, our motor system will be less activated than that of the expert when we observe the same action (Calvo-Merino et al. 2005; Haslinger et al. 2005). Given all that we have seen up to now, we could compare the understanding of actions in certain cases to a kind of private joke. We can hear the words and understand them literally, but we do not understand the hidden meaning that only the initiates understand. In the same way, we see the gymnast performing a double midair somersault with a spiral in each loop, but we only have an "abstract" representation of what we see and not a "concrete" and integral one because we have no motor neurons able to make us do such figures and thus able to resonate when we observe these figures. Consequently, we should not be able to, concretely, activate the intention to execute a double midair somersault with its motor counterpart, even if we can think about it, desire to do it, or even imagine it in some ways.

It is interesting to consider the fact that our capacity for perception, representation, and understanding of actions and of others' behaviors and intentions can be more or less dependent on not only our capacity to "receive" but also on our capacity to "produce," to act. In a certain way, to rework Piaget, it seems indeed that action forms what we are and conditions the access of what we are to the world. Moreover, "existence may indeed precede essence" (Sartre 1946), as we are not already constituted individuals who would have a preestablished reading of the world. It rather seems that we are individuals who form ourselves through our actions and, in the meantime, thanks to that, modify our capacities for representation and comprehension, that is our "*Umwelt*" (von Uexküll 1909). Thus, action constitutes both a potentiality, because it allows us to access new representations and comprehensions of the world, and a limit, because the limits of the action become those of our representations and comprehensions, as we could see through our own results and those of others. Moreover, even the potentialities opened by our actions contain their own limits, as, by allowing access to a new dimension of reality, they model this access and make it peculiar to the individual and to his or her individual capacity for action. Here is one of the major sources of subjectivity.

To illustrate my views with an anecdote, we know that certain persons are more intelligent than others and that, among these persons, some are able to represent and conceptualize things that very few other people in the world can conceptualize. Physics, among other fields, has provided famous examples from Albert Einstein to Stephen Hawking. Hawking, because of his disease (Lou Gehrig's syndrome, which lets him communicate only with a few eye movements), was able to develop some capacities of mental representation of geometrical objects unique in the world. This suggests that even the comprehension and the representation of the most abstract things can be conditioned by our physical state and by our capacities for action.

Knowing all this, the importance of the constitution of the body and of the capacities for action of individuals should be more taken into account in the education of children for the development of their intellectual and socialization capacities (cf. Sommerville and Woodward, this volume). This is a perspective that has been neglected for a long time because up to now neuroscience and the cognitive sciences in general have rather put the emphasis on sensorial and rational representations. The numerous works on mirror systems show us today, on the contrary, how we build a motor, egocentric and subjective perspective on the external world. It is a revolution per se, and we see increasingly how much of our being in the world and our perspective on the world are conditioned by our motor system in the broad sense of the word.

Acknowledgments

I want to warmly thank A. Umiltà, I. Intskirveli, L. Escola, M. Rochat, and V. Gallese for their participation in the experiment of recording mirror-neuron activities in relation to the use of tools. These experiments have taken place in the neuroscience department of Professor Rizzolatti at the University of Parma, Italy. I wish also to thank the Fyssen Foundation, which supported my stay in this department.

References

Blakemore, S. J., Decety, J. (2001). From the perception of action to the understanding of intention. *Nature Reviews Neuroscience*, 2, 561–567.

Buccino, G., Binkofski, F., Fink, G. R., Fadiga, L., Fogassi, L., Gallese, V., Seitz, R. J., Zilles, K., Rizzolatti, G., and Freund, H. J. (2001). Action observation activates premotor and parietal areas in a somatotopic manner: An fMRI study. *European Journal of Neuroscience*, 13, 400–404.

Calvo-Merino, B., Glaser, D. E., Grezes, J., Passingham, R. E., and Haggard, P. (2005). Action observation and acquired motor skills: An FMRI study with expert dancers. *Cerebral Cortex*, 15, 1243–1249.

Csibra, G. (2005). Mirror neurons and action observation: Is simulation involved? In Interdisciplines: http://www.interdisciplines.org/mirror/papers/4/.

Dinstein, I. (2008). Human cortex: Reflections of mirror neurons. *Current Biology*, 18, R956–959.

Dinstein, I., Thomas, C., Behrmann, M., and Heeger, D. J. (2008). A mirror up to nature. *Current Biology*, 18, R13–18.

di Pellegrino, G., Fadiga, L., Fogassi, L., Gallese, V., and Rizzolatti, G. (1992). Understanding motor events: A neurophysiological study. *Experimental Brain Research*, 91, 176–180.

Fabbri-Destro, M., and Rizzolatti, G. (2008). Mirror neurons and mirror systems in monkeys and humans. *Physiology (Bethesda)*, 23, 171–179.

Fadiga, L., Fogassi, L., Pavesi, G., and Rizzolatti, G. (1995). Motor facilitation during action observation: A magnetic stimulation study. *Journal of Neurophysiology*, 73, 2608–2611.

Ferrari, P. F., Rozzi, S., and Fogassi, L. (2005). Mirror neurons responding to observation of actions made with tools in monkey ventral premotor cortex. *Journal of Cognitive Neuroscience*, 17, 212–226.

Fogassi, L., Ferrari, P. F., Gesierich, B., Rozzi, S., Chersi, F., and Rizzolatti, G. (2005). Parietal lobe: From action organization to intention understanding. *Science, 308,* 662–667.

Fogassi, L., Gallese, V., Fadiga, L., and Rizzolatti, G. (1998). *Society for Neuroscience Abstracts,* 257.5.

Gallagher, S. (2007). Simulation trouble. *Social Neuroscience, 2,* 353–365.

Gallese, V., Fadiga, L., Fogassi, L., and Rizzolatti, G. (1996). Action recognition in the premotor cortex. *Brain, 119*(Pt. 2), 593–609.

Gallese, V., and Goldman, A. (1998). Mirror neurons and the simulation theory of mind reading. *Trends in Cognitive Sciences, 2,* 493–501.

Gallese, V., Keysers, C., and Rizzolatti, G. (2004). A unifying view of the basis of social cognition. *Trends in Cognitive Sciences, 8,* 396–403.

Georgopoulos, A. P., Kalaska, J. F., Caminiti, R., and Massey, J. T. (1982). On the relations between the direction of two-dimensional arm movements and cell discharge in primate motor cortex. *Journal of Neuroscience, 2,* 1527–1537.

Grammont, F., and Riehle, A. (1999). Precise spike synchronization in monkey motor cortex involved in preparation for movement. *Experimental Brain Research, 128,* 118–122.

Grammont, F., and Riehle, A. (2003). Spike synchronization and firing rate in a population of motor cortical neurons in relation to movement direction and reaction time. *Biological Cybernetics, 88,* 360–373.

Grezes, J., Fonlupt, P., Bertenthal, B., Delon-Martin, C., Segebarth, C., and Decety, J. (2001). Does perception of biological motion rely on specific brain regions? *NeuroImage, 13,* 775–785.

Grossman, E. D., and Blake, R. (2001). Brain activity evoked by inverted and imagined biological motion. *Vision Research, 41,* 1475–1482.

Haslinger, B., Erhard, P., Altenmuller, E., Schroeder, U., Boecker, H., and Ceballos-Baumann, A. O. (2005). Transmodal sensorimotor networks during action observation in professional pianists. *Journal of Cognitive Neuroscience, 17,* 282–293.

Hepp-Reymond, M. C., Husler, E. J., Maier, M. A., and Ql, H. X. (1994). Force-related neuronal activity in two regions of the primate ventral premotor cortex. *Canadian Journal of Physiology and Pharmacology, 72,* 571–579.

Iacoboni, M., Molnar-Szakacs, I., Gallese, V., Buccino, G., Mazziotta, J. C., and Rizzolatti, G. (2005). Grasping the intentions of others with one's own mirror neuron system. *PLoS Biology, 3,* e79.

Jeannerod, M., and Decety, J. (1995). Mental motor imagery: A window into the representational stages of action. *Current Opinion in Neurobiology*, 5, 727–732.

Keysers, C., Wicker, B., Gazzola, V., Anton, J. L., Fogassi, L., and Gallese, V. (2004). A touching sight: SII/PV activation during the observation and experience of touch. *Neuron*, 42, 335–346.

Kohler, E., Keysers, C., Umiltà, M. A., Fogassi, L., Gallese, V., and Rizzolatti, G. (2002). Hearing sounds, understanding actions: Action representation in mirror neurons. *Science*, 297, 846–848.

Matelli, M., Luppino, G., and Rizzolatti, G. (1985). Patterns of cytochrome oxidase activity in the frontal agranular cortex of the macaque monkey. *Behavioral Brain Research*, 18, 125–136.

Riehle, A., Grammont, F., and MacKay, W.A. (2006). Cancellation of a planned movement in monkey motor cortex. *Neuroreport*, 17, 281–285.

Riehle, A., and Requin, J. (1989). Monkey primary motor and premotor cortex: Single-cell activity related to prior information about direction and extent of an intended movement. *Journal of Neurophysiology*, 61, 534–549.

Riehle, A., and Requin, J. (1995). Neuronal correlates of the specification of movement direction and force in four cortical areas of the monkey. *Behavioral Brain Research*, 70, 1–13.

Rizzolatti, G., and Craighero, L. (2004). The mirror-neuron system. *Annual Review of Neuroscience*, 27, 169–192.

Rizzolatti, G., Fadiga, L., Matelli, M., Bettinardi, V., Paulesu, E., Perani, D., and Fazio, F. (1996). Localization of grasp representations in humans by PET: I. Observation versus execution. *Experimental Brain Research*, 111, 246–252.

Rizzolatti, G., Fogassi, L., and Gallese, V. (2001). Neurophysiological mechanisms underlying the understanding and imitation of action. *Nature Reviews Neuroscience*, 2, 661–670.

Sartre, J. P. (1946). L'existentialisme est un humanisme. Paris: Nagel.

Stevens, J. A., Fonlupt, P., Shiffrar, M., and Decety, J. (2000). New aspects of motion perception: Selective neural encoding of apparent human movements. *Neuroreport*, 11, 109–115.

Tanaka, M., Yokochi, A., and Iriki, A. (2004). *Society for Neuroscience Abstracts*, 82.14.

Umiltà, M. A., Escola, L., Intskirveli, I., Grammont, F., Rochat, M., Caruana, F., Jezzini, A., Gallese, V., and Rizzolatti, G. (2008). When pliers become fingers in the monkey motor system. *Proceedings of the National Academy of Sciences USA*, 105, 2209–2213.

Umiltà, M. A., Kohler, E., Gallese, V., Fogassi, L., Fadiga, L., Keysers, C., and Rizzolatti, G. (2001). I know what you are doing: A neurophysiological study. *Neuron, 31*, 155–165.

von Uexküll, J. (1909). *Umwelt und Innenwelt der Tiere*. Berlin: Springer.

Wicker, B., Keysers, C., Plailly, J., Royet, J. P., Gallese, V., and Rizzolatti, G. (2003). Both of us disgusted in my insula: The common neural basis of seeing and feeling disgust. *Neuron, 40*, 655–664.

7 Intention and Consciousness in Sensorimotor Automatisms

Jean Pailhous, Jozina B. De Graaf, and Mireille Bonnard

Nothing seems to be further apart from intentionality and consciousness than sensorimotor automatisms. In general, these concepts are even opposed: voluntary movement versus reflex, flexibility versus stereotypy, and, why not, cortex versus spinal cord. Although these oppositions have permitted us to ask useful questions, these days, they seem to have more inconveniences than advantages, since they do not permit the incarnation—naturalization—of the conceptual distinction between voluntary actions and automatisms. Already in 1942, Merleau-Ponty stated that

> since in the neuronal activity our least conscious reactions can never be isolated, and since these reactions always seem to be guided by the internal as well as the external situation and are able, up till a certain point, to adapt to any particularity of these situations, we can no longer maintain the classical clear-cut distinction between reflex activity and instinctive or intelligent activity: We cannot oppose blind automatism to intentional activity, between which the relation would stay, by the way, unclear.

In the present chapter, we want to argue that choosing complex rhythmic sensorimotor automatisms, such as locomotion, respiration, or mastication, and analyzing their adaptability under the influence of the intentions of the subject is a good paradigm for studying how intentions influence the motor system in order to produce the behavior desired by the subject. Indeed, the rhythmicity permits the expression in real time of intentionality (called by Searle 1983 "intention in action") in the form of modulations of the produced behavior. This modulation is the exact moment at which the cognitive processes are articulated to the sensorimotor processes in order to produce an "intelligent" movement. The cognitive processes implicated in these adaptations are often elementary and even unconscious. The intentional adaptation of automatisms implies, therefore, an articulation between a high-level controlled processing and a low-level automatic processing without a necessity of consciousness. Many studies have demonstrated that during our own actions, motor control can be achieved in the absence of awareness, even when performed intentionally. As already indicated by Leroi-Gourhan (1964),

> it is certain that most of the chains that we unroll the whole day ask for only little consciousness . . . , it takes place in a psychical half-shadow out of which the subject only comes when unexpected events appear in the course of sequences. For all the movements we make successively while shaving, eating, writing, driving, the return to consciousness, even exceptional, is very important . . . one can neither imagine a behavior asking for a continuous lucidity, nor a totally conditioned behavior without any conscious intervention; the former would ask for a re-invention of every part of the smallest movement, the latter would correspond to a totally pre-conditioned brain.

The sudden appearance of consciousness implies the existence of forces in opposition to the intention as expressed in the modulations of automatisms (these forces transform the automatism into action) but not to the automatism itself. Therefore, these opposing "forces" (external forces, habits, another person . . .) need a reattribution (a revision—see Livet, this volume) to an agent (world, yourself, another person), which is a process that can present problems in certain pathologies (e.g., schizophrenia).

In this chapter, we propose to empirically decompose the motor expression of intention (seen by correctly performing the motor task) and the consciousness of that expression with help of two complementary experiments. The first one (Varraine et al. 2002) analyzed the conditions for gaining awareness of a voluntary act; the second one (De Graaf et al. 2004) studied cerebral activities related to awareness of either the goal of the action (planning) or the means of realization of that action.

Sudden Awareness of a Voluntary Motor Act

It is often from the distinction between a high-level controlled processing and a low-level automatic processing that the notion of consciousness appears in cognitive psychology. Many studies have demonstrated that during our own actions, motor control can be achieved in the absence of awareness, even when performed intentionally (Fourneret and Jeannerod 1998; Goodale et al. 1986). For example, by giving false visual feedback about the trajectory of the hand movement, Fourneret and Jeannerod (1998) demonstrated that subjects who could not see their hand were able to voluntarily achieve the desired result of drawing a straight line on a computer screen by making deviant movements, but they were not aware of this deviation. As emphasized by Woodworth (1899), "In voluntary movement, the intention is related to the goal of action and not to the means of movement production. The movement follows from the mind of the result of action and not from the mind of movement." However, in these experiments, one can suspect that if the discrepancy between the feedback about the knowledge of result and the proprioceptive feedback from the movement were to increase, the subjects would suddenly become aware of their deviant movement. This raises questions concerning the influence of top–down mechanisms (linked to action goal) and bottom–up mechanisms (linked to sensory discrepancy) in the sudden awareness of our own movement. Insight into these processes could allow understanding of the online dialog between a high-level controlled processing and a low-level automatic processing in motor control.

Locomotion is particularly well-suited to this aim because it is an automatic behavior which can be intentionally modulated (Grillner 1981; Rossignol 1996), making it the case that the intentional processes can be clearly separated from the automatic bases. When we are walking through space, our intention is to move from one point to another in a certain period of time. Although we are conscious of the spatial goal, we are generally not aware of our leg movement, which is controlled at a spinal level by the central pattern generators (Duysens and van de Crommert 1998). When one is studying treadmill walking (i.e., walking without displacement through space), the spatial goal is removed, so, if subjects want to control their displacement, they need to focus on their leg-somatosensory feedback—the kinetic inputs coming from the generation of propulsive forces (Duysens et al. 2000) or the kinematic inputs coming from rhythmic leg movement, via muscle spindles and joint receptors (Ivanenko et al. 2000).

In the absence of external forces, walking velocity covaries with propulsive forces. However, if the external forces increase, the kinematic feedback is dissociated from the kinetic feedback. Thus, if subjects are required to walk while voluntarily maintaining their walking velocity despite increasing external forces, they will voluntarily produce the same leg movement kinematics (goal feedback), but the propulsive forces will progressively increase (sensory consequences). Inversely, if subjects are required to maintain the same propulsive forces (goal feedback), the stride length and frequency will decrease because of the increase in external forces (sensory consequences). We asked subjects to walk continuously with one or the other of these two instructions (constant walking speed or constant propulsive forces); they were sometimes faced to slow variations in resistance that they had to detect as a double task. To study the influence of the action goal (i.e., top–down mechanisms) in the sudden awareness of leg movement production (organized at a low level), we compared the thresholds of awareness of the modification of sensory afferents when these afferents (kinetic or kinematic) either were or were not linked to the goal. Finally, to know if the bottom–up mechanisms involved in the sudden awareness of movement depend on the modified sensory input, the sudden awareness of the propulsive force increase was compared with the sudden awareness of stride parameters decrease (amplitude and stride frequency).

As shown in figure 7.1, when the subject had to actively compensate for the resistance increase (compensation condition), it appeared that he had compensated for most of the resistance increase when he detected it 6 seconds after the perturbation onset. During this period, he voluntary maintained his stride length and stride frequency—that is to say, he used his kinematic afferents of leg movement as goal feedback—to maintain his walking velocity (Bonnard and Pailhous 1991). Nevertheless, he was not aware of the increase in the force he was producing. Reciprocally, when the subject was focused on voluntary maintaining of his forces (no-intervention condition), his frequency and amplitude decreased with the resistance increase, but he became aware of his kinematics modifications

Figure 7.1
The sudden awareness of low-level gait pattern production. (a) Compensation condition: Average walking velocity (WV; thick black line) and average horizontal traction force (N; thin black line) and their average within-subjects standard deviations (respectively, dashed line and dotted line) observed during a decrease of torque (gray thick line in arbitrary units). The sudden awareness of force increase (vertical continuous line) and its average within-subjects standard deviations (two vertical dotted lines). The gray area under the curve of horizontal traction force between 0 and 6.18 seconds (delimited by the starting time of the resistance increase and the detection time of the resistance increase) represents the unconsciously produced increase of force. The gray area over the curve of walking velocity represents the range of variability in which the subject is able to voluntarily maintain his walking velocity. (b) No-intervention condition: The legend is the same as before. The sudden awareness of walking velocity decrease (vertical continuous line) and its average within-subjects standard deviations (two vertical dot lines). The gray area over the curve of walking velocity between 0 and 6.20 seconds represents the unconsciously produced decrease of velocity. The gray area under the curve of horizontal traction force represents the range of variability in which the subject is able to voluntarily maintain his force (from Varraine et al., 2002).

Intention and Consciousness in Sensorimotor Automatisms

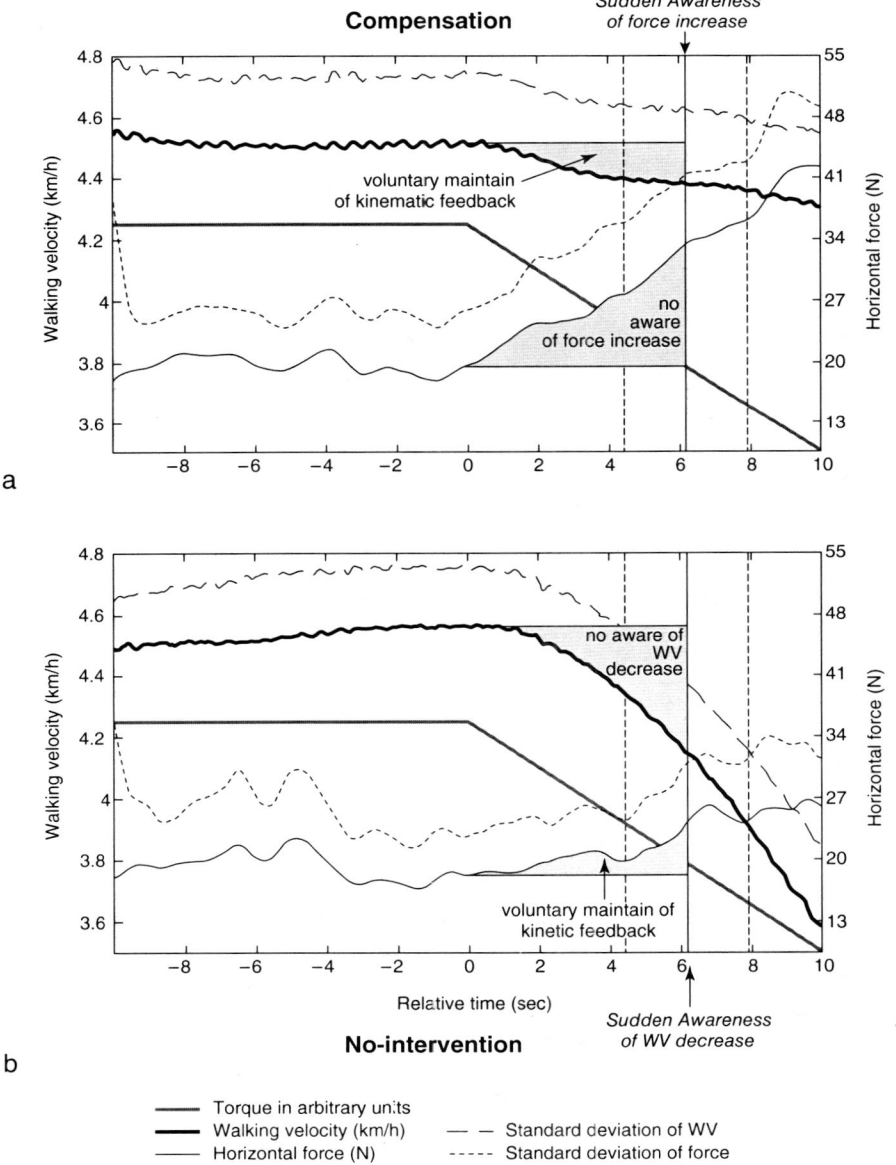

only 6 seconds later. Thus, this experiment confirms that the voluntary control of an intended action can function in the absence of awareness of the production of this action (Fourneret and Jeannerod 1998; Goodale et al. 1986; Worringham and Stelmach 1985).

The models of awareness and control of action emphasize the role of the gap between the desired state and the actual state perceived through sensorial consequences in the awareness of action (for a review, see Frith et al. 2000). For example, many patients with schizophrenia who have no awareness of their predicted consequences are not aware of controlling their action. In our experiment, the awareness of movement was not based on an error detection between the desired state and the actual state. Indeed, when the subject had to compensate for the force increase, the motor responses observed for each trial did not show any velocity gap followed by a compensation to reduce the gap. It seems (probably in order to avoid being surprised by the external perturbation—which occurred randomly with short time intervals) that the subject was concentrated on his stride parameters and adopted an online control of stride frequency and stride length to keep the same velocity (Danion et al. 1997). In both conditions, it is because the feedback of the intended action constantly informed the subject about the success of the desired state that he remained largely unaware of the modification of his other sensory inputs. In fact, there was an inertia effect of the awareness of the stability of goal feedback on the awareness of the modification of the movement sensorial consequences caused by external forces. While the resistance was not sufficient for the subject to become suddenly aware of his movement modification, the intentional control of goal feedback affected the awareness of the other sensory sources despite the attention that was turned to them. Indeed, this unawareness of the other sensory sources was all the more surprising since the subject focused on an expected modification of his movement.

One might wonder which perceptive mechanisms activate this sudden awareness. Two arguments show that the conscious perception of modification of the sensorial consequences depended on the detection of a relative discrepancy threshold between the goal feedback and any sensorial consequences of movement, rather than on an absolute detection threshold defined for each input. First, for a long time, the subject remained unaware of his force increase in the compensation condition or his walking velocity decrease in the no-intervention condition, although the modifications went largely beyond the variability range in which he is able to intentionally control his force in the no-intervention condition or his velocity in the compensation condition. Second, the conscious detection of resistance increase occurred at the same time in both conditions, although the goal control concerned the walking velocity in the compensation condition and the propulsive forces in the no-intervention condition, and although the sensory consequences of movement production were linked to propulsive forces in the compensation condition and to walking velocity in the no-intervention condition. It seems that, as force sensation is inextricably linked with position judgments (Worringham and Stelmach 1985)—because in the absence of external forces the kinetics covary with the kinematics—the subject became aware of the external forces modification beyond a discrepancy threshold between the kinetic and the kinematic afferents. Whatever the condition, for the same variation of resistance, the discrepancy between the kinetic and the kinematic afferents was the same. That is the reason why the sudden awareness occurred at the same time in both conditions.

In conclusion, the sudden awareness of a movement pattern produced at a low level emerges from the interaction between a top–down mechanism where the intentional control of goal feedback delays the aware perception of the other sensory sources and a bottom–up mechanism where high-level mechanisms of sensorimotor integration come into play beyond a discrepancy threshold between different sensory information. This could explain why, although the experimental conditions of our experiment specifically affected the kinetic afferences in the compensation condition or the kinematic afferences in the no-intervention condition, the sudden awareness occurred at the same time in both conditions, because it was caused by the no-specific-discrepancy threshold between different sensory cues which are the same in both conditions.

The conditions of the sudden emergence of voluntary acts in the field of consciousness give rise to two remarks. First, one should not confound nonconscious voluntary acts with unconscious but rather with preconscious. This means that nonconscious voluntary acts are predisposed to appear in the field of consciousness, as is well indicated by the concept of psychical half-shadow of Leroi-Gourhan (1964). Second, in the field of consciousness, "voluntary act" should not be confounded with "voluntary movement." A clear distinction between them might provide insight into their subtle relation. However, if one wants to study this relation, exclusively analyzing the behavioral level is insufficient because the voluntary movement is the behavioral expression of the voluntary act. What stays when one removes the movement from the voluntary motor act (see Searle 1983)? Analyzing cerebral activation when the movement is identical but the voluntary motor act is different might offer insight into the relation between them. We will show this in the following.

Awareness of Motor Act and Brain Activation

Consciousness can be defined as "inner, qualitative, subjective states and processes of sentience or awareness," and its essential feature is unified, qualitative subjectivity (Searle 2000). In this view, motor awareness is one subjective state of awareness being part of a unified consciousness. In the motor control literature, motor awareness is often considered as explicit knowledge about our own motor output (i.e., motor realization; Haggard et al. 2002; Tsakiris and Haggard 2003). Since it is, by definition, an "inner subjective state" and thus not directly accessible by a third person, one means of studying this, among others, has been to ask subjects to accurately reproduce a movement immediately after its production (e.g., Fourneret and Jeannerod 1998; Johnson et al. 2002). The basic assumption of such a reproduction paradigm is that the movement characteristics that we reproduce are those of which we are aware. Moreover, in order to reproduce a movement, a rough awareness is not sufficient. An awareness with a precise content is required. With such a paradigm, it has been shown that we are not necessarily aware of all aspects of our voluntary movement realization.

In the same way, one could define muscle force awareness as explicit knowledge about the muscular force applied to produce a voluntary movement. This awareness of produced muscle force should be well differentiated from awareness of movement outcome, since no univocal relationship exists between muscle force production and movement outcome. Indeed, all biological movements are the result of the integration of two types of force: active and passive (external; Bernstein 1967; Kugler and Turvey 1987; Bonnard et al. 1997). However, although the neural bases of awareness of movement outcome have been studied (Fourneret et al. 2002; Sirigu et al. 1999; Stephan et al. 2002), very little attention has been given to the neural mechanisms underlying awareness of produced muscle forces.

Awareness of produced muscular force not only is a theoretically interesting issue but seems to interfere constantly with movement production. First, studies on tongue strength and endurance postulate that muscle force sense may be a contributing factor that limits the ability to maintain a contraction (Robin et al. 1991, 1992). Second, in a patient with a stroke in the posterior limb of the internal capsule who was suffering pure motor hemiplegia, it has been shown that motor recovery was initiated only after the effort sensation was fully recovered (Rode et al. 1996). These results show, indeed, that the sense of muscle force is not simply a *consequence* of motor realization but interferes with it. The awareness of force production is also an issue of importance in the discussion about the "attribution of action judgment" (Georgieff and Jeannerod 1998; Jeannerod 1999). Many patients with schizophrenia describe "passivity" experiences in which their own actions are experienced as though made for them by some external agent (Mellors 1970). In most cases the actions made by the patient, although felt to be controlled by alien forces, are not discrepant with their intentions (e.g., Spence et al. 1997). Apparently, these patients have a problem with the relation between intention, motor outcome, and attribution of action. One might ask whether one of the causes of this problem could be related to awareness of their own produced muscular forces.

We used functional magnetic resonance imaging to address the question concerning the neural bases underlying the awareness we can have of the muscle forces we put into our voluntary movement. Subjects performed rhythmical extension–flexion hand movements and had to anticipate that in the succeeding condition, in which the resistance to the movement was higher, they would have to reproduce either their produced muscle forces (resulting in smaller amplitudes of the rhythmical movement) or the movement kinematics (resulting in higher force production to compensate for the increased external force). In these conditions, the behavioral output was similar, that is, the subjects performed a rhythmical movement with similar amplitude and frequency. However, the fact that, later on, they had to reproduce either the force or the kinematics against a higher resistance put them, as we expected, in a different cognitive context. Obviously, their awareness had not the same content, and thus their voluntary act was different. It should be noted that, contrary to the behavioral studies cited above using the reproduction paradigm, we were interested in the neural mechanisms allowing the subjects to gain awareness of their muscle forces (in the force-awareness condition) or awareness of their kinematics (in the movement-awareness condition).

It appeared that the contrast between force awareness and movement awareness was highly asymmetrical. We did not find any brain structure more activated in the movement-awareness condition than in the force-awareness condition, whereas several structures were much more activated in the force-awareness condition than in the movement-awareness condition. These are shown in figure 7.2 on a surface rendering.

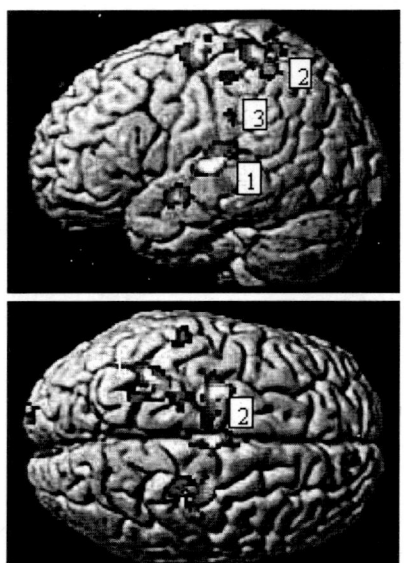

Figure 7.2
Result of the t-contrast force awareness–movement awareness. Height threshold of significance: corrected $p < .01$ (T = 4.90). The voxels are superimposed on the canonical brain surface rendering of spm. Cluster number 1 indicates the activation of left medial and posterior insula, number 2 of left primary and associative sensorimotor areas, and number 3 of left inferior parietal lobule (from De Graaf et al. 2004). Note that the activation of the cingulate gyrus is not visible on the surface rendering.

Insula

The most significant activity difference between force awareness and movement awareness was found for the posterior part of left insula (activation number 1 in figure 7.2). A collective consideration of afferents and efferents shows that the insula has connections with principal sensory areas, with association areas, with paramotor cortex (e.g., Brodmann's area [BA] 6), and cingulate areas (Mesulam and Mufson 1982; Ture et al. 1999). The topographic distribution of efferent cortical output of the posterodorsal insula suggests it to be specialized for auditory–somesthetic–skeletomotor functions (Mesulam and Mufson 1982). Indeed, intracortical stimulation of posterior insular cortex evokes somesthetic sensation (Ostrowsky et al. 2000). Moreover, patients with acute stroke restricted to the posterior insula can show somatosensory deficits (Cereda et al. 2002). Also, somatosensory tactile tasks activate the posterior insula (Sadato et al. 2000). These results strongly suggest that the posterior insula is part of a somesthetic network. The finding in our study of the important activation of the posterior insula in the force-awareness condition seems to indicate the importance of somesthetic information processing in awareness of produced muscle force.

Somatosensory Areas
An important activity in primary and associative sensory areas (number 2 in figure 7.2) was found in the force-awareness condition relative to the movement-awareness condition. Although in these two conditions the subjects received similar somatosensory information concerning their actual movements (because the movements were similar), it appears that this information had "more importance" in the force-awareness condition. Lesion (Caselli 1993; Levine et al. 1978) and stimulation studies (Penfield and Jaspers 1954) have suggested that areas posterior to SI (BA 5, 7, and 40) are necessary for the conscious processing of somatosensory stimuli. Studies in neurosurgical patients showed that subliminal stimuli (i.e., stimuli not reaching consciousness) elicit only the early component of the evoked potentials in the primary somatosensory cortex (Libet et al. 1967). Recently, it was shown in a magnetoencephalography study on tumor patients that activation of the primary somatosensory cortex alone is not sufficient to have consciousness about tactile events (Preißl et al. 2001). These patients showed an intact early (40 ms) component and an absence of later components as well as a complete lack of conscious awareness of tactile stimuli. These results together strongly suggest that activation of associative sensory areas is necessary to obtain consciousness about an (external) event.

The need to reproduce the force required an awareness with a precise content. Since the subjects had to reproduce the muscle force independent of the kinematics of the movement, the subjects had to separate the relevant from the irrelevant afferent information. Muscle spindle activity, besides the fact that it is highly influenced by kinematics, does not seem to be a good candidate for muscle force estimation (McCloskey et al. 1974). Although Golgi tendon organs give reliable information concerning intramuscular tensions, it is evident that their discharge is also influenced by the kinematics of the rhythmical movements (that, the subjects knew, was going to change). Thus, the subjects could not use these proprioceptive sources to calibrate their produced force. The only afferent information that the subject could use seems to be the cutaneous information coming from the hand pushing the handle of the manipulandum. It has been shown in experiments with skin surface anaesthetics that cutaneous information may play a role in grip force regulation (e.g., Monzee et al. 2003) and weight estimation (Gandevia and McCloskey 1977).

Anterior Cingulate Cortex

Another very important activation difference between force awareness and movement awareness was found for anterior cingulate cortex (ACC; not visible on the surface rendering in figure 7.2). A large meta-analysis of positron emission tomography studies (Paus et al. 1998) showed that the common denominator of ACC activation across many task conditions is, in fact, the amount of effort which has to be engaged in a task. ACC activation, therefore, might reflect the degree of intentional effort, motivation, or volition that is needed to carry out a task (Paus 2001; Winterer et al. 2002). Thus, the important activation difference in this region in our study probably reflects the inhabitual aspect of the force-awareness conditions: gaining awareness of the produced force underlying a movement costs an important amount of volition.

Left Inferior Parietal Lobule

The role of left inferior parietal lobule (activation number 3 in figure 7.2) in motor attention has been clearly demonstrated (e.g., Rushworth, Ellison, and Walsh 2001; Rushworth, Krams, and Passingham 2001). In parallel, the inferior parietal lobule is generally assumed to be involved in "sensory awareness." This assumption is based on the fact that neglect which constitutes an attentional rather than a sensory deficit is most commonly found after lesions of the inferior parietal lobule (Mattingley et al. 1998).

It is clear that gaining precise awareness of the produced force underlying a movement is a demanding task. At a behavioral level, all subjects reported the difficulty of the force-awareness task relative to the movement-awareness task. This, together with the very important cerebral activity in the force-awareness condition relative to the movement-awareness condition, shows that gaining awareness in such a precise way that one is able to reproduce the muscular forces we put in a movement despite changing external force is not easily accomplished.

There might be two reasons for this difficulty. First, it has been proposed that the level of processing which relates to the "public" aspects of an action (motor output) may be conscious, whereas the "private" aspects (active forces making part of the motor act) are not shareable with other individuals and, therefore, remain unconscious (Frith 1995). Indeed, awareness of forces seems to be merely related to the external (i.e., public) force ("There is wind opposing to my movement," something that can be shared with others) and not to the produced (private) force ("I had to produce more force to maintain my walking speed"). Reports concerning awareness of force production published so far are often related to weight estimation (e.g., Burgess and Jones 1997; Gandevia and McCloskey 1977; Rode et al. 1996). Weight estimation is always with respect to an object, so the awareness concerns more the object (i.e., the public aspect) than the muscular force produced by the subject (although, of course, the produced force has to be taken in account at some unconscious level in order to be able to perform the task). Thus, one difficulty of the force-awareness condition might have been to obtain awareness of some private aspect that usually does not reach consciousness.

Second, as already argued above, reproduction requires a precise and not some rough awareness. Besides the fact that during a desired action produced muscle forces change all the time, we have to separate the relevant from the irrelevant afferent information. Indeed, usually sensory signals inform us about movement dynamics "as a whole," taking also into account movement kinematics. Therefore, it seems to be difficult to obtain precise awareness of something that changes all the time, and for which we have to discriminate the different sources of sensory information.

In a review paper, McCloskey (1978) argued that the judgments of achieved muscular force are based on the magnitudes of the outgoing motor commands rather than on the real muscular tensions achieved. This hypothesis seems not to be confirmed by the present results. Indeed, all brain areas we found activated in the present experiment taken together suggest that awareness of produced force is essentially based on activation of primary and associative somatosensory structures, that is, on sensory information. Moreover, a parallel is often made between muscle force sense and effort sense (Gandevia 1987). However, it is known that the anterior insular cortex is an important cerebral cortical structure involved in the process of integrating one's sense of effort (Williamson et al. 2003), and in our study we did not find any activity difference in this structure between the force-awareness and the movement-awareness conditions. Thus, although often used interchangeably, awareness of muscular force does not seem to be based on the same mechanism as that underlying the integration of one's sense of effort.

Conclusions

In the context of this book, the two empirical illustrations we have chosen contribute to the huge debate at the interface between neuroscience and philosophy concerning agency.

The opposition "active–passive" is rather old (see Bard et al. 1992; Brouchon and Paillard 1996, for experimental studies), and its importance in the constitution of the agent (the "self") during ontogeny is well-known (Wallon 1928; Piaget 1949). Yet, at the level of the motor realization (that is considered as important in the actual debate because of the potential role of the efference copy in the attribution of an action judgment to its author), we state that it is impossible to infer the characteristics of the movement (i.e., the motor realization) from its motor command because of the presence of external forces.

Having a question about the agent ("who did what?") does not necessarily imply a disorder of agency. Indeed, it happens to everybody to be sometimes unable to attribute a movement (i.e., the active forces) to its author. Clear examples of this can be found in contact sports (such as judo), horse riding, or even car driving. This means that the executive sensorimotor areas, although they can be involved in disorders of agency, cannot be the principal brain support for such disorders. Of course, this does not imply that disorders of attribution judgment do not give rise to problems concerning the attribution of the agent.

The first experiment showed that we do not have any difficulty in the self-attribution of voluntary acts without any awareness of having them performed. At the other side, it is not difficult to find examples of attribution to ourselves of nonintentional acts (see the interesting work of Wallon 1928 concerning clumsiness). Indeed, a child goes in several months from "the spoon fell down" (so, he or she is not the agent) to "I let the spoon fall down" (he or she became the agent), and, to our knowledge, there is no temporal delay between "I took the spoon" (which corresponds to the child's intention) and "I let the spoon fall down" (being not intended, an involuntary act still attributed to himself or herself).

The second experiment showed that gaining awareness of active forces, the only ones that we can really attribute to ourselves in the realization of a movement, needs more cerebral activation in a large number of brain areas than gaining awareness of the movement outcome, although the latter is the result of an integration of active and external forces. This shows that, although we can only produce active forces, it is the movement outcome that is easily consciously controlled (concerning the difference between product control and production control, see Bonnard and Pailhous 1995). Therefore, in the debate concerning attribution of agency, one should integrate that although movement programming (using a metaphor from informatics) with its prediction of sensorial consequences might be an often accepted notion, it is not the only one, and it is not our own. Sensorimotor integration can be found at multiple levels, including the medullar, that is, far away from "intellectual syntheses" expressed by Petit (2002). With respect to the motor cortex, over the last few years several researchers have shown that the primary motor area, reputed to be executive, is, in fact, also involved in nonmotor functions, such as those reflecting the integration of cognitive and sensorimotor information (see Bonnard et al. 2003, 2004 for works from our team) also depending on emotional states. This supports well-known phenomena such as yawns, panic, and many other catching and irrepressible behaviors. Moreover, it is important that theoretical positions fit both ontogeny and phylogeny. An excess of intellectualization (computation, representation . . .) with its consequences for the supposed brain organization splits humans from their childhoods and the human species from its origin, gregarious among others. Let us take the example of mental simulation; even if it exists, it is a delayed, sophisticated process that has more elementary processes underlying it, such as inhibition of action. In order to be "empathetic," we first need to avoid being totally empathetic; otherwise, we would simply be in symbiosis (empathy is not the organizational principle of the collective behavior of a school of fish!), and, then, how could we attribute an intention to anybody without having the possibility not to be the agent?

References

Bard, C., Paillard, J., Lajoie, Y., Fleury, M., Teasdale, N., Forget, R., and Lamarre, Y. (1992). Role of afferent information in the timing of motor commands: A comparative study with a deafferented patient. *Neuropsychologia, 30,* 201–206.

Bernstein, N. (1967). *The coordination and regulation of movements.* London: Pergamon Press.

Bonnard, M., Camus, M., de Graaf, J., and Pailhous, J. (2003). Direct evidence for a binding between cognitive and motor functions in humans: A TMS study. *Journal of Cognitive Neuroscience, 15,* 1207–1216.

Bonnard, M., de Graaf, J., and Pailhous, J. (2004). Interactions between cognitive and sensorimotor functions in the motor cortex: evidence from the preparatory motor sets anticipating a perturbation. *Reviews in the Neurosciences, 15,* 371–382.

Bonnard, M., and Pailhous, J. (1991). Intentional compensation for selective loading affecting human gait phases. *Journal of Motor Behavior*, 23(1), 4–12.

Bonnard, M., and Pailhous, J. (1995). A few reasons why psychologists can adhere to Feldman and Levin's model. *Behavioral and Brain Sciences* (comment of a manuscript by Feldman and Levin), 18, 746–747.

Bonnard, M., Pailhous, J., and Danion, F. (1997). Intentional on-line adaptation of rhythmic movements during a hyper- to microgravity change. *Motor Control*, 1, 247–262.

Brouchon, M., and Paillard, J. (1996). Influence of active or passive conditions of mobilization of a limb on the precision of the locating of its final position. *Comptes rendus des séances de la Société de biologie et des ses filiales*, 160, 1281–1285.

Burgess, P. R., and Jones, L. F. (1997). Perceptions of effort and heaviness during fatigue and during the size-weight illusion. *Somatosensory and Motor Research*, 14, 189–202.

Caselli, R. J. (1993). Ventrolateral and dorsomedial somatosensory association cortex damage produces distinct somesthetic syndromes in humans. *Neurology*, 43, 762–771.

Cereda, C., Ghika, J., Maeder, P., and Bogousslavsky, J. (2002). Strokes resisted to the insular cortex. *Neurology*, 59, 1950–1955.

Danion, F., Bonnard, M., and Pailhous, J. (1997). Intentional on-line control of propulsive forces in human gait. *Experimental Brain Research*, 116, 525–538.

de Graaf, J., Gallea, C., Pailhous, J., Anton, J. L., Roth, M., and Bonnard, M. (2004). Awareness of muscular force during movement production: An fMRI study. *NeuroImage*, 21, 1357–1367.

Duysens, J., Clarac, F., and Cruse, H. (2000). Load-regulating mechanisms in gait and posture: comparative aspects. *Physiological Reviews*, 80, 83–133.

Duysens, J., and Van de Crommert, H. V. (1998). Neural control of locomotion: I. The central pattern generator from cat to humans. *Gait and Posture*, 7, 131–141.

Fourneret, P., and Jeannerod, M. (1998). Limited conscious monitoring of motor performance in normal subjects. *Neuropsychologia*, 36, 1133–1173.

Fourneret, P., Paillard, J., Lamarre, Y., Cole, J., and Jeannerod, M. (2002). Lack of conscious recognition of one's own actions in a haptically deafferented patient. *Neuroreport*, 13, 541–547.

Frith, C. D. (1995). Consciousness is for other people. *Behavioral Brain Sciences*, 18, 682–683.

Frith, C. D., Blakemore, S. J., and Wolpert, D. M. (2000). Explaining the symptoms of schizophrenia: Abnormalities in the awareness of action. *Brain Research Review, 31*, 357–420.

Gandevia, S. C. (1987). Roles for perceived voluntary motor commands in motor control. *Trends in Neurosciences, 10*, 81–85.

Gandevia, S. C., and McCloskey, D. I. (1977). Effects of related sensory inputs on motor performances in man studied through changes in perceived heaviness. *Journal of Physiology, 272*, 653–672.

Georgieff, N., and Jeannerod, M. (1998). Beyond consciousness of external reality: A "who" system for consciousness of action and self-consciousness. *Consciousness and Cognition, 7*, 465–477.

Goodale, M. A., Pelisson, D., and Prablanc, C. (1986). Large adjustments in visually guided reaching do not depend on vision of the hand or perception of target displacement. *Nature, 320*, 748–798.

Grillner, S. (1981). Control of locomotion in bipeds, tetrapods and fish. In V. Brooks (Ed.), *Handbook of physiology: The nervous system II* (pp. 1179–1236). Bethesda: American Physiological Society.

Haggard, P., Clark, S., and Kalogeras, J. (2002). Voluntary action and conscious awareness. *Nature Neuroscience, 5*, 382–385.

Ivanenko, Y. P., Grasso, R., and Lacquaniti, F. (2000). Influence of leg muscle vibration on human walking. *Journal of Neurophysiology, 84*, 1737–1747.

Jeannerod, M. (1999). To act or not to act: Perspectives on the representation of actions. *Quarterly Journal of Experimental Psychology, 52A*, 1–29.

Johnson, H., Van Beers, R. J., and Haggard, P. (2002). Action and awareness in pointing tasks. *Experimental Brain Research, 146*, 451–459.

Kugler, P. N., and Turvey, M. T. (1987). *Information, natural law, and the self-assembly of the rhythmic movement*. Hillsdale, NJ: Erlbaum.

Leroi-Gourhan, A. (1964). *Le geste et la Parole: I. Technique et langage*. Paris: Albin Michel.

Levine, D. N., Kaufman, K. J., and Mohr, J. P. (1978). Inaccurate reaching associated with a superior parietal lobe tumor. *Neurology, 28*, 555–561.

Libet, B., Alberts, W. W., Wright, E. W., and Feinstein, B. (1967). Responses of human somatosensory cortex to stimuli below threshold for conscious sensation. *Science, 156*, 1597–1600.

Mattingley, J. B., Husain, M., Rorden, C., Kennard, C., and Driver, J. (1998). Motor role of human inferior parietal lobe revealed in unilateral neglect patients. *Nature, 392*, 179–182.

McCloskey, D. I. (1978). Kinaesthetic sensibility. *Physiological Reviews*, *58*, 763–820.

McCloskey, D. I., Ebeling, P., and Goodwin, G. M. (1974). Estimation of weights and tensions and apparent involvement of a 'sense of effort'. *Experimental Neurology*, *42*, 220–232.

Mellors, C. S. (1970). First-rank symptoms of schizophrenia. *British Journal of Psychiatry*, *117*, 15–23.

Merleau-Ponty, M. (1942). *La structure du comportement*. Paris: Presses Universitaires de France Quadrige.

Mesulam, M. M., and Mufson, E. J. (1982). Insula of the old world monkey: III. Efferent cortical output and comments on function. *Journal of Comparative Neurology*, *212*, 38–52.

Monzee, J., Lamarre, Y., and Smith, A. M. (2003). The effects of digital anesthesia on force control using a precision grip. *Journal of Neurophysiology*, *89*, 672–683.

Ostrowsky, K., Isnard, J., Ryvlin, P., Guenot, M., Fischer, C., and Mauguiere, F. (2000). Functional mapping of the insular cortex: Clinical implication in temporal lobe epilepsy. *Epilepsia*, *41*, 681–686.

Paus, T. (2001). Primate anterior cingulate cortex: where motor control, drive and cognition interface. *Nature Reviews Neuroscience*, *2*, 417–424.

Paus, T., Koski, L., Caramanos, Z., and Westbury, C. (1998). Regional differences in the effects of task difficulty and motor output on blood flow response in the human anterior cingulate cortex: A review of 107 PET activation studies. *Neuroreport*, *9*, R37–R47.

Penfield, W. G., and Jaspers, H. (1954). *Epilepsy and the functional anatomy of the human brain*. London: Churchill Press.

Petit, J.-L. (2002). La constitution par le mouvement: Husserl à la lumière des données neurobiologiques récentes. In J. Petitot, F. J. Varela, B. Pachoud, and J. M. Roy (Eds.), *Naturaliser la phénoménologie* (pp. 283–311). Paris: Editions du CNRS.

Piaget, J. (1949). *La psychologie de l'intelligence*. Paris: Armand Colin.

Preißl, H., Flor, H., Lutzenberger, W., Duffner, F., Freudenstein, D., Grote, E., and Birbaumer, N. (2001). Early activation of the primary somatosensory cortex without conscious awareness of somatosensory stimuli in tumor patients. *Neuroscience Letters*, *308*, 198–196.

Robin, D. A., Goel, A., Somodi, L. B., and Luschei, E. S. (1992). Tongue strength and endurance: Relation to highly skilled movements. *Journal of Speech and Hearing Research*, *35*, 1239–1245.

Robin, D. A., Somodi, L. B., and Luschei, E. S. (1991). Measurement of tongue strength and endurance in normal and articulation disordered subjects. In C. A. Moore, K. M. Yorkston, and D. R. Beukelman (Eds.), *Dysarthria and apraxia of speech: Perspectives on management* (pp. 173–184). Baltimore: Brookes.

Rode, G., Rossetti, Y., and Biosson, D. (1996). Inverse relationship between sensation of effort and muscular force during recovery from pure motor hemiplegia: A single-case study. *Neuropsychologia, 34*, 87–95.

Rossignol, S. (1996). Neural control of stereotypic limb movement. In V. Brooks (Ed.), *Handbook of physiology: Regulation and integration of multiple systems* (pp. 173–216). Bethesda: American Physiological Society.

Rushworth, M. F. S., Ellison, A., and Walsh, V. (2001). Complementary localization and lateralization of orienting and motor attention. *Nature Neuroscience, 4*, 656–661.

Rushworth, M. F. S., Krams, M., and Passingham, R. E. (2001). The attentional role of the left parietal cortex: The distinct lateralization and localization of motor attention in the human brain. *Journal of Cognitive Neuroscience, 13*, 698–710.

Sadato, N., Ibanez, V., Deiber, M. P., and Hallett, M. (2000). Gender difference in premotor activity during active tactile discrimination. *NeuroImage, 11*, 532–540.

Searle, J. R. (1983). *Intentionality: An essay in the philosophy of mind*. Cambridge: University Press.

Searle, J. R. (2000). Consciousness. *Annual Review of Neuroscience, 23*, 557–578.

Sirigu, A., Daprati, E., Pradat-Diehl, P., Franck, N., and Jeannerod, M. (1999). Perception of self-generated movement following left parietal lesion. *Brain, 122*, 1867–1874.

Spence, S. A., Brooks, D. J., Hirsch, S. R., Liddle, P. F., Meehan, J., and Grasby, P. M. (1997). A PET study of voluntary movement in schizophrenic patients experiencing passivity phenomena (delusions of alien control). *Brain, 120*, 1997–2011.

Stephan, K. M., Thaut, M. H., Wunderlich, G., Schicks, W., Tian, B., Tellmann, L., Schmitz, T., Herzog, H., McIntosh, G. C., Seitz, R. J., and Hömberg, V. (2002). Conscious and Subconscious sensorimotor synchronization-Prefrontal cortex and the influence of awareness. *NeuroImage, 15*, 345–352.

Tsakiris, M., and Haggard, P. (2003). Awareness of somatic events associated with a voluntary action. *Experimental Brain Research, 149*, 439–446.

Ture, U., Yasargil, D. C., Al-Mefty, O., and Yasargil, M. G. (1999). Topographic anatomy of the insular region. *Journal of Neurosurgery, 90*, 720–733.

Varraine, E., Bonnard, M., and Pailhous, J. (2002). The top down and bottom up mechanisms involved in the sudden awareness of low level sensorimotor behavior. *Cognitive Brain Research, 13*, 357–361.

Wallon, H. (1928). La maladresse. *Journal de Psychologie, 35*, 72–84.

Williamson, J. W., McColl, R., and Mathews, D. (2003). Evidence for central command activation of the human insular cortex during exercise. *Journal of Applied Physiology, 94*, 1726–1734.

Winterer, G., Adams, C. M., Jones, D. W., and Knutson, B. (2002). Volition to action—An event-related fMRI study. *NeuroImage, 17*, 851–858.

Woodworth, R. S. (1899). The accuracy of voluntary movement. *Psychological Review, 3*, 1–106.

Worringham, C. J., and Stelmach, G. E. (1985). The contribution of gravitational torques to limb position sense. *Experimental Brain Research, 61*, 38–42.

8 Bodily Intention and the Unreasonable Intentional Agent

Dorothée Legrand

My Intention

In this chapter, I intend to specify what it means to be an agent of intentional action. I will argue that to be an agent is not limited to the ability to entertain the sort of mental states that are the causal sources of actions and/or that are relevant to the guidance of actions. I will question the conception of intentional action as reason based and thereby argue in favor of a conception of the agent as an "unreasonable" actor, in the following sense: the agent does not act intentionally only when he or she follows the reason he or she consciously entertains; actions are structurally intentional, and the conception of intention as mental states must be completed by a conception of intention as bodily.

Specifically, this chapter will be organized as follows: I will present in slightly more detail (in the next section, "A Bewildering Subtraction") the classical conception of intentional action: acting intentionally is considered as acting following *mental states* (reasons to act ...) that are the *causal sources* of the intentional action. I will then specifically question two points of this conception: Causalism: Is intention a causal source of intentional action? The discussion of this first point (in the "Causalism and Internalism" section) will lead me to tackle the second issue (in the section "Structurally Intentional Action: The Body Schema"): Mentalism. Is intention necessarily and only a mental state, or does it make sense to talk about bodily intention? Answering these questions, I will define bodily intention as intrinsic to intentional action. Data from cognitive neurosciences will be presented to support this position (in the section "The Neurosciences of the Intentional Body: Some More Data"). The defended conception of intentional action will in turn support (in the "Conclusion" section) the definition of the agent as one who does not have his eyes turned inwards, on his mental states only, but who is a body interacting intentionally with the world, sometimes (at least) "unreasonably."

A Bewildering Subtraction

The most classical way to begin the investigation of intentional action is to specify what it is, and, for that, to contrast it with what it is not: a mere movement. The latter is easily characterized by muscular contraction. The question thus becomes: what is an action apart from muscular contraction? After Wittgenstein (1953, §621): "What remains if I subtract the fact my arm went up from the fact that I raised my arm?" I will argue here that the lessons we can draw from this subtraction come less from its result than from the fact that we are bewildered by this calculation. Before clarifying this perplexity, let's put the subtraction as (IA − M) for "intentional action minus movement" and see how it has been interpreted:

- (IA − M = 0) thus (IA = M). There would be no distinction between intentional action and movement. This is basic reductionism, and many voices militate against this interpretation, unconditional materialists included.
- (IA − M = C); C = cause. The distinction between intentional action and movement would be intention, conceived as the cause of the action. The cause can be reduced to some physical mechanisms within the brain, or these specific neuronal activations can be interpreted in terms of action representation. Many authors have been unconvinced by causalist views of intentional action (see the following section, "Causalism and Internalism"). For now, let's just briefly mention that it has frequently been argued that intentional action would not be characterized by any type of mechanical cause but specifically by reason. This distinction between cause and reason paves the ground for other interpretations of the calculation (IA − M).
- (IA − M = R); R = reason. The difference between intentional action and movement would be a matter of point of view. For Ryle (1949), IA and M would be physically indiscernible and the difference between them would be purely mental, that is to say, in his framework, inexistent. On the contrary, Anscombe (1979) does not nullify this point of view but links it to the linguistic equipment allowing one to answer the question "Why?": Why has such a behavior been produced? The answer is considered as a reconstitution of the agent's calculation, a conventional condensation of "What-happened-in-the-mind-of-the-agent-and-led-to-the-action?" (Petit 1991, p. 160). Against such views, it has been argued that to act for a reason

is necessarily for this reason to be the cause of the action; hence the following calculation.

- (IA − M = CR); CR = causal reason. Here, the difference between what I do and what happens to me is a question of rationality. The agent can answer the question "Why did you act like this?" and from the answer we learn the reason that caused the action (Davidson 1997). But here, obviously, we are back to a type of causalist view of intentional action.

In fact, all the calculations (IA − M) rely on a common presupposition. Specifically, no matter what their alleged result, they all presuppose the possibility of dissecting intentional action and extracting from it "something" that is not intentional, called movement. However, this very possibility is rather surprising. In fact, if one wants to tackle the specificity of intentional action, (IA − M) is as absurd as (IA − I), that is, the subtraction of intention from intentional action. Indeed, intentional actions involve *intrinsically* intention *and* action. Neither the moving of a limb nor the intention can be subtracted from it. Ryle, Anscombe, Davidson, and many followers have all faced, in their own way, this subtraction denaturing intentional action. Here, I would like to tackle the problem from below. Rather than trying to give a meaning to a nonsensical and bewildering subtraction, I intend to give body to the bewildering itself. In other words, I will try to investigate intentional action given that this calculation is nonsensical, that is, given that neither M nor I can be subtracted from IA. Before that, let's clarify the problems linked to the views accepting the subtraction.

Causalism and Internalism

The presupposition that "intention" can be isolated and differentiated from some nonintentional part of intentional action is the common point underlying many contrasted conceptions of intention. In addition to the views recalled above,

in Descartes's dualism, a nonphysical mind, substantially distinct from the body, activates it as efficient cause. . . . In opposition to the dualists, materialists chose to analyze voluntary motion as one part of the body (in the brain) that, separate and distinct from the rest, activates the later. . . . And so the race was on to find the control neuron or set of neurons . . . that serves as the mechanical trigger on intentional action. (Juarrero 1999, p. 23)

In fact, the common point to all these views, as behaviorism, mentalism, or materialism, is another "*ism*": causalism. Indeed, any causalist view of action, that is, in general, any characterization of intentional action in terms of what causes it, implies the possibility of a dissociation between the cause and its effect, that is, here, between the intention and the action. This framework is compatible with the description of the cause (the intention) as mental or physical, thereby its compatibility with both mentalism and materialism. However, following one or the other of these views, the specificity of intentional action is neglected, since what is studied is either action in a disintentionalized way or intention in a mentalized way. These investigations miss the crucial point: action as intentional, intention as acted.

This failure to account for the specificity of intentional action is, in fact, inherent in the standard conception of causation. In such a framework

> for a relationship to be properly causal, agents must be other than the behavior they (powerfully) cause. Nothing can cause itself . . . it should be possible to tell the difference between the agent responsible for a certain instance of behavior and the behavior itself. The agent must be either a nonphysical mind or one part of the central nervous system that causes behavior by efficiently activating another part. What, then, is this agent? . . . The burden of proof then becomes . . . any philosopher's who advocates agent causation while simultaneously retaining the standard view of cause: find the mysterious agent. (Juarrero 1999, p. 26)

Here, I intend to dispel this "mystery." Before developing this view, let's see how the problem of the dissociation between the effect and the cause, the intention and the action, has been answered in the literature. In the aim to avoid a number of problems linked to classical causalist theories of intentional action (Pacherie 2000), Searle (1983) has introduced a distinction that has become central in the philosophy of action: prior intention versus intention-in-action. To summarize, the former triggers the action while the latter plays a continuing role in the control of the execution, until its end. Searle thus defends the idea that intention should not be conceived as an antecedent of the action, a trigger whose activity would cease once the execution has started. However, it must be underlined that Searle's view does not question the foundation of causalism: cause and effect, intention and action, are dissociable. In fact, in the present framework, the relevant difference between classical causalism and Searle's position is that intentional action is no longer characterized by a two-part mosaic (intention + movement) but by a three-part mosaic (prior intention + intention-in-action + movement). On the contrary, the conception I intend to defend here argues against the "dualism" that lies behind the possibility of dissociation between the intentional and nonintentional parts of intentional action. In this framework, it is doubtful that "trialism" is preferable to "dualism."

Against this form of dualism that allows dissecting intentional action, the conception of intention as bodily implies that intention and action cannot be dissociated. As a consequence, the subtraction between movement and action is not relevant to investigate intentional action. Importantly, this is not to say that movement and action are indistinguishable. This last position is, in fact, closely related to causalism as well. Indeed, a direct consequence of classical causal theories is that the difference between action and movement is their causal *history*, that is, they are not different in themselves, since the effects of different causal sequences can be inherently indistinguishable (Frankfurt 1997).

Apart from the detrimental question of how the dissociated intention and body could be associated at all (which is the problem of any dualism), another difficulty lurks in the classical conceptions of intentional action. We just saw that the subtraction (IA – M) relies on causalism and that the latter is itself linked to a form of dualism between intention and action. In turn, this dualism is associated with a last *"ism"* I would like to underline: internalism. In fact, internalism is only the logical follow-up of causalism: both presuppose that intentional and nonintentional parts of intentional action are dissociable. Localize the cause within, and you get internalism, in the sense at stake here: "to express fully our tendency, let's say that we suppose the existence *within* us of a kind of internal agent: volition. This agent plays the role of the operator of a machine to his dashboard: in fact *he does not have more reality than this machine itself"* (Petit 1991, p. 61, italics added).

One major problem of this internalism is that any action, be it intentional or not, is determined by a complex of factors that are only artificially situated exclusively within or outside of the body. As the classical behaviorist stimulus–response model failed by neglecting internal determinations of action, the reverse model minimizing the role of external determinations of intentional action is misleading as well. To be able to act in a goal-directed way implies not only controlling one's action as intended but also being receptive to the contextual constraints of the external environment within which the action is taking place. A triple determination of action can, in fact, be described: actions are a function of the body, of the mental intention or project of the agent, and of the constraints of the external world. It is thus artificial to separate what comes from within the agent from what comes from the world (Merleau-Ponty 1942)—in short, no reified intention within us, and its counterpart, no machine-like body. Importantly, if intention is not conceived as a mental and/or physical state within the agent, which controls its body, then this body cannot afford anymore to be a mere machine executing the orders coming "from the top."

In the remainder of this chapter, I will develop a conception of intention as bodily which relies neither on causlist dualism dissociating intentional and nonintentional parts of the intentional action nor on internalism localizing what makes an action intentional exclusively within the agent.

Structurally Intentional Action: The Body Schema

The distinction described above between intentional and nonintentional parts of intentional action overlooks the distinction between two types of intention: mental and bodily. One can hardly deny the existence of some mental states prior to the execution of intentional action. We can have some illusion about this (Wegner 2002), but my intention is not to debate this here. Rather it is to specify the conception of intention at a bodily level: to have an intention is not only to have a reason to act but also to have a body oriented toward a goal.

This bodily orientation lies between mechanism and intellectualism (Merleau-Ponty 1942, p. 41; 1945, p. 128) and implies that the body is not the object of action, representation, or reflection: it is the subject of action. That is, the body is not the instrument of intention but its organ: it allows the expression of intention in the world. Unlike desire (Grammont, this volume), which can remain unfulfilled, bodily intention is nothing but this oriented bodily expression.

The intentional orientation of the body has been described by both philosophers and neurophysiologists under the term *body schema* (often misunderstood; cf. Paillard 1973; Gallagher 1995, 2005). The body schema is a middle term between mere physiology and consciousness. It has first been described by Head and Holmes (1911–1912) as "a combined standard against which all subsequent changes of posture are measured, . . . before the changes of posture enter consciousness." It has to be differentiated from the geocentered postural reference which allows situating the body parts in relation to the head, the latter being itself situated in external space (Paillard 2005). The body schema must also be differentiated from the body image, which corresponds to an "internal representation in the conscious experience of visual, tactile and motor information of corporal origin" (Head and Holmes 1911–1912). The body schema is a reference that is both egocentric and situated geocentrically. The two frames of reference are combined: the geocentric reference allows situating the body in relation to the external environment, while conversely the egocentric reference allows situating exteroceptive information in relation to the situated body. Thereby, the body schema corresponds to the integration of sensorial information in the postural reference. It can thus only be understood as the combination of information on the stimulus and the surrounding space, and information on the body itself, provided by proprioception, vestibular receptors, and vision. The body schema is often misunderstood as the integration of these latter sets of information on the body, through, for instance, the activation of bimodal neurons (Iriki et al. 1996). However, the body schema is not about the body itself, in isolation, but about the body situated in and oriented toward the world.

This physiological conception of the body schema and its distinction from the body image has also been described in philosophy (Merleau-Ponty 1945). The body schema is conceived as "a system of processes that constantly regulate posture and movement—*sensorimotor processes* that function without reflective awareness or the necessity of perceptual monitoring" (Gallagher 2000). Conversely, the body image is defined as "a (sometimes conscious) system of perceptions, attitudes, and beliefs pertaining to one's own body" (Gallagher 2000). The body schema corresponds to the dynamical and operational performance of the body rather than to a static image, conceptual representation, or even preconceptual proto-image of the body. It is not reducible either to mere physiological mechanisms as describable in isolation. Indeed, it is selectively attuned to its environment as it organizes the incoming information from the stimuli in relation to pragmatic concerns (Merleau-Ponty 1945; Gallagher 1995). The specificity of the body schema is, in fact, to allow the execution of an adapted behavior without conscious control. The level of the body schema remains phenomenologically hidden (Gallagher 2005). However, this does not mean that the body schema is not linked at all to consciousness. Indeed, in order for the motor programs to function properly, they have to be linked to information on the environment where the action takes place, that is, to perceptual consciousness. Moreover, if the behavior monitored through the body schema does not necessitate conscious control, it is not reducible to a mere reflex either. Such behavior can indeed be precisely modulated according to the conscious intentions entertained by the agent rationally and consciously. For instance, if a subject holds out his or her hand to reach a glass of water in order to drink, the subject's hand forms a grip adapted in size to this goal automatically and in an anticipated way (Jeannerod 1986). If now the target of the movement remains the glass of water, but the goal of the action is now to move it to another place, the hand will adapt its grip aperture, but in a different manner, adapted to the new task. The conscious mental intention of the agent thus modifies the structure of the action without this structure's being itself conscious. Rather, the latter is monitored at the level of the body schema, which adapts the movement to the task in a smooth and coordinated way. In fact, the body schema operates as constraining and enabling factors that limit and define the possibilities of intentional consciousness. "The body schema, understood in this way, is not the perception of 'my' body; it is not the image, the representation, or even the marginal consciousness of the body. Rather, it is precisely the style that organizes the body as it functions in communion with its environment" (Gallagher 1986, pp. 157–158).

This distinction between body schema and body image is corroborated by data obtained with a patient suffering from deafferentation from the neck and below (Gallagher and Cole 1995). This patient, I.W., at the beginning of his neuropathy, began to lose control of his posture and movement, even with visual feedback. After two years, though, he recovered enough motor control to execute diverse precise tasks, but for that, vision is absolutely necessary. The control of his movements is an activity that requires a lot of concentration, while it is automatic in a normal subject. If I.W.'s attention is grabbed by something else, his movement loses its coherence. From these facts, the authors draw the following conclusion:

> In terms of the distinction between body image and schema, I.W. has lost the major functional aspects of his body schema, and thereby the possibility of normally unattended movement. He is forced to compensate for that loss by depending on his body image (itself modified in important aspects) in a way that normal subjects do not (Gallagher and Cole 1995, p. 375).

To specify this losing of the body schema following a losing of proprioception, it is worth differentiating the body as situated and the body as identified (Paillard 1980). The former is characterized by the body schema and can be localized even when deafferented. This is not the case with the latter, which corresponds to the body image. This dissociation between situated and identified body has been observed experimentally (Paillard et al. 1983) with a patient who suffers from a central deafferentation of her right hand and forearm. The latter is thus insensible to tactile, thermal, or painful stimulations. The performance of this patient has been tested in a localization task: the experimenter touches the arm of the patient, and she has to point to the target on the intact left arm with her deafferented right arm, or conversely. In these conditions, she is able to point, without vision, toward a tactile stimulation of a deafferented limb. Simultaneously, she reports a great surprise and an inability to feel anything at the indicated place. This behavior has been identified as a "blind-touch" (Paillard et al. 1983): in analogy with the distinction between two visual systems (what and where; see below), the location of body parts in a *body schema* (a "where" problem in the body space, here preserved) could be processed in the nervous system differently than the perceptual identification of the body features in a *body image* (a "what" problem, here perturbed; Paillard 1999). This dissociation has been confirmed by data on another patient suffering from an extensive neuropathy who shows the converse dissociation: a capacity to identify perceptually the location of a stimulated part of her body but an inability to reach the stimulated site when her vision is blocked (Paillard 1997).

In the current framework, the conclusion that can be drawn from this discussion is that the body presents a specific ability to orient intentionally toward the world, an ability summarized under the term body schema. This intentional orientation is specific in that it is dissociable from the conscious identification of the body as an image and from the conscious identification of the target of the intentional action. This conception of the body schema allows for an understanding that intentional action is not exclusively an action performed by a consciously identified body toward a consciously identified target in the world. Rather, it is a prereflective orientation of an intentionally structured action toward a place in the world thanks to the integration of geocentric and egocentric frames of reference. This mode of processing information concerns mainly that part of the physical world to which the organism is attuned by virtue of its basic sensorimotor apparatus. It maintains direct dialogues with the world and thus contributes to the continuous updating of a body-centered mapping of extracorporal space where objects are located and to which actions are directed. By contrast, the representational mode of processing information involves internal representations of the physical environment. It allows an identification of both the body and the goal of its action. The point here is that such identifications are not necessary for intentional action, while the sensorimotor mode of processing information is necessary, at least in the normal case, as evidenced by the sharp contrast between intentional actions executed by normal subjects and those controlled consciously by deafferented patients. The next section reviews some more data from the cognitive neurosciences in order to specify what it means for the body to be intentional, that is, for intention to be bodily.

The Neurosciences of the Intentional Body: Some More Data

The aim of this section is not to isolate neuronal correlates of intention. As described above, such a perspective would imply a form of internalism relying on a causalist view of intention. On the contrary, a genuine understanding of action as structurally intentional implies that the relation of intention to intentional action is not a relation of a cause to its effect. In simple terms, the neurosciences of bodily intention do not consist simply in the investigation of a top-down causality from brain to muscles. Bodily intention has been described above by the notion of body schema, which is not a correlate of it but describes it as lying between the cortical representation of the body classically discussed in neurosciences and the body image classically discussed by psychologists and philosophers (Gallagher 1995). Many other data come to specify this naturalistic description of bodily intention. My place here is not to review them (for more results, see Bonnard, De Graaf, and Pailhous; Gallese; Grammont; Legrand and Iacoboni; Tsakiris and Haggard, this volume). I will rather focus on classical results and interpret them in the framework of bodily intention proposed here.

Bodily intention has, notably, two inseparable characteristics: (1) at the level of action, the body relates to the world in a meaningful, motor and nonintellectual way, and (2) at the level of perception, the body as it is a power to act attributes a meaning to the perceived objects in terms of action goal, and it structures perceptual processes. I will present results supporting these two points, but first it must be underlined that this dichotomy between the level of perception and the level of action is artificial and only serves the clarity of the presentation. It must not hide the circular relations of perception and action. The present view of bodily intention is, in fact, fundamentally incompatible with what has been denounced as the "classical sandwich model" (Hurley 1998): the view that perception and action are separate and peripheral, the former being limited to an input system and the latter to an output system, whereas cognition would be a central slice separated from perceptual and motor processes. This unidirectional conception that goes from perception to execution through intention at a cognitive level has long been dominant in physiology. It characterizes the organism as a "machine to react" (Paillard 1994). Even if current investigations open the behaviorist black box, the latter, intention included, is still often considered as a layer of interposition between perception and action.

Against that view, the notion of bodily intention relies on a perceptivomotor network where action depends on perception that itself depends on action: "we thus have to abandon the distinction between sensorial and motor, ... the boundaries between sensation and motricity disappear" (Berthoz 1997, p. 225). Crucially, these dependencies of perception and action are not instrumental ones. Indeed, the point is not trivially that the agent moves his or her body through space and thus gets the opportunity to perceive previously hidden objects. Rather, the integration at stake here is situated at the level of perceptual and motor *processing*. This view replaces the "input–output picture" with what has been called the "two-level-interdependance view" (Hurley 1998, p. 15): the interaction between perception and action is not limited to the superficial "feeding" with data. That would imply that only the perceptual input is linked to the motor output. Rather, perception and action are interconnected at a structural level (Clark 1999, p. 4), as evidenced by the following data.

First, as already recalled above, it has been shown that actions are organized specifically according to their goal: the grip aperture is specifically correlated to the size of the target object (Jeannerod 1986). What is interesting for us here is the fact that the execution of a simple grasping action implies taking into account not only the properties of the motor system but also the properties of the object that are relevant for the action: its size, shape, texture. In this sense, we can talk here of a pragmatic representation of the object (Jeannerod 1994), by contrast with the semantic representation of the object, allowing its identification and conceptualization: "in the gesture of the hand which raises toward an object is encapsulated a reference to the object not as a represented object but as this very determined thing towards which we project ourselves, beside which we are by anticipation" (Merleau-Ponty 1945, p. 160).

This pragmatic representation of action goal has a very peculiar format: it does not reflect muscular contraction, but it nonetheless remains specifically motor. This latter claim is notably supported by an experiment in which grasping acts executed naturally with the hand were compared with grasping acts executed using a tool (Gentilucci et al. 2004). The results show that the tool grasp and the finger grasp share the kinematic parameters related to the target object (peak velocity of aperture and maximal aperture as a function of object size). In contrast, the temporal aspects of the two types of grasping differ. The authors conclude that some features of the action are specifically related to the goal to be reached and are coded independent of the used effector. However, it would not be legitimate to extend this conclusion to the claim that this peculiar representational format linking action to its goal, which is not muscular, would not even be motor, but perceptual.

To avoid such a misunderstanding, it is relevant to recall the now classical distinction between the "vision to perceive" and the "vision to act" (Milner and Goodale 1995). This distinction has received converging supports at different levels of investigation:

- At an anatomical and electrophysiological level, there exists a distinction between a ventral (inferotemporal cortex) and a dorsal (posterior parietal cortex) path, the former linked to visual identification and the latter to the visuomotor transformation (Ungerleider and Mishkin 1982).
- At a neuropsychological level, a double dissociation has been evidenced between, on the one hand, optic ataxia linked to a lesion of the dorsal path and leading to difficulties in visuo–manual tasks while description is preserved and, on the other hand, agnosia linked to a lesion of the ventral path and showing the reversed profile (Milner et al. 1991).
- At a behavioral level, classical perceptual illusions (like the "Titchener illusion") have significantly less of an effect on the reaching and grasping of the stimulus than on the perceptual judgment (Goodale et al. 1986; Gentilucci et al. 1996; Aglioti et al. 1995).

At this last level, some data are worth considering in slightly more detail. If a subject facing a perceptual illusion is asked to grasp the stimulus, the grip aperture of the hand will fit the real size of the stimulus and not its illusory perceptual size. If the subject is then asked to grasp the same target not immediately but after a 5-second delay during which the visual image is removed, the illusion now clearly affects the anticipatory scaling of the hand grip (Hu and Goodale 2000; Milner and Dyde 2003). The comparison of these two conditions suggests a difference between two types of goal-directed actions, that is, a difference between two types of intention: first, a mental intention adapting the action to the size of the object as visually identified and remembered in the second condition and, second, a bodily intention adapting the action to the real size of the object in the condition of immediate grasping.

Taken together, all these data suggest that there exists not only two types of visual perception, one to identify and the other to localize, but also two types of action, one descriptive and the other operational. It is thus relevant to differentiate, on the one hand, a descriptive capacity using perception as a source of information and action as a means to describe the received information by mimicking it in another format and, on the other hand, a capacity for sensorimotor involvement integrating action and perception in order to monitor adapted behavior (as already described by Merleau-Ponty [1945, p. 123] as "intentional arc"). Bodily intention belongs to this latter level.

Here, a potential objection may arise, which goes as follows. Even if we agree that actions are structured in an intentional way at the bodily level, and not only at the mental level, isn't it much more specific and thus relevant to qualify action as intentional only when the role played by the agent in the control of his or her action is greater than the role played by the external environment? Apart from the fact that this objection relies on a form of internalism, already discussed above, it also points to some empirical data that are worth considering here and that suggest a fundamental difference between intentional action, on the one hand, and environment-driven behavior, on the other hand. This difference is sharp in the case of utilization behavior (Lhermitte 1983): due to frontal lobe lesions, the patients execute complex actions that may appear intentional but which express an environmental dependency syndrome. On this basis, it has been argued (Rossetti and Pisella 2003) that the ability to perform complex goal-directed action is not enough to ascribe intention. The same restriction holds for the anarchic hand syndrome, or simply in the normal case of overlearned stimulus–response transformation, resulting in a deficit of intentional control of action. To summarize, these arguments hold that the specific characterization of intentional action relies on the distinction between action and reaction. Only the former would be intentional, while what I call here "bodily intention" would belong to the latter.

In fact, the description of bodily intention defended here joins this basic distinction between intentional action and mere reaction. The specific claim here is that intentional actions are structured by bodily intention, and this structuring differentiates them from purely data-driven processes. In this framework, it is worth comparing the present description of bodily intention to the following statement: "Reflex, in that it opens up to the meaning of a situation and perception, in that it does not pose first an object of knowledge and in that it is an intention of our whole being, are modalities of a preobjective view which is what we call the being-in-the-world" (Merleau-Ponty 1945, p. 94). Some data are worth mentioning to clarify this claim. I will first recall one example which specifies the distinction between action and reaction and then consider the intentional structuring of perception.

The first experiment (Paillard 1948; Paillard et al. 1989) contrasts two conditions in which the subject must always execute synchronic movements of the foot and the index finger. In the "reaction"condition, these movements must be executed as fast as possible in response to a stimulus delivered in a nonanticipated way. In the "prevision" condition, the same movements must be executed spontaneously. Subjects are very good at performing these two tasks, but the movements of the hand and of the foot are slightly asynchronous. In the reaction condition, the hand moves systematically before the foot, while the reverse is true in the prediction condition. In fact, in the reaction condition, the subject executes the task by answering as fast as possible with both effectors, without really taking care of their synchronicity. The priority of the hand over the foot is explained by a synchronous triggering at the level of the motor cortex together with a difference in the delay of efferent conduction. By contrast, the priority of the foot over the hand in the prevision condition is explained by a temporal interval at the level of the motor command, in order to obtain synchronous afferent feedback. Two additional points are worth mentioning: these results are obtained from the very first trial, and the subjects remain unaware of the nonsynchronicity of their movements. These data thus suggest that predictive motricity is managed in a specific way, involving anticipation of the sensorial consequences of the action, that is absent from spontaneous reactions (Paillard 1990). Again, we come back here to the description of a structural (rather than merely instrumental) sensorimotor integration. Just as we saw above that this structuring is a middle term between muscular contraction and perceptual identification, we see here that it is a middle term between data-driven reaction and mentally controlled intentional action. This structuring of action is what is called here bodily intention. It is not intended to replace the classical notion of mental intention's triggering and controlling some intentional actions but is rather intended to complete it.

As claimed above, bodily intention structures not only action itself but also perceptual processes. Crucially for the point at stake here, it is the *intentional* orientation of the body (and not merely its muscular contractions) that modifies its perceptual relation to its environment. This claim is corroborated by neuronal recordings in the ventral premotor cortex. Neurons called "canonical" present both a visual and a motor activity. First, they are active during the execution of a goal-directed action. This activity is goal related and not movement related: the action can be achieved with the hand or the mouth, engaging no common muscles, and the corresponding neuron will still be active, given that the goal is reached. Second, they are also active while the agent is not acting but is merely observing the goal of his or her potential action, even if this observation period is not a preparatory period, that is, even if it is not followed by an action oriented toward that goal (Murata et al. 1997). The authors argue that the visual and the motor responses would have a unique functional meaning: a representation of the action indicating precisely how to interact with the object. In other words, this representation is at the same time both a representation of the action in relation to the object and a representation of the object in relation to the action. The object is seen, through F5, thanks to motor eyes, that is, following motor constraints, and the latter are structurally intentional: they are structured according to the goal of the action.

Other data show that this specifically motor structuring of perceptual processes is highly flexible in the sense of being directly linked to the current ability to act of the agent. This has notably been shown for the representation of peripersonal space (the space within which action on the object is possible). In the particular case of this experiment, a monkey was trained to use a rake to obtain some food that was inaccessible by a simple extension of his arm, and the somatosensory and visual receptive fields (RFs) of bimodal neurons were recorded (Iriki et al. 1996; for a review, see Maravita and Iriki 2004). After the monkey learns to use the rake, the visual RF is modified. While it was previously centered on the hand, it now extends to the whole length of the rake. In the case of other neurons, the visual RF that was previously limited to the prehension space of the hand is, after learning, enlarged to the space now accessible thanks to the use of the rake. Importantly, these modifications occur only when the monkey uses the rake actively and not when he simply holds it passively in front of the target object. What is important in the present framework is to highlight that spatial organization is not fixed by some constant values of distance between the effector and the target. Rather, it depends on the capacity for action of the agent, and this dependence is structured by bodily intention, specifically, by the concrete ability to reach a goal.

The structuring role of bodily intention has been further evidenced by contrasting directly the influence on perceptual processes of active action and of passive movement. In these experiments, in a first condition, the action is executed voluntarily, at an onset chosen freely by subjects, who have to report the perceived time of their action and its sensory consequences (auditory in Haggard et al. 2002; somatic in Tsakiris and Haggard 2003). In the second condition, the same sensory consequences are produced by an involuntary movement of the subject's limb after magnetic brain stimulation. The first condition leads to an attraction of the perceived times: subjects perceive their voluntary action as occurring later and its sensory consequences as occurring earlier than they actually do. This is what has been called "intentional binding." This effect owes this name to the fact that it is specific to intentional action. Indeed, it is reversed in the case of an involuntary movement. These data evidence clearly that bodily intention structures perceptual processes. Importantly, it has also been verified that this structuring is not due to a mere prediction of the sensory consequences of the executed action but rather to an anticipation of the consequence of the intention (for a discussion of this latter point, see Legrand 2004 and Tsakiris and Haggard 2004). Moreover, the intentional binding is not observed when the intention is uncompleted, that is, when it does not play its normal role regarding the execution of the action and the production of its sensory consequences (Haggard and Clark 2003): an intention "in the head" is not enough. Taken together, these results thus point to a specific sensorimotor integration that we name here bodily intention.

Conclusion

The conception of bodily intention defended here has important consequences for the conception of the agent of intentional action:

If introspection reveals only states of consciousness of a "self" without any outcome in the world, without any incarnation in the body, it reveals an internal world closed and, besides, fictitious. If external observation collects only movement devoid of meaning and without any anchoring in the "you," it reveals only a motor décor without any connection with a subject. If on the contrary, the integral experience of cogito envelops the experience of one's own body and through it the experience to act in the world, if, on the other hand, the behavior of others is described as revealing of a subject, a "you," the notions of action and behavior that we must conceive definitely concern the action of a subject in the world "through" his body. (Ricoeur 1950, pp. 211–212)

I hope to have shown here that contemporary cognitive neurosciences provide relevant data that corroborate such a claim and the conception of intentional action as not only mental but first of all bodily intentional. This leads to a conception of the agent not only as someone acting sometimes for the reasons he or she entertains and reports but also as someone who acts intentionally without controlling reasons: that is, the agent is to be conceived of as not only rational but also "unreasonable."

References

Aglioti, S., Goodale, M. A., and DeSouza, J. F. X. (1995). Size-contrast illusions deceive the eye but not the hand. *Current Biology*, 5, 679–685.

Anscombe, G. E. M. (1979). *Intention*. Oxford: Blackwell.

Berthoz, A. (1997). *Le sens du mouvement*. Paris: Odile Jacob.

Clark, A. (1999). Visual awareness and visuomotor transformation. In R. Nunez and W. Freeman (Eds.), *Reclaiming cognition: The primacy of action, intention and emotion* (pp. 1–18). Bowling Green, OH: Imprint Academic.

Davidson, D. (1997). Actions, reasons, and causes. In A. R. Mele (Ed.), *The philosophy of action* (pp. 27–41). Oxford: Oxford Universtiy Press.

Frankfurt, H. G. (1997). The problem of action. In A. R. Mele (Ed.), *The philosophy of action.* (pp. 42–52). Oxford University Press.

Gallagher, S. (1986). Lived body and environment. *Research in Phenomenology, 16,* 139–170.

Gallagher, S. (1995). Body schema and intentionality. In J. L. Bermudez, A. Marcel, and N. Eilan (Eds.), *The body and the self* (pp. 225–244). Cambridge: MIT Press.

Gallagher, S. (2000). Phenomenological and experimental research on embodied experience. Atelier phenomenologie et cognition. Phénoménologie et Cognition Research Group CREA. Paris.

Gallagher, S. (2005). *How the body shapes the mind*. Oxford: Oxford University Press.

Gallagher, S., and Cole, J. (1995). Body image and body schema in a deafferented subject. *The Journal of Mind and Behavior, 16,* 369–390.

Gentilucci, M., Chieffi, S., Daprati, E., Saetti, M. C., and Toni, I. (1996). Visual illusion and action. *Neuropsychologia, 34,* 369–376.

Gentilucci, M., Roy, A., and Stefanini, S. (2004). Grasping an object naturally or with a tool: Are these tasks guided by a common motor representation? *Experimental Brain Research, 157,* 496–506.

Goodale, M. A., Pelisson, D., and Prablanc, C. (1986). Large adjustments in visually guided reaching do not depend on vision of the hand or perception of target displacement. *Nature, 320,* 748–750.

Haggard, P., and Clark, S. (2003). Intentional action: Conscious experience and neural prediction. *Consciousness and Cognition, 12,* 695–707.

Haggard, P., Clark, S., and Kalogeras, J. (2002). Voluntary action and conscious awareness. *Nature Neuroscience, 5,* 382–385.

Head, H., and Holmes, G. (1911–1912). Sensory disturbances from cerebral lesions. *Brain, 34,* 102–245.

Hu, Y., and Goodale, M. A. (2000). Grasping after a delay shifts size-scaling from absolute to relative metrics. *Journal of Cognitive Neuroscience, 12,* 856–868.

Hurley, S. L. (1998). *Consciousness in action*. Cambridge: Harvard University Press.

Iriki, A., Tanaka, M., and Iwamura, Y. (1996). Coding of modified body schema during tool use by macaque postcentral neurones. *Neuroreport, 7*, 2325–2330.

Jeannerod, M. (1986). *The neural and behavioral organisation of goal-directed mouvements*. Oxford: Oxford University Press.

Jeannerod, M. (1994). The representing brain: Neural correlates of motor intention and imagery. *Behavioral and Brain Sciences, 17*, 187–245.

Johnson-Frey, S. H. (Ed.). (2003). *Taking action: Cognitive neuroscience perspective on intentional acts*. Cambridge: MIT Press.

Juarrero, A. (1999). *Dynamics in action: Intentional behavior as a complex system*. Cambridge: MIT Press.

Legrand, D. (2004). Problèmes de la constitution du soi. Thèse de Doctorat en Philosophie de l'Université Aix–Marseille I.

Lhermitte, F. (1983). "Utilization behavior" and its relation to lesions of the frontal lobes. *Brain, 106*, 237–255.

Maravita, A., and Iriki, A. (2004). Tools for the body (schema). *Trends in Cognitive Sciences, 8*, 79–86.

Mele, A. (Ed.). (1997). *The philosophy of action*. Oxford University Press.

Merleau-Ponty, M. (1942). *La structure du comportement*. Paris: Presses Universitaires de France Quadrige.

Merleau-Ponty, M. (1945). *Phénoménologie de la perception*. Paris: Gallimard.

Milner, A. D., and Dyde, R. T. (2003). Orientation and disorientation: Illusory perception and the real world. In S. H. Johnson-Frey (Ed.), *Taking action: Cognitive neuroscience perspective on intentional acts* (pp. 3–28). The MIT Press.

Milner, A. D., and Goodale, M. A. (1995). *The visual brain in action*. Oxford: Oxford University Press.

Milner, A. D., Perrett, D. I., Johnston, R. S., Benson, P. J., Jordan, T. R., Heeley, D. W., Bettucci, D., Mortara, F., Mutani, R., Terazzi, E., et al. (1991). Perception and action in "visual form agnosia." *Brain, 114*, 405–428.

Murata, A., Fadiga, L., Fogassi, L., Gallese, V., Raos, V., and Rizzolatti, G. (1997). Object representation in the ventral premotor cortex (area F5) of the monkey. *Journal of Neurophysiology, 78*, 2226–2230.

Pacherie, E. (2000). The content of intentions. *Mind and Language, 15*, 400–432.

Paillard, J. (1948). Quelques données psychophysiologiques relatives au déclenchement de la commande motrice. *Année Psychologique, 46–47*, 28–47.

Paillard, J. (1973). Intervention suite au rapport de R. Angelergues sur "Réflexion sur la notion de schéma corporel." In Symposium de l'APSLF (Ed.), *Psychologie de la connaissance de soi* (pp. 143–148). Paris: Presses Universitaires de France.

Paillard, J. (1980). Le corps situé et le corps identifié. Une approche psychophysiologique de la notion de schéma corporel. *Rev. Méd. Suisse Romande, 100*, 129–141.

Paillard, J. (1990). Réactif et prédictif: deux modes de gestion de la motricité. In V. Nougier and J. P. Blanchi (Eds.), *Pratiques sportives et modélisation du geste* (pp. 13–56). Grenoble, France: SC Grenoble.

Paillard, J. (1994). L'intégration sensori-motrice et idéomotrice. In Anonymous, *Traité de psychologie expérimentale* (pp. 925–961). Paris: Presses Universitaires de France.

Paillard, J. (1997). Divided body schema and body imge in deafferented patients. *Brain and Movement: International Symposium on Motor Control. St. Petersburg. Moscow.* Abstract.

Paillard, J. (1999). Body schema and body image—A double dissociation in desafferented patients. In G. N. Gantchev, S. Mori, and J. Massion (Eds.), *Motor control, today and tomorrow* (pp. 197–214). Sofia, Bulgaria: Academic Publishing House.

Paillard, J. (2005). Sensorimotor versus representational framing of Body Space. A neural basis for a distinction between Body schema and Body image. In V. Knockaert and H. De Preester (Eds.), *Body image and body schema: Interdisciplinary perspectives* (pp. 89–109). Amsterdam: John Benjamins.

Paillard, J., Bard, C., and Fleury, M. (1989). Synchronizing hand and foot movement in a projective or reactive mode: Two contrasting schedules of motor command. *Society for Neuroscience Abstracts, 243.3*.

Paillard, J., Michel, F., and Stelmach, G. (1983). Localization without content. A tactile analogue of "blind sight." *Archives of Neurology, 40*, 548–551.

Petit, J.-L. (1991). *L'action dans la philosophie analytique*. Paris: Presse Universitaire de France.

Ricoeur, P. (1950). *Philosophie de la volonté: I. Le volontaire et l'involontaire*. Paris: Aubier.

Rochat, P., and Striano, T. (1999). Emerging self-exploration by 2 month-old infants. *Developmental Science, 2*, 206–218.

Rossetti, Y., and Pisella, L. (2003). Mediate responses as direct evidence for intention: Neuropsychology of Not-To, Not-How, and Not-There tasks. In S. H. Johnson-Frey (Ed.), *Taking action: Cognitive neuroscience perspective on intentional acts* (pp. 67–105). Cambridge: MIT Press.

Ryle, G. (1949). *The concept of mind.* London: Hutchinson.

Searle, J. (1983). *Intentionality.* Cambridge: Cambridge University Press.

Tsakiris, M., and Haggard, P. (2003). Awareness of somatic events associated with a voluntary action. *Experimental Brain Research, 149,* 439–446.

Tsakiris, M., and Haggard, P. (2004). Experimenting with the acting self. *Cognitive Neuropsychology, 22,* 387–407.

Ungerleider, L. G., and Miskin, M. (1982). Two visual pathways. In D. J. Ingle, M. A. Goodale, and R. J. W. Mansfield (Eds.), *Analysis of visual behavior* (pp. 549–586). Cambridge: MIT Press.

Wegner, D. (2002). *The illusion of conscious will.* Cambridge: MIT Press.

Wittgenstein, L. (1953). *Philosophical investigations* (Trans. G. E. M. Anscombe). New York: Macmillan.

9 Recursivity, Control, and Revisions in Intention in Action

Pierre Livet

In Livet and Petit (this volume) we have suggested that intention in action has to be thought of as a two faces-notion, one face being the reason given by default for the action and the other the control and execution aspect of the action. The two faces have to be present in order for the intention to exist as such. Intention reduced to its reason is only a reason or at best a wish; intention reduced to its control and execution implementation is only a motor skill. Now, we need to understand how congruence is ensured between the two faces. We will attack this problem from three perspectives. We first give an idea of the formal structure needed to do that job and show that this structure is a recursive one. Then, we will show how the criteria that the human observers use in order to detect a movement as intentional are congruent with this formal structure. Third, we contrast the first-person experience with the third-person experience of the observer. We will show that in action we are mainly conscious of the goal and, if they are necessary, of the revisions of the action, and the criteria for seeing or feeling a movement as an action are centered on these two properties. As a conclusion, we will examine what pieces of this reconstruction of the action are easier and what pieces are more difficult to naturalize.

The Recursive Structure of Action

The core of intention in action is the congruence between its two faces, execution control and reason. Reason seems to be a static notion, while execution control is a dynamic one. In basic actions, like grasping our glass and drinking its content, reason can be reduced to the combination of the target (the glass) and the motivation (drinking its content). We need to explain how this combination can be integrated into the dynamical functioning of control.

First, we note that the entry of the control function is not only the target (the glass) but the target as qualified by the motivation (the glass as containing water to drink). We can express this qualification by a function applied to the target taken as an argument: (*motivation* [*target*]), in which the target has itself to be explained as (content of [the glass]) and the motivation as (drinking . . .)—drinking is here an abbreviation for "desire to drink." The glass$_1$ (we mark it by the index 1 in order to distinguish further several other levels of recursion) is thus an input to the function "the content of," giving the output value: "water-in-the-glass$_1$," and this output value is the input of the motivational function "desire to drink," given the output value "water-in-the-glass$_{1)2}$-being-drunk as fulfilling my desire" (the indices $_{1)2}$ will be explained soon). What determines the execution control is not just glass$_1$ (the input of the first function), the thing seen at the present time as a thing among others, but glass$_2$, glass as related to the desired situation of drinking (the output of the motivational function). Glass$_1$ as input of the first function has now to be replaced by glass$_{1)2}$ as satisfying the execution conditions for the water-in-the glass to satisfy my desire to drinking it. It has to be carried to my mouth and tipped up so as to let the water flow in my throat.

This implies recursivity, and a complex one. Recursivity is the property that a formal process exhibits when it is able to be reapplied to its own result. It includes the possibility to have in the arguments to which the function or the functional has to be applied one of its past results. More complex recursivity opens, in addition, the possibility of taking again an input to which a function has been already applied in a previous step and reprocessing it using a new function in order to get a new kind of value (here, glass$_{1)2}$). Recursivity can be applied not only to one of its past results (here, glass$_1$), but also to one of its future results, here the water-of-the-glass$_2$-flowing-in-my-throat. Of course, as this future result is not yet known in all its details and factual properties, it has to be considered as a partly unknown x, and we have to compute what values of this x satisfy the constraints on the considered function, including its application to this partly unknown result x. By analogy, some taxes (like tax on additional value, AVT) have to be computed as a percentage not of the initial price but of the sum of the price and the unknown tax. Here, the properties of the present glass$_1$ to be selected are the ones of glass$_{1)2}$ selected by the motor execution function (the more embedding one) taking as input the properties satisfying the "drinkability" of glass$_2$, themselves selected by the drinkability of the water as a content of glass$_1$. The properties of the glass have been submitted to two steps of recursion.

The consequence of the recursivity of intention for execution control is that the agent has to coordinate the sequence of movement in a backward regression: starting from the present positions of the target (the glass) and the body, the agent has to compute the movements that allow him or her to reach the glass and then to carry it back to his or her mouth. The motor function adds by itself a new recursivity. As it changes step-by-step the respective positions of the glass and the body, it returns different values for each of the steps of the movement that it controls. It has to take into account the successive results of each step, to compare them with the satisfaction conditions of the motor-motivational function and to make the needed adjustments. This implies what can be called the "updates" of the movement: when I hold out my arm toward the glass, I have to compensate for the disequilibrium of the cantilevered mass of my arm by strengthening my muscles; when I grasp the glass, I have to compensate for the additional weight of the glass. My movement changes the very situation of the action, and I have to take these changes into account for the continuation of this very movement.

The recursive reconstruction of the constraints related to grasping the glass ($glass_1$ in our terminology) is not sufficient, as it could give any sequence of movements that grasp the glass. Not every such sequence is found admissible. For example, if I grasp the glass with my hand over its top, my hand will prevent me from swallowing the water of $glass_2$ (glass as qualified by its content as being drinkable). Or if, while carrying it up to my mouth, I do not keep $glass_2$ vertical enough, the water will be wasted. We see that the movement itself is not only transforming the situation of the target—carrying $glass_1$ toward my mouth. It is itself qualified by the motivation: drinking the water that the glass contains. We need to embed our motor function of successively grasping, carrying, and tipping up the glass into the motivational function again, reapplying to the movement and its steps the motivation that was first applied to the target:

($drinking_{2m}$ (tipping up, carrying, grasping ($drinking_1$ (content of (the glass))))).

Each of these successive motor steps selects different properties of the glass and different means of interaction between the glass and the agent's body (with the fingers, with the positions of the hand, of the arm and of the body).

The reason why we have to reapply the motivational constraints at each step of the execution control are related to the problem of how to determine what movements have to be avoided—for example, grasping the glass with my hand over it or tipping up the glass too much and pouring into my mouth too much water at a time. These peculiarities cannot be discovered just by combining one motor function and a motivational qualification: "carrying the glass toward my mouth" and "the glass as containing water to be drunk." Some variations of the movement already compatible with the motivational qualification of the glass that has to be carried happen to be incompatible not only with drinking the water in whatever way but with drinking easily and with no trouble the content of the carried glass. Here, the motivation has to be reapplied to the very movement that takes as argument the object already qualified by this motivation. In a sense, the movement as applied to the motivating object reveals some new possibilities of the motivation, its capacities to qualify some unexpected aspects of the movement itself. We have formulated this intricate relation by marking the right occurrence of "motivation" in the formula by index 1 and its left occurrence by index 2m (m for "motor"), but to be more precise we might have to repeat this splitting of motivation and the multiplication of indices for each step of the motor function (grasping, carrying, and tipping up). The process of control is then determined by this complex recursive functional, which takes as constituents the motivation function in its different roles (the first one applied only to the target, the following ones to different steps of the movement).

This recursive functional and the intricate relation of motivation function and motor function give us the way to ensure the congruence between the reason face of the intention of the action and its control face. The content of the reason for the action is given by the conditions of satisfaction that ensure that the values of our functional are kept inside some limits determined by the motivation function. Most of the time, in these kinds of basic actions, we are only conscious of their reasons under the form of schematic representations of their targets as qualified by the final anticipated situation (the water flowing into my throat). We are not conscious of the reason as determining, for example, the angle by which the glass is tipped up, even if, being the reason for this very action, it must have such a specified content. We will come back further to the reasons for this kind of neglect. To conclude this section, we have seen that the recursive functional that is our guide for formalizing action also gives the relation between reason and execution control: reason is given by the motivational parts of the functional; execution control is given by the effect of these motivational functions on the motor function. The congruence between the two is built in by the embedding of motivation$_1$ into the motor function and the embedding of motor function into motivation$_{2m}$.

Action from the Third-Person Point of View

The formal structure of action gives its full content to intention. Now is it possible that the effects of the control of action by intention (i.e., the very action) can be detected by other people, and if it is, what criteria can they rely on in order to detect a movement as intentional?

Control gives rise to fluid action, but also to adjustments and even to revisions (adjustments are small corrections that do not require reconstructing the plan of the action; revisions are corrections needed when the anticipated action encounters obstacles and incompatibilities and has to be reorganized).

These adjustments and revisions, and even this fluidity, seem essential in order for the observer to perceive a movement as intentional and as an intentional action (we need here a distinction between a movement perceived as intentional because it is orientated toward a target and a movement perceived as the movement of an agent, as an intentional action; we will call "intentional" the first aspect of the movement, and "agentive" the second one). They are essential also in the first-person perspective for the agent to feel his or her movement as his or her own action. Nevertheless, phenomenology and ways of appearing of these adjustments and revisions are very different from this first-person perspective compared with the third-person one.

Adjustments and revisions are useful for checking whether the intention of the real action fits in with two versions of the reason face of intention. We will call the first one the motivation intention and the second one the formulation intention. The content of the motivation intention is simply given by the aspect of the target as activated as salient and attractive by the agent's desire in the first-person perspective. The formulation intention is the formulation of the aspect of the final situation that summarizes the main conditions of satisfaction of the action. As we will see, its content is learned during intersubjective interactions, so that it is useful for the third-person perspective. The execution face of the intention can be seen also in two different ways: either as the control intention, when we take the agent's perspective, or as the criterion intention, when we take the observer's perspective. The activation of this function of intention on the one hand makes the agent able to control his or her movement and on the other hand gives to the observer the criteria that he or she needs to perceive the movement as an intentional action.

In what follows, we will first analyze more precisely what the criteria are that the observer uses for ascribing an intentional movement to an agent, and how essential adjustments and revisions are for the evaluation of these criteria. Then, we will analyze which of these criteria are accessible to the agent and how. At each step we will show how these criteria are related to the recursive function that is our guide for formalizing the intention in action.

The Five Criteria of Intentional Movement

From the observer's perspective, what properties of a movement could be taken as signs that it is part of an intentional action? We assume that intention is mainly intention in action, that is, a functional that ensures that the movement is (1) oriented toward a target, an aspect of which is motivating for the agent, (2) adjusted as soon as necessary when the relations between the environment and the agent change (the relations relevant for the motivational aspect), and (3) controlled in such a way that the deviations are corrected and the obstacles are either removed or bypassed. These characteristics of intention can be used as criteria for the intentionality of a movement. We have seen in Livet and Petit (this volume) that so-called prior intentions are only an extension of the possibilities offered by the cognitive architecture required for the third property, the control of the action.

It is easy to transform these characteristics into criteria. The first one is borrowed from the first embedding function of our functional: the qualification of the target by the motivation and of our movement toward the target by this motivation. This implies that a movement oriented toward a target salient for the observer is assumed to be intentional. However, in some cases this can be an illusion. Take one of Premack's experiments (Premack and Premack 2003). On a TV display, you can see things the shape of which is partly a circle and partly a triangle, which looks like a beak. When these things turn their beak toward other similar things, and when the orientation of their beak varies in accordance with the movement of these other things, we can't help perceiving these things with beaks as pointing toward the others and following their movements. If pointing and following are intentional movements, then we can't help ascribing to these things intentional movements.

However, things are not so simple. The oriented movement criterion points at a necessary property for a movement to be perceived as intentional, but it is not a sufficient criterion, at least for perceiving this movement as an *agent*'s movement, as an action. We do not see the beaked things as agents.

The second criterion is related to the motivational aspect of the action. If the observer has in his or her motivational repertoire a motivation that explains easily why the target has a salient and attractive aspect for the agent, then the observer can't help ascribing intentionality to the agent's movement. However, this ascription is an ascription by default. If this movement is followed by other movements that cannot be related to the supposed motivation, the ascription of intentionality is suspended. For example, I see a person grasping his glass of water and I suppose that he grasps it intentionally, because I have in my repertoire the motivation of drinking a glass of water. But, in fact, he does not take it to drink. He just grasps it, lets it go, then grasps it again, and so on and so forth (he is playing with it). As I cannot see what his motivation in doing so is, I hesitate to keep taking my assumption as valid.

For the observer, these two criteria are still necessary but not sufficient ones. Most of the time, they are considered as convincing enough by the observer, and we can say that they are sufficient by default, as long as they are not defeated by contrary evidence.

The third criterion also comes from an analysis of the second embedding function of our functional, the type of movement. The observer has to possess in his or her own motor repertoire the movement that the agent is exhibiting (cf. Grammont, this volume). For example, we have difficulty in assigning intentionality to the peculiarities of the movements of centipedes, spiders (why so many articulations?), and even snakes (why have they to make their way so sinuously?) and in general to animals that have a very different mode of motion. By contrast, we need not have in our motor repertoire all the variety of adjustments that are required for real skill in that domain. It is even possible that we identify a movement only when we have in our repertoire some subsequences of it, as when we identify a triple axel but are not able to do more than jump and make one turn (and without ice skates!).

The fourth criterion is a first consequence of the third embedding of our functional. If the movement is successful, its main steps will be relevant and useful from the point of view of the motivation. This implies that the motivation controls each relevant step of the movement and that the movement, in turn, specifies each application of the motivation. Such an interaction is shown by continual adjustments of the movement. If a movement is continually adjusted (or at least apparently continually for the observer), its trajectory will be smooth and its movement fluid. Nevertheless, this criterion is neither a sufficient one nor a necessary one. We ascribe intentional movements to Parkinsonians. However, we have difficulties in identifying their intention when their movement presents oscillations that are too large.

This kind of criterion can be divided into two species: first, the fluidity of the movement and, second, the movements that are necessary to adjust the posture and to keep equilibrium in order for the movement that is directed toward the target to be successful. We could call these movements the collateral movements. Rearrangements of the posture and updates of the posture as soon as our movement requires them in order to keep our equilibrium are species of collateral movements.

The fifth criterion is a necessary one only for the observer who wants to ascertain whether the movement is really an intentional one. It is a necessary criterion, but nevertheless also insufficient, as no criterion here is sufficient: criteria cannot be more than presumptive criteria, because intentionality is not directly accessible by observation. This fifth criterion corresponds to a second kind of consequence of the reciprocal specification of movement by motivation and of motivation by movement. The first kind of consequence was observed when no problem or obstacle was encountered during the action. The second one is observed in the opposite situation. If the movement is deviated, if obstacles are encountered, corrections of the movement are undertaken. They may differ from simple adjustments, as they can imply roundabout behavior, getting not nearer but at first farther off from the target, or even restarting another movement from the beginning. In order to emphasize this difference we call them revisions.

When the observer sees such a behavior, beginning with a movement toward the target, then encountering an obstacle, moving away from the obstacle, getting round it, and moving again toward the target, he or she can't help ascribing intentionality to this movement. This example presents only a revision of the orientation of the movement. A more significant revision is the one in which we refrain from reaching the target so as to save from destruction the property of the target that is its motivational aspect and that a more direct approach would have ruined.

We can put these criteria into two classes: criteria for intentional movement and criteria for agentive movement. Orientated movement and fluid movement are criteria for intentional movement. Sharing motivation, sharing the type of the movement, observing collateral movements, and observing revisions are criteria for agentive movement. Note that if intentional movements are not by themselves ascribed to a unified agent, agentive movements are not possible without reference to some center of synthesis and coordination. Besides that, agentive movements are movements that can be acknowledged as shared by other human agents.

The First-Person Perspective

How are these criteria present to the phenomenal experience of the agent? The motivation is, of course, conscious, as are the perception of the target and the main direction of the movement. However, the movement itself does not have to be conscious. When I grasp my cup, I do not need to be conscious of the quasi-automatic movement of grasping it, and, in fact, I am not conscious of some of its peculiarities, like the size of the interval between the thumb and the other fingers. But this size is fitted to the size of the cup, and this is one example of adjustment. As a consequence, adjustments are usually not conscious. The collateral movements needed to save our equilibrium are not conscious if their amplitude is not too large. And, of course, we are not conscious that a movement of another person belongs to our repertoire, but only that it does not belong to it, and only because we feel this movement as "strange."

Criteria can be unconscious and, nevertheless, necessary. Of course, the presence of a typical movement, even if unconscious, is a necessary condition, as is the presence of this movement in our repertoire. The collateral movements are also needed. Even for limited movements, like grasping a cup that is very near our hand, some collateral commands are required, other than the orientation of the direction of the movement toward the target and the grasping movement. The inertia of the limbs has to be overcome and at the end the inertial movement has to be stopped.

If adjustments like collateral movements, or like updatings of the position of the body and its limbs relative to the environment, are required both from the observer's and the agent's perspective in order to feel the movement as intentional, other adjustments like the ones that ensure the fluidity of the movement are not needed from the agent's perspective. As the agent focuses onto the target, even if his or her movements are a bit erratic (e.g., if the agent is dystonic), he or she may be used to these irregularities so that they are not for the agent a sign that the movement is not intentional. On the contrary, for the observer, the absence of fluidity is an obstacle to the identification of the movement as intentional. The observer has to wait to see the agent reaching the target in order to capture the right movement.

As mentioned earlier, corrections or revisions are not necessary for the movement to be intentional. Most of our movements are made in very usual situations and require no revisions. However, when revisions are the case, they are, in contrast to adjustments, conscious. Moreover, if the agent was not able to make revisions when deviations or obstacles occur, the agent would feel his or her intentionality as an impotent and limited one. And an observer would take for granted only a supposed intentional movement, not a confirmed intentional movement.

Revisions are salient to consciousness. Adjustments are not. But how can we distinguish them? An experiment performed by Fourneret and Jeannerod (1998) gives us some clues with respect to this distinction. Subjects had to draw a line so as to reach a point. They could not see their hand and could see the line not directly but only on a TV display. The line on the display was deviated by a program; subjects made a counter-deviation, so that the apparent line remained directed toward the target, but the real one was deviating. When asked to repeat the same gesture, subjects, who could this time see their hand and the line, drew a line leading directly to the target, and not a deviated line. One explanation could be that the visual information has priority over the proprioceptive information. However, a simpler explanation could be the following. The agent is conscious of the target and of his or her motivation (the agent wants the drawn line to reach the target). But the agent does not have to be conscious of its movement. The agent is consciously sensitive to the deviations of the line relative to the target, not to the deviations of the movements. As long as there is no major deviation from the target, there is no revision to trigger. On the display, the correction of the real deviation appears as a small adjustment, which does not make it really difficult to reach the target. When consciously monitoring the repeated movement, the subject has to take into account not the adjustments but only the revisions. As the "acquisition" of the target is visually made, the checking of the adequacy of the movement to the task of reaching the target is also mainly visual. No revision is needed according to the visual information, so that the correcting movement is assumed to belong to the class of adjustments. The distinction between revision and adjustments is then that revision is triggered by information about a salient possibility of missing the target, and adjustments are modifications of the movement in which missing the target is not directly at stake. They are changes for a more convenient movement, or they are continuous changes related to changes of the target, such that missing the target never becomes a striking possibility.

A different experiment (Varraine, Bonnard, and Pailhous 2002a, b) corroborates the claim that consciousness does not retain adjustments that do not get out of the limits inside which the target remains reachable and that it focuses either on reaching the target or on correcting the movement when these limits are exceeded. Here, the target is not a visual target; the goal is to maintain constancy in one characteristic of the movement, either the speed of a walk or the rhythm of the steps. In normal conditions, maintaining the speed is easier, because we have visual clues, but here subjects are walking on a rolling belt without visual clues about their speed. The resistance of the belt to the impulse of the walker's steps can be strengthened progressively. When this resistance increases, subjects, in order to maintain speed, have to increase their rhythm, but they also, in order to maintain rhythm, have to reduce their speed.

In addition to the main task (maintaining their speed or maintaining their rhythm), subjects have to signal the moment at which they feel a significant resistance by pressing a button. The clue for resistance, when you are trying to maintain your speed, is that your rhythm is decreasing, and the clue for resistance when you are trying to maintain your rhythm is that your speed is decreasing. In each case, the subject's sensitivity threshold is very high, and subjects take no less than 6 seconds before signaling a resistance, while they have modulated either their speed or their rhythm long before. This sensitivity threshold is much lower when the main task is the signaling. The explanation seems to be that the main task (except when it is signaling) uses the clues for the signaling task as a mean of adjustment. As long as subjects are able to cope with the requirement of the main task—say, maintaining their speed—the variations of the rhythm are considered as simple adjustments. When it becomes too tiring for subjects to satisfy this requirement, they go outside the limits of adjustments, because success in the main task is endangered. The variations of rhythm are then considered as clues that trigger revision; they become conscious, and the signaling can be done.

The striking fact is that even in conditions in which rhythm is a more accessible clue than speed (because in the absence of visual clues about our speed, we still have information about our rhythm), the behaviors of the subjects remain symmetrical: they signal with the same delay, 6 seconds. The explanation seems to be that in each case the clue for signaling is at the same time the variable of the adjustment. As it is used as a margin of adjustment for remaining in the limits in which the target task can still be satisfied, it is not salient to the agent's consciousness. In a sense, the 6-second delay shows the limits beyond which the adjustments become revisions. The main conclusion is that the assignment of modifications of the movement either to the role of adjustments or to the role of revision depends on the task, but also that in each task, we find a duality between adjustments and revisions.

Coordinating the First- and Third-Person Perspectives: Motivation Intention and Formulation Intention

We have seen how the control intention of the agent can be related to the criterion intention of the observer. However, we have not yet shown the relationship between the two modes of presentation of the other face of the intention (the reason face), that is to say the basic first-person mode, the motivation intention, and the intersubjective mode, the formulation intention. In addition, we want to evaluate how the project of naturalizing intention in action is well fitted for each of these different aspects.

Naturalizing adjustments (i.e., finding physical–chemical mechanisms that explain these adjustments), and finding a plausible evolutionary scenario according to which these mechanisms have been selected, is a task that seems possible in principle. The difficulties are empirical ones, not conceptual ones. Naturalizing revisions raises more conceptual problems. No conceptual problems are raised by the idea of a threshold of sensitivity, and of limits beyond which revision is triggered. However, revision is necessary only when the result of the movement is in danger of losing its congruence with the motivational aspect. As a motivational aspect is an intentional notion, its naturalization could be more difficult.

Basic motivations are not difficult to naturalize. They are related to the basic needs of an organism, and this organism has at its disposal perceptual clues for detecting in the environment the target the aspect of which triggers the perceptual clue that in accordance with the present state of the organism triggers in turn the motivation.

More elaborated motivations involving complex intentional aspects seem much more difficult to naturalize, because for every decidable mean assumed to make us able to identify a particular intentional aspect, we can find several possible specifications of this intentional aspect that this mean cannot distinguish. But here naturalization can take the roundabout of intersubjective coordination. Even if the aspect that one subject has in mind is difficult to grasp, the aspect on which a subject wants to coordinate with other subjects has to be accessible by external clues (note that a similar problem occurs for intrasubjective coordination over time, and has a similar solution). Indeed, the questions about the singularity of the intentional motivation, the "why" questions, are unnecessary as long as the motivational aspect that is activated by another agent corresponds to one of our motivational scenarios. They are needed only when the motor behavior of the agent satisfies the orientation constraint, the fluidity constraint, but the motivational aspect is difficult to identify: "Why are you staring in this direction?" "Why are you doing that thing?" As mentioned in Livet and Petit (this volume), the why questions asked about the action itself and not its antecedents are not supposed to have a larger scope than that of the motivation directly related with the movements executing the action. This seems to show that why questions are intersubjective coordination questions. As evolution can be assumed to have selected categorizations or schematizations of actions and motivations that are useful for coordination, the kind of motivation that is reducible to the motivation directly related with the coordination of the different movements of different agents can be naturalized.

However, coordination has a positive and a negative aspect. The positive one is the joint action, its target and its result. The negative one may be more important, even if it is mainly implicit. It is made up of the conditions in which the joint action is in danger of failure. Of course, nobody can know all these conditions in advance, but the "knowing how" that is constitutive of an agent's ability and skill consists in a list of such risky situations to avoid and of how to avoid them. This is, in fact, a list of conditions of revisions.

Naturalization encounters its limits here: a finite list of conditions of revision can be given (a list of limits conditions and of procedures telling how to change the action and the situation). However, it is impossible to give the list of all cases in advance. Some general features of the process of revision could be naturalized, but to naturalize all the possible paths of revision in advance is impossible. In another sense, taking the intersubjective coordination stance reduces here the naturalization task. Naturalization is not supposed to solve problems that are not naturally solved, and in the same way intersubjective coordination is not supposed to overcome the troubles that are ours when the situation falls outside the cases that are recognizable by at least some of the participants.

If the motivation intention can be partially naturalized as recognizable in an intersubjective coordination, this way of naturalizing is a fortiori applicable to the formulation intention (a kind of tractable and schematic summary of all the possible conditions of satisfaction of the action that can be identified either from a first- or a third-person perspective), as it also has a coordination function, for language is one of our main means of coordination. However, here we can notice an interesting fact. Consider a formulation intention like "I want to grasp my cup" or "Bring me the hammer." As is usual in a situation of communication and coordination, we only explicitly mention the contents that in the particular situation are not yet supposed to be commonly accessible in the first-person perspective and in the third- (or second-) person perspective, at least without the help of our utterance: in the former example, the target that could not have been identified by the other and, in the latter, my desire that the hammer (and not another tool) be brought to me. By contrast, the motivation, the specific movement, the adjustments and revision conditions do not have to be mentioned in a fully explicit way. The motivation is only alluded to by "want" or by the imperative form, and the typical movement by "grasp" or "bring." But in order to understand, for example, the sentence about the cup, you need to have in your motivational repertoire the desire to drink the content of a cup (or to wash it, etc.), you need to have in your perceptual repertoire the shape of a cup, and you need to have in your motor repertoire the kind of grasping that is relevant for our way to use the cup: grasping it on its sides for drinking its content or on its top for putting it away. Most of the time we use action sentences not to explain what our motivation is ("I want to drink a cup of water") but to order or suggest to other people some action: "Bring me the hammer," as in Wittgenstein's game of §2 of *Philosophical Investigations* ("Bring me a slab"). We suppose that other people have in their motor repertoire all the movements needed to bring the hammer, whatever these movements would be. This is what makes the language of action difficult to naturalize. It mentions properties that can be captured only if a lot of practical, motor, perceptual, and motivational attitudes and dispositions have been acquired first. The naturalization has to progress from the basis, from these basic motivations, motor skills, and sensitivity to perceptual shape, long before we reach the level of language. It would be a disastrous mistake to assume that language alone can supply this basis.

Finally, how are our four notions of intention articulated, the first two pertaining to the execution face of the intention (the first-person control intention and its third-person perspective version, the criterion intention), the second two pertaining to the reason face of the intention (the first-person motivation intention and the intersubjective formulation intention)?

We can study these articulations by examining cases of their failures. I am climbing and I say to myself, "Well, if I launch my right hand and grasp this right hold, and then launch my left hand and grasp this upper left hold, I will overcome the difficulty." This is a formulation intention. But when I have grasped the right hold, I discover that I cannot launch my left hand to the left, because my center of gravity is too far to the right, and losing my grasp on the previous left hold would make me pivot to the right and lose my balance. The formulation intention cannot be transmuted in a control intention. In a similar way, we may fail to recognize a formulation intention in a behavior because we do not possess sufficiently refined clues for criterion intention. For example, we could fail to identify the meaning of expressions in Asian cultures (if we take a Japanese smile as indicating agreement when it is actually a polite refusal).

Failure of articulation between motivation intention and control intention is also possible in the other sense: a controlled movement can be perfectly carried on, but the satisfaction is not there. To take the same example, my motivation was to get out of this difficult pitch. I can realize the previous plan of climbing without trouble but find that I was not at the end of the difficulties. Another possibility is that the motivation intention is very clear, and the control intention fails because of my insufficient motor skill.

Here again, in order to be able to articulate these three different kinds of intention (motivation, control, and formulation intention), we need to have at our disposal a rich repertoire of revision procedures. If I am pivoting to the right, I can use my left leg as a counterbalance, either extended to the left or, on the contrary, crossing my right one, in order to find again my balance either by gravity or by increasing the pressure on my right hold. If I am not at the end of the difficulties, I have to expend more energy and, to enhance my motivation, take the difficulty as a new challenge.

It would be a useful study of the relation between our four modes of presentation of intention to determine what the limits of our possibilities of revision are, because these limits are also the limits of the possible congruence between motivation, formulation, control, and criterion intentions. It is another way of naturalizing intention in action, and maybe the more promising one: identifying the revisions that *cannot* be done in order to overcome the failures of the articulation between these four kinds of intention. It would be a fruitful way to learn the limits of the natural processes on which the motivation intention and the formulation intention are supervenient. To show that there are natural limits that are not predictable in a purely conceptual and speculative perspective is the better argument to demonstrate that our intention in action is already in the way of being naturalized.

Revision and the Limits of Naturalization

The notion of revision can also be used in a reverse way. Suppose that a very sophisticated technique of brain imaging makes us able to observe in real time the neuronal activations of an agent during its movement. Suppose that we observe an activation in the zone of the motor preparation, and successively in all the neurons that are supposed to be implied in some movement (including the neurons involved in the efference command, the activation of the motor neurons, the reafferences, the reaction to these reafferences, etc.), and finally that we observe the movement. Then, we could say that this movement was an intentional one, this movement was an action. This assertion would be valid at least by default, as long as we have no observation at all of external causes of this movement.

Now suppose that we have built a robot that is a simulation of a human agent. Suppose that our brain (observed by brain imaging), when we perceive a movement of this robot, presents exactly the same activations as when we perceive a human movement. In this case, we could not say that the movement is an intentional one because the previous proviso (no external causes) is not satisfied (the program and the activity of programming are external causes).

Now, is it possible to observe in the same way—correlating neuron-by-neuron brain imaging and the peculiarities of the movement—the intentions of an action? We have said that in order to have intentions, an agent needs a rich repertoire of revision procedures. We could try to determine this repertoire of revisions by observing the agent making roughly the same action in different situations. However, then we are unable to be sure that what we interpret as revisions of the previous movement in the new situation were really the potential revisions that were at the disposal of the agent in the previous situation. For all that we know, the brain is a dynamical system which cannot be assumed to be in exactly the same condition at two different moments. The present variations may be considered as expressions of the previous capacities of revision, but only in a fuzzy way, by approximation. It is, by definition, impossible to make a list of all the revisions a given agent is able to make, for the agent could not trigger some revision of the list in this present situation but could trigger it in a future one—suppose he or she has not yet learned to activate this revision but at present has only the potentiality to activate it—for revisions, in contrast with adjustments, can also be done by interrupting the action, waiting for other circumstances and even for the maturation of reflection and learning. Even the death of the agent cannot exclude that he or she had such and such potentialities of revision. If the notion of an intention implies the definition of all these potentialities of revision, it is inaccessible to scientific experimentation and to naturalization in a strict sense.

However, this bad news for naturalization is, in another sense, good news. For let us suppose that our concept of intentional action would be inaccessible in a strong sense to naturalization. This would imply that we would already have at our disposal a concept of action the content of which would be completely determined and at the same time shown to be inaccessible to the naturalizing perspective. But our concept of action is not inaccessible to naturalization in this sense. It is inaccessible only because we will never be able to exhibit such a complete content, as new revisions could always appear in the future. Even this "never" is not a complete concept, because it is, of course, a "never" "by default" (for maybe no new revisions will occur). The only definite conclusion is that we cannot be sure that our content will be complete. However, this incompleteness is precisely what we can expect from a natural being whose capacities of revision are grounded in limited natural processes—limited but capable of reorganization. This incompleteness cannot be "completely" accessible to experimentation. But this does not prevent accessibility to experimentation of some limits of our present abilities of reorganization and revision, and this is plainly compatible with the conceptual possibility of intention as a naturalized notion.

References

Fourneret, P., and Jeannerod, M. (1998). Limited conscious monitoring of motor performance in normal subjects. *Neuropsychologia, 36*, 1133–1140.

Gärdenfors, P. (Ed.). (1992). *Belief revision.* Cambridge: Cambridge University Press.

Jeannerod, M., and Pacherie, E. (2004). Agency, simulation and self-identification. *Mind and Language, 19*, 113–146.

Milea, D., Lobel, E., Lehericy, S., Leboucher, P., Pochon, J. B., Pierrot-Deseilligny, C., and Berthoz, A. (2007). Prefrontal cortex is involved in internal decision of forthcoming saccades. *Neuroreport, 18*, 1221–1224.

Pacherie, E. (2006). Towards a dynamic theory of intentions. In S. Pockett, W. P. Banks, and S. Gallagher (Eds.), *Does consciousness cause behavior? An investigation of the nature of volition* (pp. 145–167). Cambridge: MIT Press.

Pacherie, E. (2007). Sense of control and sense of agency. S. Siegel (Ed.), *Psyche, 13*(1) [Special issue on the Phenomenology of Agency].

Premack, D., and Premack, A. (2003). *Original intelligence: Unlocking the mystery of who we are.* New York: McGraw-Hill.

Varraine, E., Bonnard, M., and Pailhous, J. (2002a). Interaction between different sensory cues in the control of human gait. *Experimental Brain Research, 142,* 374–384.

Varraine, E., Bonnard, M., and Pailhous, J. (2002b). The top down and bottom up mechanisms involved in the sudden awareness of low level sensorimotor behavior. *Cognitive Brain Research, 13,* 357–361.

Wiener, S. and Taube, J. (Eds.). (2005). *Head direction cells and the neural mechanism of spatial orientation.* Cambridge: MIT Press.

Wittgenstein, L. (2001). *Philosophical investigations.* Oxford: Blackwell.

Part V Interactionist and Social Perspectives

10 Of Goals and Intentions: A Neuroscientific Account of Basic Aspects of Intersubjectivity

Vittorio Gallese

Primates, and particularly human beings, are social animals whose cognitive development capitalizes upon interaction with other conspecifics (adults, siblings, etc.). During social interactions, we manifest our inner intentions, dispositions, and thoughts by means of overt behavior. We reciprocate this by trying to figure out the intentions, dispositions, and thoughts of others when we witness their behavior. Detecting another agent's intentions, or other inner states, helps in anticipating this agent's future actions, which may be cooperative, noncooperative, or even threatening. Accurate understanding and anticipation enable observers to adjust their responses appropriately. Cognitive neuroscience has started to unveil the neural mechanisms that are the basis of social cognition.

In this chapter, I will first review neuroscientific evidence on the neural underpinnings of action goals and on their ontogeny and phylogeny. In the second part of the chapter, I will clarify how action goals can be understood and will discuss the relationship between action control and action understanding by introducing mirror neurons and the notion of embodied simulation. I will conclude by proposing a model of basic aspects of social cognition: the "intentional attunement" hypothesis.

Movements, Actions, and Their Neural Underpinnings

On a nonconceptual level, actions are elementary building blocks of reality for certain living organisms: Some species of organisms have developed agent-detecting modules, and some of them also conceive of themselves as agents. Let us now define what an action is on a *conceptual* level. Let us begin by distinguishing movements, motor acts, and actions.

Bodily movements are simple physical events, and they can be represented accordingly. Motor acts are movements that are goal directed, that is, they can meaningfully be described as directed toward a set of satisfaction conditions, but without necessarily being linked to an explicit and conscious representation of such conditions. As simple movements, they also do not have a consciously experienced reward-producing component (Rizzolatti, Fogassi, and Gallese 2001, p. 668). Motor acts, such as grasping an object, can be chained in sequential patterns in order to attain an overarching, more distal goal (e.g., grasping a glass and bringing it to the mouth in order to attain the distal goal of drinking), thus constituting actions. In contrast to movements, motor acts are not necessarily isomorphic to a specific movement: the same goal can, in fact, be attained by different movements.

Actions are a specific subset of goal-directed movements. They are a series of motor acts that are functionally integrated with a currently active representation[1] of a goal state as leading to a reward. The simplest of actions can coincide with motor acts. Therefore, similarly to motor acts, an action is not isomorphic to a particular movement or specific behavioral pattern, because many different movements can constitute the same goal-directed action (e.g., one can drink by bringing a glass to the mouth following different trajectories, as well as by sipping the liquid through a straw). What individuates an action is the set of satisfaction conditions defining the content of its goal component as leading to a reward plus the special way in which it is causally linked to the actual event of overt movement generation.

The second defining characteristic is that an action in the true sense involves a representation of the perspective the system now takes on the world. That is, the selection process may well be unconscious, but it inevitably leads to a more global final stage resulting in a conscious representation of the system as a whole—as *having* an intention, as initiating and executing its own bodily movements. In other words, on the phenomenal level, we always find a corresponding global state in which the system as a whole is itself represented as an agent.

What do we know about the neural underpinnings of motor acts and actions? This will be the target of next section.

The Neural Correlates of Motor Acts and Actions

For decades, neurophysiology has been reluctant to be involved with any research program promoted to investigate the realm of the intentional–representational aspects of behavior. In particular, the target of neurophysiological research carried out on the motor system of nonhuman primates was, and by some researchers still is, uniquely focused on the study of a multilayered system characterized *exclusively* in terms of very elementary physical features such as force, direction, and amplitude. However, even in the absence of any explicit commitment to investigate the possible cognitive entailments of the neural control of motor behavior, a series of empirical results almost forces us to cope with the previously neglected cognitive aspects of action and its control.

In the following part of this section I will illustrate empirical evidence that forcefully points to a crucial role played by *interaction* in shaping, defining, and constraining the representational aspects of the dynamic interplay between organisms and environment. To do so, I will introduce the neural properties of a sector of the premotor cortex of macaque monkeys studied in our lab for more than twenty years.

The most anterior region of the ventral premotor cortex of the macaque monkey controls hand and mouth movements (Rizzolatti et al. 1981, 1988; Kurata and Tanji 1986; Hepp-Reymond et al. 1994). This sector, which has specific histochemical and cytoarchitectonic features, has been termed area F5 (Matelli et al. 1985). A fundamental functional property of area F5 is that most of its neurons do not discharge in association with elementary movements but are active during *motor acts* such as grasping, tearing, holding, or manipulating objects (Rizzolatti et al. 1988).

What is coded in premotor area F5 is not simply a physical parameter of movement such as force or movement direction but rather the relationship, in motor terms, between the agent and the object of the action. Furthermore, this relation is of a very special kind: a relation leading to success. A hand reaches for an object; it grasps it or manipulates it. F5 neurons indeed become active only *if* a particular type of effector–object relation (e.g., hand–object) is executed until the relation leads to a different state (e.g., to take possession of a piece of food, to throw away an object, to break it, to bring it to the mouth, etc.). Particularly interesting in this respect are grasping-related neurons that fire any time the monkey *successfully* grasps an object, regardless of the effector employed, be it either of his two hands, the mouth, or both (Rizzolatti et al. 1988; see also Rizzolatti, Fogassi, and Gallese 2000).

The independence between the nature of the effector involved and the end state that the same effector is supposed to attain seems to suggest that the motor system contains an *abstract* kind of means–end representation. A formal quantitative testing and validation of this hypothesis was recently carried out by Umiltà et al. (2008). In this study hand-related neurons were recorded from premotor area F5 and the primary motor cortex (area F1) in monkeys trained to grasp objects using two different tools: "normal pliers" and "reverse pliers." These tools require opposite movements to grasp an object: with normal pliers the hand has to be first opened and then closed, as when grasping is executed with the bare hand, while with reverse pliers the hand has to be first closed and then opened. The use of the two tools enabled researchers to dissociate the neural activity related to hand movement from that related to the goal of the motor act. All tested neurons in area F5 and half of neurons recorded from the primary motor cortex discharged in relation to the accomplishment of the goal of grasping—when the tool closed on the object—regardless of whether during this phase the hand opened or closed, that is, regardless of the movements employed to accomplish the goal. The data of Umiltà et al. (2008) indicate that goal coding structures the way action is mapped in area F5 and, although to a minor extent, even in the primary motor cortex.

The presence in the motor system of a specific neural format for motor acts' *goal states*, allows, on the one hand, for a much simpler selection of a particular motor act within a given context (Rizzolatti et al. 1988). Either when the motor act is self-generated or when it is externally driven, only a few representational elements need to be selected.

On the other hand, within the context of a *motor, interactive* code for goal states, motor acts aimed to a specific goal can be represented in the brain just as such, as goal states, and not in the far less economical terms of the specification and control of individual movements. Thus, we have a neural format that generalizes across different instances in which a particular successful end state of the organism (the goal state) can be achieved. In accord with information theory, the informational narrower state has been reached by getting rid of redundant information, such as the load of information about *all* the dynamic patterns under which a given motor act can be characterized.

Beyond purely motor neurons, which constitute the overall majority of all F5 neurons, area F5 also contains two categories of "visuomotor" neurons. Neurons of both categories have motor properties that are indistinguishable from those of the above-described purely motor neurons, while they have peculiar "visual" properties. The first category is made up of neurons responding to the presentation of objects of a particular size and shape in the absence of any detectable action aimed toward them, either by the monkey or by the experimenter. These neurons have been termed "canonical neurons" (Rizzolatti and Fadiga 1998; Rizzolatti, Fogassi, and Gallese 2000; Raos et al. 2006; Umiltà et al. 2007).

The second category is made up of neurons that discharge when the monkey *observes* an action made by another individual and when it *executes* the same or a similar action. These latter visuomotor neurons were called "mirror neurons," which will be addressed in the next sections (Gallese et al. 1996; Rizzolatti et al. 1996; for a review, see Rizzolatti, Fogassi, and Gallese 2001; Rizzolatti and Craighero 2004; Gallese et al. 2004).

Let us have a closer look at canonical neurons. Because most grasping actions are executed under visual guidance, a relationship has to be established between the most important relational features of three-dimensional (3D) visual objects (their affordances) and the specific motor specifications they might engender *whenever* the individual is aiming at them. The appearance of a graspable object in the visual space will retrieve immediately the appropriate "motor schema" of the intended type of hand–object relation. This process, in neurophysiological terms, implies that the same neuron must be able not only to code the motor acts it is supposed to control but also to respond to the situated visual features triggering them.

Indeed, canonical neurons respond to the visual presentation of objects of different size and shape in the absence of any detectable movement of the monkey (Rizzolatti et al. 1988; Jeannerod et al. 1995; Murata et al. 1997; Rizzolatti, Fogassi, and Gallese 2004; Raos et al. 2006; Umiltà et al. 2007). Very often, a strict congruence has been observed between the type of grip coded by a given neuron and the size or shape of the object effective in triggering its "visual" response. The most interesting aspect, however, is the fact that in a considerable percentage of neurons a congruence is observed between the response during the execution of a specific type of grip and the visual response to objects that, although differing in shape, nevertheless all "afford" the same type of grip that excites the neuron when executed (see Murata et al. 1997; Raos et al. 2006).

The first conclusion we can draw is that such canonical neurons contribute to a *multimodal representation of an organism–object relation*.

The function of F5 canonical grasping neurons can therefore hardly be defined in purely sensory or motor terms alone. At this stage, object representations seem to be processed in *relationally specified* terms (Gallese 2000a, 2000b). Within the operational logic of such a neural network, a series of physical entities, 3D objects, are identified, differentiated, and *represented* not in relation to their mere physical appearance but in relation to the effect of the interaction with an acting agent. In my opinion, this qualifies as an *intentional* type of representation: a representation specifically and exclusively coded under a distinct type of motor neural activity pattern, one involving dynamic organism–object relations.

This evidence is also important because it sheds light on important aspects of how the brain maps intentional actions. The limited "vocabulary" (Rizzolatti et al. 1988; see also Rizzolatti, Fogassi, and Gallese 2004; Gallese et al. 2009) of motor acts represented in area F5 of the macaque monkey suggests that the intentional character, the "aboutness" of the representational format of our mind, could be deeply rooted in the intrinsic relational character of body action, which, in turn, suggests the intrinsic *intertwined character* of action, perception, and cognition (Gallese 2000b; see also Hurley 1998).

Representational content cannot be fully explained without considering it as the result of the ongoing modeling process of an organism *as currently integrated with the object to be represented, by intending it*. This integration process between the representing organism and the represented object is articulated in a multiple fashion, for example, by intending to explore it by moving the eyes, by intending to hold it in the focus of attention, by intending to grasp it, and ultimately, by *thinking* about it (see Gallese 2000b; Gallese and Metzinger 2003; see also Metzinger 1999, 2000, 2003).

The intrinsic need of any organism to control its dynamic interaction with the environment also determines the way these interactions are modeled, hence represented. Nature seems to have operated during the course of evolution according to a principle of parsimony. The same *sensorimotor* circuits that control the ongoing activity of the organism within its environment also map objects and events in that very same environment, thus defining and shaping their representational content. It is no coincidence that our representation of the world is a *model* of it that *must* incorporate our idiosyncratic way of interacting with it. This stems from the peculiar and unique way biological organisms are supposed to gain information about the world, that is, by transducing its energetic nature into neural action potentials, through a peculiar type of active interaction with the world, in turn shaped by how living organisms' bodies are built and how the world is. Our take on the reality of the world cannot be but a *model of the world* just for that reason.

Mammals, because of the way they are, can only represent the world by modeling it. We have learned also that this model can be conceived of as an integrated dynamic interplay between situated organisms and their natural playground. From that follows that (1) the representational content resulting from the use of neural information for control purposes and (2) that same neural information both share the same ontological status. It must be emphasized, however, that such equivalence holds only if we qualify neural information as shaped and determined by the peculiar nature of the organisms making use of it. To put it in different words, the producer and the repository of representational content is not the brain per se, but the brain–body system, by means of its interactions with the world of which it is a part.

Action Goals: Ontogeny and Phylogeny

The neuroscientific data so far presented make it necessary to answer the following question. What is a goal? From a scientific point of view, no such things as goals exist in the world. All that exists are goal representations, for instance, as previously shown, goal motor representations activated by biological nervous systems. Goal representations are representations of goal states. What functionally *makes* such a state a goal state is the fact that its internal representation is structured along an axis of valence: it possesses a value *for* the system. A value is anything that is conducive to preserving an organism's integrity (e.g., homeostasis), to maintaining integration on higher levels of complexity (e.g., cognitive development and social interaction), and to achieving procreative success. Therefore, the reward system is a second important element of the way in which a goal representation can be implemented in a causally effective way. Goal states imply values on the level of the individual organism, and values are made causally effective through the reward system.

It is interesting to note how infants construe goal relatedness differently when witnessing the intentional actions of other individuals as opposed to physical events not involving human agents. When 18-month-old infants see a person slip and fail to complete an intended action, they imitate the intended action and not the actual movements that the actor made. However, if the action is displayed by a mechanical device, they fail to successfully reproduce it (Meltzoff 1995). A further argument favoring the hypothesis that goal relatedness is differently perceived by infants in social and physical event configurations is provided by some findings of Amanda Woodward and collaborators (Woodward et al. 2001; Sommerville and Woodward, this volume). These researchers have shown that 6-month-old infants react differently to observed grasping actions according to the biological (human hand) or artificial (mechanical claw) nature of the grasping agent. Only the former are considered as goal-directed actions. It appears, therefore, that infants' early propensity to attend to goals seems to be specific to human actors.

According to some theorists, specialized developmental mechanisms that are in place at birth (Premack 1990; Leslie 1994; Baron-Cohen 1994) allow infants to interpret actions as goal directed very early in life. Innate sensitivity to ostensive behavioral cues like animacy, self-propelledness, temporal contingency, and equifinal variations of action would enable infants to ascribe goal relatedness to the action of a wide range of entities, largely encompassing their experience-related knowledge.

In a similar vein, Gergely and Csibra's teleological stance hypothesis (Gergely et al. 1995; Csibra et al. 1999; Csibra et al. 2003) posits that by 9 months of age, infants are equipped with an inferential system applied to factual reality (action, goal state, and current situational constraints) for generating nonmentalistic goal-directed action representations. According to these authors, an action is represented as teleological only if it satisfies a *"principle of rational action,"* stating that an action can be explained by its goal state if the agent reaches its goal through the most efficient means given the contextual constraints.

A different theoretical view on the emergence of infants' goal-directed action interpretation stresses the intrinsic link between action understanding and experience. Several scholars emphasize the constructional effect of observational and self-agentive experience on infants' understanding of actions' goal relatedness (see Sommerville and Woodward 2005). In particular, infant research employing habituation–dishabituation paradigms showed that previous motor experience facilitates 3-month-old infants' perception of goal-directed actions performed by others (Sommerville et al. 2005). Moreover, 10-month-old infants' ability to construe an action representation as hierarchically organized toward a distal goal strictly depends on their ability to perform similarly structured action sequences (Sommerville and Woodward 2005).

Interestingly, congruency between the observed action and the observer's motor repertoire seems to be crucial for goal prediction. In a recent study, it was shown that just like adults using their own action plans to anticipate the actions of others (Flanagan and Johansson 2003), infants produce proactive goal-directed eye movements when observing a placing action only to the extent they can perform it (Falck-Ytter et al. 2006). The results of Sommerville and Woodward (2005) and Falck-Ytter et al. (2006) suggest that in the case of specific goal-related interactions (such as hand–object interactions typical for reaching and grasping), it is simpler and more plausible to construe infants' understanding of intentions in terms of their own motor knowledge than to call on a "pure reason"-based inferential system such as that assumed by Gergely and Csibra's teleological stance hypothesis.

Goal detection is thought to form the core ability of action understanding and social learning through imitation. Both adults (Baird et al. 2001) and children represent actions as constituted by units hierarchically organized with respect to an overarching goal. Ten-month-old children share with adults the ability to parse actions in units whose boundaries correspond to the completion of a goal (Baldwin et al. 2001). Imitation tasks clearly reflect children's ability to represent actions' units as organized toward a distal goal. When asked to imitate the action of another person, preschoolers reproduce the higher order goal of the action (Bekkering et al. 2000). Eighteen-month-old infants reproduce the goal they inferred from the failed attempts of a human demonstrator (Meltzoff 1995). Carpenter and colleagues (2005) showed that infants could flexibly interpret the goal of an observed sequence of movements according to the context and therefore reenact either the goal of an observed action or the means by which it had been produced. Similarly, Gergely et al. (2002) found that 14-month-old infants reproduce both observed means and goal only when the reason according to which the agent chose a specific means appeared to surpass children's knowledge. Underlying this cognitive flexibility is the fundamental ability to discriminate between means and ends.

Rochat and colleagues (2008) recently investigated the ability of macaque monkeys to evaluate and predict the goal-directed action of others. Nonhuman primates' ability to discriminate between means and end and to use contextual cues to evaluate the ecological validity of a chosen mean has been tested by adapting a looking-time paradigm previously used with human babies (Gergely et al. 1995). Results showed that macaque monkeys, similarly to 9- to 12-month-old human infants, detect the goal of an observed motor act and, according to the physical characteristics of the context, construe expectancies about the most likely action the agent will execute in a given context. This, however, is true only to the extent that observed motor acts are consonant with the observer's motor repertoire, whereas inadequate motor acts, non-goal-related movements, or unfamiliar goal-related motor acts do not allow any simulation and prediction. It is reasonable to hypothesize that monkeys evaluate the observed acts by mapping them on their own motor neural substrate, through the activation of the mirror neuron system (see below). The results of Rochat et al. (2008) provide the first evidence for the presence through phylogeny of the ability to evaluate the contextual adequacy of an action directed to a particular motor goal.

These results reveal that nonhuman primates are endowed with the ability to understand the intentional meaning of others' behavior by relying upon visible behavioral cues; hence, they seriously argue against the traditional dichotomous account of primate social cognition based on a sharp evolutionary discontinuity between behavior readers and mind readers (Gallese and Umiltà 2006; Gallese 2007). It appears that motor behavior contains elements that can be detected and used to understand it and construe predictions about it, without necessarily relying on mental representations in propositional format, certainly precluded in nonhuman primates. Altogether, the results of Woodward, Sommerville, and coworkers on human infants and those of Rochat et al. on macaque monkeys suggest that in the case of specific goal-related interactions (such as hand–object interactions typical of grasping) the understanding of basic action intentions is based on the observer's own motor knowledge.

The neurophysiological discovery that goal relatedness is the functional organizing principle of primates' motor systems provides a possible phylogenetic explanatory framework for these empirical findings, lending support to a deflationary, motor account of the development of intentional understanding.

Mirror Neurons in Monkeys: The Understanding of Action Goals and Intentions

About seventeen years ago, we discovered in the macaque monkey brain a class of premotor neurons that discharge not only when the monkey executes goal-related hand actions like grasping objects but also when observing other individuals (monkeys or humans) executing similar actions. We called them "mirror neurons" (Gallese et al. 1996; Rizzolatti et al. 1996a; see also Gallese 2000a, 2000b, 2001, 2003a, 2003b; Gallese 2004). Neurons with similar properties were later discovered in a sector of the posterior parietal cortex reciprocally connected with area F5 (see Gallese, Fadiga, Fogassi, and Rizzolatti, 2002).

The observation of an object-related action leads to the activation of the same neural network that is active during its actual execution. Action observation causes in the observer the automatic simulated reenactment of the same action. We proposed that this mechanism could be at the basis of a direct form of action understanding (Gallese et al. 1996; Rizzolatti et al. 1996; see also Gallese 2000, 2000a, 2000b, 2003b; Gallese, Fadiga, Fogassi, and Rizzolatti 2002; Gallese, Ferrari, Kohler, and Fogassi 2002).

The relationship between action understanding and action simulation is even more evident in the light of the results of two other studies carried out in our laboratory. In the first series of experiments, F5 mirror neurons were tested in two conditions. In the first condition, the monkey could see the entire action (e.g., a hand grasping action); in the second condition, the same action was presented, but its final critical part, that is, the hand–

object interaction, was hidden. Therefore, in the hidden condition the monkey only "knew" that the target object was present behind the occluder. The results showed that more than half of the recorded neurons also responded in the hidden condition (Umiltà et al. 2001).

These results seem to suggest that predictions or "motor inferences" about the goals of the behavior of others appear to be mediated by the activity of motor neurons coding the goal of the same actions in the observer's brain. Out of sight is not "out of mind" because, by simulating the action, one can fill in the gap.

Some transitive actions are characteristically accompanied by a specific sound. Often this particular sound enables us to understand what is going on even without any visual information about the action producing the sound. The perceived sound has the capacity to make an invisible action inferred and, therefore, present and understood.

We showed that a particular class of F5 mirror neurons, "audiovisual mirror neurons," discharge not only when the monkey executes or observes a particular type of noisy action (e.g., breaking a peanut) but also when it just listens to the sound produced by the action (see Kohler et al. 2002). These audiovisual mirror neurons not only respond to the sound of actions but also discriminate between the sounds of different actions. The actions whose sounds maximally trigger the neurons' discharge when heard are those that also produce the strongest response when observed or executed. The activation of the premotor neural network normally controlling the execution of action "A" by sensory information related to the same action A, be it visual or auditory, can be characterized as simulating action A.

The multimodally driven simulation of action goals instantiated by neurons situated in the ventral premotor cortex of the monkey instantiates properties that are strikingly similar to the symbolic properties characteristic of human thought. The similarity with conceptual content is quite appealing: the same conceptual content ("the goal of action A") results from a multiplicity of states subsuming it, sounds, observed and executed actions. These states, in turn, are subsumed by differently triggered patterns of activations within a population of audiovisual mirror neurons.

The *action simulation* embodied by audiovisual mirror neurons is indeed reminiscent of the use of predicates. The verb "to break" is used to convey a meaning that can be used in different contexts: "seeing someone breaking a peanut," "hearing someone breaking a peanut," "breaking a peanut." The predicate, similarly to the responses in audiovisual mirror neurons, does not change depending on the context to which it applies nor depending on the subject–agent performing the action. All that changes is the context to which the predicate refers (Gallese 2003c; Gallese and Lakoff 2005).

A major step forward in the research on mirror neurons consisted in the discovery that not only do parietal mirror neurons code the goal of an executed–observed motor act, like grasping an object, but they also discriminate identical motor acts (like grasping) according to the final goal of the action in which the act is embedded (e.g., grasping an object to bring it to the mouth or into a container; Fogassi et al. 2005). Mirror neurons map integrated sequences of goal-related motor acts (grasping, holding, bringing, placing) so as to obtain different and parallel chained sequences of motor acts properly assembled to accomplish a more distal goal state. Each embedded motor acts appears to be facilitated by the previously executed one, reorganizing itself so as to map the fulfillment of the overarching goal. These results suggest—at least at the level of basic actions—that the "prior intention" of eating or placing the food is also coded by parietal mirror neurons. Of course, this doesn't imply that monkeys explicitly represent prior intentions as such. Preliminary results show that similar properties are instantiated by F5 mirror neurons (Ferrari et al. 2006).

The general picture conveyed by these results is that the sensorimotor integration supported by the premotor–parietal mirror neuron system instantiates simulations of transitive actions utilized not only to generate and control goal-related behaviors but also to map the goals and purposes of others' actions by means of their simulation. This account doesn't entail an explicit declarative format. It is meaningful, implicit, and direct.

Mirroring Mechanisms in Humans

Several studies using different experimental methodologies and techniques have documented the existence of a common neural activation during action observation and execution also in the human brain (for reviews, see Rizzolatti et al. 2001; Gallese 2003a, 2003b, 2005a, 2005b, 2006, 2007; Gallese et al. 2004; Rizzolatti and Craighero 2004).

Neuroimaging studies have demonstrated that the observation of actions activated the likely human homologue of the monkey areas in which mirror neurons were originally described. In humans, the lower part of the precentral gyrus, the posterior part of the inferior frontal gyrus, the rostral part of the inferior parietal lobule, and regions within the intraparietal sulcus are described as "forming the core of human mirror system" (Rizzolatti and Craighero 2004). During the observation–execution of mouth-, hand-, and foot-related acts, the activation of distinct cortical regions within the premotor and posterior parietal cortices reflect the presence of a coarse somatotopic organization, similar to the one found in monkeys' homologue areas (Buccino et al. 2001; Aziz-Zadeh et al. 2006). Similar results have been found using transcranial magnetic stimulation (see Rizzolatti and Craighero 2004). Furthermore, Fadiga et al. (2002) showed that listening to speech is associated with an increase in motor-evoked potentials recorded from the listener's tongue muscles when the presented words strongly involved tongue movements.

Experimental evidence seems to suggest that the involvement of the mirror neuron system during action observation is strictly correlated with species' and individuals' motor history. Mirror areas are significantly more activated when observing goal-directed actions executed by conspecifics (Buccino et al. 2004a). Moreover, several neuroimaging studies have underlined the formative role played by motor experience in modeling action comprehension (Järveläinen et al. 2004; Calvo-Merino et al. 2005, 2006). Those results corroborate the hypothesis that actions may be differently perceived—and understood—on the basis of the individual's motor capabilities and experience.

The existence of shared neural and cognitive representations of one's own and another's action could at least partially account for the human ability to imitate actions. Functional magnetic resonance imaging (fMRI) evidence shows that mirror areas in humans are selectively activated during simple movement imitation (Iacoboni et al. 1999) and during imitation learning of complex skills (Buccino et al. 2004b; Vogt et al. 2007). Buccino and colleagues (2004b) proposed that during learning of new motor patterns by imitation, the observed actions are decomposed into elementary motor acts that automatically activate the corresponding motor maps. The prefrontal cortex would then recombine the activated motor maps according to the observed model. A recent study by Buxbaum et al. (2005) on posterior parietal neurological patients with ideomotor apraxia not only showed that these patients were disproportionately impaired in the imitation of transitive as compared to intransitive gestures but also found a strong correlation between imitation deficits and the incapacity to recognize observed goal-related meaningful hand actions.

We do not have a clear neuroscientific model of how humans can understand the intentions prompting the actions of others they observe. A given action can be originated by very different intentions. Suppose one sees someone else grasping a cup. Mirror neurons for grasping will most likely be activated in the observer's brain. A simple motor equivalence between the observed action and its motor representation in the observer's brain, however, can only tell us *what* the action is (it's a grasp) and not *why* the action occurred. Determining why action A (grasping the cup) was executed, that is, determining its intention, can be equivalent to detecting the goal of the still not executed and impending subsequent action (say, drinking from the cup).

In an fMRI study (Iacoboni et al. 2005), subjects watched three kinds of stimuli: grasping hand actions without a context, context only (a scene containing objects), and grasping hand actions embedded in contexts. In the last of these conditions, the context suggested the intention associated with the grasping action (either drinking or cleaning up). Actions embedded in contexts, compared with the other two conditions, yielded a significant signal increase in the posterior part of the inferior frontal gyrus and the adjacent sector of the ventral premotor cortex where hand actions are represented. Thus, premotor mirror areas—areas active during the execution and the observation of an action—previously thought to be involved only in action recognition are actually also involved in understanding the "why" of an action, that is, the intention promoting it. Detecting the intention of action A is equivalent to predicting its distal goal, that is, the goal of the subsequent action B.

Similar to what is observed in macaque monkeys (Fogassi et al. 2005), the mirror neuron system in humans seems to also be involved in the detection of action intentions. These results seem to suggest that even humans do not necessarily need to explicitly represent intentions as such when understanding them in others. Action intentions *are embedded* within the intrinsic intentionality of action—that is, its intrinsic relatedness to an end state, a goal. Most of the time we do not *ascribe intentions to others*; we simply detect them. By means of embodied simulation, we can, when witnessing others' behaviors, directly grasp their motor intentional contents without the need to represent them in propositional format.

Humans can easily detect the statistical frequency of action sequences as they are habitually performed or observed in the social environment. Such detection can trigger preferential paths of motor inferences–predictions. It can be hypothesized that this can be accomplished by chaining different populations of mirror neurons coding not only the observed motor act but also those that in a given context would normally follow. Ascribing intentions would therefore consist in predicting a forthcoming new goal. If this is true, it follows that one important difference between humans and monkeys could be the level of recursivity attained by the mirror neuron system in our species. According to this perspective, action prediction and the ascription of intentions are related phenomena, underpinned by the same functional mechanism. In contrast with what mainstream cognitive science would maintain, action prediction and the ascription of intentions do not belong to different cognitive realms. Both pertain to embodied simulation mechanisms underpinned by the activation of chains of logically related mirror neurons.

Embodied Simulation

The notion of simulation is employed in many different domains, often with different, not necessarily overlapping, meanings. Simulation is a functional process that possesses certain content, typically focusing on possible states of its target object. In philosophy of mind, the notion of simulation has been used by proponents of the simulation theory of mind reading (see Gordon 1986, 1995, 2000, 2005; Goldman 1989, 1992a, 1992b, 1993a, 1993b, 2000, 2005, 2006; Gallese and Goldman 1998; Goldman and Gallese 2000) to characterize the pretend state adopted by the attributer in order to understand another person's behavior. Basically, according to this view, we use our mind to put ourselves into the mental shoes of others.

In contrast to standard accounts of simulation theory, I qualify simulation as *embodied* in order to characterize it as a mandatory, prerational, nonintrospectionist functional mechanism. Simulation, as conceived of in the present chapter, is therefore not necessarily the result of a willed and conscious cognitive effort, aimed at interpreting the intentions hidden in the overt—and supposedly intentionally opaque—behavior of others, but rather a basic functional mechanism of our brain. The folk-psychological model of mind reading proposed by standard accounts of simulation theory (Goldman 2006) does not apply to the prelinguistic and nonmetarepresentational character of embodied simulation (Gallese 2003a, 2003b, 2005a, 2005b, 2006). My embodied simulation model is, in fact, challenging the notion that folk psychology is the sole account of interpersonal understanding. Before and below mind reading is *intercorporeity* as the main source of knowledge we directly gather about others (Gallese 2007).

A direct form of understanding of others from within, as it were, is achieved by the activation of neural systems underpinning what others and we do. Parallel to the detached third-person sensory descriptions of the observed social stimuli, internal nonlinguistic "motor representations" associated with actions are evoked in the observer as if he or she were performing a similar action. By means of an isomorphic format, we can map others' actions onto our own motor representations. This is what I mean by embodied simulation when applied to the action domain.

To what extent is embodied simulation *solely* a motor phenomenon? According to the use I make of this notion, embodied simulation is not conceived of as being exclusively confined to the domain of motor control but rather as being a more general and basic endowment of our brain. It applies not only to actions or emotions, where the motor or visceromotor components may predominate, but also to sensations like vision and touch. I posit that embodied simulation is a crucial functional mechanism for empathy. It is mental because it has content (see Gallese 2003c, 2005b). It is embodied not only because it is neurally realized but also because it uses a preexisting body model in the brain realized by the sensorimotor system and, therefore, involves a nonpropositional form of self-representation.

The Intentional Attunement Hypothesis

Our seemingly effortless capacity to conceive of the acting bodies inhabiting our social world as *goal-oriented persons* like us depends on the constitution of a "we-centric" shared meaningful interpersonal space. This shared manifold space (see Gallese 2001, 2003a, 2003b, 2005a, 2005b) can be characterized at the functional level as embodied simulation, a specific mechanism likely constituting a basic functional feature by means of which our brain–body system models its interactions with the world.

The mirror neuron systems and the other nonmotor mirroring neural clusters in our brain mapping emotions and sensations represent a subpersonal instantiation of embodied simulation. With this mechanism we do not just "see" an action, an emotion, or a sensation. Side by side with the sensory description of the observed social stimuli, internal representations of the body states associated with these actions, emotions, and sensations are evoked in the observer, "as if" he or she were performing a similar action or experiencing a similar emotion or sensation.

Social cognition is not *only* explicitly reasoning about the contents of someone else's mind. Our brains, and those of other primates, appear to have developed a basic functional mechanism, embodied simulation, which gives us an experiential insight into other minds. It must be added that the notion of neural mirroring and the related functional mechanism of embodied simulation do not imply that what is mirrored and simulated in the observer's brain has to be an exact replica of its object. The mirror metaphor is perhaps misleading. The more we study mirroring mechanisms, the more we learn about their plasticity and dependence upon the personal history and situated nature of the "mirroring subject."

The phenomenal content of the intentional relations of others can be grasped by means of the activation of the mirroring mechanisms here described, which enable our "intentional attunement" to others. Intentional attunement, in turn, by collapsing the other's intentions into the observer's ones, produces the peculiar quality of familiarity we entertain with other individuals. This is what "being empathic" is about. By means of intentional attunement, the "objective other" becomes "another self."

This, of course, doesn't account for all of our social cognitive skills. Our most sophisticated mind reading abilities likely require the activation of large regions of our brain, certainly larger than a putative domain-specific theory of mind module. The same actions performed by others in different contexts can lead the observer to radically different interpretations. Thus, social stimuli are also understood on the basis of the explicit cognitive elaboration of their contextual aspects and of previous information.

The point is that these two mechanisms are not mutually exclusive. Embodied simulation is experience based, while the second mechanism is a cognitive description of an external state of affairs. When embodied simulation is not present or is malfunctioning, as perhaps in autism (see Gallese 2006), the propositional, more cognitively sophisticated mind-reading abilities can—at best—only provide a pale, detached account of the social experiences of others. It is an empirical issue to determine how much of social cognition, language included, can be explained by embodied simulation and its neural underpinnings.

This proposal also opens new, interesting perspectives for the study of the neural underpinnings of psychopathological states (Gallese 2003b, 2006) and psychotherapeutic relations (Gallese 2008; Gallese et al. 2007) and of other aspects of intersubjectivity such as aesthetic experience (Freedberg and Gallese 2007).

Conclusions

Many scholars in the cognitive sciences focus exclusively on clarifying differences between humans and other primates with respect to the use of propositional attitudes. According to this mainstream view, humans have theory of mind, and nonhuman primates don't. This paradigm, so pervasive in contemporary cognitive science, is too quick in establishing a direct and nomological link between our use of propositional attitudes and their supposed neural correlates. No one can deny that we use propositional attitudes, unless embracing a radical eliminativism (which is not my case). However, it is perfectly possible that we will never find boxes in our brains containing the neural correlates of beliefs, desires, and intentions as such. Such a search qualifies, in my opinion, as a heuristically poor form of reductionism.

As pointed out by Allen and Bekoff (1997), this "all-or-nothing" approach to social cognition, this desperate search for a "mental Rubicon" (the wider the better), is strongly arguable. When trying to account for our cognitive abilities, we forget that they are the result of a long evolutionary process. It is reasonable to hypothesize that this evolutionary process proceeded along a line of continuity (see Gallese and Goldman 1998; Gallese et al. 2002; Gallese and Umiltà 2006).

It is perhaps more fruitful to establish to what extent different cognitive strategies may be underpinned by similar functional mechanisms, which in the course of evolution acquire increasing complexity. The empirical data briefly reviewed in this chapter are an instantiation of this strategy of investigation. The data on mirror neurons in monkeys and mirroring circuits in the human brain seem to suggest that the ease with which we are capable of understanding others and recognizing them as similar to us—in other words, our "intentional attunement" to others—may rely on a series of matching mechanisms that we have just started to uncover.

Acknowledgments

This work was supported by Ministero Italiano dell'Università e della Ricerca, by the European Union (EU) grant NESTCOM, and by the EU Marie Curie—Research Training Network 035975 "DISCOS—Disorders and Coherence of the Embodied Self."

Note

1. In the present chapter the notion of representation is used very differently from its standard meaning in classic cognitive science and analytic philosophy. It refers to a particular type of content, generated by the relations that our situated and interacting brain–body system instantiates with the world of others. Such content is prelinguistic and pretheoretical but nevertheless has attributes normally and uniquely attributed to conceptual content.

References

Adolphs, R. (2003). Cognitive neuroscience of human social behaviour. *Nature Reviews Neuroscience*, 4, 165–178.

Adolphs, R., Damasio, H., Tranel, D., Cooper, G., and Damasio, A. R. (2000). A role for somatosensory cortices in the visual recognition of emotion as revealed by three-dimensional lesion mapping. *Journal of Neuroscience, 20,* 2683–2690.

Allen, C., and Bekoff, M. (1997). *Species of mind.* Cambridge: MIT Press.

Aziz-Zadeh, L., Wilson, S. M., Rizzolatti, G., and Iacoboni, M. (2006). Congruent embodied representations for visually presented actions and linguistic phrases describing actions. *Current Biology, 16,* 1818–1823.

Baird, J. A., and Baldwin, D. A. (2001). Making sense of human behavior: Action parsing and intentional inferences. In B. F. Malle, L. J. Moses, and D. A. Baldwin (Eds.), *Intentions and intentionality* (pp. 193–206). Cambridge: MIT Press.

Baldwin, D. A., Baird, J. A., Saylor, M. M., and Clark, M. A. (2001). Infants parse dynamic action. *Child Development, 72,* 708–717.

Baron-Cohen, S. (1994). How to build a baby that can read minds: Cognitive mechanisms in mindreading. *Cahier de Psychologie Cognitive/Current Psychology of Cognition, 13,* 1–40.

Bekkering, H., Wohlschläger, A., and Gattis, M. (2000). Imitation of gestures in children is goal-directed. *Quarterly Journal of Experimental Psychology, 53A,* 153–164.

Buccino, G., Binkofski, F., Fink, G. R., Fadiga, L., Fogassi, L., Gallese, V., Seitz, R. J., Zilles, K., Rizzolatti, G., and Freund, H.-J. (2001). Action observation activates premotor and parietal areas in a somatotopic manner: An fMRI study. *European Journal of Neuroscience, 13,* 400–404.

Buccino, G., Lui, F., Canessa, N., Patteri, I., Lagravinese, G., Benuzzi, F., Porro, C. A., and Rizzolatti, G. (2004a). Neural circuits involved in the recognition of actions performed by nonconspecifics: An fMRI study. *Journal of Cognitive Neuroscience, 16,* 114–126.

Buccino, G., Vogt, S., Ritzl, A., Fink, G.R., Zilles, K., Freund, H.-J., and Rizzolatti, G. (2004b). Neural circuits underlying imitation learning of hand actions: an event-related fMRI study. *Neuron, 42,* 323–334.

Buxbaum, L. J., Kyle, K. M., and Menon, R. (2005). On beyond mirror neurons: Internal representations subserving imitation and recognition of skilled object-related actions in humans. *Cognitive Brain Research, 25,* 226–39.

Calvo-Merino B., Glaser, D. E, Grezes, J., Passingham, R. E., and Haggard, P. (2005). Action observation and acquired motor skills: An FMRI study with expert dancers. *Cerebral Cortex, 15,* 1243–1249.

Calvo-Merino, B., Grèzes, J., Glaser, D. E., Passingham, R. E., and Haggard, P. (2006). Seeing or doing? Influence of visual and motor familiarity in action observation. *Current Biology, 16,* 1905–1910.

Carpenter, M., Call, J., and Tomasello, M. (2005). Twelve-and-18-month-olds copy actions in terms of goals. *Developmental Science, 8,* F13–F20.

Cisek, P., and Kalaska, J. (2004). Neural correlates of mental rehearsal in dorsal premotor cortex. *Nature, 431,* 993–996.

Csibra, G., Birò, S., Koòs, O., and Gergely, G. (2003). One-year-old infants use teleological representations of actions productively. *Cognitive Science, 27,* 111–133.

Csibra, G., Gergely, G., Birò, S., Koòs, O., and Brockbank, M. (1999). Goal attribution without agency cues: The perception of "pure reason" in infancy. *Cognition, 72,* 237–267.

Fadiga L., Craighero L., Buccino G., and Rizzolatti G. (2002). Speech listening specifically modulates the excitability of tongue muscles: A TMS study. *European Journal of Neuroscience, 15,* 399–402.

Falck-Ytter, T., Gredeback, G., and von Hofsten, C. (2006). Infant predict other people's action goals. *Nature Neuroscience, 9,* 878–879.

Ferrari, P. F., Bonini, L., Ugolotti, F., Simone, L., Rozzi, S., Rizzolatti, G., and Fogassi, L. (2006). Coding of motor intention in monkey parietal and premotor grasping neurons. *Society for Neuroscience Abstracts,* 255.1/X13.

Ferrari, P. F., Gallese, V., Rizzolatti, G., and Fogassi, L. (2003). Mirror neurons responding to the observation of ingestive and communicative mouth actions in the monkey ventral premotor cortex. *European Journal of Neuroscience, 17,* 1703–1714.

Flanagan, J. R., and Johansson, R. S. (2003). Action plans used in action observation. *Nature, 424,* 769–770.

Fogassi, L., Ferrari, P. F., Gesierich, B., Rozzi, S., Chersi, F., and Rizzolatti, G. (2005). Parietal lobe: From action organization to intention understanding. *Science, 302,* 662–667.

Freedberg D., and Gallese V. (2007). Motion, emotion and empathy in esthetic experience. *Trends in Cognitive Sciences, 11,* 197–203.

Gallese, V. (2000a). The acting subject: towards the neural basis of social cognition. In T. Metzinger (Ed.), *Neural correlates of consciousness: Empirical and conceptual questions* (pp. 325–333). Cambridge: MIT Press.

Gallese, V. (2000b). The inner sense of action: Agency and motor representations. *Journal of Consciousness Studies, 7*(10), 23–40.

Gallese, V. (2001). The "shared manifold" hypothesis: From mirror neurons to empathy. *Journal of Consciousness Studies, 8*(5–7), 33–50.

Gallese, V. (2003a). The manifold nature of interpersonal relations: The quest for a common mechanism. *Philosophical Transactions of the Royal Society of London, Series B, Biological Sciences, 358,* 517–528.

Gallese, V. (2003b). The roots of empathy: The shared manifold hypothesis and the neural basis of intersubjectivity. *Psychopathology, 36*(4), 171–180.

Gallese, V. (2003c). A neuroscientific grasp of concepts: From control to representation. Phil. Trans. Royal Soc. London B., 358, 1231–1240.

Gallese, V. (2004). From mirror neurons to the shared manifold hypothesis: A neurophysiologycal account of intersubjectivity. In J. Langer, S. Taylor-Parker, and C. Milbrath (Eds.), *Biology and knowledge revisited: From neurogenesis to psychogenesis* (pp. 179–203). Mahwah, N.J.:Lawrence Erlbaum.

Gallese V. (2005a). "Being like me": Self–other identity, mirror neurons and empathy. In S. Hurley and N. Chater (Eds.), *Perspectives on imitation: From neuroscience to social science* (Vol. 1, pp. 101–118). Cambridge: MIT Press.

Gallese, V. (2005b). Embodied simulation: From neurons to phenomenal experience. *Phenomenology and the Cognitive Sciences, 4*, 23–48.

Gallese, V. (2006). Intentional attunement: A neurophysiological perspective on social cognition and its disruption in autism. *Brain Research, 1079*, 15–24.

Gallese, V. (2007). Before and below theory of mind: Embodied simulation and the neural correlates of social cognition. *Philosophical Transactions of the Royal Society of London, Series B, Biological Sciences, 362*, 659–669.

Gallese, V. (2008). Empathy, embodied simulation and the brain. *Journal of the American Psychoanalytic Association, 56*, 769–781.

Gallese, V., Eagle M. E., and Migone P. (2007). Intentional attunement: Mirror neurons and the neural underpinnings of interpersonal relations. *Journal of the American Psychoanalytic Association, 55*, 131–176.

Gallese, V., Fadiga, L., Fogassi, L., and Rizzolatti, G. (1996). Action recognition in the premotor cortex. *Brain, 119*, 593–609.

Gallese, V., Fadiga, Fogassi, L. L., and Rizzolatti, G. (2002). Action representation and the inferior parietal lobule. In W. Prinz and B. Hommel (Eds.), *Common mechanisms in perception and action: Attention and performance XIX* (pp. 247–266). Oxford: Oxford University Press.

Gallese, V., Ferrari, P. F., Kohler, E., and Fogassi, L. (2002). The eyes, the hand, and the mind: Behavioral and neurophysiological aspects of social cognition. In M. Bekoff, C. Allen, and G. Burghardt (Eds.), *The cognitive animal: Empirical and theoretical perspectives on animal cognition* (pp. 451–461). Cambridge: MIT Press.

Gallese, V., and Goldman, A. (1998) Mirror neurons and the simulation theory of mind-reading. *Trends in Cognitive Sciences, 12*, 493–501.

Gallese, V., Keysers, C., and Rizzolatti, G. (2004). A unifying view of the basis of social cognition. *Trends in Cognitive Sciences, 8*, 396–403.

Gallese, V., and Lakoff, G. (2005). The brain's concepts: The role of the sensory-motor system in reason and language. *Cognitive Neuropsychology, 22*, 455–479.

Gallese, V., and Metzinger, T. (2003). Motor ontology: The representational reality of goals, actions, and selves. *Philosophical Psychology, 16*, 365–388.

Gallese, V., Rochat, M., Cossu, G., and Sinigaglia, C. (2009). Motor cognition and its role in the phylogeny and ontogeny of intentional understanding. *Developmental Psychology, 45*, 103–113.

Gallese, V., and Umiltà, M. A. (2006). Cognitive continuity in primate social cognition. *Biological Theory, 1*(1), 25–30.

Gergely, G., Bekkering, H., and Kiràly, I. (2002). Rational imitation in preverbal infants. *Nature, 415*, 755.

Gergely, G., and Csibra, G. (2003). Teleological reasoning in infancy: The naive theory of rational action. *Trends in Cognitive Sciences, 7*, 287–292.

Gergely, G., Nàdasdy, Z., Csibra, G., and Bìrò, S. (1995). Taking the intentional stance at 12 months of age. *Cognition, 56*, 165–193.

Goldman, A. (1989). Interpretation psychologized. *Mind and Language, 4*, 161–185.

Goldman, A. (1992a). In defense of simulation theory. *Mind and Lnguage, 7*, 104–119.

Goldman, A. (1992b). Empathy, mind and morals: Presidential address. *Proceedings and Addresses of the American Philosophical Association, 66*, 17–41.

Goldman, A. (1993a). The psychology of folk psychology. *Behavioral Brain Sciences, 16*, 15–28.

Goldman, A. (1993b). *Philosophical applications of cognitive science*. Boulder, CO: Westview Press.

Goldman, A. (2000). The mentalizing folk. In D. Sperber (Ed.), *Metarepresentation*. Pp. 171–196, London: Oxford University Press.

Goldman, A. (2005). Imitation, mindreading, and simulation. In S. Hurley and N. Chater (Eds.), *Perspectives on imitation: From neuroscience to social science* (pp. 79–93). Cambridge: MIT Press.

Goldman, A. (2006). *Simulating minds*. Oxford, UK: Oxford University Press.

Goldman, A., and Gallese, V. (2000). Reply to Schulkin. *Trends in Cognitive Sciences, 4*, 255–256.

Gordon, R. (1986). Folk psychology as simulation. *Mind and Language, 1*, 158–171.

Gordon, R. (1995). Simulation without introspection or inference from me to you. In M. Davies and T. Stone (Eds.), *Mental simulation* (pp. 53–67). Oxford: Blackwell.

Gordon, R. (1996). "Radical" simulationism. In P. Carruthers and P. Smith (Eds.), *Theories of theories of mind* (pp. 11–21). Cambridge: Cambridge University Press.

Gordon, R. (2000). Sellar's Rylean revisited. *Protosociology, 14*, 102–114.

Gordon, R. (2005). Intentional agents like myself. In S. Hurley and N. Chater (Eds.), *Perspectives on imitation: From cognitive neuroscience to social science* (pp. 95–106). Cambridge: MIT Press.

Hauser, M. D., Chomsky, N., and Fitch, W. T. (2002). The faculty of language: What is it, Who has it, and How did it evolve? *Science, 298*, 1569–1579.

Hauser, M. D., and Fitch, W. T. (2004). Computational constraints on syntactic processing in a nonhuman primate. *Science, 303*, 377–380.

Hepp-Reymond, M.-C., Hüsler, E. J., Maier, M. A., and Qi, H.-X. (1994). Force-related neuronal activity in two regions of the primate ventral premotor cortex. *Canadian Journal of Physiology and Pharmacology, 72*, 571–579.

Hurley, S. (1998). *Consciousness in action.* Cambridge: Harvard University Press.

Iacoboni, M., Woods, R. P., Brass, M., Bekkering, H., Mazziotta, J. C., and Rizzolatti, G. (1999). Cortical mechanisms of human imitation. *Science, 286*, 2526–2528.

Iacoboni, M., Molnar-Szakacs, I., Gallese, V., Buccino, G., Mazziotta, J., and Rizzolatti, G. (2005). Grasping the intentions of others with one's own mirror neuron system. *PLoS Biology, 3*, 529–535.

Järveläinen, J., Schlurmann, M., and Hari, R. (2004). Activation of the human primary motor cortex during observation of tool use. *NeuroImage, 23*, 187–192.

Jeannerod, M., Arbib, M. A., Rizzolatti, G., and Sakata, H. (1995). Grasping objects: The cortical mechanisms of visuomotor transformation. *Trends in Neuroscience, 18*, 314–320.

Kohler, E., Keysers, C., Umiltà, M. A., Fogassi, L., Gallese, V., and Rizzolatti, G. (2002). Hearing sounds, understanding actions: Action representation in mirror neurons. *Science, 297*, 846–848.

Kurata, K., and Tanji, J. (1986). Premotor cortex neurons in macaques: Activity before distal and proximal forelimb movements. *Journal of Neuroscience, 6*, 403–411.

Leslie, A. M. (1994). ToMM, ToBy, and agency: Core architecture and domain specificity. In L. A. Hirschfield and S. A. Gelman (Eds.), *Mapping the mind: Domain specificity in cognition and culture* (pp. 119–148). New York: Cambridge University Press.

Matelli, M., Luppino, G., and Rizzolatti, G. (1985). Patterns of cytochrome oxidase activity in the frontal agranular cortex of the macaque monkey. *Behavioral Brain Research, 18*, 125–137.

Meltzoff, A. N. (1995). Understanding the intentions of others: Re-enactment of intended acts by 18-month-old children. *Developmental Psychology, 31,* 838–850.

Metzinger, T. (1999). *Subjekt und Selbstmodell* (2nd ed.). Paderborn: mentis.

Metzinger, T. (2000). The subjectivity of subjective experience: A representationalist analysis of the first-person perspective. In T. Metzinger (Ed.), *Neural correlates of consciousness—Empirical and conceptual questions* (pp. 285–306). Cambridge: MIT Press.

Metzinger, T. (2003). *Being no one: The self-model theory of subjectivity.* Cambridge: MIT Press.

Metzinger, T., and Gallese, V. (2003). The emergence of a shared action ontology: Building blocks for a theory. *Consciousness and Cognition, 12,* 549–571.

Murata, A., Fadiga, L., Fogassi, L., Gallese, V., Raos, V., and Rizzolatti, G. (1997). Object representation in the ventral premotor cortex (Area F5) of the monkey. *Journal of Neurophysiology, 78,* 2226–2230.

Premack, D. (1990). The infant's theory of self-propelled objects. *Cognition, 36,* 1–16.

Raos, V., Umiltà, M. A., Fogassi, L., and Gallese, V. (2006). Functional properties of grasping-related neurons in the ventral premotor area F5 of the macaque monkey. *Journal of Neurophysiology, 95,* 709–729.

Rizzolatti, G., and Craighero, L. (2004). The mirror neuron system. *Annual Review of Neuroscience, 27,* 169–192.

Rizzolatti, G., Fogassi, L., and Gallese, V. (2000). Cortical mechanisms subserving object grasping and action recognition: A new view on the cortical motor functions. In M. S. Gazzaniga (Ed. in Chief), *The new cognitive neurosciences* (2nd ed., pp. 539–552). Cambridge: MIT Press.

Rizzolatti, G., Fogassi, L., and Gallese, V. (2001). Neurophysiological mechanisms underlying the understanding and imitation of action. *Nature Neuroscience Reviews, 2,* 661–670.

Rizzolatti, G., Fogassi, L., and Gallese, V. (2004). Cortical mechanisms subserving object grasping, action understanding and imitation. In M. S. Gazzaniga (Ed. in Chief), *The new cognitive neurosciences* (3rd ed., pp. 427–440). Cambridge: MIT Press.

Rizzolatti G, Scandolara C, Matelli M, Gentilucci M. (1981). Afferent properties of periarcuate neurons in macaque monkeys. II. Visual responses. *Behavioral Brain Research, 2,* 147–63.

Rizzolatti, G., Fadiga, L., Gallese, V., and Fogassi, L. (1996). Premotor cortex and the recognition of motor actions. *Cognitive Brain Research, 3,* 131–141.

Rizzolatti, G., Camarda, R., Fogassi, M., Gentilucci, M., Luppino, G., and Matelli, M. (1988). Functional organization of inferior area 6 in the macaque monkey: II. Area F5 and the control of distal movements. *Experimental Brain Research, 71*, 491–507.

Rochat, M., Serra, E., Fadiga, L., and Gallese, V. (2008). The evolution of social cognition: Goal familiarity shapes monkeys' action understanding. *Current Biology, 18*, 227–232.

Schubotz, R. I., and von Cramon, D. Y. (2004). Sequences of abstract nonbiological stimuli share ventral premotor cortex with action observation and imagery. *Journal of Neuroscience, 24*, 5467–5474.

Sommerville, J. A., and Woodward, A. (2005). Pulling out the intentional structure of action: The relation between action processing and action production in infancy. *Cognition, 95*, 1–30.

Sommerville, J. A., Woodward, A., and Needham, A. (2005). Action experience alters 3-month-old perception of other's actions. *Cognition, 96*, 1–11.

Umiltà, M. A., Kohler, E., Gallese, V., Fogassi, L., Fadiga, L., Keysers, C., and Rizzolatti, G. (2001). "I know what you are doing": A neurophysiologycal study. *Neuron, 32*, 91–101.

Umiltà, M. A., Brochier, T., Spinks, R. L., and Lemon, R. N. (2007). Simultaneous recording of macaque premotor and primary motor cortex neuronal populations reveals different functional contributions to visuomotor grasp. *Journal of Neurophysiology, 98*, 488–501.

Umiltà, M. A., Escola, L., Intskirveli, I., Grammont, F., Rochat, M., Caruana, F., Jezzini, A., Gallese, V., and Rizzolatti, G. (2008). How pliers become fingers in the monkey motor system. *Proceedings of the National Academy of Sciences, 105*, 2209–2213.

Vogt, S., Buccino, G., Wohlschläger, A. M., Canessa, N., Shah, N. J., Zilles, K., Eickhoff, S. B., Freund, H. J., Rizzolatti, G., and Fink, G. R. (2007). Prefrontal involvement in imitation learning of hand actions: Effects of practice and expertise. *NeuroImage, 37*, 1371–1383.

Watkins, K. E., Strafella, A. P., and Paus, T. (2003). Seeing and hearing speech excites the motor system involved in speech production. *Neuropsychologia, 41*, 989–994.

11 Intersubjective Intentional Actions

Dorothée Legrand and Marco Iacoboni

The other transforms me into an object and denies me, I transform him into an object and deny him. In fact the other's gaze transforms me into an object, and mine him, only if both of us withdraw into the core of our thinking nature, if we both make ourselves into an inhuman gaze, if each of us feels his actions to be not taken up and understood, but observed as if they were an insect's. This is what happens, for instance, when I fall under the gaze of a stranger. But even then, the objectification of each by the other's gaze is felt as unbearable only because it takes the place of possible communication.
—Maurice Merleau-Ponty (1962), pp. 360–361

Intentions and intentional actions are a fundamental ingredient of our social interactions. The aim of this chapter is to better understand the role of intentional action in the constitution of intersubjectivity. We will develop our view in three parts. The first part addresses the fundamental distinction between interaction with others and representation of others, that is, between others as subjects and others as objects. We will see how the discussion of philosophical arguments on this issue has important implications for the recently established social neurosciences. The second and the third parts of this chapter will be concerned with the role of intentional action as the foundation of the type of intersubjectivity that considers not only the self but also others as subjects. The second part argues that the intersubjective relation primarily involves the sharing of a common world. We will describe a process according to which the relation of the self with objects offers the basis for the sharing of the world with others. This is made possible through the performance of goal-directed actions represented within a shared framework. The third part investigates direct self–others interactions. We argue that these intersubjective relations are not primarily based on inferences but are rather anchored to concrete coordinated intentional actions.

Others as Subject

The Sovereign Self and Philosophical Autism

In philosophy, others are often considered as a problem. In a Cartesian perspective, the very possibility of other subjects questions the model of the sovereign self: the existence of other consciousnesses contradicts the conception of the cogito as the radical foundation (Descartes 1641). Husserl (1929) restates this foundational problem in a different framework. His phenomenology notably[1] advocates bracketing the existence of the objective world, *others included*. Through the *epoche*, others become the ego's phenomenon. Thus, as for Descartes, in this framework, others are only thinkable within the primordial and prior perspective of the self. This view has been described as some sort of "philosophical autism" because its consequences are such that "my experience of the other person is something that blossoms only within the garden of my own mind" (Gallagher 2000).

This position gives priority to the self over others and prevents one from understanding others as subjects. Indeed, "the other person is another subjectivity that refuses to be captured by the epistemic perspectives available to the self-sufficient ego" (Gallagher 2000). To understand others as subjects in their own right, it is necessary to account for the reciprocity of the self–other relation: not only is the self a subject in relation to the other, but the other is also a subject related to the self.

Self–Other Reciprocity

The reciprocity of the self–other relation plays a crucial role in Hegel's (1807) philosophy. Without going into a detailed analysis of his position, it is interesting to note that Hegel proposes that the self does not preexist to its relation with others, no more than the other consciousness preexists to this relation. In other words, consciousness reduced to a self-sufficient identity would only be an abstraction. Nevertheless, Hegel's framework does not allow considering others for themselves. Others are only considered as the means of objectifying one's subjectivity. The focus remains the constitution of the self, rather than a coconstitution of self and other. The self–other relation, as Hegel conceived it, is indeed reciprocal but also asymmetrical.

As shown by Hegel's position, reciprocity is both a central feature of the self–other relation and an important problem to solve. This issue comes out more clearly in Sartre's account (1943, p. 303). Sartre underlines that "the 'being-seen-by-the-Other' is the truth of 'seeing the Other.'" However, in a Sartrean context, this reciprocity becomes a problem, if not an impossibility. Indeed, Sartre insists on the fact that the other's look freezes the self as an object in the world. I recognize that I am as the other sees me. The other's perspective thus immobilizes all my possibilities. I get trapped in the image that the other has of me. Again, this position denies the specificity of intersubjective relations, since the self loses its subjectivity, as he or she is objectified by the other's perspective.

The Objectification of the Self and Others

An important point to note is that the conception of the self–other relation classically implies an objectification of the self and/or the other: either others are alienated to the self's perspective, being only a means for its own constitution, or the self is alienated to the others' perspective. Such an objectification makes any genuine encounter of the self and others impossible: either the other is considered as subject, a free consciousness, and thus the self is its reified object, or the self takes the other as its object, and the "other as subject" vanishes.

The objectification of the self and/or others takes at least two different forms. As stated by Gallagher,

from either perspective [first- or third-person perspective], the other appears as an object. From a strict first-person perspective, it appears as an object constituted within the transcendental realm of ownness (e.g., Husserl). From a third-person perspective, it appears as an object that we theorize to be different from all other objects insofar as we hypothesize for it a mental interior (a position psychologists refer to as "theory of mind"[2]). (Gallagher 2000)

The other is both the self's intentional object, providing the content of the self's consciousness, and a particular object of the world, that is, a physical body. As well, the self may consider that it can be taken as the other's intentional object of consciousness as far as it is also a physical object of the world. Through this dual process of objectification, the self may frame itself as an objectified subject and the other as a subjectified object. However, under this scenario, self–other relationships are reduced to subject–object[3] relationships. In this framework, when I as subject recognize that the other entertains some mental states, I recognize that the particular object that the other is, is also a subject. However, this does not make me interact directly with him or her as subject (see also Gallagher 2001). I only attribute some qualities to a particular object that passively receives these qualities. Also, when I consider that the other is taking me as his or her intentional object of consciousness, this is a relation between subject$_{other}$ and object$_{me}$. Again, this is not a subject–subject relationship, since I am only the receiver of the other's attribution of some quality. Here, we would like to highlight that this is a commonly held position which misses a crucial point: the subject–subject relationship that is typical of the genuinely reciprocal and dynamical self–others inter*subjective* relations that we experience in our everyday life.

Subject–Subject Interrelations

Intersubjectivity literally means "between subjects." Thus, genuine intersubjectivity implies that both the self and others are subjects, and are subjects for each other. Far too trivial. However, as we just saw, the meaning of this fact is also far too neglected in the literature: self–other relations are, in fact, most often described as the objectification of the other and of the self through their relation. In contrast, the subject$_{me}$–subject$_{other}$ relation, by definition, implies considering that, at any given time, both the self and the other are subjects in a full sense (Butcher 2003). An important peculiarity of intersubjective relations, compared to subject–object relations, is that both the self and the other are more than only receivers of some qualification: both the self and the other are active in an intersubjective relation. Not only is the self active in what he or she receives and gives, but crucially the other is too. Thereby, the self (or the other) alone cannot constrain the whole relation.

This position is consistent with the claim that what the self is, the mental states he or she entertains, and the behavior he or she shows are not fully determined by himself or herself as taken in isolation. Rather, it also depends on the other and on the self–other relation. What the self is cannot be established statically, prior to its relation with others, if inter*subjective* relations are at all possible, since such an a priori fixation would allow only a subject–object relation. In other words, intersubjective relation engages the two interacting subjects in a process of auto- and interconstitution. The other participates in the organization of the self (the organization of his or her mental and behavioral states), and the self participates in the organization of the other as well.

In the next two parts of this chapter we discuss the subject–subject giveand-take processes under a naturalistic framework.

From Philosophy to Social Neurosciences

At this point, a nonphilosopher cognitive scientist may wonder what the concrete implication of such a view is for his or her own discipline. Are all these considerations only worth elaborating within a purely philosophical framework? We think not. Indeed, the field of cognitive neuroscience has recently merged with social neuroscience into the exciting field of social cognitive neuroscience, and we propose that the distinction between other as object and other as subject is crucial for social cognitive neuroscience. This distinction has to be taken into account in experimental design and in the interpretation of empirical data and may help in reconciling apparently inconsistent results in the literature. Some empirical findings seem to contradict each other, partly because what is measured is not sufficiently specified. We propose distinguishing three levels of self–others relation, on the basis of whether it involves (1) noninteractional observation of others, (2) interactional observation of others, or (3) online interaction with others. Only the last of these involves a genuine subject–subject relation, allowing one to investigate the role of intentional action in the constitution of intersubjective relations between self and others. The rest of this chapter will focus on this issue. However, before doing so, let us discuss briefly how the three levels of self–others relation have been implemented more frequently in social cognitive neuroscience.

Observation and Attribution

The first case (1: noninteractional observation of others) implies a $subject_{me}$–$object_{other}$ relation. It is in place in any experiment where the subject has to make some judgment about the other. It is the equivalent of experiments where subjects have to make some judgment about themselves, taking themselves as their own object. In fact, these two types of experiments are often combined together. For example, the subject can be given the following instruction: "If the face on the screen looks more like you, press the right button with your right index finger; if the face looks more like the other person, press the left button with the left index finger" (Kircher et al. 2001). As noted elsewhere (Uddin et al. 2005), if a blocked design is used for this task, there is no emphasis on the discrimination component of the task, since each block contains mostly stimuli from one category. There is no direct comparison between the self's and another's face.

The simple use of an event-related design changes the task dramatically (Uddin et al. 2005), creating an "interactional" (even if restricted) context. Indeed, the event-related design forces subjects to make "self–other" discriminations at each trial. Thus, the event-related design invokes self–other discrimination more than the blocked design. In other words, the blocked design is better described as a case of noninteractional observation (1), while the event-related design would rather correspond to a case of interactional observation (2).

The distinction between these two protocols may appear insignificant but, in fact, they produce different brain activations. In Kircher et al. (blocked design), the processing of self's face images, compared with the processing of other's face images, reveals greater responses in left fusiform gyrus, left inferior frontal gyrus, left supramarginal gyrus/inferior parietal lobule, right middle temporal gyrus, right insula, and right hippocampal formation. In Uddin et al. (event-related design), the self–other discrimination task modulates activity in a network involving frontoparietal structures described as part of the human "mirror neuron system" in the right hemisphere, and in two areas of the so-called "default/resting state." These two large-scale neural systems have been identified as crucial systems for the processing of social relations (Iacoboni et al. 2004), thus supporting our interpretation on the interactional nature of Uddin's task.

A similar distinction between noninteractional observation of others and interactional observation of others can be made in the case of two other experimental tasks: observation of another's actions to imitate them and observation of another's actions to later recognize them. Only the former corresponds to what we call here interactional observation of others. While observation in order to imitate strongly activates frontoparietal systems for action control, the observation of action for recognition purposes activates mostly medial temporal structures associated with memory processes (Decety et al. 1997; Grezes et al. 1998, 1999). These data strongly suggest that a context of imitation,[4] implying interaction between self and others, emphasizes neural systems quite different from the ones engaged by explicit action recognition tasks.

Online Interaction

We just differentiated noninteractional and interactional observations of others. We now differentiate both of them from (3) online interaction. In contrast to the first two cases, online interaction does not involve judgment and attribution, but coordinated actions. Obviously, interacting with others also requires perceiving others. However, this perceptual process is rather different from the ones invoked by noninteractional and interactional observations of others, because the perception of the other is specifically made in an interactional context and does not reduce the other to an object of observation and attribution. As stated by Gallese (2005), when we are involved online with social transactions, we experience a totally different attitude toward the objects of our perceptions. There is actually a shift of the object of our intentional relation. We are no longer directed to the content of a perception in order to categorize it. We are just *attuned to the intentional relation displayed by someone else*. . . . By means of *intentional attunement*, "the other" is much more than a different representational system; it becomes a *person*, like us.

What is relevant in order to differentiate observational and interactional relations with others is the context in which the other is encountered. Some data suggest that the mere looking at other subjects and/or agents involves what we call here an online interaction. It is indeed well-known that observing another's action and executing the same action activates in both cases the so-called mirror neuron system (Gallese et al. 1996; Rizzolatti and Craighero 2004; Rizzolatti and Sinigaglia 2007; Iacoboni 2008). This suggests that even when the task is merely to watch other agents, an interactional link between the self and the other is activated. This same link may not be activated in full in more constrained tasks, for example, when the subject has to attribute some mental and/or physical properties to the other, thus considering the other as an object of observation, judgment, and attribution (Legrand 2007).

The claim that simply facing others in ecological situations already involves an interaction is also supported by data recorded during an experiment where the subject had simply to look at movies showing people interacting (Iacoboni et al. 2004). Interestingly, brain regions that are typically activated in nonecological laboratory situations are not activated by the presentation of the naturalistic social stimuli used in this experiment. The dorsolateral prefrontal cortex, often associated with reasoning, monitoring, and control; the anterior cingulate cortex, also associated with monitoring and control; and the lateral aspect of the posterior parietal cortex, often engaged in attentional tasks, are not activated by the observation of the movie clips, whereas the mirror neuron system is strongly activated together with midline structures that are typically deactivated by almost any task (including the self–other task by Uddin et al. 2005). Overall, the pattern of results obtained by Iacoboni et al. (2004) suggests that watching social interactions continuously engages online (nonattributional) interactions between subject$_{me}$ and subject$_{others}$ rather than a controlled inferential process.

Our point here is to clarify the differences between the three types of self–other relations we have described rather than ironing them out under what could be called a "neuronal signature of other consciousness."[5] The differences between noninteractional observation, interactional observation, and online interaction are not only nominal, as they are reflected at the level of brain activations as we just saw. To further support our position, we will now detail which roles intentional actions and interactions play in online inter*subjective* self–other interactions. Specifically, the next section will bring some content to the claim that the give-and-take processes playing a role in the constitution of intersubjective relations is primarily based on the sharing of a common world between two subjects, through the mediation of their respective goal-directed actions. The third part of this chapter will investigate direct intersubjective relationships and provide some data from cognitive neuroscience suggesting that they are not restricted to inferential attribution of mental states to others (as classical theories of mind suggest) but crucially involve the coordination of self's and others' intentional actions.

Sharing a Common World

Being in a World of Others

Our previous discussion has allowed us to support the idea that genuine intersubjective relations primarily involve two subjects interacting online. This part intends to show that such intersubjectivity allows the understanding of a basic form of self–others relation: the sharing by the self and the other of a common world upon which they can both act.

The idea that some intersubjectivity can be found in the subject's relation to the world has been defended in different forms in phenomenology. As recalled by Zahavi (2001, p. 156, note 2),

> in *Being and Nothingness*, Sartre nicely sums up Husserl's position in the following manner: "Thus, each object, far from being constituted as for Kant, by a simple relation to the *subject*, appears in my concrete experience as polyvalent; it is given originally as possessing systems of reference to an indefinite plurality of consciousnesses; it is on the table, on the wall that the Other is revealed to me as that to which the object under consideration is perpetually referred—as well as on the occasion of the concrete appearances of Pierre or Paul" (Sartre 1943, p. 278).

In other words, for these authors, objects of the world are experienced as public. They cannot be reduced to being the self's own intentional objects because they are also experienced by others. This position implies that, prior to the concrete perceptual encounter with another subject, intersubjectivity already exists in the perception of the world. This coreference to a common world bases Husserl's notion of *transcendental intersubjectivity*, which involves the idea that intersubjectivity allows the constitution of the world as objective. Indeed, when the self is able to consider that objects are also experienced by others, his or her relation to those objects is modified: being accessible to others, objects can be experienced as objective.

Although we agree that "Under normal circumstances we understand each other well enough through our shared engagement in the common world" (Zahavi 2001, p. 155), we also acknowledge that this position suffers from an important problem: defining intersubjectivity *beyond* the concrete encounter with other subjects, this view may neglect the specificity of real online interactions (Zahavi 2005). Here, we would like to argue that a "middle course" may be considered, which suggests that intersubjectivity can be based on a real encounter with others mediated by their relations to objects. We will now develop this position.

To better understand the link between oneself, the world, and others, let us first give an example. A predator is pursuing a prey. At one point, the environment presents a hole, providing a potential hiding place for the prey. Both the attentive predator and the despairing prey perceive the hole and act accordingly. The predator changes his trajectory in order to intercept the prey before it enters the hole, and the prey is thus forced to modify its trajectory according to the predator's trajectory. Consider now the next day. The now starving predator is hunting a bigger prey. They cross the same place as the day before, the prey orienting by chance its course toward the hole. This time, however, the hole is too small to hide the prey. The predator thus continues with a direct trajectory toward the prey, not taking into account the hole as a possible hiding place. Thus, what the predator perceives and how he organizes his behavior has changed, according to the relevance of the environment *for the prey*. It means that the way one perceives and acts in the world is modified according to how others perceive and act themselves in the same shared world.

This example provides us with an illustration of the idea that one's being in the world depends on others and on their own relation to the world. What a subject perceives is also made relative to what others can perceive or not: the world is shared. Being in the world is notably for the self to be in a world of others. Here, we thus find the idea that intersubjectivity can be mediated by the self's and other's relations to a common world.

Triangular Relation

The crucial point of our proposal is that a form of intersubjectivity would be based on a triangular relation between the subject, the object, and the other. Indeed, three links are essential: first, the subject is linked to the object, as it perceives it and acts on it; second, the other subject is linked to the object as well; third, the subject is linked to the other in that it recognizes that it is linked to the object. The link between the subject and the other is made through the mediation of the object, by virtue of the fact that the object is reachable not only by the subject itself but also by another subject. Through the inclusion of the other's perspective, the object now exists beyond the context of the self's own restricted access to it. The world is "understood" as reachable by others, and, in that, as exceeding the self's own perspective. This new perspective changes fundamentally one's representation of the world: the world is not for myself exclusively but for "us." In this sense, the self's relation to the world is basically intersubjective. Importantly, this intersubjectivity of one's being in the world as a being in a common world is not produced by a direct link between the self and the other. Rather, self and others are here related through their relation to the world, by the sharing of it. This is what we mean by "triangular relation."[6]

Sharing by Acting

We hold here that a primary form of intersubjectivity takes the form of a sharing of a common world, thanks to the simultaneous existence of both one's and the other's perspective on objects. To clarify the notion of triangular relation we propose here, let us consider the most basic way of having a perspective on the world. To have a perspective is to have an access to the world, access that is particular, limited in that it does not give the whole reality. Our proposition is that the most primary, concrete, and observable way to consider others' perspectives on the world is to consider others' motor accesses to the world, that is, to observe others acting. This approach is the most parsimonious and most relevant to a naturalizing approach, in particular as compared to the ability to imagine that an action could take place or that a perspective could be held (Grush 2001).

The subject accesses the world through its action not only by reaching and grasping objects physically but also by constituting motor representations of objects (Berthoz 1997; Gibson 1979; Paillard 1971, 1991; Varela, Thompson, and Rosch 1991). This position is supported by some electrophysiological recordings, specifically, the recordings of a category of visuomotor neurons in area F5 of the cortex of the macaque monkey (Rizzolatti et al. 1988; Murata et al. 1997). These neurons, called "canonical neurons," show two types of activity. They are active during the execution of a goal-directed action, and they are also active even though the monkey does not execute any movement but is just observing an object that is potentially a goal of action. This period of observation does not have to be followed by any execution of action for these neurons to be activated. Such a pattern of neuronal activity suggests that the subject sees the object through "motor eyes," that is, following motor constraints. The potential interaction of the actor with the object is what gives a meaning to the pictorial description of objects and environment given by the visual system. The activity of canonical neurons illustrates the role of (potential) action for the constitution of the meaning of the world. Indeed, the meaning of the object is not what the subject reads passively from the already written open book of the world. Rather, the subject is the very actor of the content of his or her perception of the world. We are thus in a position to say that, at least in part, the subject sees the object in the context of its own (potential) action. This fact provides the basis for our investigation of the sharing of the world with others at the level of action.

To share the world requires that the motor representation of the object is not limited to one's own action only. More precisely, the subject must be able to entertain a motor representation of the object that is dependent on his or her own action as well as on actions executed by others. This is a way to detach the object from one's own action only and, thus, to share it with others.

The idea that action execution and observation correspond to a triangular relation as described here is strengthened by some neurophysiological evidence, namely, the recording of mirror neurons activity in area F5 of the cortex (Gallese et al. 1996; Rizzolatti et al. 1996; Fadiga et al. 1995; Rizzolatti and Craighero 2004). Mirror neurons activity is widely known as involving a representation of action that provides a link between oneself and others (Gallese and Goldman 1998; Gallese 2001). Here, we will specify how this link can be understood in relation to one's being in the world and being in a world of others.

A first characteristic of mirror neurons, which is where their name comes from, is the mirroring of the actions of the agent and of the observer. Indeed, mirror neurons are active when the subject executes a goal-directed action as when he or she merely observes another agent (the experimenter or another monkey) doing a similar action. This suggests that a partly common representation of action is activated both during action execution and action observation. Moreover, mirror neuron activity is most often correlated with the reaching of the goal, rather than with the way the goal is reached: some neurons are active when the action to grasp a piece of food is done with the hand as well as when it is done with the mouth. Mirror neurons are not active during the observation of the object alone (in contrast to canonical neurons, described above) nor during the observation of the agent alone. Nor are they active in a situation in which the action is mimicked without achieving the goal (Gallese et al. 1996). In this case, the action takes place, but the link between the agent and the object is not completed.

According to this collection of data, mirror neuron activation can be said to correspond to the representation of goal-directed actions. This characteristic of mirror neurons clarifies the sense in which these neurons can be said to "mirror." Indeed, mirror neuron activity links oneself and others through their goal-directed actions, that is, *through their relations to the world*. This is why action execution and action observation correspond to a triangular relation: mirror neurons are active when an agent acts on an object, and when he or she observes another agent acting toward an object, that is, both for the link between the agent and the object, and for the link between another agent and the object. It seems that these neurons provide a basis for the sharing of common representations of the world, through actions directed toward goals. In this sense, these neurons could have been named "sharing neurons." Such a sharing of the world implies a basic intersubjectivity that is acted in concrete self–others encounters mediated through the relation to objects.

Acted Intersubjective Relations

Our approach centered on action makes clear that the process of triangular relation we discuss here, and thus the basic intersubjectivity based on it, does not imply the ability to attribute mental states to oneself nor to others. Rather, what is involved here is motor access to the world and not a mental perspective on it. Agents are related to objects by acting on them, and they are related to each other by observing these goal-directed actions.

In addition, it must be clear that the process of triangular relation described here does not presuppose the ability to entertain interindividual linguistic communication. Moreover, our position highlights the role of others in the cognitive development of an organism—for example, through cooperation or imitation.[7] At a behavioral level, it is evident that the actions of others are taken into account before the development of language. This is especially true for highly social species like humans but is also the case for nonsocial species: most animals have to consider others' action in the environment in order to be efficient predators and not easy preys.

To summarize, our proposal is that a primary intersubjective relation is made possible through the sharing of a common world, by virtue of the execution and observation of goal-directed actions: the goal of one's action becomes represented as something that can be shared in the sense that the object is not only one's own intentional object but also the intentional object of others. Obviously, though, intersubjective relations are not limited to this basic level of triangular relations. We investigate more sophisticated and direct self–others interactions in the next section of the chapter.

Sharing Coordinated Actions

Untheoretical Practice

In developmental psychology, the most classical way to investigate the ability to entertain intersubjective relations uses the so-called false-belief task (Wimmer and Perner 1983). In this kind of experiment, the subject is asked what another person would think and do in the described situation. For example, the subject is told or shown (with drawings) that a person moves a piece of chocolate from a box to a cupboard. Later, a second person, who did not see the piece of chocolate being moved, enters the room. The subject has to tell whether the second person will search for the chocolate in the box or in the cupboard. Four-year-olds generally answer correctly that the second person thinks that the chocolate is in the box, whereas three-year-olds are unable to consider that the other person has different knowledge, and thought, from themselves. They thus answer that the second person thinks that the chocolate is in the cupboard.

Gallagher (2001, 2005, 2008) has raised questions about certain background assumptions that shape the design of such experiments and the interpretation of their results. He points out that in these experiments the task is to predict the mental states and behavior of others with whom the subject is *not* interacting. However, as stated above, a third-person observation does not adequately capture the way we interact with others directly in second-person relationships. Moreover, theories of mind imply that our understanding of others is based on theories or internal simulation. As pointed out by Reddy and Morris (2004), this view hides a mind–behavior dualism, whereas "we do not interpret our action on either an abstract physiological level (I am activating a certain group of muscle) or in terms of a mentalistic performance (I believe P so I will do X). . . . Rather quite naturally we understand our own actions on the highest pragmatic level possible" (Gallagher 2001, p. 88). The same goes for others: "we interpret their actions in terms of their goals and intentions set in contextualized situations, rather than abstractly in terms of their muscle performance or their beliefs" (p. 88). It is "body reading, rather than mind-reading" (p. 90). Far from being only mediated by theories of mind, intersubjective relations rather rely on "practice of mind" (Gallagher 2001).

This position joins the Heideggerian (Heidegger 1927) existential phenomenology in that it conceives our way of being in the world as primarily pragmatic (based on action and interaction according to environmental and contextual factors) rather than mentalistic or conceptual (based on prediction and attribution, mediated by mental contents): "the less we just stare at the hammer-Thing, and the more we seize hold of it and use it, the more primordial does our relationship to it become, and the more unveiledly it is encountered as that which it is" (Heidegger 1927, p. 98). Our position holds the same view on self–others intersubjective relations.

Intersubjective Actions: The Case of Imitation
Neuroscientific experiments investigating online self–others interactions are not easy to implement, since they require that subjects interact online in a scanner, which is practically very difficult at this stage (see also Gallagher 2001, note 18). In this framework, imitation provides an interesting approach for the investigation of this level of online interaction between self and other.

Imitation provides a good example of embodied intersubjective practice. It also makes particularly clear the idea that humans unfold their activities according to a coordinated framework of actions, gestures, and beliefs, expectations that go beyond the individual expression of intentional relations. Imitation is a key factor in the emerging ways of achieving social coordination among toddlers.

What are the neural and cognitive underpinnings of imitation? A variety of systems and cognitive neuroscience approaches, from functional magnetic resonance imaging and positron emission tomography to transcranial magnetic stimulation and neurophysiological recordings, suggest a "minimal neural architecture" for imitation. This minimal neural architecture provides critical computations for imitative behavior and is composed of superior temporal, posterior parietal, and inferior frontal cortex (Iacoboni 2005). The information flow within this large-scale network would go as follows:

• The superior temporal cortex provides a visual description of the observed action to be imitated to posterior parietal neurons matching observation and execution of action (*mirror* neurons).
• The posterior parietal *mirror* neurons provide additional somatosensory information regarding the action to be imitated (Iacoboni et al. 1999), and this information is sent to inferior frontal *mirror* neurons.
• Inferior frontal *mirror* neurons code the goal of the action to be imitated (Iacoboni et al. 1999; Koski et al. 2002).

- Efferent copies of motor commands providing the predicted sensory consequences of the planned imitative actions are sent back to superior temporal sulcus (STS; Iacoboni et al. 2001).
- In STS occurs a matching process between the visual description of the action and the predicted sensory consequences of the planned imitative actions; if there is a good match, the imitative action is initiated; if there is a large error signal, the imitative motor plan is corrected until convergence is reached between the superior temporal description of the action and the description of the sensory consequences of the planned action.

This neural architecture maps onto a computational architecture for motor control composed of internal models (Iacoboni et al. 2007). Internal models are neural mechanisms that can mimic the input–output characteristics of the system. Inverse models are important for motor control, whereas forward models are important for motor learning. An inverse model retrieves the motor plan necessary to reach a desired sensory state. The input of the inverse model is the desired sensory state, and the output of the inverse model is the motor plan necessary to reach that desired sensory state. In our case, the imitator desires to imitate the action of the actor, and an inverse model is created by STS inputting the visual description of the observed action into frontoparietal mirror areas that produce the output of the inverse model, the motor command necessary to imitate the actor. An efferent copy of the motor command (from frontoparietal mirror areas) is fed into STS to create a forward model that allows prediction of the sensory consequences of the planned imitative action. A forward model is a mimic of the motor system, and if the prediction is confirmed by reafferent feedback, then the forward–inverse model pair is reinforced by a "responsibility signal" that assigns high responsibility for imitating that given action to that specific forward–inverse model pair.

Coordinated social activity and complex intentional interactions emerge from this subpersonal architecture for motor control and imitation. The key factor is the thick fabric of our shared social practices. We have observed and performed ourselves the actions that form our shared social practices and our everyday coping skills over and over again. They provide the background against which meaning in social interactions emerge.

The main claim here is that we are at first, originally, initially, in a primal way, agents embedded in interactions. The interactions are made out of a fabric of subpersonal acts, gestures and goals, forward and inverse models. From this fabric, a coordination process emerges at a suprapersonal level, forming the social relation between interacting humans. In all this, the third-person, noninteractional observation of others is oftentimes interfering, clumsily, in the flow of give and take that makes an interaction possible.

Conclusion

The view defended here does not restrict social understanding to inferential mechanisms borrowed from "nonsocial" cognition. Rather, social understanding is embedded in "nontheoretical" cognition, and it does not correspond only to the attribution of mental states to others. Specifically, social understanding is anchored to intentional action, as it implies, in the first place, the understanding of others' action as intentional. That is, the others are not only endowed with mental states but are also agents executing intentional actions toward goals. At this level, self–other relations are interactional, in the sense that they involve two (or more) subjects interacting with each other and with the world through the coordination of their intentional actions.

Notes

1. Note that Husserl has developed different considerations of others, at different levels. He notably introduced the concept of "transcendental intersubjectivity" (Zahavi 2001). We consider this view in more detail in the second part of this chapter.

2. Cf. the third part of this chapter.

3. This distinction between subject and object is not ontological but phenomenological: "object" here means "object of intentional consciousness," and "subject" means "subject of intentional consciousness."

4. More data on imitation are presented in the third part of this chapter.

5. The same is true as well for self-consciousness (Legrand 2003).

6. A similar notion of "triangulation" is also central in Davidson's (1991) theory. By this idea, Davidson argues that knowledge of oneself, knowledge of others, and knowledge of a common objective world form an interdependent set of concepts, no one of which is possible in the absence of the other ones. We will not detail his theory here, since his aim is principally to understand linguistic behavior and thus differs from ours. What remains common is the focus on the relationships between a subject (a speaker, for Davidson; an agent, in our position) and both its social and physical environments.

7. Cf. the third part of this chapter.

References

Berthoz, A. (1997). *Le sens du mouvement*. Paris: Odile Jacob.

Butcher, M. (2003). The subject subject relationship. *Aporia, 13.2*.

Davidson, D. (1991). Three varieties of knowledge. In A. P. Griffiths (Ed.), *A. J. Ayer: Memorial essays* (pp. 153–166). Cambridge: Cambridge University Press.

Decety, J., Grezes, J., Costes, N., Perani, D., Jeannerod, M., Procyk, E., Grassi, F., and Fazio, F. (1997). Brain activity during observation of actions: Influence of action content and subject's strategy. *Brain, 120*, 1763–1777.

Descartes, R. (1641). *Les méditations métaphysiques*. Paris: Nathan. 1983.

Fadiga, L., Fogassi, L., Pavesi, G., and Rizzolatti, G. (1995). Motor facilitation during action observation: A magnetic stimulation study. *Journal of Neurophysiology, 73*, 2608–2611.

Gallagher, S. (2000). Ways of knowing the self and the other. *Arobase, 4*(1–2). [Introduction to the special issue on Ipseity and Alterity; online journal.]

Gallagher, S. (2001). The practice of mind: Theory, simulation or interaction? *Journal of Consciousness Studies, 8*(5–7), 83–108.

Gallagher, S. (2005). *How the body shapes the mind*. Oxford: Oxford University Press.

Gallagher, S. (2008). Direct perception in the intersubjective context. *Consciousness and Cognition, 17*, 535–543.

Gallese, V. (2001). The "shared manifold" hypothesis: From mirror neurons to empathy. *Journal of Consciousness Studies, 8*(5–7), 33–50.

Gallese, V. (2005). Embodied simulation: From neurons to phenomenal experience. *Phenomenology and the Cognitive Sciences, 4*, 23–48.

Gallese, V., Fadiga, L., Fogassi, L., and Rizzolatti, G. (1996). Action recognition in the premotor cortex. *Brain, 119*(Pt. 2), 593–609.

Gallese, V., and Goldman, A. (1998). Mirror neurons and the simulation theory of mind-reading. *Trends in Cognitive Science, 2*, 493–501.

Gibson, J. J. (1979). *The ecological approach to visual perception*. Boston: Houghton Mifflin.

Grezes, J., Costes, N., and Decety, J. (1998). Top down effect of strategy on the perception of human biological motion: A PET investigation. *Cognitive Neuropsychology, 15*, 553–582.

Grezes, J., Costes, N., and Decety, J. (1999). The effects of learning and intention on the neural network involved in the perception of meaningless actions. *Brain, 122*, 1875–1887.

Grush, R. (2001). Self, world and space: The meaning and mechanisms of ego- and allocentric representation. *Brain and Mind*, 1(1), 59–92.

Hegel, G. W. F. (1807). *Phénoménologie de l'esprit*. Paris: Vrin, 1997.

Heidegger, M. (1927). *Being and time* (Joan Stambaugh, Trans.). Albany: State University of New York Press, 1953.

Husserl, E. (1929). *Les méditations Cartésiennes et les Conférences de Paris*. Paris: Presses Universitaires de France, coll. Epiméthée, 1994.

Iacoboni, M. (2005). Understanding others: Imitation, language, empathy. In S. Hurley and N. Chater (Eds.), *Perspectives on imitation: From mirror neurons to memes*. Cambridge: MIT Press.

Iacoboni, M. (2008). *Mirroring people*. New York: Farrar, Straus and Giroux.

Iacoboni, M., Kaplan, J., and Wilson, S. (2007). A neural architecture for imitation and intentional relations. In K. Dautenhahn and C. Nehaniv (Eds.), *Imitation and social learning in robots, humans and animals: Behavioural, social and communicative dimensions*. Cambridge: Cambridge University Press.

Iacoboni, M., Koski, L., Brass, M., Bekkering, H., Woods, R. P., Dubeau, M.-C., Mazziotta, J. C., and Rizzolatti, G. (2001). Re-afferent copies of imitated actions in the right superior temporal cortex. *Proceedings of the National Academy of Sciences USA*, 98, 13995–13999.

Iacoboni, M., Lieberman, M. D., Knowlton, B. J., Molnar-Szakacs, I., Moritz, M., Throop, C. J., and Fiske, A. P. (2004). Watching social interactions produces dorsomedial prefrontal and medial parietal BOLD fMRI signal increases compared to a resting baseline. *NeuroImage*, 21, 1167–1173.

Iacoboni, M., Woods, R. P., Brass, M., Bekkering, H., Mazziotta, J. C., and Rizzolatti, G. (1999). Cortical mechanisms of human imitation. *Science*, 286, 2526–2528.

Kircher, T. T., Senior, C., Phillips, M. L., Rabe-Hesketh, S., Benson, P. J., Bullmore, E. T., Brammer, M., Simmons, A., Bartels, M., and David, A. S. (2001). Recognizing one's own face. *Cognition*, 78, B1–B15.

Koski, L., Wohlschläger, A., Bekkering, H., Woods, R. P., Dubeau, M.-C., Mazziotta, J. C., and Iacoboni, M. (2002). Modulation of motor and premotor activity during imitation of target-directed actions. *Cerebral Cortex*, 12, 847–855.

Legrand, D. (2003). How not to find the neural signature of self-consciousness. *Consciousness and Cognition*, 12, 544–546.

Legrand, D. (2007). Naturalizing the acting self: Subjective vs. anonymous agency. *Philosophical Psychology*, 20, 457–478.

Merleau-Ponty, M. (1962). *Phenomenology of perception* (Trans. Colin Smith). London: Routledge.

Murata, A., Fadiga, L., Fogassi, L., Gallese, V., Raos, V., and Rizzolatti, G. (1997). Object representation in the ventral premotor cortex (area F5) of the monkey. *Journal of Neurophysiology*, 78, 2226–2230.

Paillard, J. (1971). Les déterminants moteurs de l'organisation de l'espace. *Cahiers de psychologie*, 14, 261–316.

Paillard, J. (1991). Knowing where and knowing how to get there. In J. Paillard (Ed.), *Brain and space* (pp. 461–481). Oxford: Oxford University Press.

Reddy, V., and Morris, P. (2004). Participants don't needs theories: Knowing minds in engagement. *Theory and Psychology*, 14, 647–665.

Rizzolatti, G., Camarda, R., Fogassi, L., Gentilucci, M., Luppino, G., and Matelli, M. (1988). Functional organization of inferior area 6 in the macaque monkey: II. Area F5 and the control of distal movements. *Experimental Brain Research*, 71, 491–507.

Rizzolatti, G., and Craighero, L. (2004). The mirror-neuron system. *Annual Review of Neuroscience*, 27, 169–192.

Rizzolatti, G., Fadiga, L., Gallese, V., and Fogassi, L. (1996). Premotor cortex and the recognition of motor actions. *Brain Research: Cognitive Brain Research*, 3, 131–41.

Rizzolatti, G., and Sinigaglia, C. (2007). *Mirrors in the brain*. Oxford: Oxford University Press.

Sartre, J. P. (1943). *L'être et le néant: Essai d'ontologie phénoménologique*. Paris: Gallimard.

Uddin, L. Q., Kaplan, J. T., Molnar-Szakacs, I., Zaidel, E., and Iacoboni, M. (2005). Self-face recognition activates a frontoparietal "mirror" network in the right hemisphere: An event-related fMRI study. *NeuroImage*, 25, 926–935.

Varela, F., Thompson, E., and Rosch, E. (1991). *The embodied mind: Cognitive science and human experience*. Cambridge: MIT Press.

Wimmer, H., and Perner, J. (1983). Beliefs about beliefs: Representation and constraining function of wrong beliefs in young children's understanding of deception. *Cognition*, 13, 103–128.

Zahavi, D. (2001). Beyond empathy: Phenomenological approaches to intersubjectivity. *Journal of Consciousness Studies*, 8(5–7), 151–167.

Zahavi, D. (2005). *Subjectivity and selfhood: Investigating the first-person perspective*. Cambridge: MIT Press.

12 Intention-in-Interaction

Albert Ogien

In the chapter entitled "Are Meanings in the Head?" of his book *Intentionality*, John Searle totally rejects the anti-internalist conceptions of intention which, according to him, falsely "suggest that in order to account for the relations between words and the world we need to introduce ... external contextual, non-conceptual, causal relations between the utterance of expressions and the features of the world that the utterance is about" (Searle 1983, p. 199). He claims that the term intention must exclusively be used to refer to the mental state of an individual. He thus asserts that

> some form of internalism must be right because there isn't anything else to do the job. The brain is all we have for the purpose of representing the world to ourselves and everything we can use must be inside the brain. ... Intentionality is a biological phenomenon and is part of the natural world like any other biological phenomenon. (Searle 1983, p. 200)

The kind of naturalization Searle advocates here is too embracing to be convincing. In particular, it does not solve a problem: How is an intention to be identified? Searle gives an unsteady answer to this question. He pleads for a "dualist conception" which combines, on the one hand, a Background (which is like a warehouse where all the contents that might be attributed to an intentional state at a given time and in a given society are stored) and a Network (which is a kind of predetermined set of desires and beliefs defining the conditions of satisfaction related to a particular intentional state), and, on the other hand, an intention-in-action (the actualization in a social relation of an appropriate ready-made intention that has been picked up from the Background).[1] For all its merits, Searle's theory offers no explanation of where this stock of intentions comes from in the first place; how is a specific intention picked out by an individual to fit the actual circumstance in which it is used; what kind of reactions does this use elicit from others? These questions are sociological in nature rather than philosophical.

Sociology—or the type of interactionist approach advocated by Goffman (1974) and Garfinkel (2002) at least—defends a "monist" conception of intention, which denies the validity of the kind of cognitive division of labor Searle has introduced between Background and intention-in-action. A mass of sociological data has yet demonstrated that coordination of action seldom requires computation or deliberation by individuals engrossed in interaction since they possess a sufficiently accurate sense of what is going on between them—that is, they approximately know what their mutual intentions are. Moreover, the sociological tradition supplies very plausible arguments allowing the assertion that no individual is free to decide by himself or herself—that is, irrelatively to the actual circumstances of an ongoing interaction—what his or her or somebody else's intention is or should be. Thus, instead of assuming that intention is a subjective state or the cause of an individual behavior, sociologists—when they adopt an externalist stance—would rather consider it as a justification individuals are accustomed to use *in and for* action.

From a sociological point of view, then, intention is *public* (what one is able to intend in a given circumstance is an element of commonsense knowledge and is therefore probably shared by all the partners in interaction), *anticipated* (the intention one might entertain in a given situation has to be appropriate to the type of activity in which one is engaged), and *reflexive* (the goal one initially aims at can be radically modified in the course of an interaction to match up to unexpected events and new orientations). (One can pretend that these three properties respecify sociologically G. E. M. Anscombe's [1957] groundbreaking definition of intention.)

The externalist stance rules out that intention should be found in an individual's brain (the place where Searle would locate it). Where, then, should the sociologist turn to approach the phenomenon and to give an empirical description of it: in the world, in language, or elsewhere? To outline the answers sociology is qualified to give to that question, I will first try to demonstrate the current availability to individuals of what I call "social identification criteria of intention" (which are incorporated in these "social things" that are roles, situations, and concepts of ordinary language). I will then hypothesize that these criteria exert logical constraints on the process of intention imputation occurring in specific contexts of action. And, to conclude, I will briefly argue that there is no need to consider these social identification criteria as "repertoires" comparable (both in objectivity and efficiency) to those neurophysiology or developmental psychology have discovered in the sensorimotor sphere.

Intention in Sociology

When a sociologist views intention as a justification devised to account for action rather than as a mental state or as a cause of behavior, he or she has to stand the test of objectivity: How would the sociologist demonstrate that two individuals understand the intention an action is supposed to express in the "same way"? This question is usually turned into an empirical problem that is addressed by collecting appropriate data about the ways individuals manage to "read" somebody else's "intentions" and correctly adjust their reaction to them even though these intentions are not explicitly stated in the course of action.

Max Weber has suggested a theoretical solution to this problem, claiming that the possibility of understanding the reasons which might account for individual behaviors depends on the fact that the intentions these behaviors are supposed to express have a collective dimension. According to him, there only exists a specified "chance" (in the probabilistic sense of the term) for an intention (or what he calls a "motive") to be apprehended as such. This chance is measured by two variables: expectations based on past regularities which have never been deceived and rules of rationality and intelligibility supposedly shared by every member of a social group (Turner and Factor 1981). Understanding others in the course of an action is then, according to Weber, a kind of bet one directly makes on the chance (or degree of probability) a motivated and legitimated event or behavior has to occur in a given circumstance. Weber's position is externalist in a very unusual sense: it advocates that the reasons that can be given to explain an action (or an intention) are socially predefined but only in a probabilistic way. The trouble with Weber's outlook is that it ultimately relates this predefinition to a mechanism: socialization, which produces a belief in the legitimacy of a system of norms and values imposed by a society (or a social group) on its members.

G. H. Mead (1934) urged, at about the same time, consideration of socialization from a "social behaviorist" standpoint. He conjectured that it originates in an evolutionary process founded on a basic human faculty: the "ability to be the other at the same time as he is himself" (Mead 1922, p. 161). Mead did conceive of this ability as a natural property of joint action, or, to use his words, of a "conversation of gestures" in the course of which an act made by an individual awaits the response it gets from relevant others to achieve its significance. Moreover, Mead claimed that the responses that fit the act—which are distributed in the environment—are directly given so that the process of "act completion" requires neither deliberation nor computation on the part of individuals. Mead's claim is reciprocal: fitting responses can be anticipated since individuals are drilled to pick them up when they find themselves in the position of the other (Ogien 2007b, pp. 157–177). Expanding Mead's conception of the human ability "to take the place of the other" in a way he would probably have disallowed, one can derive an argument for an externalist conception of intention—namely, that one should not define an intention without considering the process through which individuals take into account the expectations that they suppose are those of their partners in interaction (Ogien 2007a). In other words, an externalist conception should admit that typicality is a fundamental feature of intention—which means that one is not free to have intentions that a social group of reference deems inacceptable for one of its member to entertain.

Inspired by Weber's and Mead's insights, an "interactionist" sociology has developed, the aim of which was to discover and analyze the social organization of interaction, that is, the inner constraints guiding the accomplishment of practical activities as they get actualized in the sequentiality of joint action. One knows that this approach has been devised to challenge a tradition largely dominated by the determinist thesis according to which social order is enforced by a system of norms imposed by "the" society on its members, the prescriptions of which are mechanically enacted by subservient individuals.

The interactionist approach grants, on the contrary, a certain degree of autonomy to actors. It claims that individuals have to accomplish the joint action they are engaged in, and that to do so they necessarily have to give some intelligibility to what's going on between them, that is, to instate a relation between observed behaviors (which implies an ordering procedure) and the intentions these behaviors are supposed to express (which implies a categorization procedure). When a sociologist adopts this perspective, he or she ceases to view intention as a mental state: he or she admits instead that it has to be empirically accounted for through a description of the procedures individuals make use of to recognize and attribute an intention in an appropriate and acceptable way.

The interactionist approach hypothesizes that an essential feature of these procedures is the multitude of identification criteria that are to be sifted out from the direct environment of action to inform the ordinary methods individuals use to recognize and attribute an intention. This hypothesis may seem circular or tautological. To put it to test, this chapter will thus focus on three questions:

1. Do a class of identification criteria exist the use of which enables individuals to attribute intentions (to themselves and to others) in such or such circumstance of action?
2. Can one say that these criteria guide the practical reasoning of all the members of a social group in an identical way, that is, that they are collectively shared?
3. Do such procedures of practical reasoning make individuals produce "moves" in interaction that are adjusted in advance to the changing intentions of their partners?

To answer these questions, two empirical propositions will be discussed: (1) identification criteria of intention are inherent to three constitutive elements of a context of action, namely, roles, situations, and the concepts of ordinary language, and (2) the compelling use of these criteria plays a major part in shaping the practices of ordering and categorizing through which coordination of joint action emerge. Let us turn now to the analysis of the three "social things" that have just been referred to.

Roles

Though a reference to the notion of role can be found in the works of Pareto and Weber, and appears in the social behaviorism of Mead, it is R. Linton (1936) who gave it a sociological definition, introducing the now famous distinction between status and role. According to Linton, the first of these two notions should qualify the sum of rights and duties structurally attached to an institutionalized position in a social system, and the second one would name the type of behavior that should be adopted by the individual who puts these rights and duties in application. This distinction, and the corollary assertion that the two notions are complementary, has turned to be a standard component of the social theory of action.

According to S. Nadel (1957), Linton's distinction is troublesome since no methodological rule instructs the analyst in how to draw a clear separation between status and role. To overcome the confusion, he proposes specifying the notion of role, claiming it has to be used only to qualify a *class* of individuals, constituted on the basis of a finite list of attributes and properties. Nadel then turns to another puzzlement: does every action require the endorsement of a role? According to him, a behavior (riding a bike, eating, or reading) can refer to a role only when those who accomplish it are viewed in relation to an institutionalized way to actualize this behavior (professional cyclist, gastronomical critic, or manuscript reader in a publishing house). He consequently contends that the obligations attached to a role emanate from a socially organized form of practical activity. In other words, playing a role amounts to acting in accordance with principles and maxims that can be explicitly stated, and abiding by them should normally guarantee that an individual behavior is appropriate to the ongoing flux of social transactions.

Goffman's theory of interaction (1961a) pushes Nadel's analysis a step further. He decomposes the notion of role into three constitutive dimensions: its normative side, its typical side, and its representation (in the theatrical sense of the term). The normative side of role is defined by ideal rules of conduct one should follow to adequately perform the function a particular role is supposed to fulfill in a specific sphere of action. Its typical side refers to the qualities currently associated with the individual who plays such or such role. An important point Goffman hints at here is the following: since the way the qualities affixed to a role are to be displayed is never codified, the correctness of a representation is only and entirely assessed by the partners of interaction. For example, a police officer should keep his nerve, know and enforce the law, and be polite and trustworthy, and a physician should speak and dress in an elegant fashion, have good manners, show perfect mastery of medical skills, and know how to adequately write his prescriptions. The smoothness of the transactions in which police officers or physicians are involved will depend on the assessment citizens or patients make about the correctness their behavior exhibits. The third dimension of role, representation, has more specifically to do with the sequentiality of the interaction during which an individual occupies a given position trying neither to breach the ideal norms nor to fail to display the typical expected but unstated qualities.

This decomposition leads Goffman to formulate three propositions: (1) there is no strict codification of the behavior that should be adopted concerning an essential part of the role (its typical side and its representation): one has to behave in the way one believes fits the expectations that others would probably entertain about the role one plays; (2) a role has necessarily a practical nature, since it is always within a "system of situated activity" that it is actualized in the unique representation that is given of it; (3) a role exists independent of the individual who happens to play and represent it.

These propositions turn the use of the notion of intention into a rather problematical exercise. According to Goffman, the same person can be described in a thousand different ways almost at the same time; and he or she is able to switch from one to another of his or her multiple facets in the course of the same interaction, the only condition being that these shifts do not jeopardize the central role this individual plays in a specific situated activity. Here is the example Goffman gives to illustrate his "simultaneity of multiple identities" thesis (Ogien 1999): a surgeon can publicly express the most common human desires while practicing surgery as long as he or she performs the surgical operation in the most professional way.

Goffman's role theory decomposes the identity of the subject in such a dramatic way that it seems to entirely dissolve what we think constitutes the individual: his or her moral responsibility. If a human being is just a succession of roles, which can be contradictory and incoherent and from which one can always distance oneself (Goffman 1961a), it seems difficult, or doubtful, to confer a consistent identity to anyone or even to know who is to be held as responsible for the representation of all these roles. Goffman does not really solve this problem: he simply acknowledges that since human beings obviously have a physical identity, they can be described in terms of a single individual biography (Goffman 1964). However, this acknowledgement appears to be more a concession to reality than a plain conception of individual identity.

Since Goffman admits that the essential dimension of role is its representation (in the theatrical sense of the term), the model of interaction he favors combines four principles: (1) the role is a set of practical rules (instructions, principles, maxims) one has to learn and follow correctly if one intends to play it the adequate way in a given context; (2) behaving according to these rules cannot merely be reduced to drill or interiorization: if one knows what rules are supposed to govern the representation of a role, one knows, by the same token, those governing the representation of the complementary and rival roles that are typically associated with it (e.g., being a patient implies knowing what being a physician should be); (3) the representation of a role is always accomplished in the presence of others (who unremittingly assess the appropriateness and quality of the performance) and calls for the reckoning of the prerogatives normally attached to the other roles involved in this circumstance of action; and (4) knowing what is required to perform a role implies also learning to deal with uncertainty and ambiguity: if playing a role amounts to endorsing a "social identity" during the time a sequence of action lasts, it is also, as Goffman reminds us, endorsing a typical character one can play *at* (which is a condition of the possibility of deception).

It is time now to return to identification criteria of intention. If one accepts the relevance of Goffman's dynamic and realist model of interaction, one can claim that a first series of such criteria are constitutive of the roles that we necessarily endorse in our everyday dealings. One can assert that these criteria are probably shared by a majority of the members of an organized community, since everyone has to play a multiplicity of roles in his or her current life. Playing a role does not simply amount to acting mechanically according to a status but requires the mobilization of the social knowledge needed to take the complementary roles into account and to live up to the expectations of others. As already mentioned, a physician can understand the way such or such patient is going to behave because he or she has already been one or is susceptible to becoming one someday; and inversely, the patient has an idea about the way a physician should behave because he or she has already met one or has some clues about what a physician is supposed to do. One of the lessons that can possibly be drawn from Goffman's role theory is the following: identification criteria of intention are inherent to the idea everyone has about what endorsing such or such role should imply and the way these criteria should be used in such or such context. These ideas are regularly reinforced and updated in the unceasing flow of interactions which constitutes everyday life. Let's turn now to the second "social thing" that supposedly encapsulates another series of identification criteria of intention: the situation.

Situations

Goffman has imposed the idea that interaction is an order of reality which incorporates the principles of its organization in itself. His analyses have demonstrated that the mere material requirements inherent in copresence and in the necessities of cooperation create a regime of constraints to which all the parties to a social relationship do defer, as long as they intend to honor the engagement they have contracted. These immanent requirements are the foundations on which interaction can emerge, unfold, and stop in a mutually satisfying way (A. W. Rawls 1987). A first series of these inner constraints lies in the obligation to abide by the rules of politeness and reciprocity. According to Goffman, these constraints are not mandatory: they are embedded in a constantly kept in mind principle which commands one to always act so as to "save the face of the other." Another series of constraints derives from an essential condition of possibility of social transactions: the a priori admission of the other's truthfulness, that is, one has to admit, though not unconditionally, that others really do what they seem to be doing and really mean what they say. A third series of constraints is linked to the nature of the activity actualized by the ongoing interaction, that is, by the "situation." According to Goffman, the mere fact that one knows what kind of activity one is involved in implies a reference to a set of "acceptability constraints" (Ogien 1991) which compels those who act to follow partially defined norms, of conduct or of talk, allowing them to give and preserve intelligibility to what they do—either by conjecture or on the basis of an explicit mutual agreement. What, then, is a situation? It is a kind of envelope (a "membrane" says Goffman) which cuts off a fragment of the social world and operates as a filter which selects, among all the obligations individuals have to defer to, those which are relevant to the actual circumstances of action.

In sum, the notion of situation qualifies, for Goffman, a typical and relatively stable frame which organizes beforehand the kind of behavior that must, at a certain time, occur in it. These frames preexist with respect to the engagement of individuals in an interaction and survive to its termination. In this sense, the situation possesses the sociological features of an institution and thus provides some of the identification criteria (impersonal and supposedly shared) that are used to attribute (to oneself and to others) intentions in a specific context of action.

Let's go a step further. Even though the situation circumscribes a specific modality of action and defines the form a particular activity might take, these pregiven limits do not work in a deterministic fashion: they are always transitory references in permanent rearrangement. One can admit that an individual caught in a situation more or less knows what he or she has to do in such or such case (sending a letter, drinking coffee, drawing a circle on a paper, sawing a piece of cloth, discussing the terms of a contract, teaching a class, etc.) but that the way in which he or she does it builds itself up step-by-step in the course of doing it, and by reconsidering, at each of these steps, the unity and coherence of the ongoing action. Each situation represents a kind of field of variation, and what distinguishes one of these fields from another is only the number and complexity of the constraints it imposes:[2] sending a postcard, organizing a mass meeting, doing an arithmetical exercise, or ruling a nation are situations the form and nature of which impose different obligations on those who accomplish them. And insofar as one can think that members of the same social group are currently involved in a multitude of similar practical activities, one can say that they share, even though very approximately, a similar knowledge about the situations they find themselves in and the acceptability constraints attached to each of them. One is then allowed to suppose that the "moves" individuals might make in a situation have a good chance of being sufficiently adequate to let coordination emerge. This is probably why Goffman conceives of interaction as an "order *sui generis*" (to use A. W. Rawls's qualification), that is, the obligations entailed in it are not thought of as external constraining forces but inhere in the social principles of cooperation and reciprocity that any human being necessarily masters. Goffman writes as follows:

The elements and processes [the individual] assumes in his reading of the activity often *are* ones that the activity itself manifests—and why not, since social life itself is often organized as something that the individuals will be able to understand and deal with. A correspondence or isomorphism is thus claimed between perception and the organization of what is perceived, in spite of the fact that there are likely to be many valid principles of organization that could but don't inform perception." (Goffman 1974, p. 26)

Let's sum up. For Goffman, the situation is a structure of constraints which (1) imposes the use of a given range of descriptive categories as a means of ordering the things, events, and behaviors observed in the course of practical activity; (2) defines adequate ways to play the roles that are specific to this activity; and (3) provides indications about the propensities of the action[3] that can possibly be accomplished in it. This structure of constraints controls the engagement in action as well as the assessments of the moves and utterances produced by the interacting partners. It also provides a series of rules of transformation[4] that enable individuals to revise, when needed, the way a criterion is used or the practical significations conferred to these things, events, and intentions.

According to this conception, what one is able to think one should do in a given circumstance cannot outreach the limits of a "possible" which is entailed *in* a situation. Though one can admit that such a "possible" is never entirely defined, one has nevertheless to acknowledge that the situation exerts a compelling force simply by virtue of being a typical and approximately stabilized form of environment which specifies what each activity it frames might be and the directions in which it should evolve. Hence, a situation incorporates a series of identification criteria that allow individuals to confer (to themselves and to others) intentions in context.

Concepts

A third kind of "social thing" can be considered as a source of identification criteria of intention: the concept. To assess the relevance of this proposition, one has to evoke Cassirer's theory of the concept, which strangely echoes the way Durkheim has defined the sociological properties of the concept as well as the ethnomethodological considerations on the reflexive nature of practical reasoning (Ogien 2007b, pp. 79–106).

A generally admitted view asserts that knowledge has two sources: intuition and concept (Heidegger 1971). According to Cassirer, this classical distinction rests upon another one, which, he claims, is of greater importance: whereas intuition is related to perception, conceptual knowledge is directly associated with the capacity of thought (Cassirer 1953). In *Substance and Function*, Cassirer (1923) rejects the validity of this second distinction: he contends that intuition is, just like conceptual knowledge, a construction resting on a form of thought. He then proposes a theory of conceptualization based on an analysis of the operation which constitutes knowledge: abstraction. For Cassirer, this operation consists in relating

a present content to a past content and to comprehend the two as in some respect identical. This synthesis, which connects and binds together the two temporally separated conditions, possesses no immediate sensible correlate in the contents compared. According to the manner and direction in which this synthesis takes place, the same sensuous material can be apprehended under very different conceptual forms." (Cassirer 1923, p. 15)

Cassirer does not stop his description of abstraction here. His analysis further reveals a more primitive operation, which is constitutive of the activity of abstraction itself: the ordering of perceptions into "series of similar." He writes as follows:

Without a process of arranging in series, without running through the different instances, the consciousness of their generic connection—and consequently the abstract object—could never arise. This transition from member to member, however, manifestly presupposes a *principle* according to which it takes place, and by which the form of dependence between each member and the succeeding one, is determined. Thus from this point of view also it appears that all construction of concepts is connected with some definite form of construction of series. We say that a sensuous manifold is conceptually apprehended and ordered, when its members do not stand next to one another without relation but proceed from a definite beginning, according to a fundamental generating relation, in necessary sequence. It is the identity of this generating relation, maintained through changes in the particular contents, which constitutes the specific form of the concept. (Cassirer 1923, p. 15)

In Cassirer's detailed analysis, the activity of abstraction consists *simultaneously* in continuously instating relations between the elements of the "perceptual given" and maintaining their stability through the vicissitudes and contextual variations that put their precarious acceptability to test. Cassirer's conception of abstraction is reflexive (in the sense ethnomethodology gives to the notion): to know is to connect elements of an environment, and the form taken by this connection depends on the circumstances in which it occurs. From this point of view, a concept does not refer to an entity defined in terms of sufficient and necessary conditions. Its variable content emerges in a movement in which each former arrangement of elements sets the conditions under which the latter might be ordered. Cassirer proposes, then, a dramatic change in the conception of the concept:

> What lends the theory of abstraction support is merely the circumstance that it does not presuppose the contents, out of which the concept is to develop, as *disconnected particularities*, but that it tacitly thinks them in the form of an ordered manifold from the first. The concept however, is not deduced thereby, but presupposed; for when we ascribe to a manifold an order and connection of elements, we have already presupposed the concept, if not in its complete form, yet in its fundamental function. (Cassirer 1923, p. 17)

Arguing that the concept is presupposed rather than derived—that is, that it organizes and controls knowledge instead of resulting from it—Cassirer further topples the classical theoretical construction: not only does he claim that intuition and conceptual knowledge rest on the same procedures of abstraction but he furthermore adds that the concept must preexist with respect to intuition if an object is to be apprehended. From this point of view, the concept does not refer to a *substance* that could be defined in terms of necessary and sufficient conditions but to the *function*[5] it directly fulfills in the activity of abstraction; and that function consists in instating a particular type of nomological relationship. According to Cassirer,

> the characteristic feature of the concept is not the "universality" of a presentation, but the universal validity of a principle of serial order. We do not isolate any abstract part whatever from the manifold before us, but we create for its members a definite relation by thinking of them as bound together by an inclusive law (Cassirer 1923, p. 20).

I have probably said enough by now on Cassirer's theory of the concept. What we have been reminded of here allows us to suggest that using a concept is at the same time establishing a given relationship between particulars (an occurrence in an environment) and a generality (the class of things this occurrence can immediately be related to), and such a relationship must be instated within the bounds of a specific "realm of acceptability" which is itself in constant rearrangement in the dynamics of action. In other words, the mere fact of making use of a concept sets about an unnoticed procedure: the implementation of nonformal logic operations. From this point of view, the concept possesses an irreducible duality: it entails both the elements of a definition of the entity it qualifies *and* the modalities according to which one instates a relationship between these elements that is adjusted to the circumstances *in and for* which it has been instated.

If Cassirer's thesis about the constitutive duality of the concept[6] can be viewed as a contribution to the description of knowledge as it expresses itself in action, it still confronts the traditional contradiction which burdens the notion of definition: Would it be possible to identify an object without possessing any a priori idea about the identity of this object? Just as all those who advocate the essential variability of significations and admit the irremediable reflexivity of practical reasoning (like Wittgenstein or Garfinkel inter alia), Cassirer claims that to make use of a concept is an activity in which a word, *and* the objects it might name, *and* the acceptable uses it might accept are indistinctly intermingled. And when one accepts that no straightforward separation can be introduced between language, world, and thought, one comes to think that it is acknowledging such a separation, which is inane. Another way to consider the dynamics of the concept can be discovered in Durkheim's theory of knowledge, which gives, as it were, a sociological twist to Cassirer's.

The original question Durkheim (1995) tries to answer in *The Elementary Forms of Religious Life* is the following: How is one to account for the passage of the concepts which are created by society into the minds of individuals? Durkheim's answer is formulated in the same outdated terminology as the one used in his question: he claims that a slow process of individualization of the faculty of thought has taken place which has brought forth the inscription of the "collective representations" a society develops into each of its members' brain. One has to recall that, in Durkheim's thesis, the general categories of the understanding and the concepts of ordinary language that constitute the human faculty of thought emanate directly from social life. In contemporaneous terms, Durkheim's radical and still stimulating claim is that cognition is social through and through (Bloor 1983; Livet 2002; A. W. Rawls 2004).

Durkheim's argument is simple: since it entails the principle of an obligation, the concept is an institution. And, as such, it has two indivisible properties: immovability (a word survives as long as it is part of a lively lexicon) and universability (a concept can, according to the circumstances, be used to qualify a multitude of unexpected entities). Durkheim claims that these properties are dynamically connected: they confer at the same time sufficient stability and sufficient variability to the terms of ordinary language so as to enable individuals to assign and maintain a sense of mutual understanding about what is going on when they act together. A question remains unanswered though: What kind of constraint does the concept exert, and how does it exert it? Let's now turn to that question.

Whether it refers to an object, a property, or a function (Peacocke 1991), the concept has an essential feature: it always is "the concept of something" (Pettit 1991).[7] The sociologist is inclined to complement this philosophical statement by insisting that all the "somethings" concepts do refer to are unfailingly apprehended and named in the course of an action accomplished in common and in pubic. Empirical inquiry has shown, as I said earlier, that each form of practical activity and each situation set in advance the specific conditions in which concepts can be used in ordinary descriptions and circumscribe the range of acceptable significations one can give to them.

Let's summarize what has been suggested so far. Though the idea that the content of a concept is susceptible of multiple rearrangements (even surprising ones) in the course of social interactions came finally to be largely accepted, such an acknowledgement does not allow claiming that these rearrangements are boundless. Should it actually be possible to mean something by using whatever term in whatever circumstance, one would soon find oneself in a world that one is simply unacquainted with. We still have no good reason to believe that the numerous uses of the same word can vary inconsistently. One might better suppose that the procedures implemented to order the way we apprehend the world to act jointly are loosely defined and controlled. This is the stand I have taken in the description of the three regimes of constraints which supposedly incorporate social identification criteria of intention: roles, which specify the kind of intention one can possibly attribute (to oneself or to others) in relation with the social identity one has temporarily endorsed; situations, which restrict the area within which an acceptable justification can be given by invoking such or such intention; and concepts, the mere existence of which delineates a space of variability of the significations one can give to the word intention in a description.

The condensed analysis I have submitted here has tried to explain what allows a sociologist to say he or she is founded to claim that conceptual constraints impose, on a group of partners in interaction, the use of sufficiently similar identification criteria of intention, and that this enables them to make sense, in the course of action, of what everyone is doing. However, does this claim really entitle one to assert that individuals are able to attribute intentions supposedly expressed in behavior in the same mutually intelligible way?

The Invocation of Intention and Its Logical Constraints

Intentional concepts are words one usually uses to relate an individual behavior to the desires, beliefs, aims or ambitions that have motivated it. The use of such a word is guided by the logical constraints governing the attribution of mental predicates. These constraints have been accurately described by G. Ryle (1949) in his grammatical analysis of dispositions.

Ryle's idea is that dispositional concepts are used, as intentional concepts are, in a specific type of phrase: lawlike sentences, the essential feature of which being to refer to both justifications and empirical propositions. On the one hand, these sentences instate a relation between two elements[8] by placing one in the position of a "cause" and the other in the position of its "effect"; on the other hand, this relation has a particular content since it refers to a given disposition—or intention—which has supposedly been displayed in a given circumstance. Ryle notices that dispositional or intentional sentences cannot be considered as lawlike sentences since "they do not refer to particular objects or human beings," whereas laws only apply to generalities. Nevertheless, he claims that one can consider these two types of sentences as if they were belonging to the same kind since they are about phenomena or events regularly "causing" predictable effects, even though not in the absolute and certain way science gives to causation.

Ryle admits, then, that a proposition invoking a disposition or an intention provides, as lawlike sentences do, what he calls an "inference ticket": it allows someone to draw practical conclusions and to act according to them. The sociologist may suggest that these inference tickets are issued and used *in and for* ongoing interactions, and henceforth that their content depends on the practical circumstances in which "doing an inference" occurs. This claim is also cogent for intention. Making use of a "vocabulary of intentionality" is seldom an operation done in an office or in a laboratory, nor is it a computation accomplished by a mind totally severed from all social relations (though it is still possible and legitimate to define intention in a purely abstract or theoretical way). It is more often a public phenomenon: the acceptability of any imputation of intention is systematically put to the test in the ongoing action and can be revised at will when a failure, a misunderstanding, or an error are supposed to have occurred or have actually been noticed by others.

Ryle's inferential conception of intention and the sociological conception of intention as justification can be juxtaposed. One may then contend that the imputation of an intention emerges within a structure of constraints which circumscribes, beforehand, the approximate content such an imputation might take, that is, a pregiven structure sets the objective limits (in the sense of seemingly mutually shared) within which an intention can actually be imputed. And in what precedes, I have tried to demonstrate that a set of identification criteria of intention (incorporated in roles, situations, and concepts) do circumscribe these objective limits.

When one admits that invoking an intention serves as a justification one makes use of in an ongoing action and within a set of logical and sociological frames that constrain it, one is led to propose an enlarged definition of the notion of intention. Instead of reducing it to a particular substantial content to which a dubious causal efficiency is granted, it should better be apprehended by considering the function the vocabulary of intentionality fulfills in ordinary practical reasoning as it manifests itself in social interactions.

Common Repertoires of Social Things?

Three questions were asked at the beginning of the analysis:

1. Do a class of identification criteria exist the use of which enables individuals to attribute intentions (to themselves and to others) in such or such circumstance of action?
2. Can one say that these criteria guide the practical reasoning of all the members of a social group in an identical way, that is, that they are collectively shared?
3. Do such procedures of practical reasoning make individuals produce "moves" in interaction that are adjusted in advance to the changing intentions of their partners?

I hope the concise answers that have been given to these questions in this chapter have offered some arguments in favor of sociology's externalist conception of intention. These answers may have suggested that an internalist view of intention has to be far more intricate than the version Searle advocates in his intention-in-action theory. More specifically, I hope they have demonstrated that internalism does not simply amount to a matter of locating intention in the brain of an individual. In the light of the advances made in neurosciences (Fodor 2000; Berthoz 2003), it is also a matter of accounting for the neurophysiological mechanism explaining the emergence of intention.

Such cognitive models are discussed in other chapters of this book. Summarily, these models define intention as (1) a smooth movement (2) oriented toward a single target which (3) never changes its goal and (4) is executed, in a mechanical or deliberate way, by an individual—or an organism or a system—(5) by making use—even if unconsciously—of "repertoires" of movements that are stored somewhere in the cognitive apparatus to accomplish (or recognize) it. One immediately senses the abyss that separates this conception of intention from sociology's conception. In the latter, intention refers to (1) a "move" in a game which (2) takes place within a certain type of practical activity, (3) the relevance of which is tested during action itself and (4) the content of which can change, since interacting with others involves unceasing adjustments to unpredictable aims, desires, beliefs, and projections emerging as action unfolds.

Viewed from a sociological perspective, intention is a justification or an endlessly revisable judgment formulated, in the course of an action, about the anticipated rationale of an individual behavior. To produce such a judgment, identification criteria of intention are available which are incorporated in these social things one cannot ignore as soon as he or she acts with others: roles, situations, and concepts. Moreover, the capacity to make use of these identification criteria in a sufficiently quick and satisfying manner inheres to the everyday practices of the members of a social group, and the relevance and efficiency of such uses is unremittingly put to practical test in social interactions.

However, even if this dynamic conception of intention is correct, does it really allow the sociologist to contend that these identification criteria constitute true "repertoires," which are stored in some hypothetical "social memory" and do mechanically produce an appropriate attribution of intention in each and every context? Is there any sense in introducing a notion drawn from neurophysiology ("repertoire of movements") in sociology to explain how a "move" in a joint action sequence is perceived as intentional and agentive? Is it necessary to postulate that such a perception is only possible when an individual possesses a "similar movement scheme in his or her repertoire" and is able to "coactivate this scheme to perceive the function this movement fulfills"?

The sociological arguments explored in this chapter dictate a negative answer to that question. Why? If one acknowledges that identification criteria of intention do exist and are part of ordinary knowledge, one can claim that they endow individuals with a vocabulary of intentionality rich enough to categorize even the faintest move. When one assumes that ordinary knowledge allows individuals to identify intentions so keenly and so directly (even if falsely), one might ask what sense would there be to conceive of such a capacity as a cognitive mechanism or a set of neural correlates. A final question has thus to be asked: Does one really need, even from a purely evolutionist point of view, to go down to a phylogenetic level to explain intention, as it is currently invoked in everyday life at least?[9] A good answer to this question has been given, I think, by sociology and philosophy of action, which have by and large demonstrated that ordinary knowledge,[10] as it manifests itself in the mastery of language, is a human capacity—which can otherwise be apprehended as a biological function—enabling individuals to solve their everyday problems of attribution of agency in an economical and efficient way.

Notes

1. A quotation illustrates the confusion between forms and levels of knowledge in Searle's definition of the Background: "A minimal geography of the Background would include at least the following: we need to distinguish what we might call the 'deep Background,' which would include at least all those Background capacities that are common to all normal human beings, in virtue of their biological makeup—capacities such as walking, eating, grasping, perceiving, recognizing, and the preintentional stance that takes account of the solidity of things and the independent existence of objects and other people—from what we might call the 'local Background' or 'local cultural practices,' which would include such things as opening doors, drinking beer from bottles, and the preintentional stance that we take toward such things as cars, refrigerators, money and cocktail parties. . . . Now within both the deep and the local Background, we need to distinguish those aspects which have to do with 'how things are' from those aspects that have to do with 'how to do things'" (Searle 1983, pp. 141–142). He adds to the confusion by stating the following: "The Background, therefore, is not a set of things, rather it is simply a set of skills, stances, preintentional assumptions and presuppositions, practices, and habits. And all of these, as far as we know, are realized in human brains and bodies. There is nothing whatever that is 'transcendental' and 'metaphysical' about the Background, as I am using that term" (Searle 1983, p. 154).

2. These properties are of two kinds: material (location, dress, topography, physical distribution of the objects and participants, etc.) and interactional (rules of reciprocity and deference, temporal order of transactions, asymmetrical dimensions of a relation, etc.).

3. In the sense given to that notion by F. Jullien (1992) or K. Popper (1992).

4. According to Goffman: "The process of mutually sustaining a definition of the situation in face-to-face interaction is socially organized through rules of relevance and irrelevance. These rules for the management of engrossment appear to be an insubstantial element of social life, a matter of courtesy, manners, and etiquette. But it is to these flimsy rules, and not to the unshaken character of the external world that we owe our unshaken sense of realities" (Goffman 1961b, p. 81).

5. In the mathematical sense of the term.

6. A modern formulation summarizes it this way: "The concept is at the same time *act* and *object* of thought. . . . As 'object of thought,' it is essentially characterized by its aptitude to dissociate into elements or parts, hence by the application of ordered procedures of analysis and composition. As 'act of thought,' it is the rule according to which these procedures are implemented" (Granger 1989, p. 530).

7. Petit (1991) claims that the "dependence" of a concept on its context of use is a constitutive and irremediable phenomenon.

8. Following Descombes (1996), one could claim that this relation has a "tryadic structure": the action of aiming at something, the object aimed at, and the content of the aiming itself. In other words, making use of an intention might amount to arranging these three elements *as well as* the relation that links them together in the particular context of its use.

9. This point brings to mind the controversy on mental reductionism, and, in particular, two arguments Davidson (1980) opposed to the naturalization of the mind: the anomaly of the mental and the multiple realizability of mental concepts. To illustrate: whereas it seems highly improbable to ever discover the specific set of neural firings that would account for the intention to eat some milk chocolate with hazelnuts of a given brand on a full moon night on a sandy beach with a particular girlfriend dressed in white (Seron 1997), one does easily account for it by using the rudimentary resources of ordinary language.

10. Which undeniably rests on a neural substratum.

References

Anscombe, G. E. M. (1957). *Intention*. Oxford: Basil Blackwell.

Berthoz, A. (2003). *La décision*. Paris: Odile Jacob.

Bloor, D. (1983). *Wittgenstein: A social theory of knowledge*. New York: Columbia University Press.

Cassirer, E. (1923). *Substance and function*. Chicago: Open Court.

Cassirer, E. (1953). *The philosophy of symbolic forms* (Vol. 1). New Haven: Yale University Press.

Davidson, D. (1980). *Essays on actions and events*. Oxford: Clarendon Press.

Descombes, V. (1996). *Les institutions du sens*. Paris: Ed. de Minuit.

Durkheim, E. (1995). *The elementary forms of religious life*. New York: Free Press, 1912.

Fodor, J. (2000). *The mind doen't work that way*. Cambridge: MIT Press.

Garfinkel, H. (2002). *Ethnomethodology's program*. Lanham: Rowman and Littlefield.

Goffman, E. (1961a). Role distance. In *Encounters* (pp. 85–152). Indianapolis: Bobbs Merrill.

Goffman, E. (1961b). Fun in games. In *Encounters*. Indianapolis: Bobbs Merrill. 17–81.

Goffman, E. (1964). *Stigma*. Englewood Cliffs: Prentice Hall.

Goffman, E. (1974). *Frame analysis*. New York: Harper and Row.

Goffman, E. (1983). The interaction order. *American Sociological Review, 48*(1), 1–17.

Granger, G. G. (1989). Catégories et raison. In A. Jacob, *L'univers philosophique*. Paris: Presses Universitaires de France.

Heidegger, M. (1971). *Qu'est-ce qu'une chose*. Paris: Gallimard (TEL).

Jullien, F. (1992). *La propension des choses*. Paris: Le Seuil.

Linton, R. (1936). *The study of man*. New York: Appleton Century.

Livet, P. (2002). *Emotions et rationalité morale*. Paris: Presses Universitaires de France.

Mead, G. H. (1922). A behavioristic account of the significant symbol. *Journal of Philosophy, 19*, 157–163.

Mead, G. H. (1934). *Mind, self and society*. Chicago: University of Chicago Press.

Nadel, S. (1957). *The theory of social structure*. London: Cohen and West.

Ogien, A. (1991). L'acceptable et le pertinent. *Critique*, 524–525.

Ogien, A. (1999). *Sociologie de la déviance*. Paris: Armand Colin.

Ogien, A. (2007a). *Les formes sociales de la pensée*. Paris: Armand Colin.

Ogien, A. (2007b). *Les règles de la pratique sociologique*. Paris: Presses Universitaires de France.

Peacocke, C. (1991). The metaphysics of concepts. *Mind, C*(400), 525–546.

Pettit, P. (1991). Realism and response-dependence, *Mind, C*(400), 622–626.

Popper, K. (1992). *A universe of propensities*. Bristol: Thoemmes Press.

Rawls, A. W. (1987). The interaction order *sui generis*: Goffman's contribution to social theory. *Sociological Theory, 5*(3), 136–149.

Rawls, A. W. (2004). *Epistemology and practice*. Cambridge: Cambridge University Press.

Ryle, G. (1949). *The concept of mind*. Chicago: University of Chicago Press.

Searle, J. (1983). *Intentionality*. Cambridge: Cambridge University Press.

Seron, X. (1997). *La neuropsychologie cognitive*. Paris: Presses Universitaires de France (Que sais-je?).

Turner, S., and Factor, R. (1981). Objective possibility and adequate causation in Weber's methodological writings. *Sociological Review, 29*(1), 5–29.

Part VI   Intention and Intentionality: Neuroscientific and Philosophical Perspectives

13 Intention in Phenomenology and Neuroscience: Intentionalizing Kinesthesia as an Operator of Constitution

Jean-Luc Petit

The advances in cognitive sciences over the last thirty years used to be so enthusiastically applauded by the practitioners of these same sciences that it did not occur to an outside observer to note a lack of clarity in the assumed representation of the relationship between conscious conduct and its hypothesized neural bases. An ever growing number of researchers are even trying to apply the tools of information theory to the encoding, translating, and decoding (presumably performed by specialized brain areas) of signals impinging on the body. Nevertheless, the brain cell (the so-called "grandmother cell" or "cardinal cell") responsible for coding a significant item of daily activities or an important concept of the mind has still not been found. And an ever growing wealth of substitutes for this cell are in the offing—"population coding," "temporal coding," "volume coding," and so forth—an excess of competitors that makes it even more difficult to determine what patterns in brain tissue can be held responsible for what behavioral patterns, warned the neuroscientist Horace Barlow.[1] Other researchers, more reluctant to launch out into neurocomputational constructions (or the same researchers in popularizing works), limit themselves to borrowing ordinary, personal conduct predicates and boldly reusing these predicates in reference to brain functioning. Mental verbs, besides expressing what a person might be doing on some occasion of experience, are thus employed to label the brain. This is a simple renaming procedure that, for want of agreement on an interpretative model in neurosciences, a default that Alain Berthoz recently deplored,[2] cannot but postpone a satisfactory explanation, given the dubious intelligibility of common speech mental vocabulary in this new context. In such a situation, the classic three-stage transition of the genesis of scientific knowledge—ordinary language metaphor, hypothetical model, theoretical concept—fails and leaves us stuck either in metaphors or in computational tricks with no bearing on mental life.

From the phenomenological viewpoint,[3] this epistemological blockage might be interpreted as a failure to understand the intentionality of the *sense-giving acts,*[4] or *constitutive operations,*[5] to which any component of a person's experience owes its *sense of being.*[6] At first sight, and at the very least, the main purpose of these acts is to orient the field of vision toward an object of interest and to grasp or maintain the object in question within arm's reach. A rather trite accomplishment apparently! However, by constantly repeating the process by which one directs one's gaze in ever changing directions and learns to handle things in a variety of different ways, these acts contribute to the emergence and constant updating of a certain *field of vivid actuality*[7] against a background or under *a horizon*[8] of indifferent inactuality—a field to which things have to have access in order that they acquire fully fledged being for the perceiving–acting person. Only in such a context do things really acquire significance for the agent. And as for the agent itself, its biography is composed of little else but such acts. Thus, the being, the reality or objectivity of absolutely anything whatsoever (for the subject interacting with the thing in question), is contingent upon acts that have to be accomplished for this *pretended value of being* to be sustained.[9]

To set the matter in a specifically philosophical light, Husserl's later writing investigates the possibility of making use in his theory of intentionality of consciousness of the psychophysiological notion of *kinesthesia*[10] by blending James's peripheral sensations of movement and Wundt's central *Innervationsgefühle.*[11] To remain constantly aware of the way in which we will the movements of our body, this is the task of the "kinesthesia of the I." To remain constantly aware of the sensory contact of the skin of our hands or other limbs with any external thing or other part of the body, this is the task of "organ kinesthesia." This doubly oriented kinesthesia was granted a major role in the constituting of that sense of being which gives us the things we perceive or act upon in daily life. However, in stressing this aspect of constitution, my proposal is not to stick to an interpretation of kinesthesia from a strict phenomenological perspective, that is, as pure interiorities of conscious experience. What I propose is to rethink kinesthesia as a possible link between the subjectivity of experience and the objectivity of functional activation patterns in the brain.

I base this proposal on the fact that kinesthesia happens to be one of the more primitive ways in which an embodied consciousness can manifest itself in space and time. This, to the extant that it "expands or retracts" through its material inscription, locally, in *neural map*[12] shaping and, at a distance, in synchronizations or desynchronizations of *cortical oscillatory patterns*.[13] Such map changes and pattern shifting initiate a process of "spatialization and temporalization of the mind." Whatever its final destiny as a factor of structuring *the lived world*[14] at large, this process begins modestly. It begins in body–brain transactions that subtend motivations, emotions, intentions, or anticipations of inner, mental life emerging into bodily gestures without needing the mediation of verbal expression or reflective thinking. Kinesthesia is thus our best candidate for endowing with experiential value the patterns of activation of brain regions elicited by any behavioral conduct on the part of the subject. Sure enough, not each and every activation pattern of brain can be convincingly correlated in this manner with kinesthesia. We have to concede that most brain events stand in no provable correlation to kinesthetic experience. Nevertheless, it remains (1) that at least some of these patterns are already currently acknowledged as *neural signatures of intentions*[15] or similar acts, and these are indeed typical kinesthesia, and (2) that the same acts, by exerting some measure of feedback, *top–down*,[16] *frontoparietal*[17] control over the whole functional dynamics of brain machinery, recategorize it as kinesthetic. In fact, a few but well-authenticated neurobiological results (reviewed hereinafter) indicative of the modifying influence of intention and attention on the topologic organization not only of the motor but also the primary sensory areas, provide us with indispensable empirical proof of the well-foundedness of our suggestion.

In so funneling the dynamics of brain activation patterns through the kinesthetic channels of experience, we hope to find an embodiment of intentionality that goes farther than dodging the issue like current cognitive theory of mind by implementing mental representations (its fake substitutes) in the brain. In the staggering entanglement of *horizontal*,[18] *vertical*,[19] and *diagonal*[20] connecting loops that the present state of research has kept track of, kinesthetic constitution theory would be a welcome Ariadne's clue. It will be an Ariadne's clue, insofar as it would help us to organize data under the heading of kinesthesia in three fundamental ontological domains: things, body and others. To put the matter in a nutshell (not without paying tribute to Merleau-Ponty), our way out is to admit gesturing, effectively accomplished in bodily movements or kept inchoate in purely internal acts, as a schema for furthering an impending reconciliation between the objective "materialism" of the neurosciences and the subjective "idealism" of a phenomenology of consciousness.

A Sampling of Constitutive Analyses in Phenomenology

Now, let's get back to examples of intentionally constituted objects: a sound, a cube. A sound is not a simple "acoustic stimulus" in the physical environment captured by a passive receptor in the internal ear (cochlea) to give us automatically an auditory representation. A sound is a temporal objectivity which appears as endowed with the following sense of being: an objective entity temporally extended across the flux of my experience. This object owes its constitution to its being placed at the center of *positings*,[21] a system of subjective tensions and projections of the living subject.[22] As for the place that this object occupies in objective time, it results from a later abstraction of the axioms of physical time measurement from the experience to which this system owes its structure—an abstraction purchased at the cost of obliviousness to the original structure of that constituting time which lies at the root of habitual time. Adopting the Husserlian metaphor of the comet, one might say that when a sound sounds it is possible to distinguish a core made up of original sensorial experience and a tail of retentions consisting of its "just having been" and of the "just having been" of its "just having been," and so on. The latter is thereby prolonged in a continual series of overlapping temporal fields right up to that limit beyond which the sound trails away and a new act is needed in order for it to be recalled in memory. The present of the actual sound is not a fixed point but a generative origin from which there arises a constantly renewed sensorial material, each of whose newly engendered phases is subject to a process of *modification*[23] which stretches out into an ever increasing distance from the present "now." This point is not the limit of an approximation which once attained would provide a definitive term but an incessant source of novelty. This novelty is neither a simple diversity nor a pure successive dispersion. Rather, the series of present "nows" of the sound is embraced and firmly upheld in its unity of sense as being "the same sound" by an act of *apprehension of identity*[24] which is effected in the actual now. The circularity between an original self-identity maintained through distance and a distance which increases up to the point of nonretention is a pre-empirical (*transcendental*)[25] structure. The actualization of such structure in the acts of the subject perceiving a sound is the condition of the possibility of his or her experiencing "the sound."

In the same way, a cube (a gaming dice) is not simply "an optical stimulus" whose passive impression on our retina gives us automatically the corresponding spatial representation. A cube[26] is a spatiotemporal objectivity which is never given in any actual sensorial content because it only presents its frontal aspect, while its lateral aspects run off into perspectives, if they are not completely closed off. As any and every object of spatial perception, it is the product of the constituting activities of the perceiving subject whose contribution is indispensable for the appearance of the thing in its full range of aspects.[27] At the outset, nothing like "the thing" is given; there are only *adumbrations*,[28] shadowy or phantom bearers of objective pretensions in the course of being confirmed (or the reverse) through the further course of experience. These series of adumbrations enter our instantaneous visual fields, go through them, and leave them up at the pace of the movements of our sensory and motor organs. They only get organized for the perceiving subject into a permanent configuration bearing the value of being "a thing" because the subject enfolds them all in a positing of identity. By means of this act, they are retained and connected in such a way as to form "a manifold." That is a series of a sensorially laden phases of experience which is no longer arbitrary and dispersed but "definite" under expectations of the subject. On the objective side of this experience its *noematic correlate*[29] is the identical and unique thing.

Once again this structure of multiplicity is a system emerging from the flux of sensations, principally visual but also kinesthetic. The realization of such a system requires a tight synchronization of the series of adumbrations with the *running off*[30] of kinesthetic sensations under the control of the objectifying posit. By contrast with the sound example, what produces the diversity of spatial perception can no longer be identified with the impressional sensation (the *hyletic material* of the sensory content of acts)[31] nor with the positing of identity. Here, the "empty" positing of a regular (normal) running off of the adumbrations of the hidden sides of the thing in conformity with what is anticipated in advance of the flux of experience is sensorially fulfilled (or not fulfilled) with the production of new aspects "of the same thing." We are always waiting "to know more" about the object, an expectation of more that is nevertheless confined to aspects of the same type as before. My contention is that these new aspects are constantly provided and motivated by the sole free functioning of the kinesthetic system. Thus, we have to distinguish the physical stimulus from the thing in space: the first illustrates our passive sensibility, the second our active (transcendental) constitution of the sense of being.

Reassessing the Intentionality of Kinesthesia in Constitution Theory

Bearing in mind these findings concerning the constitution of the temporal object and the constitution of the spatial object, we would like to draw attention to the fact that this theory of constitution is propelled in two contrary directions by the desire to satisfy two mutually conflicting, if not incompatible, requirements. A first requirement was for Husserl to found the meaning of being for any subject of experience upon the transcendental subject, the ultimate source of all meaning giving. For he saw it as necessary to maintain the transcendental dimension of the back-reference to the I-pole of all those acts constitutive of the value of being for . . . and so as not to mechanically pile up one layer of constitution upon another, in oblivion with respect to the organic tension by which all layers are referred to the I, a criticism that Husserl made to empirical psychology, but rather to recover the ultimate, subjective constituting sources of sense. The second requirement was to deploy the system of subjective operations in such a way as to bring to light the manner in which each product is constituted from scratch with the meaning of being that belongs to it for the subject of experience. Incorporating the constituting subject into the total system of kinesthetic activity was a matter of not allowing subjectivity to detach itself from the flux of constituting activity—and so precisely because a detached subjectivity would be incapable of expressing itself in such acts. These two requirements are incompatible at least in the following respect. The former requirement tends to refer all meaning giving activity to a unique transcendental subject by conferring an absolute value upon the latter through a species of abstraction—an abstraction which makes it difficult to understand the relation of this subject to the constituted formations of sense and so call in question its right to be regarded as constitutive of the latter. The second requirement tends to render the constitution of sense as operational as possible by grounding these constitutive processes in the immanence of an uncontroversial psychophysiological experience—a layer of experience which lends itself to be conceived as so primitive as to make its attribution to a subjectivity seem gratuitous. As a result, the fundamental dilemma for a theory of constitution which claims to have surmounted the subject–object opposition remains the following: that the process by which subjectivity gets objectified and that by which objectivity gets subjectified, instead of concurring to bring about the same result, seem torn between opposite trends.

In the direction of subjectification, the trend is to denaturalize subjectivity—a subjectivity reduced accordingly to its function of conferring (or refusing) validity upon the pretention of any possible entity to possess a value of being for someone. Such reference to an ultimate arbiter is so fatally drawn upward through reflection as to lose all effective support. In the direction of objectification, the trend is to incarnate the productive activity in the immanence of natural life in which it is rooted and which furnishes its motivational preconditions. And again along this route there can be no halting point, for any and every motivational component, no matter what the level at which it contributes to the hierarchy of behavioral determinants—will, desire, effort, instinct, feeling, impulse, tendency, and so on—remains a possible candidate for the status of contingent somatic precondition of the transcendental.

However, what is truly remarkable is that Husserl refuses to make a choice as between these two requirements. Right to the end, he struggles to do justice to them both, thereby engaging in a sort of heroic confrontation with the tension imposed upon him by his attempt to remain true to his foundational program. In his kinesthetic theory of constitution, developed especially in unpublished manuscript material from the 1930s, he tried to retain the transcendental approach, even though he is, in effect, deepening his understanding of the rootedness of concrete experience in the structure of embodiment. He ceaselessly worked against himself (and against the transcendental tradition) by bringing the subjectivity of the transcendental subject back down into felt movements and the practical intentions of an acting body. "Qua primitive, consciousness is formed on the basis of the activity itself"[32]: this solution comes down to saying that the objective world is primarily that with which we stand in relation, that toward which we are consciously oriented in perception and action, to the extent that it remains the constant correlate of all those postures, movements intentions, and dispositions to action which give us access to the identity and the permanence of objects—and this solely by featuring as the horizon of perceptual presentations for an I and the field of its practical interventions, manipulations, and transformations.

For all that, in the constitution of the temporal object, the apprehension of identity which traverses the instantaneous temporal fields of the just having been is directly referred to an act of the I, an act which itself does not run off in time but enjoys the privilege of atemporality. We find a parallel presupposal in the constitution of the spatial thing concerning the grasping of the unity and identity of "the same thing": an intentional apprehension which runs through the definite manifold of the adumbrations of its sides to the extent that they are exhibited in the instantaneous visual fields associated with the running off of the kinesthesia relative to the different perceptual and motor organs. Such apprehension is also directly referred to an I which itself remains invariable. The progress made by Husserl in his ever deeper understanding of the incarnate character of the theory of constitution leads him to call in question such fixity of the

I—and to plunge the latter back into the dynamic process of the constitution of sense in which it nevertheless remains the pole of identity.

While appearing to remain faithful to the Cartesian ego, one notices several attempts at an immersion of the I in the constituting flux of the experience of an activity which is initially "without an I"—but an activity which remains such that it enables an I to arise, and so to bring to consciousness the existence of a unitary and self-identical I. Through the process of constitution, kinesthetic sensations begin to acquire a status which they did not enjoy before, for instance, in *Ding und Raum*, which explicitly refused to treat them as intentional.[33] All intentionality could claim then were images of the visual field, since it is only across these series of images and to the extent that they refer to each other in a progressively more adequate approximation to the point of an optimal presentation that something can be present as an appearance. With regard to this presentative function of visual images, the kinesthetic movements of the eyes, of the head, and of the whole body are reduced to a function of motivation, understood in a very narrow sense. Kinesthetic movement and rest had to take account of external and accompanying circumstances, circumstances[34] whose variation brought with them a diversification of those aspects of the field necessary for a satisfactory presentation of the thing. However, this diversity was subordinated to the intentionality of the perceptual apprehension, an apprehension which both dictated its realization and imposed upon it its own attentional orientation by selecting those kinesthetic routings capable of unfolding the series of adumbrations leading to the confirmation of its expectations.

Insofar as it is reduced to figuring as an optimum for a series of suboptimal presentations which tend toward this optimum, an optimum associated with quite determinate kinesthetic sensations, such an intentionality would remain purely visual,[35] a provisional limitation to be corrected by taking into consideration the role of touch and the sense of posture in conjunction with the movements accomplished by the body in its constituting activity, which latter is precisely tactilokinesthetic and not visual. Over and beyond the abstract apperceptive apprehension, over and beyond the regularity with which a series of adumbrations is connected in the visual field, it is in terms of the free possibilities of a running off of kinesthetic sensations for the return to the same thing in perception, or the positing of the same goal in action, that intentionality has to be rethought.

With regard to the period 1905–1907, the period 1930–1933 puts into effect a dramatic redirection of intentionality toward kinesthesia. *Ideen II*, which could be cited as a work of transition, does not bridge the gap because it fails to compensate for the deficit in intentionality of kinesthesia. The significance of this evolution might be missed if one failed to take into account the specific use Husserl makes of the term *Kinästhese*, for he does not use the word in the sense of modern physiology, which gave James preference over Wundt. For physiologists, kinesthesia designates a proprioceptive sensibility, whether muscular or articulatory, which follows centripetal sensorial paths to keep the brain informed about the movements of the body once these movements have been carried out.[36] Husserl, on the contrary, does not even mean by kinesthesia sensations of movement, that is, physical movements relative to the displacements in space of the limbs and of the muscular masses of flesh that coat skeletal bones of which the limbs are composed. He means rather the feeling that the agent has in an immediate and continuous way of his or her intentions to move and of their conception and realization in effective movements. His kinesthesia is not the effects felt in the body with respect to movements actually completed but a drama, a Passion, or even a phenomenology (of Spirit)[37] of the development of an intention in and through its motor realization. Is this an archaic conception? Certainly, but one which has turned out to be premonitory, as will be convincingly shown hereinafter.

In spite of the peripheralist sensualist ideology which has impregnated physiology and psychology for some time now, evidence for such a feeling of acting and of the acting self and of its contribution to the functioning of the perceiving self has not been wanting. Now, that kinesthesia is attributable to an I and that the I is, before all else, the I of kinesthetic sensations was Husserl's main idea. What are kinesthesias in themselves, he asked?[38] And what relation do they bear to those acts of the I by which they are accompanied, of that I which includes them in their running off? Inasmuch as it consists in an "I move" rather than an "I feel," surely this form of kinesthesia already belongs to the I. But then what does the subjectivity in question here really mean?[39] Is the I anything at all over and above its concrete acts? And is a concrete act thinkable other than as a running off, or as something which unfolds actively and which could therefore also be unfolded inactively? Or again, could it consist in a core which is self-unfolding in an immediately active way?[40]

In the light of the above, one is in a better position to understand the intentionalization of kinesthesia, the fact that the meaning of being self-identical can be conferred upon things and upon the self not just by a law of association linking their images one with another but by the fully concrete sense we have of moving toward them. The thing proves to be the same because I can always come back to it and find myself again alongside of it. No need to posit, in the abstract, an arrow of visual attention directed apperceptively toward . . . an attentional arrow which would be the privilege of a cogito without its being possible to say how the latter succeeds in materializing across the sensorial material and so conferring a unitary orientation upon it. This kinesthetic power grants being to beings: whatever simply is, is only meaningful as such by virtue of its *being actively made to be* itself. Kinesthesia is the unique sphere of a power whose exercise is immediately constitutive.[41] Just as perception interpreted as the reception of a sensory stimulus subjects us to the external object, so its reinterpretation as constituting the meaning of the being of the thing in its kinesthetic activities confirms our freedom. Obtaining what is identical depends upon my freedom of movement, upon the immediate evidence I have of being free in the course of exercising it.

A purely visual world remains a world of images devoid of materiality, due to the absence of forces and of resistances to these forces. It is still remote from being an inertial world composed of masses in movement defined in terms of their equilibrium or disequilibrium, their accelerations, torques, and so forth—and this for an agent who is himself or herself embodied and feels in his or her bones, sinews, and muscles the constantly changing strain of the surrounding field of forces as a reflex of his or her own intervention in this field. The transition from the former visual world to the latter real, fully material world depends, in effect, upon my active intervention through an effectuation of the entire system of kinesthesia over and beyond oculomotor kinesthesia. While I don't have to overcome an inertia to move my eyes, and might accordingly dream as if a pure spirit hovering over the world, suffice it that "I move my head, my body, and so forth" for me to acquire a fully material sense of the object as that object which stubbornly remains the same through the free realization of the totality of kinaesthesia.[42] As the unity and identity of the entire series of adumbrations unfolded for me by the sensorial fields of my organs in proportion as they are displaced through my exploratory and manipulative maneuvers, the real object becomes the point toward which all these paths lead. It turns out to be for me the index of my capacity to enter these paths as and when I want—hence, the solution to the problem of perceptive synthesis (*binding problem*): the aspects are only aspects of something to the extent that they are constantly available to me through my free kinesthetic activity.[43] By going back to my former posture, something unique and identical is given to me.[44] Thus, there can be no question of detaching such a thing from those subjective perceptive–motor activities which give me access to it, as had to be the case with the physical object of classical physics.[45] In and through these modes of appearance of things, one finds the "I alongside" of the functioning of my perceptual organs.[46] That there is a world for the subject of experience therefore presupposes the freedom to run through such kinesthetic manifolds.[47] The thingliness of the world is the precipitate of human intentions. All that is issues from my (our, intersubjective) activity.[48]

Light might be cast on such intentionalization of kinesthesia if we fix the relationship of Husserl's theory of kinesthesia to the Dilthey–Scheler controversy on the origins of the reality of external world.[49] Dilthey aptly put forward the role of our experience of willing and of the will impulse's being countered by the resistance of the thing. However, he did not distinguish sufficiently clearly such experience from the sensory feeling of a feedback pressure exerted on the moving limb by the object, noted Scheler—a Scheler who, for his part, stressed the importance of an impulsory experience of the acting I, whose nonsensory intention went right through any accompanying sensory experience (an intention, he insisted, that was solely responsible for the giving of the thing itself to the perceiving subject). In this controversy, Husserl's position can be expressed quite straightforwardly: he agreed with both parts. And there is no paradox in that, because his "kinesthesia of the I" stems from the same source as the voluntary intention to act, while his "organ kinesthesia" derives either from peripheral sensations of limb postures and movements or from proprioceptive feelings. It is true that in the visual constitution of spatial things the arrow of attention is detached from the eye–head–body kinesthetic system and attributed to a still disincarnate I. However, in the tactilokinesthetic constitution of the body, the motor, voluntary kinesthesia of the I and the somatosensory, tactile organ kinesthesia are finally tightly intertwined, thanks to a full embodiment of the I in the *pulsional intentionality*[50] of motivation.

Correlating Phenomenology with New Findings in Neuroscience

The models of phenomenological description invoked above did not take into account the possibility of other fields than the complete visual field or the whole temporal field of the perceiving subject. Is this a limitation, and are these analyses out of date in consequence? The most important contribution of the neurosciences of vision[51] has certainly been to multiply and distribute these fields by relating the reception of the signal to the "receptive fields" (RFs) of the cells responsible for the different neuronal relays in the hierarchic processing of visual information (from V1, occipital calcarine area, to the polar inferotemporal region). The functions said to be of a "high level" (attention, individuation, objectivation, binding, recognition of identity) were supposed to intervene at later stages in the process and not in the primary sensorial regions. The functional architecture of the latter seemed to be devoted to maintaining the topography of the receptors: retinotopy of V1, primary visual area; tonotopy of A1, primary acoustic area in the temporal cortex; somatotopy of SI, primary somesthesic area along the posterior margin of central sulcus. However, the widespread admission of a reentrant feedback hypothesis,[52] thanks to which the information extracted in superior regions would modify (facilitate or inhibit) the reception of the signal in primary sensorial regions, has called in question the uniqueness of this hierarchy, thereby inviting us to think again about the integral unity of the processing of sensory data.

Everything happens on the level of the neural correlates of attentive perception as if the cells of the primary receptive regions "refused to be" limited to simply encoding and decoding the relevant stimuli falling in their RF—and this because they "knew something" about what was going on outside this RF, therefore within the total field, which now also has to be taken into account. By indulging in such metaphors, we are not lapsing into the same bad habit of mentalistic renaming of the subpersonal substrate. On the contrary, the discharge rate of the cell which RF is localized on a segment of a curve on a screen in front of the monkey is modulated by the endpoint of this curve, despite the fact that it is situated outside the RF, if only this endpoint is the target of an ocular saccade that the monkey has learned to make at the fading of the fixation point.[53] Far from inflating mental language, such a way of bringing intelligence back down from the plane of supramodal (not visual nor auditory nor tactile) associations to the sensorial plane makes it possible to get by with fewer mental representations. This is because it becomes less tempting to introduce such representations if the receptive activities are already fully interpretative. But, by the way, any unitary theory (the theory of constitution included) which attempted to account for the continuing integration of perception in and through the dynamic of the global visuo-attentional or audio-attentional or tactilo-attentional field would also become more plausible.

Our vision of the (nonanatomical) functional architecture of the transitory activation patterns of the cerebral circuits recruited by the processing of visual or auditory perception is no longer limited to the the linear bottom–up retino–, or cochleo–, thalamo–cortical hierarchy. This functional architecture is conceived as intersecting such hierarchy with a double feedback. A feedback of the superior stages onto the primary sensorial regions, on the one hand, and, on the other, upon the horizontal (corticocortical, i.e., frontoparietal) and oblique (cortico–subcortical) modifying factors. With regard to the biological significance of perception as the individuation of an external object, these processes stem from acts which intervene *in advance* of "the reality of the object" and of the cognitive or affective values which it bears. It is this precedence with regard to habitual reality which makes it possible to talk of a biological foundation for operations constitutive of perceptual experience. If these pre-empirical operations do not float in a vacuum, it is not enough to attribute them to "the transcendental subject." To provide them with a foundation, it suffices to attribute them to the patterns of transitory activation in the functional loops recruited by perceptual activity in the brain of a perceiving subject.

We will particularly stress the evidence for the modifying influence of *attention* on the primary visual and auditory cortex as well as the modifying influence of *action* and *intention* on the plasticity of maps of the somatosensory cortex.

Attention Modulates Audition

Electroencephalographic recordings show a negative deflection of the curve representing electric potentials in brain tissue reacting to an unpredictable interruption of regular patterns of alternation between two tones that differ in pitch. Until recently, such *mismatch negativity* (MMN) was considered to be automatic and so independent of attention.[54] The deviant stimulus was viewed as standing out against a background of representations of formerly regular series of stimuli retained in memory, thereby causing attention to be oriented toward this stimulus. A process of this kind tended to conceive of attention as purely passive in relation to external stimuli and to abstract attention from the interests, motivations, and intentions of the subject. In fact, what the combination of a deviant stimulus and a voluntary orientation of attention revealed is that when the subject has to attend to a sound in one ear while ignoring the sounds in the other, the MMN registered in the case of attention is no less than two times greater than in the case of inattention.[55]

Such results prove the early influence of an internal activity of the listener upon his of her perception of auditory regularities. This perception can no longer be attributed to a mechanism of automatic detection of irregularities released by the physical properties of stimuli. A special recruitment of cognitive resources is required for the selection of the deviant stimulus, as the mere contrast it creates with the regular series of tones does not suffice for its perceptual recognition. Perceiving it implies that it is recognized *as deviant*, and this by a focusing of attention upon its occurrence. We can see here the importance of the notion of an identifying act in the theory of perception, an act without which a true realization of the identity of the object would be out of the question.

Magnetoencephalographic recordings confirm these findings by registering the electromagnetic fields evoked by the sounds perceived in the attentive, in contradistinction to the unattentive, ear.[56] It has been found that the activity evoked by attentive hearing of a tone is situated next to, not to say confounded with, the activity evoked by an inattentive audition. Both can be referred to the auditory primary cortex, that is, *planum temporale* in Heschl gyrus near the Sylvius fissure—a localization of the source that fuels the hypothesis of a control exercised by attention on the cortical treatment of the auditory signal, a control that bears upon the very first stages of this treatment, including that of stimulus selection at the point of entry of the auditory cortical system. In fact, some measurable incidence was registered in this auditory primary cortex no later than 20 milliseconds poststimulus.

Attention Modulates Vision

The functional organization of the primary visual area (V1) in the occipital cortex retains the topography of the retina (retinotopy), a structural homology that tends to disappear in the temporal and parietal cortical regions, deemed to be more concerned with interpretation than with the reception of visual information. Such a disposition was thought to be indicative of a purely receptive functioning of V1, where we find cells devoted to a passive detection of elementary signals impinging on their receptive field.

A recent piece of brain research using functional magnetic resonance imaging succeeded in disassociating and comparing the activations of the visual cortex correlated with shifts in visual attention and those evoked by passive exposure to identical stimuli.[57] Successive shifts of attention toward progressively more peripheral sectors of a circular target induce a transitory amplification of activation that sweeps the cortex from its occipital pole (V1) to ventromedial extrastriate regions. This progression conforms to the known retinotopic pattern of cortical representations of the visual field in the visual cortex, despite the fact that it reflects a movement of attention and not of the gaze, which remains fixed on the center of the target. A remarkable locational concordance is observed between the enhancements of activations of whatever origin: passive exposure to stimuli or voluntary displacement of visual attention. Such "attentional retinotopy" suggests an influence of attention on the first stages of the cortical treatment of visual stimuli, and possibly even before the beginning of this treatment (20 milliseconds poststimulus again).

These data call for a reconsideration of the role of so-called "primary" or "inferior" visual areas. Far from being limited to the pure reception of an external signal, they prove to be the locus of *a decision to see* what the perceiving subject wants to see. At the very least, the same primary regions (V1, V2) are controlled in a feedback loop by modulatory influences from higher regions (V3, V4), influences that could be traced back to internal sources in the prefrontal and parietal cortex that are themselves relaying subcortical, *limbic*[58] sources. As regards the adaptive value of this *functional architecture*,[59] it is thought to speed up the recognition of objects in visual scenes by projecting onto the sensory material some kind of organizing preperceptions, informed by survival motives.

Attention and Intention Shape the Body Schema

Electroencephalographic recording of the fields of local intracortical potentials in the representational area of the hand has brought to light mutually coherent oscillations of a frequency of 25 to 35 Hz correlated with the execution of precise movements of the fingers requiring an effort of attention.[60] They appear most clearly in connection with the monkeys' attempts to retrieve grapes in the holes of a *Klüver board*.[61] However, their frequency does not vary as a function of the nature of the task. Not being synchronized with the bursts of electromyographic activity of the forearm muscles, these oscillations cannot be attributed to the motor order nor to the preparation of an action. The important fact is that such oscillations have been recorded in sites of implantation of electrodes located along an anteroposterior axis overlapping the central fissure. This suggests that they signal a synchronization of activities between the precentral regions devoted to the elaboration of motor orders and the postcentral regions of the somatosensory cortex where the sensorimotor signals are integrated. This frontoparietal synchronization does not necessarily intervene with each movement but only when the task requires a concerted effort of attention. In such circumstances, the sensorimotor integration could be facilitated by a coordination of the oscillatory activities of the somatosensory and motor cortices, a global activity whose coherent pattern organizes the contributions of the interactions of the large population of individual cells recruited for the task. An analogous hypothesis was initially advanced in vision by C. von der Malsburg.[62]

Brain plasticity studies of hand maps in the somatosensory postcentral cortex have established a reorganization of these maps due to cortical *deafferentation*[63] by limb amputation or nerve injury. Recent experiments[64] evidenced an influence of attention on this map reshaping. An electric stimulation was applied to digits 1 and 5 of subjects while the other digits were anaesthetized by an injection, a condition that spontaneously focuses attention on the disagreeable sensation in the anaesthetized digits. Electroencephalographic recording of electric potentials elicited in the brain by these stimulations revealed that the cortical maps of hands tend to expand when the subjects attend to their anaesthetized digits and to retract when their attention is redirected toward a stimulus applied on the back of the hand.

The experience of one's arm's being prolonged by the use of a tool was correlated with the plasticity of the functional architecture.[65] A monkey was trained to retrieve food pellets using a rake. Electrodes were placed in the intraparietal sulcus, a region of convergence of somatosensory and visual information, in which neurons react not only to tactile stimuli applied to one hand but also to visual stimuli moving around the same hand. When the experimenter moves a food pellet over the monkey's hand, the places in the surrounding space at which a registered neuron fires are normally concentrated above the hand. However, surprisingly, the locus of these firings shifted along the axis of the rake when (and only when) the monkey actually used it, as if, suggest the authors, this visual field expansion were "associated with the monkey's immediate intention to use it."

After a stroke in the right hemisphere, patients frequently suffer from *hemineglect*[66] of space on the left, a deficit in attention, not in vision, that affects the *contralateral*[67] part of the visual field.[68] The influence of action and intention on attention was taken advantage of for the functional recuperation of the cortical representations of peripersonal space supposed to be deafferented, but not suppressed, by the lesion.[69] Patients were trained to seize a stick presented horizontally with the right hand and then to lift it repetitively. Tests of inattention (line bisection, letter cancellation, figure copying, drawing) evinced a sensible amelioration in performance due to the training. The conflict between the intention to seize a stick at its center and the sensorimotor feedback of the stick held, in fact, out of equilibrium prompts subjects to correct their skewed phenomenal space. Here again, the intention to act exerts a regulatory influence upon the body schema.

Conclusion

We concede willingly that we have not given above "an empirical proof" but have only made a gesture, even if a not merely symbolic one, in the direction of such a proof. The data that we gathered are, in effect, for the most part referring to the effects of attention and an extension of the conscious control of awareness on the precocious stage, low-level neural treatment of sensory signals, while the influence of the genesis of intention or action on perception is largely only in the offing.[70] However, as we track back their ultimate determinants, the correlates of attention in perception tend to requalify under a more inclusive category to the extent that they pertain to the same long-range circuit as the correlates of intention in action. Accordingly, to be honest, the present conclusions are more in the way of a bet on future research—but, for all we know at this time, this is not wishful thinking but a perfectly reasonable bet.

Thus, what we expect to see, in fact, is the emergence of a large-scale reorientation in neuroscience and cognitive science generally. Up to now, neuroscientific labs have been concentrating upon preattentional, rigid, automatic modular systems of perception and decision.[71] From now on, they will compete in finding preperceptive or proactive, dynamic interacting systems of attention and intention.[72] The former conception of a mind that is essentially unconscious in most, not to say all, of its functions[73] will be replaced by a new theory of the full embodiment, the rootedness of consciousness and intentionality in the body.[74] Inasmuch as one tends to find in the end what one is looking for, the cognitive impact of consciousness is likely to appear ever more precocious, contrary to the previous assumption that consciousness could only be encountered much later on in the hierarchy of cognitive functioning.

If our forecast is correct, this redirection of empirical research will change the terms of the relationship between cognitive science and phenomenology. As we have seen, the antinaturalism of the phenomenology of transcendental constitution was not, after all, incompatible with a physiology of anticipation and action—a physiology that would try to unearth the biological foundations of those constitutive operations without which an acting subject would be unable to attribute to objects of its experience the meaning of being distinct and independent of consciousness.[75] In fact, recent empirical research has already begun to implement just such a neurophysiology of constitutive consciousness, thereby heading in the same direction as Husserl when he called for a science of the constitution of any kind of objectivity by an essentially active, conscious being.

Acknowledgment

I express my gratitude to Dr. Christopher Macann for the translation.

Notes

1. In Gazzaniga (1995, p. 428), a warning that questions any advance toward a more liberal understanding of the coding theory of neurons, those particularly by Bach-y-Rita, Georgopoulos, Gilbert, Rolls, Singer, and Tanaka.

2. Berthoz (2003, pp. 40–41).

3. For the reader not familiar with phenomenology, we provide explanatory notes.

4. *Sinngebende Akte:* mental acts which confer to an objet the meaning it has for a subject.

5. *Konstituirende Leistungen:* the same acts, to the extent that they provide to their object any contributory layer of its "reality" for a subject.

6. *Seinssinn:* value of "reality" of something for a subject.

7. *Lebende Gegenwart:* proximal, peripersonal space and minimum length of time of experience in which any object has to appear or any event to occur in order to be dealt with by the subject.

8. *Horizont:* limit of the personal space–time which is finite, closed under the acts of the subject, but also open as source of novelty and the recess for things past to sink out of sight.

9. *Sinngebung:* the value "truly real" has to be given to the candidate object by acts that a subject accomplishes in interacting with it.

10. *Kinesis*: movement + *aesthesis*: sensation.

11. Feeling of innervations, a notion that confounded a sensitivity of motor nerves to the passing through of motor command that was disconfirmed and a now accepted "corollary discharge" or feedback of the motor command on sensory centers in brain—a feedback thanks to which the organism is aware of his action ahead of any returning signal from the moving limb.

12. For the reader not familiar with neuroscience, let us note that electophysiologists using intracerebral recordings evidenced a topologic, even if plastic, pattern of organization ("homunculus") of functional activity around central sulcus denoting some correspondence between the region of the skin covering each body part and its territory of representation in brain cortex tissue.

13. The neurodynamic school of neuroscientists registering global activities on the scalp have noted in certain bandwidths transitory coherent patterns of oscillations

in correlation with mental experiences such as the reversal of ambiguous figures (Necker cube).

14. *Umwelt*: the world of all objects of perception and aims of action for a given living being.

15. Ex. *Bereitschaftpotential*: potential of preparation of Kornhuber, a deflection of the curve representative of neural activity at scalp sites above premotor and motor areas a half second before the emission of a motor command.

16. Flow of neural modulatory influence oriented from higher cortical centers to primary areas and/or the periphery of muscular effectors or sensory captors. It is opposed to the "bottom–up" flow of treatment of sensory information from outside by progressively higher centers.

17. Brain circuit that links the frontal, motor area and the postcentral, parietal area, the latter a zone of convergence of visual and tactile and motor signals.

18. Corticocortical circuits that link together regions of cortex at different layers.

19. Thalamocortical connections by which sensory signals from the retina and other captors are relayed by the thalamus, an ontogenetically ancient nucleus of cerebrum, to their target of projection in the sensory primary areas of ontogenetically recent cortex.

20. Cortico–subcortical circuits connecting the higher cognitive regions of cortex to the lower, primitive brain nuclei of basal ganglia, that contribute to affective-conative motivation of behavior.

21. *Setzen, Setzung:* full, wholehearted assertion of belief in the reality of the object of perception or judgment, as opposed to doubt, delusion, or fiction.

22. A system to which Husserl devoted his 1905 lectures (Husserl 1966).

23. *Modifikation*: constant alteration of vivid sensation into past impression as retained in consciousness.

24. *Auffassung:* identity, or other formal property of an object of perception has to be imposed to the multiplicity of transitory aspects by an act of grasping, or relating, or unifying its sensorial diversity under the relevant ruling principle. A principle that could not possibly be found in the actual sensory content of consciousness.

25. *Transzendantal:* The scaffolding of all possibility of objective knowledge for the subject.

26. Referring to the analyses of the 1907 Lectures (Husserl 1973).

27. *Erscheinungsmodi*: aspects under which an object appears to a viewer as he or she moves around and changes his or her viewpoint in relation to this object.

28. *Abschattungen*: series of transitory, incomplete appearances bearing any pretention of objective validity beyond the limits of their actual sensory content.

29. *Noesis–noema*: from the act of perceiving we distinguish that which is aimed at by this act, that is, not the physical thing, but the object precisely as it is targeted and prefigured by the act oriented toward it.

30. *Kinästhetische Verlaufen*: free percourses of kinesthesia, the phases of which are prescribed by the anatomic constraints of our organs and go from a normal, rest posture to a maximum of tension and back to rest.

31. *Hyle:* matter of an act, its purely sensory content, so characterized despite the impossibility of taking this content apart from the formal aspect of this act.

32. Ms D 12 IV, p. 9.

33. Husserl (1973, p. 181): "Ganz anders verhält es sich mit der Reihe der K; sie weisen aufeinander nicht hin, sie laufen ab, sie sind aber nicht Träger durch sie hindurchgehender Intentionen wie sie die f (Figuren im Feld) haben, nicht ein durch sie gehendes Einheitsbewusstsein."

34. An expression we find in *Ideen II* §18, texts that Husserl did revise up to 1928. See Husserl (1952, p. 57), where visual sensations are distinguished from kinaesthesia: the former being the objects of an (intentional) apprehension to the extent that they are functioning as sketches of the thing; the latter being the objects of *eine ganz andersartige Auffassung,* that is, a kind of apprehension devoid of intentional character because it all boils down to a quasi-causal *if–then* correlation—a correlation in virtue of which "*if* the eye orients itself in such and such manner, *then* the 'image' is modified in such and such manner" (p. 58).

35. Ms D 12 V, p. 3.

36. For a reassessment of the role of kinesthesia in neurophysiology, see J.-P. Roll in Petit (2003, pp. 49–66).

37. Referring to Hegel's dramatic stage setting of the experience of consciousness in *Phänomenologie des Geistes*.

38. Ms D 10 IV (dated 1932), p. 9.

39. Ibid., p. 11–12.

40. Ibid., p. 13–14.

41. Ms D 10 I (dated 1932), p. 25.

42. Ms D 10 III (dated 1932), p. 9.

43. Ms D 13 I, p. 14.

44. Ibid., p. 17.

45. Ms D 13 X (dated 1923), p. 27.

46. Ms D 10 I (dated 1932), p. 3.

47. Ms D 13 XV (dated 1918), p. 3.

48. Ms B I 16 (dated 1931), p. 8.

49. Dilthey (1890/1924); Scheler (1926).

50. *Triebintentionalität:* ultimate roots of motivation prior to the subject–object, will–desire, feeling–acting distinctions, albeit not without an orientation toward something.

51. Zeki (1993).

52. Edelman (1992).

53. Roelfsema et al. (1998).

54. Winkler and Czigler (1998).

55. Alain and Woods (1997).

56. Woldorff et al. (1993).

57. Brefczynski and DeYoe (1999).

58. The limbic system includes nuclei of lower brain important in affective-conative motivation of behavior.

59. Variable, but coherent patterns of activation that straddle the frontiers between different cell types of brain cortex rather than being enclosed in these frontiers.

60. Murthy and Fetz (1992).

61. A presentation board that provides to monkeys a gradual difficulty in the retrieving of grains with the digits from holes of different diameters.

62. As a solution to the "binding problem" of the various modalities of the visual scene or object: a transitory coordination of the cellular activations selected for different features and extracted from the visual signal by hierarchically ordered neuronal links in V1, V2, V3, and so forth could help to integrate these features in one unique percept (von der Malsburg and Schneider 1986).

63. An experimental disconnection of cortical areas of projection of sensory nerves from their sources of afferent signals, that is, from the region of skin supporting the receptor organs. Here a transsection or crushing of median nerve that innervates digits 1, 2, and 3 of the hand induces reorganizations of cortical hand maps.

64. Buchner et al. (1999).

65. Iriki et al. (1996).

66. Unilateral negligence of one half of visual space, a syndrome manifested in eating only the food on half of one's dish or drawing on half of the page or shaving half of one's face.

67. Contralateral–ipsilateral: hemifield of visual space of the opposed–same side to the lesioned brain hemisphere.

68. Bisiach and Luzzatti (1978, p. 132).

69. Robertson et al. (1995); Robertson et al. (1997); Harvey et al. (2003).

70. We cannot perceive any default of parallelism between phenomenology and neurobiology as regards the data on our awareness of embodiment in agency, on the one hand, and our conscious scanning of scenes in the outside world, on the other, because the two conditions belong equally to a nonreflexive prethematic consciousness.

71. For example, in attention research the literature on the MMN of electric potentials evoked in auditory cortex by a deviant tone in a series (Näätänen 1992).

72. See the above references.

73. In essence, the bulk of the modularity of mind paradigm, up to recently in fashion in labs (Fodor 1983).

74. Thompson and Varela (2001); Varela and Shear (1999); Petitot et al. (1999).

75. Berthoz and Petit (2008).

References

Alain, C., and Woods, D. L. (1997). *Psychophysiology*, *34*, 534–546.

Berthoz, A. (2003). *La décision*. Paris: Odile Jacob.

Berthoz, A., and Petit, J.-L. (2008). *The physiology and phenomenology of action*. Oxford: Oxford University Press.

Bisiach, E., and Luzzatti, C. (1978). Unilateral neglect of representational space. *Cortex*, *14*, 129–133.

Brefczynski, J. A., and DeYoe, E. A. (1999). A physiological correlate of the "spotlight" of visual attention. *Nature Neuroscience*, *2*, 370–374.

Buchner, H., Reinartz, U., Waberski, T. D., Gobbelé, R., Noppeney, U., and Scherg, M. (1999). Sustained attention modulates the immediate effect of de-afferentation on the cortical representation of the digits: Source localization of somatosensory evoked potentials in humans. *Neuroscience Letters*, *260*, 57–60.

Dilthey, W. (1890/1924). Beiträge zur Lösung der Frage vom Ursprung unseres Glaubens an die Realität der Aussenwelt. *Gesammelte Werken.* Leipzig: Teubner.

Edelman, G. M. (1992). *Bright air, brilliant fire: On the matter of mind.* New York: Basic Books.

Fodor, J. A. (1983). *The modularity of mind.* Cambridge: MIT Press.

Gazzaniga, M. S. (Ed.). (1995). *The cognitive neurosciences.* Cambridge: MIT Press.

Harvey, M., Hood, B., North, A., and Robertson, I. H. (2003). The effects of visuomotor feedback training on the recovery of hemispatial neglect symptoms: Assessment of a 2-week and follow-up intervention. *Neuropsychologia, 41,* 886–893.

Husserl, E. (1913). *Logische Untersuchungen* (Vol. 2). Halle a.d.S: Niemeyer.

Husserl, E. (1952). *Ideen zu einer reinen Phänomenologie und phänomenologischen Philosophie: Vol. 2. Phänomenologische Untersuchungen zur Konstitution.* The Hague: Martinus Nijhoff.

Husserl, E. (1956). *Erste Philosophie.* The Hague: Martinus Nijhoff.

Husserl, E. (1966). *Zur Phänomenologie des inneren Zeitbewusstsein* (1893–1917). The Hague: Martinus Nijhoff.

Husserl, E. (1973). *Ding und Raum: Vorlesungen 1907,* Husserliana XVI, Martinus Nijhoff. Husserl, E., Mss B I 16; D 10 I, III, IV, V; D 12 IV, V; D 13 I, V, X, XV.

Iriki, A., Tanaka, M., and Iwamura, Y. (1996). Coding of modified body schema during tool use by macaque postcentral neurones. *NeuroReport, 7,* 2325–2330.

Jackson, F. (1982). Epiphenomenal qualia. *Philosophical Quarterly, 32,* 127–136.

Lycan, W. G. (Ed.). (1990). *Mind and cognition.* Cambridge: Basil Blackwell.

Martinez, A., DiRusso, F., Anllo-Vento, L., Sereno, M. I., Buxton, R. B., and Hillyard, S. A. (2001). Putting spatial attention on the map: Timing and localization of stimulus selection processes in striate and extrastriate visual areas. *Vision Research, 41,* 1437–1457.

McGinn, C. (1991). *The problem of consciousness.* Oxford: Basil Blackwell.

Murthy, E. N., and Fetz, E. E. (1992). Coherent 25- to 35-Hz oscillations in the sensorimotor cortex of awake behaving monkeys. *Proceedings of the National Academy of Sciences USA, 89,* 5670–5674.

Näätänen, R. (1992). *Attention and brain function.* Hillsdale, NJ: Erlbaum.

Nagel, T. (1974). What it is like to be a bat ? *Philosophical Review, 83,* 435–451.

Petit, J.-L. (Ed.). (2003). Repenser le corps, l'action et la cognition avec les neurosciences. *Intellectica* n° *36–37,* 15–372.

Petitot, J., Varela, F. J., Pachoud, B., and Roy, J.-M. (Eds.). (1999). *Naturalizing phenomenology: Issues in contemporary phenomenology and cognitive science*. Stanford, CA: Stanford University Press.

Robertson, I. H., Nico, D., and Hood, B. M. (1995). The intention to act improves unilateral left neglect: Two demonstrations. *NeuroReport, 7*, 246–248.

Robertson, I. H., Nico, D., and Hood, B. M. (1997). Believing what you feel: Using proprioceptive feedback to reduce unilateral neglect. *Neuropsychology, 11*, 53–58.

Roelfsema, P. R., Lamme, V. A., and Spekreijse, H. (1998). Object-based attention in the primary visual cortex of the macaque monkey. *Nature, 395*, 376–381.

Scheler, M. (1926). *Die Wissensformen und die Gesellschaft*. Leipzig: Der Neue-Geist Verlag.

Thompson, E., and Varela, F. J. (2001). Radical embodiment: Neural Dynamics and Consciousness. *Trends in Cognitive Sciences, 5*, 418–425.

Varela, F. J., and Shear, J. (Eds.). (1999). The view from within: First-person approaches to the study of consciousness. *Journal of Consciousness Studies*, Vol. 6 (2–3).

von der Malsburg, C., and Schneider, W. (1986). A neural cocktail-party processor. *Biological Cybernetics, 54*, 29–40.

Winkler, I., and Czigler, I. (1998). *NeuroReport, 9*, 3809–3813.

Woldorff, M. G., Gallen, C. C., Hampson, S. A., Hillyard, S. A., Pantev, C., Sobel, D., and Bloom, F. E. (1993). Modulation of early sensory processing in human auditory cortex during auditory selective attention. *Proceedings of the National Academy of Sciences USA, 90*, 8722–8726.

Zeki, S. (1993). *A vision of the brain*. Oxford: Blackwell.

14 Cognitive Neuroscience of Action and the Pragmatist Conception of Intentionalism

Jean-Michel Roy

Cognitive Intentionalism and the Pragmatist Claims of Cognitive Neuroscience

From a clearly identifiable sector of the cognitive community that one might call the cognitive neuroscience of action, an insistent claim has emerged, in the last ten years or so, to the effect that action is essential to intentionality, thereby advocating what is known in the traditional philosophical debates as a pragmatist conception of intentionalism. Although not mainstream, this pragmatist claim has now achieved sufficient quantitative importance to require a careful critical examination. Strangely enough, however, the specialists in the problem of cognitive intentionalism—namely, the set of issues raised by the property of intentionality in the context of a scientific theory of cognitive phenomena—have so far paid little attention to it. This negligence is all the more surprising since, far from being a point of minor importance, the question of the adequacy of a pragmatist conception cuts across almost all aspects of the problem of cognitive intentionalism and is therefore of major theoretical significance. Assessing the validity of the claim put forward by the cognitive neuroscience of action is consequently all the more pressing a need. It involves, in particular, assessing the extent to which it is indeed supported by the empirical data invoked in its favor, as well as the extent to which it is theoretically consistent. Can there really be, after all, such a thing as a pragmatist theory of intentionality?

The answer to these questions clearly depends on what one takes such a theory to be, beyond the general thesis that action is essential to intentionality. And in this regard, the critical analysis to be undertaken faces a special difficulty. Indeed, the content of the pragmatist claim put forward by the cognitive neuroscience of action is not without substantial imprecision, fluctuation, and variety—to the point where it sounds preferable to refer to it with a plural rather than a singular. Accordingly, an important preliminary to the assessment of the validity of these pragmatist claims of the cognitive neuroscience of action is the careful elaboration of an interpretation of what they really mean.

And it is to this preliminary task that the following pages limit their ambition. In fact, because of obvious space constraints, they are restricted to the clarification of no more than a limited sample of pragmatist claims deemed particularly important and representative (cf. "A Theoretical Analysis of the Pragmatist Conception of Intentionalism" below). Given that these claims are statements about intentionality emanating from a certain area of cognitive neuroscience, it is however important, for grasping their real content, to first provide a definition both of the general problem of cognitive intentionalism, and of what a specifically neurocognitive formulation of it amounts to (cf. "The Neurocognitive Turn of the Problem of Cognitive Intentionalism" section below). In addition, the best strategy consists in examining these claims at the light of a theoretical investigation of what a pragmatist approach to the problem of cognitive intentionalism so understood could in principle be: accordingly, their analysis is also preceded (cf. the section "The Pragmatist Claims of Cognitive Neuroscience") by a presentation of the different possible pragmatist options that they might incarnate, and that is used as guide to determine which ones they do, in fact, incarnate, if any.

The Neurocognitive Turn of the Problem of Cognitive Intentionalism

The problem of cognitive intentionalism is a multifaceted one; it is a set of logically interrelated questions. Four of these, at least, are central and, therefore, more likely to play a crucial role in defining the essence of the pragmatist approach to cognitive intentionalism:

1. *The cognitive relevance of the property of intentionality* The most basic aspect of the problem of cognitive intentionalism consists in determining whether a scientific theory of cognition should view a Brentanian[1] property of intentionality, as well as a number of related ones to be grouped under the general label of intentional properties, as relevant or irrelevant to its elaboration. A theory that sees it as relevant is an intentionalist one, while a theory that does not is an *eliminativist* (regarding intentionality) one.

2. *The nature of the property of intentionality* One of the essential goals of an intentionalist theory of cognition is clearly to reach a scientific specification of the nature of the property of intentionality (and of intentional

properties at large) that it considers as relevant, just as one of the goals of an atomistic physics is to obtain a scientific model of the nature of the atom. This question of definition is, however, a two-stage one: before an ultimate specification of the nature of intentionality can be reached, a preliminary and operational characterization of it must first be provided in order to solve the question of relevance.

One acceptable preliminary characterization is that the general idea of Brentanian intentionality is simply that *of one thing relating to another as a subject to an object*. A state of a cognitive system should accordingly be seen as intentional, if (a) it is relational and (b) the relation thereby established can be characterized as a subject–object one.[2] It is important to underline that, according to this characterization, the notion of intentionality is, at its most general level of specification, free from any reference to the concepts either of representation or of symbol and also that the notion of relation should be taken in a provisional way for lack of a better intuitive word, since it is, in fact, disputable that intentionality is a relation in the logical sense of the word.[3]

An alternative preliminary definition can be obtained by substituting the notion of aboutness or reference to that of subject–object relation. In this perspective, the notion of intentionality simply designates the fact that something refers to, or is about, something else. In wide use in the literature, this definition offers the substantial advantage of being simpler, since it is neutral with regard to the notion of relation and, similarly, makes no explicit mention of the difficult concepts of subject and object. However, it can only be preferred to the previous one under the condition that the notions of reference and aboutness are not understood as designating intrinsically semantic properties (i.e., properties of symbolic entities), a condition almost universally ignored in the contemporary literature. Indeed, it is arguable that the specificity of symbolic reference—classically defined as the fact of standing for something else, of being *aliquid quod stat pro aliquo*—should not be incorporated into a general definition of intentionality.[4] In order to avoid this widespread confusion, I will stick here to the first one of the two definitions just proposed. They are not *prima facie* equivalent, although it is an open question whether one can be reduced to the other.

3. The determination of intentionality The third main issue involved is about the determination of intentionality. Two different questions have, in fact, to be distinguished. One deals with the sheer existence of intentionality: What is it that brings intentionality into being? The other one is about the specificity of the intentional object: What is it that makes a

cognitive state relate intentionally to such or such specific object? These two questions need not necessarily receive a similar answer, and it is conceivable that action plays an essential role in only one of them.

4. The naturalization of intentionality   One can argue favorably about the cognitive relevance of intentionality and yet reject that of naturalism for cognitive science, embracing thereby a nonnaturalist form of cognitive intentionalism. Adopting a *non*naturalist perspective on cognitive science amounts to saying, at a minimum, that a natural cognitive system is not a cognitive system in virtue of what makes it a natural system and, consequently, that there is, between the natural and the cognitive properties of a natural cognitive system, an ontological and epistemological discontinuity, such that (a) in order for this system to have cognitive properties, it is not necessary that it have natural ones (a system can be a cognitive one without being a natural one) and, correspondingly, (b) the fact that it has cognitive properties cannot be scientifically accounted by the fact that it has certain natural properties.

From this characterization, one can easily derive by contrast a general specification of what embracing both an intentionalist and a naturalist approach to cognitive science amounts to through the following definitional steps:

1. Natural property of a system S   A property of a system S is a natural one either if it is included in a set of primitive natural properties Pn_1 or if it can be scientifically accounted for by the properties Pn_1 possessed by S. In this case, it is called a nonprimitive natural property, all of which form the set of properties Pn_2. If it has natural properties Pn, and inasmuch as it has them, a system is said to be a natural system.

2. Cognitive property of a natural system S   A cognitive property Pc of a natural system S is a property that characterizes it as a cognitive system: it designates what makes it a cognitive kind of natural system (a natural cognitive system).

3. Natural cognitive property of a natural cognitive system S   A cognitive property Pc of a natural cognitive system S is transformed into a natural property P, if (a) it is attributed to S *qua* natural system (*qua* having Pn) and (b) its instantiation in S is scientifically accounted for by the primitive and/or nonprimitive Pn properties of S. Pc is then said to be a naturalized cognitive property.

4. Naturalist theory of cognition   A cognitive theory is a naturalist one if *all* the cognitive properties that it makes use of are naturalized cognitive properties in the sense just defined.

5. Naturalist cognitive intentionalism A naturalist cognitive theory is intentionalist if a subset of the set Pc of cognitive properties it makes use of are intentional ones (and consequently includes the property of intentionality).

On the basis of this definition, the problem of naturalizing the property of intentionality appears to be simply that of determining whether it can be accounted for on the basis of the properties of cognitive systems that characterize them as natural systems. A general answer to this question is what is known as a principle of naturalization. The task of formulating such a principle is not to be confused with that of actually accounting with its help for specific intentional properties on the basis of specific natural properties, that is to say, of working out detailed naturalistic intentional explanations of cognition. This task has been the central concern of foundational studies in cognitive science for the past thirty years, and almost every major philosopher in the field has made relevant proposals. The most well-known are psychoneural reductionism, functionalist nonreductionism, and emergentist nonreductionism.

These core aspects of the problem of cognitive intentionalism have been so far predominantly approached from a cognitivist perspective in contrast to a neurocognitive one. The development of a neurocognitive approach is, however, one of the major transformations of the cognitive field since the 1990s. The notion of cognitive neuroscience can indeed be understood in two different ways. In its first sense, it means nothing else than the study of the neurobiological dimension of cognitive processes and is, accordingly, just one cognitive discipline among others. In its second sense, it designates a specific approach to the overall internal architecture of cognitive science, which thus is better designated in a capitalized form as Cognitive Neuroscience. This approach was articulated in a variety of ways in the mid 1980s by a number of scientists and philosophers, chief among whom are Michael Gazzaniga,[5] Steve Kosslyn and Olivier Koenig,[6] Michael Posner,[7] and Michel Imbert,[8] as well as Paul and Patricia Churchland.[9]

The difference between cognitivism and Cognitive Neuroscience can be seen as being fundamentally one of degree of abstraction of psychological hypotheses with respect to neurobiological ones, as well as one of explanatory strategy.[10]

Cognitivism merely imposes neurobiological *plausibility* on psychological hypotheses; these hypotheses should postulate cognitive mechanisms that neurobiological systems *can* have, but many other natural entities as well. Accordingly, psychological hypotheses are highly abstract with respect to neurobiological ones, in the sense that the states and processes that they postulate do not depend on the specific nature of those postulated by neurobiological hypotheses. As a consequence, neurobiological considerations only step in at the last stage of the explanation of cognition, once psychological hypotheses have been formulated. In other words, cognitive psychology is *heuristically independent* from neurobiological data and hypotheses.

Cognitive Neuroscience imposes, on the contrary, a constraint of neurobiological *reality* on psychological hypotheses and sees them as postulating cognitive mechanisms that neurobiological systems *do* have. Accordingly, the dependence of the psychological level of cognition on the neurobiological one is seen as much stronger, and its degree of abstraction with respect to it as much lower. As a consequence, neurobiological data and hypotheses step in right at the start of the explanation of cognitive phenomena. In other words, the psychological investigation of cognition is not purely behavior based and is *heuristically dependent* on neurobiological considerations. In such a perspective, there is actually no such thing as a purely psychological hypothesis anymore: hypotheses about psychological properties of cognition always are implemented ones, and neurobiological hypotheses are therefore fully integrated into the science of cognition.

A consequence of the development of Cognitive Neuroscience is that the implications of adopting a neurocognitive approach on the problem of cognitive intentionalism should be investigated. To what extent does submitting the property of intentionality to the twofold requirement of neurobiological reality and of heuristic dependency just indicated transform the meaning of such issues as the relevancy, nature, determination, and naturalization of the property of intentionality, and to what extent can this approach facilitate their resolution? With the noticeable exception of the Churchlands and Kathleen Atkins, who raise it in the most explicit manner,[11] this question has generated only modest interest to this day, even though an important amount of empirical neurocognitive research speaks directly to it, in particular in the area of binding theory. And in order to fully address it, a critical analysis of the work already engaged in this direction is needed. The specific interest of the pragmatist claims to be found in the cognitive neuroscience of action literature is that they precisely belong to this category of work. In other words, they are linked to a Cognitive Neuroscience approach and therefore amount to claiming that a neurocognitive form of intentionalism should also be a pragmatist one.

A Theoretical Analysis of the Pragmatist Conception of Intentionalism

Before attempting to clarify what such claims really mean in vindicating an essential role for action in solving the problem of cognitive intentionalism, it will prove useful to determine what such a role could in principle be. In other words, it is important to clarify the very idea of a pragmatist conception of intentionalism, and the main forms it could take, in the domain of cognition.

If the core tenet of such a theory is to make action essential for intentionality, it can clearly vary according to two crucial variables at least: the aspect of the problem of cognitive intentionalism taken into consideration and the conception of the nature of action involved.

A. Aspects of the Problem of Intentionalism

Regarding the first variable, the most important aspects of the problem of cognitive intentionalism that can influence the theory are no less clearly the four ones examined above.

Indeed, action could first be seen as essential for deciding about the cognitive relevance of intentionality. In this perspective, a pragmatist conception of intentionalism is one that considers that the notion of intentionality is only, or at least fundamentally, relevant to account for the pragmatic dimension of cognition, namely, action, as opposed to its nonpragmatic dimensions, such as perception, language... Which is to say that a cognitive intentionalism is of a pragmatist kind by virtue of solely, or fundamentally, granting relevance to the property of intentionality in the context of the cognitive explanation of action: in other words, by only or fundamentally recognizing action as an intentional phenomenon. It thereby differs from any form of cognitive intentionalism that either rejects the relevance of intentionality in accounting for action or at least does not put any fundamental emphasis on it but nevertheless resorts to it in accounting for other aspects of cognition. A natural way of defending this first form of pragmatist intentionalism is, for instance, to argue that one cannot explain action without introducing the notion of a target, understood as the object on which the action is performed. It is, for example, hard to see how one could analyze the action of grasping without making room for the concept of the object of grasping.

A different possibility is to recognize action as essential for the nature of intentionality, so that its nature cannot be analyzed without making reference to the nature of action. In this second perspective, a pragmatist conception of intentionalism is a theory that sees the nature of intentionality as essentially related with the characteristics of action.

It is important to see that admitting that the nature of only one specific form of intentionality among others is essentially related with action does not suffice by itself to turn a cognitive intentionalism into a pragmatist one in this second sense of the term. A theory that sees, for instance, intentionality as relevant to the explanation of all cognitive phenomena, but only sees the nature of action intention, understood as a specific form of intentionality, as essentially related to movement, does not qualify as such a pragmatist theory. In order to obtain in this case a pragmatist theory in the second sense, it is, in fact, necessary to limit the relevance of the property of intentionality to the explanation of action, that is to say, to also subscribe to the first form of pragmatist theory. Otherwise the theory would recognize specific types of intentionality whose nature is free from any essential relation with action, and for which, consequently, action is not essential, as far its nature is concerned. An alternative solution is to accept that the nature of all forms of intentionality is somehow essentially related with action, although one of them, like action intention, is more dramatically so. When the essential link with action is located in the nature of intentionality, it is therefore clear that a cognitive intentionalism can only be considered as pragmatist if all the forms of intentionality that it admits, however numerous or limited they are, are so linked with action.

There is, in addition, quite a bit of latitude for variation in the spelling out of the notion of an essential link between the nature of intentionality and the nature of action. One of the most natural ways to do so, although certainly not the only one, is to locate this link in the objective component of intentionality, in what an intentional state is about. A first strategy consists in arguing that every type of intentionality ascribes specific features to its objective component, but that these specific features are nevertheless systematically correlated with certain properties of action. It can be claimed, for instance, that in perception an object is referred to with certain specific features, different from the ones that characterize the object of a desire, or a judgment . . . , but that these features are also systematically correlated with features that the object has qua target of certain gestures (so that there is no such thing as a pure perception, in the sense of a perception detached from action; perception is inseparable from potential action). A stronger strategy consists in substituting the notion of subordination for that of correlation. The idea, then, is that not only, for instance, is the perceptive apprehension of an object inseparable from its apprehension as a potential action target but it is subordinated to it, so that we only, or least fundamentally, perceive in an object what is useful for acting on this object. In this perspective, perception, and intentionality in general, is essentially an instrument of action. A further step can be taken by claiming that not only does the nature of all types of intentional relations reveal a subordination to action but certain characteristic features of action are also present in them. And, accordingly, it makes literal sense, in the case, for instance, of perception, to say that an object is perceived as graspable as if we would perceptively apprehend an object qua target of a grasping.

In the last two cases just mentioned, the nature of intentionality not only is essentially related with action but is, in addition, determined by it in the general sense that it is the result of a constraint of action and that it can accordingly be said to be constituted by action. Consequently, it might seem useless, in elaborating a classification of pragmatist approaches to intentionality, to distinguish the essentiality that action might have from the point of view of the nature of intentionality and the essentiality it might have from the point of view of the determination of intentionality, the third main aspect of the problem of cognitive intentionalism according to the analysis presented in the previous paragraph. However, two reasons at least militate against such a decision. First, essential links to actions in the nature of intentionality are not necessarily the result of a constraint of action on intentionality. For instance, systematic correlations between the characteristics of an object of perception and those of a target of an action might just be the indirect product of other relations of determination. Similarly, not every constraint of action on intentionality necessarily results in a feature of intentionality whose nature is essentially linked to that of action. The second reason is that there is also more to the determination of intentionality by action than the determination of its nature. Action can also more simply, but more radically, determine the existence of intentionality. In this perspective, action determines and constitutes intentionality in the sense that it is what makes the very fact of objective reference possible, even if it puts no further constraints on its nature. A pragmatist theory of intentionality, according to this third possibility, is thus one claiming that a cognitive system deprived of action would be deprived of intentionality altogether, and not of an intentionality of a certain nature.

A fourth possibility is, finally, that action is essential for the naturalization of intentionality. In this perspective, in order to understand how intentionality can belong to a system with natural properties, the mediation of action is in one way or another needed. By virtue of the definition of naturalization previously offered, this means more technically that the properties of action are natural properties (primitive or derived) that offer the right basis for the naturalist explanation of intentional ones. And a theory of cognition is a pragmatist kind of intentionalism to the extent that it advocates this form of naturalist explanatory (and therefore also ontological) primacy of action properties.

B. The Nature of Action

Another crucial source of variation is the conception of the nature of action involved, since two pragmatist theories of intentionality will evidently count as different if they take, under the name of action, two different things to be essential for intentionality. And it is an all the more important one in that the question of the nature of action has always been, and continues to be, a hotly debated issue. There is, accordingly, no consensus on what its essential components are. Consequently, not only might it be that two pragmatist theories of intentionality sharing a common analysis of the nature of action differ by the element of action that they consider to be essential, but it might also happen that they differ more radically in their decomposition of action.

In spite of this diversity of analyses, there are clearly some recurrent candidates in the decomposition of action. Movement is one of them. One way of defending a pragmatist approach to intentionality is therefore to argue, for instance, that movement is constitutive of the very fact of objective reference, so that a cognitive system deprived of the capacity for movement would also be deprived of the capacity to refer to some things as objects. Another way, based on the notion of a target, is to argue that every intentional object is apprehended as the target of a potential action.

Another frequently invoked important component of action is not without an important difficulty. Indeed, as emphasized in many overviews of action theory,[12] action is often defined in reference to intention. In the dominant causalist perspective that locates the specificity of action in its causes, action is, for instance, often defined as a movement caused by intention. Similarly, Davidson[13] has famously proposed that "actions are doings that are intentional under some description," and Searle that there are no "actions without intentions."[14] If intention itself is not defined in terms of intentionality, claiming that intention is essential for intentionality is not problematic. But if it is, such a claim obviously raises the risk of making in certain cases the pragmatist theory of intentionality fall into a vicious circle, since the very notion of intentionality seems to be already contained in that of intention.

Indeed, intention is most often analyzed in terms of intentionality, either through its reduction to such central types of intentional relations as belief and desire[15] or through its assimilation with a sui generis form of intentional relation sharing with other ones the general features of intentionality.[16] A pragmatist theory claiming that intention is essential for understanding the nature of intentionality and based on a notion of intention so analyzed is clearly inconsistent and, therefore, impossible—unless the analysis of intention in terms of intentionality does not consist in applying to it previously intentional notions, but in forging these notions, and in such a way that every form of intentionality retains something of the specificity of intention as an intentional component of action. An example of such a theory is one claiming, for instance, that intentionally apprehending an object is always somehow intending to act upon it. The problem is also avoided by all forms of pragmatist theory that see intention as essential from any other angle than the elucidation of the nature of intentionality. Elucidating the concept of intention by means of previously established intentional notions is in particular perfectly consistent with considering action as essential for determining the cognitive relevance of intentionality: it shows that the concept of intentionality is precisely necessary for making sense of the concept of intention.

It is clear that these two series of criteria, in addition to not being exhaustive, are combinable and also possibly entertain certain forms of dependency to be taken into consideration in an effort to develop the full matrix of pragmatist theories of intentionality. The main elements of the outline of such a matrix just presented can be summarized as follows:

TA_1: Action is essential to the cognitive relevance of intentionality.
↳ B_1: Movement is essential to the relevance of intentionality.
    ↳ B_2: Intention is essential to the relevance of intentionality.

TA_2: Action is essential to the nature of intentionality.
1. = the nature of intentionality is correlated with the nature of
↳ B_1: movement
    ↳ B_2: intention
2. = the nature of intentionality is subordinated to the nature of
↳ B_1: movement
    ↳ B_2: intention
3. = the nature of intentionality integrates certain features of
↳ B_1: movement
    ↳ B_2: intention

TA$_3$: Action is essential to the determination of intentionality.
↳ B$_1$: Movement is essential to the determination of intentionality.
  ↳ B$_2$: Intention is essential to the determination of intentionality.

TA$_4$: Action is essential to the naturalization of intentionality.
↳ B$_1$: Movement is essential to the naturalization of intentionality.
  ↳ B$_2$: Intention is essential to the naturalization of intentionality.

The Pragmatist Claims of Cognitive Neuroscience

Which ones of these different possible forms of pragmatist intentionalism, if any, do the pragmatist claims of cognitive neuroscience actually exemplify?

In delineating the claims to be taken into consideration for answering this question, attention must be paid to the fact that a thorough critical examination cannot be limited to explicit pragmatist claims, although these must clearly constitute its main point of focus. Indeed, it might very well be that a neurocognitive theory of action does not explicitly defend a pragmatist form of intentionalism and yet makes statements with important implications in its favor. Accordingly, an appropriate way of delineating the corpus to be examined is to count as relevant any claim formulated in the context of a neurocognitive investigation of action that implies that action is essential for intentionality. Even though the corpus so delineated is not of unmanageable proportions, it is still beyond exhaustive reach in the context of this study, in which only a sample of representative works can therefore be made amenable to analysis. This sample includes studies by K. Atkins, A. Berthoz, J. Decéty, M. Goodale, V. Gallese, M. Jeannerod, B. Libet, A. Milner, G. Rizzolatti, and F. Varela.

In principle, each one of these studies should be successively examined and then compared with the others. However, as such a strategy would lead to obvious difficulties of expository redundancy, it appears to be more appropriate to extract from them a series of general claims in the form of a basic argument that is more or less present in all of them and then determine the extent to which, and the specific way how, each one exemplifies it.

This fundamental argumentation can be reconstructed as the following sequence of claims:

Claim 1: Intention is relevant to the explanation of action.
Claim 2: Intention is a pragmatic form of intentionality.
Claim 3: Intentionality is therefore relevant to the explanation of action.

Claim 4: Pragmatic intentionality or intention has a specific nature.
Claim 5: The relevance of intentionality can be extended to the explanation of other cognitive phenomena than action.
Claim 6: Action is essential to the nature of visual intentionality.
Claim 7: The essentiality of action is de facto but not de jure limited to the nature of visual intentionality.
Claim 8: Action is also essential to the naturalization of visual intentionality.

The Argument in Favor of Cognitive Intentionalism
This sequence should, in fact, be divided into two different parts. The first one covers claims 1 to 5 and amounts to no more than the vindication of the relevance of the property of intentionality to the explanation of action, as well as to other aspects of cognition, visual perception in particular. In other words, it amounts to no more than a defense of cognitive intentionalism from the perspective of cognitive neuroscience, with a strong emphasis on pragmatic intentionality, although not limited to it. It can be further analyzed in the following way:

Claim 1: Intention is relevant to the explanation of action This first claim asserts that, by laying bare specific neurobiological correlates that can only be made sense of psychologically in terms of intention, cognitive neuroscience of action gives support to postulating a psychological property of intention of the explanation of action. That a fundamental tenet of the cognitive neuroscience of action is to advocate the relevance of the notion of intention in the explanation of action is perhaps best illustrated by the work of Jeannerod. Indeed, his main self-proclaimed objective is to defend the idea that action should be viewed as a representation-governed process, as opposed to a process "determined by external forces."[17] Moreover, the representations involved in action are, in his opinion, in large part specifically motor ones, whose "internal structure, ... functional rules, and ... relations to movements"[18] constitute the very object of the discipline. His concept of motor representation is fairly complex, but it is clear that it chiefly involves the representation of a goal as well as a target. In the synthesis of his views offered in *The Cognitive Neuroscience of Action*, Jeannerod writes as follows:

> The representation of an action cannot be limited to the parameters and constraints dictated by execution of the action by the motor system. The goal of the action also must be encoded ... the idea will be developed that the goal of an action includes an internal representation both of the external object toward which the action is directed and the final state of the organism when this object is reached.[19]

And although he seems to also accept a more restricted sense of the concept of intention,[20] these notions of goal and target representation undoubtedly contain the essentials of the traditional notion of intention. To consider action as a representation-governed process thus implies seeing it as an intention-governed one.

Libet's work is even more focused on the notion of intention, although its approach to the problem of action is not as broad as that of Jeannerod. Indeed, one of his central concerns can be described as determining whether the property of conscious intention is a relevant one in the explanation of voluntary acts conducted from a neurocognitive perspective. Libet accepts that it is relevant from a first-person point of view: a person acting voluntarily captures adequately the content of his or her experience in saying that his or her acting is caused by an "intention" (Libet also speaks of a "will," an "urge," or a "decision") to act that way and to achieve something by doing so.[21] However, in order to be validated from a neurocognitive point of view, this first-person perspective notion should have a neurobiological correlate. And Libet demonstrates that the readiness potential discovered by Kornhuber and Deecke,[22] an increase of electrical activity located in the motor cortical regions about 1 second before the beginning of willed action, is an adequate candidate, given its absence in subjects reporting acting unintentionally, where it is replaced by a significantly more delayed potential. However, in order to fit this role, the 1-second readiness potential should be in synchrony with the experience of intention. Accordingly, Libet took as the starting point of a series of famous experimental investigations the following question: "When is the subject aware of his/her intention to act, in relation to the onset of RP [readiness potential] and to the expression of the voluntary process by the muscles (as seen in the recorded electromyogram)?"[23] These investigations demonstrated that the awareness of intention only occurs, on average, at 206 milliseconds before movement onset. Consequently, Libet's work can be taken to show that the property of intention can only be validated from a neurocognitive point of view if it is treated as unconscious. Libet nevertheless refuses this half-hearted defense of intention and makes the further hypothesis that the property of conscious intention can still play a role in the explanation of voluntary action if it is understood not as the primary cause of it but as a control factor that either validates or stops the unconsciously initiated process.

Similarly, the equally well-known investigations of Rizzolatti and Gallese on the neurons of premotor area F5 in monkeys are first and foremost a neurobiological justification of the relevance of the property of intention in the explanation of action. Their fundamental discovery, before demonstrating that such motor neurons are involved in perception, is that their activity is specifically correlated with the apprehension of a goal. Indeed, the specific feature of this activity is that the discharge only occurs when the action can be described from a psychological point of view as directed toward the achievement of something; in other and better words, the activity of F5 neurons only makes sense from a psychological point of view if it can be interpreted in terms of intention or goal directedness. They write, for instance, as follows:

What is coded is not simply a parameter such as force or movement direction, but rather the relationship, in motor terms, between the agent and the object of the action. F5 neurons become active only if a particular type of action (e.g., grasp, hold . . .) is executed to achieve a particular type of goal (e.g., to take possession of a piece of food, to throw away an object, . . .).[24]

And also: "premotor neurons . . . actually correlate with events that we can only understand if we move to the most abstract level of description of the action: its purpose."[25]

Claim 2: Intention is a pragmatic form of intentionality This property of intention is then analyzed as a form of intentionality in the Brentanian sense of the word, that is to say, as a form of objective reference. That it is so analyzed is already made clear in the illustrations of the previous claim. Intention is indeed obviously conceived as a certain form of reference to something apprehended as an objective element, be it a target object or the projected state of affairs of a goal, according to the theory taken into consideration. Gallese uses, for instance, a typically intentional terminology when he defines a goal as a "willed relational *attitude*."[26] The frequent connection established between the notion of intention and that of representation is also revealing in this respect, since the second one is often equated with the Brentanian notion of intentionality. No direct explicit connection with that specific notion is made, however, so that one could legitimately consider that this second claim remains implicit.

Claim 3: Intentionality is therefore relevant to the explanation of action This third claim follows directly from the two previous ones but is no more explicitly stated than they are in spite of its theoretical importance. It is indeed through this third claim that the neurocognitive analysis of action subscribes to the thesis of cognitive intentionalism. The cognitive intentionalism thereby espoused by the cognitive neuroscience of action remains, however, limited to the explanation of action. In other words, it is no more than a pragmatic form of cognitive intentionalism, not a general one.

Claim 4: Pragmatic intentionality or intention has a specific nature A more detailed analysis of some specific aspects of this pragmatic form of intentionality is then provided, although there is a significant variation in this respect among theorists. Some just fall short of making any real move in that direction, like Libet, whose interest is essentially limited to the question of whether conscious intention can be correlated with the 1-second readiness potential and who provides not even the outline of an analysis of what an intention to act might be. Gallese shows more concern for the nature of intention and even attempts to provide a technical definition of the idea of goal relatedness in his paper "Motor Ontology."[27] However, the main emphasis of his work and of Rizzolatti's is not on the nature of intention but on its relations with perception.

By contrast, Berthoz and Jeannerod attempt to provide a more developed analysis of the nature of pragmatic intentionality in simulatory terms, even though the term of intention per se does not play a key role in their writings. Berthoz's fundamental hypothesis is that intentional action is guided by an anticipatory simulation involving the movements to be executed and the environment in which they take place, as well as the final situation to be obtained. If there is more to this simulatory process than the idea of an intention to act, it is nevertheless clearly included in it and more or less corresponds to the simulation of the final situation. Jeannerod has pioneered similar principles of analysis, although it is only recently that he moved to a full simulatory approach to action.[28] His 1997 book restricts, in fact, the theoretical role of simulation to the analysis of the phenomenon of motor imagery, although it gives it a crucial methodological one in the study of intention itself, Jeannerod's contention being indeed that motor imagery gives us conscious access to the content of the motor representations guiding action. And, as already indicated, the resulting analysis of these motor representations is directly focused on the notions of goal and target, and it distinguishes between simple "object-oriented" actions, like reaching and grasping, and elaborate ones with a more complicated goal, involving the realization of a richly structured state of affairs. Intentional actions of this second sort include a special element of planning.

Claim 5: The relevance of intentionality can be extended to the explanation of cognitive phenomena other than action Finally, the relevance of intentionality is extended to the analysis of other cognitive phenomena closely related with action, and most of all to perception, which is a key determinant of action. However, just as it is hard to find in these studies any explicit recognition of the relevance of intentionality to the analysis of intention, it is—naturally enough—similarly difficult to find in them any explicit extension of the relevance of intentionality to the analysis of other cognitive phenomena. It is nevertheless beyond any possible dispute that it is so extended and, in particular, to perception and motor imagery.

The work of Atkins, however, constitutes a noticeable exception, both because of the more philosophical way in which she approaches the problem of the implications of the neurocognitive turn of cognitive intentionalism and because of the conclusions that she draws about it. Indeed, in her article "Of Sensory Attributes and the 'Aboutness' of Mental States,"[29] her project is to provide a critical analysis of the hypothesis of a generalized cognitive intentionalism as formulated by mainstream philosophy of cognitive science. Accordingly, she readily and explicitly acknowledges the general relevance of the property of intentionality and cannot therefore confront the issue of its possible extension from the explanation of action to the explanation of other cognitive phenomena. In fact, she confronts the reverse issue, namely, that of the limitation of the relevance of intentionality. Even though she considers that pragmatist conclusions about the nature of perception can legitimately be drawn from the data uncovered by the cognitive neuroscience approach to cognition, these data also speak, in her opinion, against the intentional character of perception. Akin's work should thus be seen as starting with claim 5, to which she gives a maximal extension, and then arguing that the pragmatist conception of perception suggested by cognitive neuroscience invites the exclusion of perception from its range of application.

The crucial point of the analyses just offered is that, in spite of Atkins' singularity, these first five claims result in a cognitive theory that is not of a pragmatist sort. As a matter of fact, as emphasized in the above section "A Theoretical Analysis of the Pragmatist Conception of Intentionalism," they only amount to a theory that advocates the general relevance of intentionality for explaining cognition, with a special emphasis on action, but does not vindicate the essentiality of action for all types of intentionality, in any of the possible ways reviewed in that section.

In particular, no essential link between perceptive intentionality and action has been yet demonstrated. Consequently, if the cognitive neuroscience of action does speak indeed in favor of a pragmatist kind of cognitive intentionalism, it is not to the extent that it adopts this first bundle of claims.

The Pragmatist Move

And it is indeed only through the second step of the argument, namely, through claims 6 to 8, that a move from a neurocognitive type of intentionalism to a neurocognitive *and pragmatist* type of intentionalism is made by some the studies under consideration. This *propio sensu* pragmatist part of the argument can in turn be analyzed as follows:

Claim 6: Action is essential to the nature of visual intentionality What most of the studies under consideration advocate forcefully is that the nature of visual intentionality can only be adequately understood if it is seen as essentially linked, in part or in totality, to action, thereby moving to a pragmatist theory of intentionality of the TA_2 kind. This claim is in many respects their most central one and lies at the core of their pragmatist commitment. It is also pervasive, since only Libet's work really makes exception to it, as well as to any other form of pragmatist intentionalism. The question is thus to determine the exact form it is given by the other studies.

In Berthoz's *The Sense of Movement*, this pragmatist move is clearly illustrated by the passage from the simulation theory of action to the motor theory of perception. As a matter of fact, Berthoz claims his book to be not only about action but also about the "relation between action and perception."[30] The motor theory of perception is first a TA_22 kind of pragmatist theory, since it advocates that the nature of perception is subordinated to action and locates this subordination mainly in the content of what is perceived. According to Berthoz, we essentially perceive what action requires in order to be possible. His favorite illustration of this hypothesis is the visual apparatus of toads that only detects longitudinal movements of elongated shapes and a large size general shape, corresponding, respectively, to the basic possible movements of their preys and to the figure of their predators, which trigger the two basic forms of their behavior. A toad facing an immobile although alive fly will let itself die of hunger.[31] Perception is, in other words, the servant of action. However, Berthoz also goes further in the direction of perceptive pragmatism by claiming that perception is active, is itself action. He writes, "We have to give up the distinction between sensory and motor.... I am saying that the frontiers between sensation and motricity are getting blurred."[32] This more radical claim, characteristic of a TA_23 form of pragmatism, is to be understood in at least two complementary ways. First, perception is, for Berthoz, an element of action, so that one should not consider them as two separate although closely linked cognitive phenomena, as they have traditionally been thought of, but as a single "perceptive–motor" one. The main reason invoked is that perceptive captors are used, on the one hand, to elaborate the simulations that guide action and, on the other hand, as instruments of verification of these simulations. The skier slaloming down the slope does not constantly construct anew his or her perceptive scene but contents himself or herself with verifying the adequacy of a simulated one and with making the necessary adjustments to it. Second, perception is an active process, and not a passive one: perceptive captors are not mere recorders but inquirers that cognitive systems modulate according to their needs and interests.

These two forms of pragmatist intentionalism ($TA_2 2$ and $TA_2 3$) are also present in Jeannerod's work, although under a different version and with different neurobiological arguments.

Jeannerod gives crucial attention to the two visual systems hypothesis of L. Ungerleider and M. Mishkin,[33] according to which visual stimuli are processed at the cortical level along two main paths, the dorsal one and the ventral one, and he reinterprets it in the context of the relation between perception and action. This reinterpretation, consonant with some investigations of Goodale and Milner,[34] is tantamount to distinguishing between two different kinds of perceptive intentionality. One is mainly, but not exclusively, based on the dorsal path and is directed at object attributes that are essentially linked to the guidance of the basic forms of action, such as grasping and reaching. The other one is mainly, but not exclusively either, based on the ventral path and is directed at object attributes that are also used in guiding action, but in a less immediate way, and that have other cognitive uses as well. This distinction between what Jeannerod calls the pragmatic visual representations and the semantic ones[35] is corroborated by pathological cases of dissociations, where the patients are dysfunctional at performing actions that involve only one of these two sorts of visual representations.

The admittance of a specifically pragmatic type of visual intentionality is definitely a pragmatist hypothesis of the $TA_2 2$ kind, since it is tantamount to admitting that the nature of what we visually perceive is relative to the requirements of action. The pragmatic form of vision mainly involved in what Jeannerod calls the visuotransformation is a vision *for* action. His perceptive pragmatism is, however, more limited than that of Berthoz, since it only concerns one aspect of the visual dimension of perception.

Similarly, Jeannerod also moves from this first type of perceptive pragmatism to a more radical one of the $TA_2 3$ kind, but in a more limited and cautious manner than Berthoz. He makes no explicit claim to the effect that, beyond being subordinated to action, pragmatic visual representations *are* in some sense action, and that the frontier between perception and action should be abolished in the case of visuomotor transformation. However, in the quotation reported above, he makes clear that the notion of motor representation applies to visual elements such as pragmatic visual representations, since the apprehension of something as a goal is indeed in most cases a partially visual one. Consequently, if the pragmatic visual representations correspond to the specifically pragmatic dimension of visual intentionality, and if motor representations are an essential element of the definition of action, it seems that the pragmatic part of visual perception should be considered as an element of action. In this perspective, Jeannerod is also, although in a more partial way, pleading for a unification by integration of action and perception.

The work of Gallese and Rizzolatti seems closer in this respect to the clear-cut pragmatist radicalism of Berthoz. Gallese and Rizzolatti were inevitably led to the analysis of the relations between action and perception by the further discovery that the premotor neurons correlated with intention were also in large part activated either during object visual perception (canonical neurons) or during the visual perception of the execution by others of similar actions (mirror neurons).

The canonical neurons case lends itself to a weak pragmatist reading of the TA_21 type that seems to be endorsed by Gallese and Rizzolatti in certain contexts, such as a synthesis article of 1997.[36] According to this interpretation, the canonical neurons are the basis of an intention to act present in action execution as well as correlated with object vision through a simple associative mechanism. When I perceive certain objects, I systematically evoke an intention to act dealing with them, although in an unconscious way, such that I cannot perceive these objects without also considering them as the target of a possible action. In such a perspective, a canonical neuron is not, strictly speaking, bimodal, since it is, in fact, the basis of a specific element of action, namely, intention, that simply happens to be coactivated by the neural mechanisms of object perception. However, Rizzolatti and Gallese clearly want to go further into pragmatism and move, in fact, to a TA_23 kind of theory of a radical sort, according to which perception is not simply correlated with action through an associative mechanism but is integrated with it. Indeed, the activation of the canonical neurons in object perception is considered by Rizzolatti and Gallese as responsible for a crucial component of object perception that they call the apprehension of its "meaning." In other words, the intention to act linked to the activation of canonical neurons is not simply correlated with object perception but is constitutive of object perception, in the sense that it is an element of the apprehension of an attribute of the perceived as such, namely, object meaning, that is itself assimilated thereby to the fact of being the target of certain possible actions. This more radical reading is essentially associated with Gallese, who, in later articles, makes frequent statements such as the following one:

> An object, as coded by canonical neurons, is transformed from a physical textured pattern of given shape, size and color into something that acquires a meaning in virtue of being constituted as the target of an action. The physical object becomes an intentional object. . . . The object ceases to exist by itself, but acquires a meaning in virtue of its relation with the acting subject."[37]

And also: "Representation is intrinsically related to action control," to the point that there is "an impossibility of drawing a sharp line between acting and perceiving."[38]

This analysis is extended to the case of mirror neurons and the perception of action. Just as canonical neurons are the basis of the apprehension of the meaning of objects, mirror neurons are claimed to be the basis of the apprehension of the meaning of actions. This extension is not without difficulties, in fact, since the analogy cannot be pushed all the way, given that the meaning of an object and the meaning of an action can hardly be taken as being of the same type. The point is not addressed, however, by Rizzolatti and Gallese and does not affect the analysis of the pragmatist character of their theory proposed here.

According to the interpretation just offered, the strongest element of pragmatism contained in the claims of the cognitive neuroscience of action is not therefore that perceptive intentionality is simply relative to action, or even subordinated to it, but that something of action is literally present in it—in a way that varies according to authors—so that perceiving is already acting, although not fully.

Claim 7: The essentiality of action is limited de facto but not de jure to the nature of visual perceptive intentionality An additional characteristic feature of the pragmatism of the cognitive neuroscience of action is its de facto limitation to perceptive intentionality. No explicit claim to the effect that it cannot be further extended to other kinds of intentionality is made. However it has so far almost exclusively focused on perceptive intentionality. The only attempts at extending this pragmatist perspective beyond visual intentionality to be found in the literature examined here are in the direction of motor imagination. The work of Decéty[39] is important in this regard, and it is used by Jeannerod (who collaborated directly with him on this issue) and, to a minor extent, by Berthoz. Indeeed, Decéty has conducted a series of investigations showing that the same areas that are activated in the preparation of an action, and accordingly are at the basis of its guiding intention, are also activated under certain conditions, not only in the perception of action but also in the imagination of that action. Similar neurobiological considerations naturally inviting similar conclusions, it can be inferred that action is integrated with imagination in the same fashion as it is with perception—a conclusion that only Jeannerod can be credited with drawing fully, with his claim that motor imagery is, in fact, nothing else than a motor representation turned conscious.[40] However, no pragmatist theory of motor imagination has so far emanated from the neurocognitive community of action in the way in which a pragmatist theory of perceptive intentionality has.

That the limitation underscored here is mostly viewed as a factual one is corroborated by the enlarged pragmatist perspective on the neurocognitive theory of cognition advocated by certain authors. The claim of a general essentiality of action for cognition is well illustrated by Berthoz, who revealingly states in the introductory pages of *The Sense of Movement*, "At the beginning was action."[41] The book itself is, however, restricted to the study of the relations between action and perception. The enactive approach of Varela should also be mentioned in this context, since it can be read as implying a generalized pragmatist intentionalism that also remains essentially theoretical. Indeed, the problem of intentionality is at the heart of the theory of enaction, which shares in addition the distinguishing features of cognitive neuroscience. As made clear in *The Embodied Mind*,[42] the theory of cognition is viewed in substance as an answer to the question, "What does it mean for a cognitive state to be about the world?" Varela criticizes the contemporary cognitive theories for assuming not so much that there is an independent world, but that this world is what a cognitive system is about and tries to capture. Instead, cognition should be understood, in his eyes, as an intentional activity of a constructive kind, whereby a cognitive system elaborates or enacts a referential world needed for adaptation to the real one. Accordingly, Varela's intentionalism also establishes an essential link of the most radical sort between intentionality in general and action. Being an enactive process, intentionality also is an active one. However, the two notions of enaction and action should not be conflated. The first is broader than the second. In the terminology of Varela, taken from the dynamical systems theory, enaction takes the form of a dynamical coupling between the environment and the cognitive system. And action certainly is one important aspect of such coupling as shown by the emphasis that Varela puts on the body and its movements, but it has also many other aspects, starting at the cell level. As a consequence, the most adequate way of characterizing the enactive approach with respect to the issue under scrutiny seems to say that it implies a general pragmatist intentionalism of a nonrealist sort. However, this implication is not spelled out in detail by Varela, either theoretically or empirically.

Claim 8: Action is also essential to the naturalization of perceptive intentionality
Finally, none of these studies demonstrates how a pragmatist conception of the nature of perceptive intentionality makes its naturalist explanation more amenable. Few of them, in fact, even endorse a well-defined principle of naturalization, although almost all seem to share an inclination for some form of neurobiological emergentism, the most detailed formulation of which is provided by Varela. However, all are also explicitly on the naturalist side and, therefore, cannot but share the conviction that a pragmatist approach to the nature of intentionality means a progress toward its naturalization, since it is impossible to naturalize a phenomenon whose nature is misconceived in the first place. They also share, therefore, the conviction that action is essential to the naturalization of intentionality, although this claim still stands in need of a fully explicit and detailed formulation. Atkins is, of course, an exception to this further conclusion, since she rejects the intentional character of perception. But she is certainly sympathetic to it if it is reformulated as the more general thesis that action is essential to the naturalization of perception.

Notes

1. The notion of intentionality at stake in the problem of intentionalism is indeed the philosophical one introduced by the nineteenth-century philosopher Franz Brentano in his landmark *Psychology from an Empirical Viewpoint* (see Brentano 1973) and not the more restricted one familiar in the psychology literature, that is, in fact, equivalent to the ordinary expression of intention.

2. Such a definition corresponds to one way of reading Brentano's original characterization of intentionality; it is also in accordance with the characterization later provided by Russell in 1913, in a fairly different philosophical context, through the closely related notion of acquaintance. See Russell (1913).

3. As shown by the long-standing issue of nonexistent intentional objects, that at one point led Brentano to explicitly characterize intentionality as a "quasi-relation."

4. Cf. Roy (1999).

5. Cf. Gazzaniga et al. (1998).

6. Cf. Kosslyn and Koenig (1992).

7. Cf. Posner et al. (1982).

8. Cf. Imbert (1992).

9. Cf. Churchland (1986).

10. Cf. Roy (2000, 2004).

11. Cf. Atkins (1996).

12. See, for instance, Davis (1994), Mele (1997), and Wilson (2002).

13. Cf. Davidson (1963).

14. Cf. Searle (1983, p. 82).

15. Cf., for example, Davidson (1963).

16. Cf., for example, Searle (1983).

17. Cf. Jeannerod (1990, p. 353).

18. Ibid.

19. Cf. Jeannerod (1997, p. 94).

20. Cf. ibid., chapter 6.

21. Cf. Libet (1985, §1).

22. Kornhuber and Deecke (1965).

23. Cf. Libet 1993 (p. 111).

24. Cf. Gallese (2000a).

25. Cf. Gallese (2000b).

26. Cf. Gallese (2000a).

27. Cf. Gallese (2003).

28. Cf. Jeannerod (2001).

29. Cf. Atkins (1996).

30. French edition (p. 12).

31. Cf. French edition (p. 180).

32. Cf. French edition (p. 229).

33. Cf. Ungerleider and Mishkin (1982).

34. Cf. Milner and Goodale (1995).

35. Cf. Jeannerod (1997, p. 76).

36. Cf. Rizzolatti and Gallese (1997).

37. Cf. Gallese (2000b, p. 1).

38. Ibid. (pp. 6, 16).

39. Cf. Decéty (1996).

40. Cf. Jeannerod (1997, chapter 4).

41. Cf. French edition (p. 10).

42. Cf. Varela et al. (1993).

References

Atkins, K. (1996). On sensory systems and the "aboutness" of mental states. *Journal of Philosophy*, 96, 337–372.

Berthoz, A. (2000). *The brain's sense of movement*. Cambridge: Harvard University Press.

Brentano, F. C., Kraus, O. et al. (1973). *Psychology from an empirical standpoint*. London: Routledge and Kegan Paul; Humanities Press.

Churchland, P. S. (1986). *Neurophilosophy: Toward a unified science of the mind–brain*. Cambridge: MIT Press.

Davidson, D. (1963). Actions, reasons and causes. In *Essays on actions and events* (1980, pp. 3–19). Oxford: Oxford University Press.

Davis, L. (1994). Action. In S. D. Guttenplan (Ed.), *A companion to the philosophy of mind* (pp. 111–117). Oxford: Blackwell.

Decéty, J. (1996). Possible involvement of primary motor cortex in mentally simulated movement: A FMRI study. *NeuroReport*, 7, 1280–1284.

Gallese, V. (2000a). The acting subject. In T. Metzinger (Ed.), *Neural correlates of consciousness* (pp. 325–334). Cambridge: MIT Press.

Gallese, V. (2000b). The inner sense of action: Agency and motor representations. *Journal of Consciousness Studies*, 7(10), 23–40.

Gallese, V. and Metzinger, T. (2003). Motor ontology: The representational reality of goals, actions and selves. *Philosophical Psychology*, 13, 365–388.

Gazzaniga, M. S., Ivry, R. B., and Mangun, G. R. (1998). *Cognitive neuroscience: The biology of the mind*. New York: W. W. Norton.

Imbert, M. (1992). Neurosciences et sciences cognitives. In D. Andler (Ed.), *Introduction aux sciences cognitives* (pp. 53–69). Paris: Gallimard.

Jeannerod, M. (1990). The representation of the goal of an action and its role in the control of goal-directed movements. In E. Schwartz (Ed.), *Computational neuroscience* (pp. 352–365). Cambridge: MIT Press.

Jeannerod, M. (1997). *The cognitive neuroscience of action*. Oxford: Blackwell.

Jeannerod, M. (2001). Neural simulation of action: A unifying mechanism for motor cognition. *NeuroImage, 14*, S103–S104.

Kornhuber, H., and Deecke, L. (1965). Hirnpotentialländerungen bei Willkürbewegungen und Passiven des menschen: Bereitschaftspotential und reaffarente Potentiale. *Pflügers Archiv für die gesamte Physiologie des menschen und Tiere, 284*, 1–17.

Kosslyn, S., and Koenig, O. (1992). *Wetmind: The new cognitive neuroscience*. New York: Free Press.

Libet, B. (1985). Unconscious cerebral intiative and the role of conscious will in voluntary action. *Behavioral and Brain Sciences, 8*, 529–566.

Libet, B. (Ed.). (1993). *Neural processes in the production of experience*. Ciba Foundation symposium; 174. Chichester: Wiley.

Mele, A. R. (1997). *The philosophy of action*. Oxford: Oxford University Press.

Milner, A. D., and Goodale, M. A. (1995). *The visual brain in action*. Oxford: Oxford University Press.

Posner, M., Pea, R., and Volpe, B. (1982). Cognitive neuroscience: Developments toward a science of synthesis. In J. Mehler, E. Walker, and M. Garrett (Eds.), *Perspectives on mental representations* (pp. 251–275). Hillsdale, NJ: Erlbaum.

Rizzolatti, G., and Gallese, V. (1997). From action to meaning: A neurophysiological perspective. In J.-L. Petit (Ed.), *Les neurosciences et la philosophie de l'action* (pp. 217–229). Paris: Vrin.

Roy, J.-M. (1997). Res cogitans sive res movens: Remarques sur une neuroscience cognitive de l'action. Unpublished manuscript.

Roy, J.-M. (1999). Saving intentional phenomena: Intentionality, representation and symbol. In J. Petitot, F. J. Varela, B. Pachoud, and J.-M. Roy (Eds.), *Naturalizing phenomenology: Issues in contemporary phenomenology and cognitive science* (pp. 111–147). Stanford, CA: Stanford University Press.

Roy, J.-M. (2000). Naturalización de la mente y autonomía de la explicación mentalista. In J. Botero, J. Ramos, and A. Rosas (Eds.), *Mentes reales* (pp. 31–56). Bogota: Siglos del Hombre.

Roy, J.-M. (2001). L'émergence de la neuroscience cognitive. *Cahiers Alfred Binet*, 667.

Roy, J.-M. (2004). Cognitive neuroscience and the unity of the study of cognition. In J. Larrazabal and J. A. Miranda (Eds.), *Language, knoweldge, and representation* (pp. 113–134). Dordrecht: Kluwer.

Russell, B. (1913/1992). *Theory of knowledge: The 1913 manuscript*. London: Routledge.

Searle, J. R. (1983). *Intentionality, an essay in the philosophy of mind*. Cambridge: Cambridge University Press.

Ungerleider, L., and Mishkin, M. (1982). Two cortical visual systems. In J. Ingle, M. Goodale, and R. Mansfield (Eds.), *Analysis of visual behavior* (pp. 549–586). Cambridge: MIT Press.

Varela, F., Thompson, E., and Rosch, E. (1993). *The embodied mind: Cognitive science and human experience*. Cambridge: MIT Press.

Wilson, G. (2002). Action. *Stanford encyclopedia of philosophy.* http://plato.stanford.edu/.CSLI, Stanford University.

Part VII Synthesis

15 Externalist Naturalization of Intention in Action

Dorothée Legrand

The present volume is entitled *Naturalizing Intention in Action*. As the diversity of the specific contributions of the chapters illustrates, the notions of "naturalization" and "intention" can be understood in a number of different ways. Here, I will argue that beyond this apparent diversity of approaches, the content of each chapter of this volume can be interpreted and exploited to propose and justify a uniform way to naturalize intention in action.[1]

Naturalization

First, what is it to naturalize? There are different ways of conceiving of such an enterprise (see J.-M. Roy, chapter 14), but an obvious common point of all naturalistic approaches is to avoid Cartesian dualism, which ontologically separates the mind from the body, the thinking substance from the physical extended substance. For example, a dualist conception would define intention purely in terms of mental states and would further conceive the latter as ontologically dissociated from physical states. Contemporary cognitive sciences intending to naturalize intention explicitly dismiss Cartesian dualism. However, some naturalistic positions remain implicitly and surprisingly dualist. This contemporary form of dualism is mostly methodological rather than ontological. It relies on the characterization of the mind primarily in terms of mental properties. On the basis of this first step that is common with Cartesian dualism, they fundamentally differ from it by correlating these mental states with states of the body (mostly states of the brain). However, this relation to the physiological counterpart of mental state is only secondary. For example, the attempt to naturalize intention classically starts from a (more or less fine-grained) description of the phenomenon under investigation (intention) in terms of mental states only (reasons, beliefs, desires) and then, and only then, considers how these mental states are correlated with cerebral states. In this view, intention is fundamentally mental, conceived in isolation from physical constraints, even if correlated with neurophysiological states. What I want to point out here is that this methodological dualism is not satisfactory to achieve naturalization. Indeed, what naturalists want is an understanding of what intention is in the natural world, not the mere understanding of the correlation of mental and physical states conceived in isolation from each other. Descartes already pursued this methodology by linking the "mind" to the pineal gland. Rather than proposing more plausible and detailed correlates, I here intend to propose an alternative methodology.

Importantly, this alternative methodology cannot simply be reductionist–eliminativist. Indeed, the latter would merely amount to pushing further the two-step methodology just described above in order to eliminate the mental states and retain only their neurophysiological correlates. Such reductionism is, in fact, no more satisfactory than dualism in achieving naturalization. Indeed, what naturalists want is an explanation of what intention is (including the subjective experience of intention), not an elimination of intention in favor of neuronal activations.

On the basis of these considerations, what is needed is a naturalistic alternative to both "methodological dualism" and reductionism. In the framework at stake here, that is, the naturalization of intentional action, one way to overcome these two problematic approaches is to reconsider their common ground: the first methodological step conceiving of (e.g.) intention primarily as internal (mental and/or neuronal) states. According to such an "internalist" view, these states (e.g., intention) are detached from behavioral states (e.g., action) and are prior to them.

Methodologically, it is important to note that the correlation of mental states with neuronal activations preserves the internalist conception following which some internal (neuro–mental) states cause some ensuing (external) behavior. As stated by J.-L. Petit about his own project: "we hope to find an embodiment of intentionality that goes farther than dodging the issue like current cognitive theory of mind by implementing mental representations (its fake substitutes) in the brain." In the same vein, I here intend to answer the following questions: What would be a noninternalist conception of mental states in general and of intention in particular? And would such an "externalist" conception allow for a nonreductionist naturalization of intention in action?

Note that in the following, the terms "internalism" and "externalism" will be considered specifically as, respectively, naming characterizations of mental states only in terms of what happens inside the head (mental and/ or neuronal) or also in terms of what happens in the behavioral interaction between a subject and its world. There are many other different conceptions of "internalism" and "externalism" debated in philosophy.[2] In particular, some conceptions of "externalism" are defined as incompatible with the naturalization of mental states. I obviously want to avoid this connotation here. Rather, I hope to contribute to some reconsideration of the very enterprise of naturalization as going beyond (reductionist or dualist) correlations: naturalizing as I understand it here does not merely amount to correlating mental states to neuronal states but also to understanding mental states as constrained and expressed by physical states, the latter including neurons, behavior, and the outside world.

Intention

As far as naturalistic considerations are concerned, why specifically focus on the investigation of intention? One reason is that it seems to provide a particularly relevant starting point for the enterprise of "externalist naturalization." Indeed, intuitively, the canonical form of intention is defined by a double aspect: mental (an intention is characterized by a set of reasons, beliefs, desires . . .) and behavioral (an intention leads to an intentional action performed in the outside world). My proposal here is that understanding the mental aspects of intention as anchored into the behavioral aspects will allow the *naturalization of intentions by externalizing them into action*. This project can take (and does take throughout this volume) different forms. As clarified by J.-M. Roy in his account of pragmatist conceptions of intentionality, mental and/or cognitive states can be conceived of as essentially related to action or as, in addition, determined or constituted by it. Of course, detailing all possibilities goes far beyond the scope of this chapter, where I will only consider some of the many links between intention and action.

From Mental Intention to Intentional Action

Traditionally, intentions are conceived of in terms of prior mental states that are causally and/or rationally linked with the intentional action, hence differentiating the latter from unintended movements or passive happenings. P. Livet and J.-L. Petit review classical philosophical problems in theories of action and argue that these problems are caused in part by the separation of intention from action. In chapter 8, I also underline the limitation of causal conceptions of intention, arguing that the specificity of intention is to be acted and that this aspect remains beyond the scope of the classical dissociation between intention (cause) and action (effect). From an empirical perspective, F. Grammont argues that desires should be distinguished from intention and that the latter is constitutively linked to action: you can have a desire but not an intention to perform an impossible action. Learning to perform a new action would not change your desire, but it is the condition for you to entertain the intention to perform it, the latter being specifically linked to action plan, execution, and recognition.

All these positions converge on a criticism of "a traditional philosophical analysis of intentional action according to which intentional action is behavior that is appropriately (rationally) motivated by beliefs and desires" (C. Allen, chapter 5).

Planning Intentional Action

As C. Allen clarifies, one might reject this view altogether and argue that intention would not be a set of mental states but would rather correspond to "motor patterns" (chapter 5). However, this would amount to a form of behaviorism that a genuine naturalization of intention must avoid. Indeed, one cannot deny the existence of intentional states prior to and determinant for the execution of intentional action. Moreover, these prior states cannot simply be reduced to mere behavioral patterns. Indeed, and as C. Allen makes clear from an ethological point of view, one should differentiate precisely between mind reading and intentional-action reading, as monkeys might be capable of the latter without being capable of the former. Intention does not merely correspond to the execution of intentional action, and intention reading does not merely correspond to behavior reading: "there seems to be a need to attribute cognitive representations that are prior to action, even if the content of these states intricately involves the animals' own possibilities for action" (C. Allen; cf. also below F. Grammont and J. Sommerville and A. Woodward, who make this same point on the basis of experiments in neurophysiology and in developmental psychology, respectively). This last issue is one of the questions I intend to clarify here: How (and how much) does "prior intention" depend on action (potential) execution?

Some answers are suggested by results obtained in the cognitive neurosciences of intentional action. Indeed, "it has been documented that magnetic stimulation over SMA [supplementary motor area] can alter the choice of the movement to be executed" (M. Tsakiris and P. Haggard). Activation of SMA is prior to and disconnected from the actual execution of the intentional action: "SMA activity precedes M1 activation during the generation of voluntary movement, and it is present even when no actual movement occurs. Moreover, its activity seems to reflect a higher level representation of motor preparation and execution, since it is not correlated to the actual muscle activity" (M. Tsakiris and P. Haggard). Therefore, these prior states seem to determine *action* and action plan, even if they are detached from *movement* (muscular contraction).

Nonetheless, it is important to underline that these basic prior internal states are not fixed a priori but notably depend on motivational states (P. Livet). As suggested by V. Gallese, goal states are represented "along an axis of valence." This valence is notably based on an innate "logic of survival," but it is also updated continuously and online, through the encounter of resisting or rewarding situations in the physical and social environment. In other words, intention (even prior intention) is regulated, modulated by the outcome of previously executed action. From a genetic (developmental) perspective, these prior states would (have to) be constrained by action execution. This is the position P. Livet argues for in terms of a "recursive genesis" from action to intention.

Goal Directedness

As just argued, prior intentions are "incarnated" (following a term used by J. Pailhous, J. DeGraaf, and M. Bonnard) in that they are partly determined (modulated) by action execution. Moreover, intention is not restricted to prior intention. Indeed, prior intention is not even necessary to the execution of intentional action. As I argue in chapter 8, what is necessary is a bodily intention. The latter is built-in action execution in the sense that the execution of action is itself intrinsically structured as goal directed. This goal-directed structure is not decided by the agent, but it remains the necessary ingredient of any intentional action. At this level, to have an intention is thus not only to have a reason to act but also to have a body oriented toward a goal.

This point is coherent with the data reported by V. Gallese, who does not investigate the properties of action execution per se but rather the (neuronal and phenomenal) characteristics of action representations. The experiments he reports suggest that intentional action is characterized by inner states which depend on the agent's embodiment and anchoring in its physical and social environment. This position thus differs both from behaviorism and from pure internalism (in the sense defined above). Specifically, neurons in the premotor area F5 are activated when a motor relationship holds between the agent and the object of the action, independent of physical parameters of movement such as force or movement direction. The point I wish to underline here is that representation of intentional actions is specifically structured in relational terms: "The appearance of a graspable object in the visual space will retrieve immediately the appropriate 'motor schema' of the intended type of hand–object relation" (V. Gallese). In more detail, "canonical neurons" are activated both when the agent acts and when he or she merely visually observes the potential target of such an action. In that sense, they "contribute to a *multimodal representation of an organism–object relation*" (V. Gallese; cf. also D. Legrand and M. Iacoboni). Objects are thus represented as action related, and actions are represented as goal directed. These representations are "internal" (neuronal activation in the premotor cortex), but their specificity is that they are modeled by the "dynamic interplay between situated organisms and their natural playground" (V. Gallese). As recalled by V. Gallese, this conception of the high-level criterion for intentional action is also suggested by M. Iacoboni's data showing in a functional magnetic resonance imaging study that premotor mirror areas are specifically more activated for actions embedded in a significant external context rather than when presented outside any context (see also F. Grammont). In other words, even at this "high" (representation of why the action is performed) and "internal" (representation within the head) level, intentional actions cannot be conceived as a private affair, as they are intrinsically structured as open (intentionally related) to the external world (physical, but also social, as I will detail below).

Executing Intentional Action

Acting intentionally is not merely representing a goal nor initiating a goal-directed action. Rather, intentional action is also an action controlled by its agent (P. Livet). Here again, this criterion of intention should not be reduced to mental states (e.g., a reason held by the agent, controlling the intentional action and justifying it up to its end). Rather, P. Livet argues that it is better understood in terms of adjustments and revisions of the execution of the action up to its end (reaching its goal). This criterion of intention is thus, here again, bodily in that it corresponds to a characteristic of action execution. At this level, an intentional action is a controlled action, that is, an action whose execution is adapted to the reaching of the goal. If the execution is not adapted to the reaching of the goal, the action is revised, and this is what makes it intentional and recognized as such. Intention is thus a characteristic of action (revisions of action execution justifying the intention recursively) rather than a mental characteristic (reasons to act justifying the action in a top–down manner).

Experiencing Intentional Action as Intentional

Another important aspect of intention and intentional action is experiential: an intentional action is an action experienced as intentional by the agent. Therefore, an "externalist–naturalist" account of intention and intentional action must be able to specify how much the experience of intentional action as intentional relies on action execution (vs. how much it relies on experiencing internal prior mental states). Specifically, the conception of intention (built-)in action defended so far would be coherent with (and strengthened by) the fact that being conscious of intentional actions is not only being conscious of "internal" intention but is also being conscious of actions specifically as they are intentionally structured. This is what I will check now: What is it like to be conscious of one's intentional action as intentional?

It has been shown that perceiving intentional action as intentional notably depends on perceiving action as goal directed. Specifically, J. Sommerville and A. Woodward show that 12-month-old infants can represent an action on an intermediary object (a cloth on which an object is placed) as a mean to reach a more distal goal (the toy), implying that they construe simple action sequences with respect to higher order goals. This suggests that perceiving an intention does not rely only on the understanding of the mental source or justification of the observed intentional action. It does not rely only on the processing of the specific means (movement) used to execute the intention, either. Rather, perceiving an intention primarily relies on the perception of the action's end as such (the goal the action is directed toward). This position is coherent with C. Allen's proposition that intentional action can, in fact, be understood without relying on the understanding of mental intention. As underlined above, behavior reading would not correspond to full-fledged intention, but this has nonetheless to be taken into serious consideration as a landmark in the development of "higher" cognitive capacity.

The understanding of intentional action that I present here differs from behaviorism and is fully coherent with the fact that agents are not easily conscious of the means with which they reach their goal, the movement force, for example. Interestingly, J. Pailhous, J. DeGraaf, and M. Bonnard investigate the delay in becoming conscious of the parameters of one's intentional modulation of one's automatic behavior (this experiment is also interpreted by P. Livet). They show that the agent has only a weak consciousness of the means as long as these means allow the goal to be achieved in a controlled way. This suggests that being aware of one's intentional action is first and foremost being aware of achieving the intended goal.

Intentional Action beyond the Agent's Conscious Control

Up to now, intentional action has been described as controlled and consciously experienced by its agent. However, it should also be underlined that intentional action at least partly slips out of the agent's hands. Indeed, as argued by J. Pailhous, J. DeGraaf, and M. Bonnard, the reaching of a goal is determined not only by controlled (mental and/or physical) states but also uncontrolled states of oneself (physical and/or mental) and of the external physical environment (muscle fatigue, gravity etc.) and also by the social environment (cf. A. Ogien's position described below). Controlling one's intentional action thus does not imply only being able to apply guiding mental states to the execution of action. Rather, it is also to be able to take into consideration constraints due to the body the intention is acted with and due to the environment the intentional action is acted in (J. Pailhous, J. DeGraaf, and M. Bonnard), in order to adjust and revise the execution of the action when necessary (P. Livet). In this view, intention comes as a regulator of what is already going on and not as a mere controller of what will ensue. In line with this conception, knowing (being conscious of) the intention does not amount to knowing the agent's reasons for acting. Rather, it is to know how much a motivation can be carried out given the current state of the body (position, muscular fatigue . . .) and given the current state of the environment (physical and social).

This view suggests that being conscious of one's intentional action as intentional implies being conscious not only of one's prior mental states, not only of one's intentionally acting body, but also of one's world (the perception of the world where one acts intentionally). If this extended-to-the-world view of intention is correct, the prediction is that acting intentionally has consequences for the perception of the world one acts intentionally in and on. This can be checked at the level of the physical environment and at the level of the social environment as I will detail below.

The Intentional Agent's Perception of the External World

Again coherently with an "externalist" conception of intention, M. Tsakiris and P. Haggard provide arguments in favor of the idea that intentions have perceptual counterparts. First, they have evidenced the phenomenon of "intentional binding" following which an intentional action (and not a passive movement) and its sensory outcomes are perceived as being closer together in time than they are in reality. Moreover, they also recall the phenomenon of "sensory suppression" following which the subject is less conscious of the sensory consequences of his or her own intentional action. They also specify that the subject is more conscious of the effect of the action when this action is not under his or her control. These results suggest that being a conscious intentional agent is far from being restricted to being conscious of causal intentional mental states. Rather, it is also being conscious of the world in a way that is specifically "filtered" by one's intentional action.

In this perspective, intentional action is not restricted to something in the head (mental and/or physical). Rather, being an intentional agent intentionally structures one's own action execution (in the world) and one's perception of the consequences (in the world) of one's action. It is thus open to motor and perceptual modifications of the external world. This is coherent with J.-L. Petit's approach, which intends to account for the attentional and intentional constitution of the intentional object through kinesthesia.

Perceiving Others' Intentional Action

Being an intentional agent is all the more "extended" (situated in the external world) in that it also structures the perception of actions other than one's own. As such, it is open not only to the physical world but to the social world as well.

Understanding others' intention(al action) relies on (F. Grammont) and is enhanced by (J. Sommerville and A. Woodward) one's own ability to perform controlled goal-directed actions. As predicted by P. Livet, "the observer has to possess in his or her own motor repertoire the movement that the agent is exhibiting." This has been shown empirically in the following ways.

F. Grammont investigates the properties of mirror neurons, a class of premotor neurons that discharge not only when the monkey executes goal-related actions but also when the monkey observes other individuals (monkeys or humans) executing similar actions. He shows that an action that does not belong to one's own motor repertoire, that is, an action that can only be observed but not performed by the observer himself, is not represented in intentional motor terms. Specifically, mirror neurons are not active during the observation of "impossible" actions. However, once these actions become possible, after motor learning, mirror neurons are active both when the agent observes and when the agent executes these actions. This result suggests that action execution participates in the constitution of representations of the goal directedness of action, these representations being later on available for one's action as well as others'.

J. Sommerville and A. Woodward investigate this same question from the perspective of developmental psychology. In particular, they argue that the infants' own production of goal-directed actions provides a powerful source of information allowing them to understand the actions of others as goal directed. To test this hypothesis, they put a sticky mitten on the hand of 3-month-old infants. This experimental setup provides these infants with new opportunities to reach and grasp, or rather reach and stick, different toys, whereas they are normally too young to do so. The results show that only infants who received the training are more interested in the goal reached than in the way it is reached. This finding suggests that "first-hand" experience of action execution facilitates the perception of the goal directedness of another's action: the acting body is a motor for the constitution of action representation and, in turn, for action perception and the understanding of intention.

This view also coheres with the pattern of activation of mirror neurons. These visuomotor neurons are activated both when the agent acts and when he or she passively observes another agent executing similar actions. As recalled above, V. Gallese argues that the representation of intentional action corresponds to the representation of the relation between means and ends. Given that the same neurons are activated for the representation of one's own action and others' action, he also claims that this representation remains neutral as to who the agent is. However, is such activation enough to claim that intentional actions are represented from *no* particular perspective (V. Gallese)? Whether this claim is secured by empirical data or not (this issue is also discussed by M. Tsakiris and P. Haggard with respect to the notion of "naked intention"), it remains that both one's own and others' intentional action are represented in a relational way linking means and ends. In other words, independent of social or intersubjective interpretations of the activity of mirror neurons, it remains that their activation is fully coherent with an understanding of intention as "situated."

Interacting Intentionally with Others

The different studies mentioned up to now suggest that intentional action is not exclusively determined by prior mental states but is fundamentally related to action execution: action execution determines prior intention; it is itself structured intentionally; it determines consciousness of one's and others' intentional action and perception of the world. Pushing this same line of thought one step further (i.e., continuing the opening of intentional action to the external world rather than restricting it to the states internal to the agent's head), it should be noted that being an intentional agent does not only structure one's observation of others, that is, it does not only relate one's action execution and one's perception of others. In addition, there is also a relation between one's action execution and the other's action execution.

This point joins the reconsideration of intention that I propose here to a reconsideration of intersubjectivity: just like intention does not come from inside out, intersubjectivity does not come from oneself toward the observed others; just like intention is built-in action execution, intersubjectivity is built-in interactions between two (or more) subjects (D. Legrand and M. Iacoboni). Indeed, understanding others' intention is not (or at least not only, and not primarily) observing others and inferring from their behavior their internal (hidden, prior, and causal) mental states thanks to some theories of mind (theory or simulation). Rather, D. Legrand and M. Iacoboni argue both philosophically and empirically that it has to rely also on interactive behavior. What is shared is a repertoire of action (P. Livet; F. Grammont), a common goal (D. Legrand and M. Iacoboni), and/or a "similar knowledge about the situations they find themselves in . . . [letting] coordination emerge" (A. Ogien).

In more detail, A. Ogien reverses the arrow from intention toward interaction: individual intentional behavior does not constraints social interaction unidirectionally; the other way around is constraining too. He argues that "no individual is free to decide by himself or herself—that is, irrelatively to the actual circumstances of an ongoing interaction—what his or her or somebody else's intention is or should be. Thus, instead of assuming that intention is a subjective state or the cause of an individual behavior, sociologists—when they adopt an externalist stance—would rather consider it as a justification individuals are accustomed to use *in and for* action" (A. Ogien). According to this interactionist conception, role, situation, and concepts "preexist with respect to the engagement of individuals in an interaction and survive to its termination" (A. Ogien). In other words, action and interaction are shaped by these social values and constraints.

Conclusion

M. Tsakiris and P. Haggard recall that "recently, Wegner (2002) suggested that free will is an illusory reconstructive perception of the relationship between unconscious brain processes and events that occur in the world around us at the right time and the right place," and they argue that this view is not supported by some empirical data. In addition, I would like to underline that this eliminativist view is symptomatic of some classical problems that I wished to underline in this chapter on the basis of an integration of the different ideas and data presented in this volume as a whole.

First, the view advocated by Wegner confuses naturalization and elimination. That a phenomenon is naturalized does not justify its elimination. Rather, and at least at the present stage, the phenomenon under investigation should be described from mutually constraining perspectives, including experiential, conceptual, behavioral, functional, and neurophysiological descriptions.

Second, the eliminativist view is also internalist in that it proposes to eliminate the notion of "free will" (or intention, for that matter) in favor of unconscious brain processes prior to any consciousness of the intention and to action execution. Perception would come only as a nonconstitutive verification.

Here, I propose something different: the "external" aspects of intention make intention neither an illusion nor a mere verification. Rather, they are constitutive of intention. The view advocated here is both recursive (from action to intention, which might superficially look like a "reconstructive" view) and nonverificationist (thus it differs from reconstructive views based on a posteriori perceptual verification). It is recursive because it is notably based on the perception of intentional behavior and its consequences. However, it is nonreconstructive since intentional states (from representations within the head of the agent to social situations) constitute and modulate this perception in the first place. To put it differently, intention is not merely before the action but corresponds to the intentional structuring of action and perception: intention is (built-)in action and perception. By the same token, this position implies that intention is not something that comes after the action either (it is not a reconstruction *à la* Wegner).

As a conclusion, I would like to "close the loop" and mention that in the present framework, intention is "naturalized" in the specific sense that it is explained (not eliminated) in terms that are all fully compatible with natural sciences. On the one hand, it is a *weak* form of naturalization, since it does necessitate pinning down specific neuronal processes that would ultimately correspond to intention. Far from that, the present approach even makes such an enterprise harder, since it does not support a view of intention as internal mental states that can "easily" be correlated with internal neuronal activations. On the other hand, what I propose is a *strong* form of naturalization, since it is neither reductionist nor dualist: in the end, there remains only one "thing" (non-dualism) that is the intention (non-eliminativism) described in a way fully compatible with natural sciences (naturalization): it corresponds to a specific (intentional) structure of action and perception (of the physical and social world). Crucially, this view allows the consideration of all levels of intention. Here, and in this volume as a whole, intention is not reduced to its primary form but includes intentional justification, prior intentional states, representation of goal-directed action, action execution, ascription of intention to oneself and others, perception of the consequences of intentional actions, and social intentional interactions. None of these levels can be reduced to internal (mental and/or neuronal) states; they are rather also constituted by the intentional structuring of the relation between the body the agent acts with and the world the agent acts in.

Notes

1. In this chapter I rely exclusively on ideas, data, or interpretation presented in the different chapters of this volume. It thus corresponds more to an integrative reading of this material rather than to a fully developed argumentation of the point at stake. All references refer to this volume.

2. The argument is roughly the following: since the relevant states are "out there," how could we pin them down and reduce them to some measurable physical states, in particular to some neuronal activation?

Contributors

Colin Allen
Department of History and Philosophy of Science
Indiana University
Bloomington, Indiana

Mireille Bonnard
Institut de Neurosciences Cognitives de la Méditérannée
Université de la Méditerranée
Marseille, France

Jozina B. De Graaf
Institut de Neurosciences Cognitives de la Méditérannée
Université de la Méditerranée
Marseille, France

Vittorio Gallese
Dipartimento di Neuroscienze
Universita degli studi di Parma
Parma, Italy

Franck Grammont
Laboratoire J.A. Dieudonné
Université des Sciences de Nice
Nice, France

Patrick Haggard
Institute of Cognitive Neuroscience
University College of London
London, England

Marco Iacoboni
Ahmanson-Lovelace Brain Mapping Center
David Geffen School of Medicine at UCLA
Los Angeles, California

Dorothée Legrand
Centre de Recherche en Épistémologie Appliquée (CREA)
École Polytechnique
Paris, France

Pierre Livet
CEPERC
Université de Provence
Aix-en-Provence, France

Albert Ogien
Centre d'Étude des Mouvements Sociaux
EHESS
Paris, France

Jean Pailhous
Institut de Neurosciences Cognitives de la Méditerranée
Université de la Méditerranée
Marseille, France

Jean-Luc Petit
Université Marc Bloch
Strasbourg, France
Laboratoire de Physiologie de la Perception et de l'Action
Collège de France
Paris, France

Jean-Michel Roy
Université de Lyon
ENS Lettres and Sciences Humaines
Lyon, France

Jessica A. Sommerville
Department of Psychology and I-LABS
University of Washington
Seattle, Washington

Manos Tsakiris
Department of Psychology
Royal Holloway University of London
Egham, England

Amanda L. Woodward
Department of Psychology
University of Maryland
College Park, Maryland

Index

Abstraction, 257. *See also* Concepts
Acceptability constraints, 254–255
Action, 26. *See also* Intentional
 action(s); Motor system
 Aristotelian and teleological approach
  of, 22–26
 control of, by intention, 185
 defined, 118, 201–202, 302, 312
 as essential to naturalization of
  perceptive intentionality, 315
 as essential to the nature of visual
  intentionality, 310–315
 intentional, 161–163
  defined, 161
 folk concept of, 31
 intention as relevant to the
  explanation of, 305–307
 intention before, 21
 intention in, 30, 33, 141, 165, 181,
  186, 247, 302 (*see also* Intentional
  action(s))
 Background and, 248
 defined, 11, 29
 efference and, 43, 57, 59
 embodying and objectifying, 117
 naturalizing, 3–5, 40, 192, 195,
  323–325
 vs. prior intention, 21, 22, 29, 164
  (*see also* Prior intention)
 translating motivational states into,
  41

 two faces of, 33, 181
 vs. movement, 21, 23–25, 118–120,
  162, 165, 327
 nature of, 302–304
 perception and, 171, 172
 perception of the effects of, 40
 principle of rational, 208
 problems caused by separation of
  intention from, 325
 problems of the contemporary theory
  of, 28–36, 36n1
 from third-person point of view,
  185–188
Action awareness. *See also* Awareness
 reconstructive account of, 52
Action-event, homogenous causal
 theory of, 23
Action experience
 facilitates detection of behavioral
  manifestation of goals, 71–72,
  81–82
 restructures representations of other's
  actions, 82–83
 yields introspective insight, 83
Action goals, 171
 mirror neurons in monkeys and,
  210–212
 ontogeny and phylogeny,
  207–210
Action perception. *See under* Action;
 Action production

Action production, 81
  action perception and, 69–72, 77–81, 83–84
  natural variability in, 71–77
  as engine in development, 71–72
  and role of agency, 81–84
Action recognition, defined, 7
Action simulation, 210–212
Action understanding, 93, 94, 102, 208, 210
  action production and, 71
  action simulation and, 210–212
  defined, 7–8
  experience and, 208
Adjustments of movement, 187, 190–191. *See also* First-person perspective; Third-person point of view
  defined, 8
Adumbrations, 273, 275, 276, 278
Affordance, 35, 205
  defined, 8
Agency, 50, 51f, 58
  action production and the role of, 81–84
  defined, 8
  parietal cortex and sense of, 46
  phenomenology of, 40, 41
Agent (of intentional action), 161, 176
  defined, 161–162
  as "unreasonable" actor, 161, 176
Akins, K., 315
Allen, Colin, 326
"All-out judgment," 34
"Anakastic" restraint, 25
Andersen, R. A., 45
Anscombe, E., 22, 24, 27, 31, 34, 162
Anterior cingulate cortex (ACC), 41–42, 152
  defined, 8
Anterior insular cortex, 153

Anticipated intention, 248, 263.
  See also under Intentional states motivating actions of others; Time awareness
  defined, 8
Anticipating the end of an action, 41.
  See also under Intentional states motivating actions of others; Time awareness
Anticipation vs. prediction, 102
Aristotelian approach of action, 22–26, 91
Aristotle, 23–25, 35, 35
Attention
  defined, 8
  and intention shape the body schema, 283–284
  modulates audition, 281–282
  modulates vision, 282–283
Attribution of intentions, observation of another's action and, 120–123
Audiovisual mirror neurons, 211
Auditory cortex, attention and, 281–282
Automatisms. *See* Sensorimotor automatisms
Awareness. *See also* Conscious intention; Time awareness
  of motor act, and brain activation, 148–153
  of a voluntary motor act, sudden, 142–148

Beer, R., 104
Being, sense of, 270
Beliefs
  defined, 8
  intentional actions and, 107
  motivating others' actions, knowledge of, 99–100 (*see also* Intentional states motivating actions of others)
Berthoz, A., 308, 310–311, 314
"Blind-touch," 169

Index

Bodily intention, 40, 165, 166, 172–176
  characteristics, 170–176
  defined, 8, 161
  vs. mental intention, 166, 172
  structuring role, 170–176
Bodily movements, 201
Body, neurosciences of the intentional, 170–176
Body image, 166, 167, 169, 170. *See also* Body schema
  vs. body schema, 166–169
  defined; 8, 166, 167
Body reading
  vs. theory of mind, 239
Body schema, 166–170
  vs. body image, 166–169
  defined, 8, 166, 167
Bottom-up vs. top-down mechanisms, 143, 144, 147
Brentanian intentionality, 295, 307
Buneo, C. A., 45

Canonical form of intention, 325
Canonical neurons, 205, 236–238, 312–313
  defined, 9, 204
  and multimodal representation of organism-object relation, 205
  visual and motor activity, 174–175
Cassirer, E., 256–259
Causalism, 163–166
Causal role of intentions, 39
Causation(s), 261
  wayward, 34
Causes (of actions), 39
  defined, 9
  formal and logical, 24
Causes-reasons debate, 22, 23
Cerebellum, 54
"Chance." *See also* "Lucky" actions
  for an intention, 249
  goal reached by, 10

Charles, David, 23
Children. *See also* Action production
  action processing in, 68 (*see also* Infancy)
Cingulate cortex. *See* Anterior cingulate cortex
"Classical sandwich model," 170
Cognition, social, 99, 216
Cognitive intentionalism. *See also* Intentionalism
  argument in favor of, 305–309
  neurocognitive turn of the problem of, 294–298
  and pragmatist claims of cognitive neuroscience, 293–294
Cognitive neuroscience
  vs. cognitivism, 297
  pragmatist claims of, 293–294, 304–305, 313
  argument in favor of cognitive intentionalism, 305–309
Collateral movement, 188, 189
Concepts, 256–260, 264n6
  vs. intuition, 256–257
Conditions of satisfaction for action, 184, 185, 193, 202, 247
  defined, 9
Conscious intention, 47–49. *See also* Awareness; Will, conscious
  defined, 9
Consciousness, 176
  defined, 148
Constitution theory, 280
  reassessing the intentionality of kinesthesia in, 273–279
Control intention, 185, 192, 194, 195
Cortical oscillatory patterns, 271
Criterion intention, 185
Csibra, G., 208

Davidson, D., 27–28, 32, 242n6, 265n9
Decéty, J., 313–314
Decision to move, defined, 9

Deecke, L., 42
Deliberation, 23, 26
  defined, 9
Desires, 107, 117. *See also* Intentional states motivating actions of others
  defined, 9
  vs. intentions, 326
Dilthey-Scheler controversy, 279
Distal goals, 202, 208, 209, 212, 214
  defined, 10
Dorsolateral prefrontal cortex (DLPFC), 44–46
Dualism, 25–28, 163–165, 323, 324
Durkheim, Émile, 259

Efference, raw, 43, 59
"Efferent consciousness," 58
Efferent copy, 53, 55, 57, 59, 241
  defined, 10
Efficient causes, 23
Effort sense, 149
  defined, 16
  vs. muscle force sense, 153
Eimer, M., 48
Eliminativist view, 294, 334
Ethology, 107–108
Ex-afference, 53
Execution, intention and, 30
Executive representation, 29
Externalism, 248–250
  vs. internalism, 262, 324–325
Externalist-naturalist account of intention and intentional action, 329
Externalist naturalization, 325, 334

False-belief task, 239
First-person perspective, 189–191
  coordinating the third-person and, 192–195
Fluidity
  of action, 185
  of movement, 187, 188

Formulation intention, 192–195
Forward model, 12
Free will, 39, 40, 47, 334
Future action, evoking the intention of, 30
Future- vs. present-directed intention, 29, 30

Gallagher, S., 229, 239
Gallese, Vittorio, 308, 312–313, 328
  on goal as willed relational attitude, 307
  on goal states, 327
  on intentional attunement, 102–103, 108, 232–233
  on prediction of action outcomes, 102
Gergely, G., 208, 209
Ginet, C., 32
Goal detection, 208–209
Goal-directed action, 121–122, 127, 165, 173, 174, 238–239. *See also* Topocinetic actions
  ability to evaluate and predict others', 209
  defined, 10
  in infants, 71, 72, 76, 78, 79, 81, 84, 207, 208
  mirror neurons and, 237–238
Goal-directed agents. *See* Agency; Agent
Goal-directed grasping and reaching, 78, 81, 92, 203–205, 207. *See also* Motor system
Goal-directed movements, actions and, 202
Goal directedness, 327–328
Goal reached by chance, 10
Goal relatedness, 207, 308
Goal representations, 83, 207. *See also* Motor representations; Representation, of goal states
Goals, 26. *See also* Action goals
  defined, 10, 207, 307
  distal, 10, 202, 208, 209, 212, 214

Index

Goal states, 204, 207
  motor, interactive code for, 204
Goffman, Erving, 248, 252–256, 264n4
Goldberg, G., 44
Goldman, Alvin, 36n1
Grammont, Franck, 104, 331–332
Granger, G. G., 264n6
Grasping. *See* Goal-directed grasping and reaching

Habituation paradigm, 77–78
  cloth-pulling, 73–76, 74f
  mittens, 78–81, 80f
Haggard, Patrick, 48–52, 51f, 54, 334
Hare, B., 99–100
Hegel, Georg Wilhelm Friedrich, 228
Heidegger, Martin, 240
Hemineglect, 284
Higher order goal, 67, 69, 72, 74–75, 209, 329
  defined, 10
Husserl, Edmund, 228, 270, 274–276
  comet metaphor, 272
  on kinesthesia, 274–277, 279, 288nn33–34

Iacoboni, Marco, 333
Identity(ies), 253
Imagination, 117, 124, 313–314
  defined, 10
Imitation, 93–94, 213, 232, 240–242
  definitions, 10–11, 93
"Incarnated" intentions, 327
Infancy. *See also* Action production
  state of action processing in, 68–69
Inferential conception of intention, 261
Inhibition, 30
"Input-output picture," 171
Insula, 150–151
  anterior part of, 8
  posterior part of left, 14, 150–151, 150f

Insular cortex, anterior, 153
Intention, 325. *See also specific topics*
  characteristics, 248
  defined, 9, 40, 247, 262–263
  dual status/two faces of, 28–31, 34
  historical perspective on, 3–4
  identification criteria, 251–260
  integrative view of, 5, 6f, 7
  invocation of, and its logical constraints, 260–262
  "monist" conception of, 335
  types of, 29–30
Intention (Anscombe), 24, 31. *See also* Anscombe
Intentional action(s)
  aspects/elements of, 40, 55–56
  beyond the agent's conscious control, 330
  executing, 328–329
  experienced as intentional, 329–330
  functional signatures of, 40–41, 47
  sensory attenuation as occurring only for predicted efferent events, 55–56, 56f
  sensory suppression, 52–55
  time awareness of action and intentional binding, 49–52
  time awareness of intention and anticipation, 47–49
  from mental intentions, 325–326
  of monkeys, as understood by other monkeys, 91–99
  perceiving others', 329, 331–333
  phenomenological signature of, 41, 56–57
    constructing agency, 58–60
    reconstructing agency, 57–58
  planning, 326–327
Intentional agent's perception of external world, 331
Intentional arc, 172
Intentional attunement, 102–103, 108, 217, 218

Intentional attunement hypothesis, 216–217
Intentional behavior, phenomenology of, 39–40
Intentional binding, 9, 50, 51f, 52, 175–176
Intentionalism. *See also* Cognitive intentionalism
  aspects of the problem of, 299–302
Intentionality. *See also* Cognitive intentionalism; Kinesthesia; Visual intentionality
  basic, 96–97
  Brentanian, 295, 307
  defined, 11, 295
  determination of, 295–296
  intention as pragmatic form of, 307
  naturalization of, 296, 301–302
  perceptive, 315
  pragmatic, 308 (*see also* Pragmatist theories of intentionality)
  property of
    cognitive relevance of, 294
    nature of, 294–295
  relevance of, extended to explanation of other cognitive phenomena, 308–309
  as relevant to explanation of action, 307–308
"Intentional maps," 45
Intentional processes
  links to action, 6f, 7
  model of, 6f, 7
Intentional states motivating actions of others, knowledge of
  monkeys as lacking, 99–100
  as necessary for action understanding, 101–106
Intention understanding, defined, 11
Interacting intentionally with others, 333–334

Interaction, 231. *See also* Intersubjective relations; Sharing
  defined, 11–12
  Goffman's theory of, 248, 252–256
  online, 232–234
  role of, 203
Interactional vs. noninterational observations of others, 231–234
Interactionist approach to intention, 248, 250, 252–253
Intercorporeity, 215
Internalism, 165–166, 170, 247
  vs. externalism, 324–325
Internal models, 52–53, 241
  defined, 12
Intersubjective actions, 227, 240–242
Intersubjective relations, 229–231, 234, 236. *See also* Sharing
  ability to entertain, 239
  acted, 238–239
  triangular relation, 235–237
Intersubjectivity, 192–194, 217, 234–236
  defined, 12, 235
  transcendental, 234–235, 242n1 (*see also* Constitution theory)
Intuition vs. conceptualization, 256–257
Inverse model, 12
Involuntary action, defined, 12
Involuntary movements, 40, 49–51, 55, 56f, 176

Jeannerod, M., 57–58, 305, 308, 311–312
Joint action. *See* Interaction
Jones, S. S., 105
Juarrero, A., 163, 164
Justification for action, 27

Kinesthesia, intentionality of, 270–271
  reassessing, in constitution theory, 273–279

Index

Knowledge of other's role, defined, 12

Lateralized readiness potential (LRP), 48
Legrand, Dorothée, 333
Leroi-Gourhan, A., 142, 147
Libet, B., 39, 47–48, 306
Linton, R., 251
Livet, Pierre, 327, 331
Locomotion, 143
"Lucky" actions, 31–32, 35

"Master of the action," 35, 36
Mead, George Herbert, 249–251
Melden, A. I., 27
Mental states that are causal sources of intentional action, acting following, 161–163
Merleau-Ponty, Maurice, 141, 171, 173, 227
Mind, theory of, 91, 99, 100, 217, 229. *See also* Mind reading; Simulation theory, of mind
 vs. body reading, 239
 folk-psychological model of, 215
 vs. theory of simulation, 122–123 (*see also* Simulation theory)
Mind reading, 93, 96, 98, 102, 107, 326. *See also under* Simulation theory
 defined, 12
 folk psychological model of, 102, 215
Mirroring mechanisms in humans, 212–215
Mirror neurons, 70, 98, 124–126, 240
 audiovisual, 211
 characteristics, 237
 defined, 12, 205, 210
 F5, 91–98, 203–205 (*see also* Canonical neurons)
 discovery of, 119
 goal-directed action and, 237–238
 in monkeys, 126, 210–212 (*see also* Intentional action(s), of monkeys)
"Mirror system," 124
Mismatch negativity (MMN), 281
Motivation, 186, 188
 defined, 13
 pulsional intentionality of, 279
Motivation aspect of action, 186–187
Motivation intention, 185, 192–195
Motivation target, 182
Motor acts, 201–203
Motor awareness. *See* Awareness
Motor cortex, 118–119
Motor evoked potentials (MEPs), 54, 56f
Motor inferences, 211
Motor intention, 46
Motor mental imagery, 30
Motor model of intention, 40
Motor repertoire, 119, 121, 187, 194, 208, 209, 331–332
Motor representations, 82, 124, 213, 215, 236, 237
 action and, 312
 activating, 82, 122–124, 130, 133, 207, 215
 defined, 13
 internal nonlinguistic, 215
 Jeannerod on, 305, 312
 motor imagery and, 314
Motor schemas, 29–30, 205
Motor system, observation of unknown action activating one's, 126–128, 128–132f, 130, 132–134. *See also under* Observation
Movement
 adjustments of, 8, 187, 190–191
 defined, 13
 intentional
  five criteria of, 186–188
  vs. nonintentional movement, 21, 25, 29

Movement (cont.)
  intentional and agentive aspects, 183
  intention and, 21–22
  separation between, 29
  modification of (*see* Revision)
  "updates" of, 183
Movement awareness. *See also*
    Movement outcome awareness
  vs. force awareness, 148–154, 150f
Movement outcome awareness, 148,
    154. *See also* Movement awareness
  defined, 13
Muscle force awareness, 148–149, 151,
    153. *See also under* Movement
    awareness
  defined, 13, 148

Nadel, S., 251–252
"Naked intentions," 57–58
Naturalist cognitive intentionalism,
    297
Naturalist theory of cognition, 296
Naturalization, 323–325, 335. *See also*
    Externalist naturalization; *specific
    topics*
  definition and nature of, 296–297,
    301–302, 323
  vs. elimination, 334
  of intentionality, 296, 301–302
  of perceptive intentionality, 315
  principle of, 297
Naturalizing. *See also under* Revision
  intention, 117
  intention in action, 3–5, 40, 192, 195,
    323–325
Needs, defined, 13
Neural correlates
  of mental states, 323–324
  of motor acts and actions, 40, 119,
    202–207
Neural map shaping, 271
Neural signature of intentional actions,
    40, 271
  from motives to intentions, 41–44
  planning and perception of self-
    generated actions, 45–47
  selecting an action, 44–45
Neural states preceding conscious
    decision to act, 39
Neural underpinnings of movements
    and actions, 201–202
Neurocognitive turn of the problem of
    cognitive intentionalism, 294–298
Neuroscience(s), 107, 269, 271
  of the intentional body, 170–176
  from philosophy to social, 230–234
"Nolition," 33

Objectification of self and others, 229–
    230, 274–275
Observation (of another's action)
  as activating one's motor system in
    same way, 123–126
  and attribution, 120–123, 231–232
  of unknown action activating one's
    own motor system, 126–128, 128–
    132f, 130, 132–134
Observer perspective, defined, 13
Ogien, Albert, 333–334
Online interaction, 232–234
Organ kinesthesia. *See* Kinesthesia
O'Shaughnessy, B., 32, 59–60
Others. *See also* Intersubjective
    relations
  as objects, 227
  defined, 13
  as subject(s), 227–230
  defined, 14

Pacherie, E., 29–30, 57–58
Pachoud, B., 41
Parietal cortex, 45–47
Parietal lobule, left inferior, 152–153
Parietal operculum, 54
Perceived environment, defined, 14
Perceived time. *See* Time, perceived

Perceiving others' intentional actions, 329, 331–333
Perception. *See also under* Action; Action production
  pragmatist conception of, 309–312, 314, 315
Perceptive intentionality, action as essential to naturalization of, 315
Petit, Jean-Luc, 165, 324
Phenomenology
  constitutive analyses in, 272–273
  correlated with new findings in neuroscience, 279–284
  Heideggerian existential, 240
"Philosophical autism," 228
Philosophy and social neurosciences, 107, 230–234
Planful strategies in infants, 76
Planning, 42, 308
  defined, 14
Posterior parietal cortex (PPC), 45–46
"Practical syllogism," 23–25, 101, 104
Pragmatic being in the world, defined, 14
Pragmatic intentionality or intention as having a specific nature, 308
Pragmatic representation of action goal, 171
Pragmatic visual representations, 311–312
Pragmatist and neurocognitive type of intentionalism, move to a, 310–315
Pragmatist approach to cognitive intentionalism, 294–296
Pragmatist conception of intentionalism, 293, 298, 314
  theoretical analysis of, 299–305
Pragmatist conception of perception, 309–312, 314, 315
Pragmatist theories of intentionality, 293, 301–303
  TA_12, TA_22 and TA_23 forms of, 310–312

Preconscious voluntary acts, 147
  defined, 14
Predator-prey interaction, 235
Present-directed intention, 30. *See also* Action, intention in
Prior intention, 21, 22, 29–31, 186, 212. *See also* "Pure intention"
  action (potential) execution and, 326
  defined, 14
  as incomplete (intentions of action), 31
  in infants, 83
  intentional binding and, 9, 52
  vs. intention in action, 21, 22, 29, 164
  transition to action from, 33
Propositional attitudes, 217
Proximal goal, defined, 14
Psychical half-shadow, 147
Public intention, 248
  defined, 15
"Public" vs. "private" aspects of actions, 152–153
Pulsional intentionality of motivation, 279
"Pure intention," 34
Purposefulness, 101. *See also* Intentionality, basic

Qualia of intentions, defined, 15

Rational action, principle of, 208
Reaching. *See* Goal-directed grasping and reaching
Reactions, 141
  vs. actions, 173–174
  defined, 15
Readiness potential (RP), 9, 42, 48
Reafference, 52–53
Reasons (for actions), 22, 192. *See also* Causes (of actions); "Why questions"
  vs. causes, 22, 23, 25–28

Reasons (cont.)
  defined, 15
  intention and, 28, 29
Reciprocity, self-other, 228–229
Recursive functional, 184, 186
  defined, 15
Recursive structure of action, 181–184
Recursivity
  of intention, 183
  nature of, 182
Reflexes, 141, 173
  defined, 15
Reflexive intention, 248
  defined, 15
Repertoire of actions, 119, 187, 189, 262, 263, 333. *See also* Motor repertoire; Motor system
  defined, 15
Representation
  of goal states, 202, 204, 207, 327
  (*see also* Goal representations)
  defined, 15
  of others (*see* Others)
Responsibility, 23, 24, 25, 27, 32, 253
  defined, 15
"Responsibility signal," 12, 241
Retinotopy, attentional, 282–283
Revision (of actions), 185–186, 188–191, 328
  vs. adjustment, 190, 191
  defined, 16
  naturalizing, 192, 193, 194
  and the limits of naturalization, 195–197
Reward system, 202, 207
  defined, 16
Ricoeur, Paul, 176
Rizzolatti, G., 312
Roles, 251–254, 260
  defined, 16, 251
  dimensions of, 252, 253
Ryle, G., 261

"Sandwich model," 170
Sartre, Jean-Paul, 228–229, 234
Schizophrenia, 146, 149
Schopenhauer, Arthur, 39, 59
Searle, John, 41, 164, 247, 264n1
Second-order intentionality, 95
Self-other discrimination, 231–232
Self-other reciprocity, 228–229
Self-others relation. *See also* Intersubjective relations
  types/levels of, 231–234
Self-produced experience, 81, 82
Sense-giving acts, intentionality of, 270
Sensorimotor automatisms, 141. *See also* Awareness
  defined, 16
  intentional adaptation of, 141–142
  defined, 11
Sensorimotor circuits, 206
Sensory attenuation
  as occurring only for predicted efferent events, 55–56, 56f
  reasons for, 52–53
Sensory awareness, 152. *See also* Awareness
Sensory bias, 56
Sensory consequences, 11. *See also* Intentional action(s), functional signatures of
  defined, 16
Sensory suppression, 52–56
  neural source of efferent signal used for, 54–55
Shared coordinated actions, 240–242
  untheoretical practice, 239–240
Shared manifold space, 216
  defined, 16
Shared representations model, 57–58
Sharing
  by acting, 236–238
  a common world, 234–242
    being in a world of others, 234–235

Index

Simulation, 215
  embodied, 211–212, 214–217
  defined, 10
Simulationist view of social cognition, 99
Simulation theory
  of action, 310
  of mind (reading), 12, 102, 122–123, 215
Situations, 254–256
  defined, 16
Social behaviorist view, 249
Social cognition, 216
  simulationist view of, 99
Social identity, 253
Social referencing, defined, 16
Society. *See also* Sociology
  defined, 16
Sociology, 263
  intention in, 248–251, 262–263
  interactionist, 250
Somatosensory areas, 151–152
Somatosensory cortex, plasticity of maps of, 281
Sommerville, Jessica A., 78, 107, 332
Sovereign self, model of, 228
Status, 251, 254
  defined, 17
  vs. role, 251
Subjectivity and subjectification, 274–275
Subject-subject interrelations, 230. *See also* Intersubjective relations
Superior temporal sulcus (STS), 11, 123, 241
  defined, 17
Supplemental motor area (SMA), 42–44, 54, 326–327
  defined, 17
Syllogism, practical, 23, 24

Teleological function, 25–26
Teleological stance hypothesis, 208

Third-person point of view. *See also under* First-person perspective
  action from, 185–188
Time, perceived, 49–50, 175
  defined, 14
Time awareness
  of action and intentional binding, 49–52
  of intention and anticipation, 47–49
Top-down vs. bottom-up mechanisms, 143, 144, 147
Topocinetic actions, 119. *See also* Goal-directed action
Transcendental intersubjectivity, 234–235, 242n1. *See also* Constitution theory
Triangular relation, 235–237
Triangulation, 242n6
Tsakiris, Manos, 50, 334
Two-level interdependence view, 171

Unconscious intention, 29, 147, 153, 202, 306, 312
  defined, 17
Unconscious vs. nonconscious voluntary acts, 147
"Updates" of movements, 183

Varela, F., 314–315
Ventral premotor (F5) cortex. *See* Mirror neurons, F5
"Vision to perceive" vs. "vision to act," 172
Visual cortex, attention and, 282–283
Visual intentionality
  action as essential to the nature of, 310–315
  pragmatic type of, 311–312
Visuotransformation, 311
Volition, 21–22, 26, 32–33, 50, 165
  anterior cingulate cortex and, 152
  defined, 17
  Schopenhauer on, 59

Voluntary acts vs. voluntary movements, 147. *See also under* Awareness
Von Wright, G., 25

Weber, Max, 249
Wegner, D. M., 39, 334
Whitford, B., 54
"Who system," 57, 58
"Why questions," 33–34
Will, 39
 conscious, 48
 weakness of, 35
  causes of, 35, 36
"Willed" responses, 44–45
Wittgenstein, Ludwig, 21, 24, 26, 29
Woodward, Amanda L., 78, 107, 332
Woodworth, R. S., 143
Wright, Larry, 25

Zahavi, D., 234, 235

BF 311 .N36 2010

Naturalizing intention in action

MAR 26 2010